Bernhard Neumärker, Jessica S

Financial Issues of a Universal Basic Income (UBI)

12/04/23

Thank you for coming to Freiburg and sharing your thoughts on UBI with us at FRIBIS!

FRIBIS eventmanagement
&

Studien des Freiburger Instituts
für Grundeinkommensstudien (FRIBIS)
an der Albert-Ludwigs-Universität Freiburg

Freiburg Studies on Basic Income

Herausgegeben von
Edited by

Prof. Dr. Bernhard Neumärker
Freiburger Institut für Grundeinkommensstudien (FRIBIS)
an der Albert-Ludwigs-Universität Freiburg

Band/Volume 1

LIT

Financial Issues of a Universal Basic Income (UBI)

Proceedings of the
FRIBIS Annual Conference 2021

edited by

Bernhard Neumärker
and
Jessica Schulz

LIT

Cover Illustration:
Mark Rothko: Untitled, 1957
Catalogue Raisonné #582
© Kate Rothko-Prizel & Christopher Rothko / VG Bild-Kunst, 2022

Bibliographic information published by the Deutsche Nationalbibliothek
The Deutsche Nationalbibliothek lists this publication in the Deutsche Nationalbibliografie; detailed bibliographic data are available on the Internet at http://dnb.dnb.de.

ISBN 978-3-643-91512-2 (pb)
ISBN 978-3-643-96512-7 (PDF)

A catalogue record for this book is available from the British Library.

© LIT VERLAG Dr. W. Hopf Berlin 2022
Contact:
Fresnostr. 2   D-48159 Münster
Tel. +49 (0) 2 51-62 03 20   Fax +49 (0) 2 51-23 19 72
e-Mail: lit@lit-verlag.de   https://www.lit-verlag.de
Distribution:
In the UK: Global Book Marketing, e-mail: mo@centralbooks.com
In North America: Independent Publishers Group, e-mail: orders@ipgbook.com

Contents / Inhalt

Bernhard Neumärker, Jessica Schulz
Introduction: Financial Aspects of a UBI   9

I Basic Income in Economic Discourse   15
*Das Bedingungslose Grundeinkommen
im ökonomischen Diskurs*

Alex Howlett
The Natural Rate of Basic Income   17
Facilitating Financial Instability and Labor Productivity

Tobias Jäger
Basic Income and Industrial Relations   37
A Theoretical Literature Survey

Marcel Franke, Tobias Jäger
Nash Bargaining with a Social Preference   71
A Preference for Equal Reference Points in Bargaining

II Basic Income: Models and Experiments 107
Das Bedingungslose Grundeinkommen: Modelle und Experimente

Bernhard Neumärker, Jette Weinel

The Implications of UBI on Utility Functions and Tax Revenue 109

Towards Time Sovereignty and Consumption Taxation

Lida Kuang

Basic Income as a Just Social Contract 135

An Experimental Approach

Thiago Monteiro de Souza

Maricá Citizen's Basic Income 155

An Overview of the Pilot

Tobias Jäger

Foreign Aid Basic Income 169

The Concept of Aid and a Short Overview

III Basic Income: Multidisciplinary perspectives 193
Das Bedingungslose Grundeinkommen aus multidisziplinären Perspektiven

Leon Hartmann

Universal Basic Income as a Discursive Formation of the Future 195

Sketch of a Discourse Analysis

Michael von der Lohe

The Enterprise Basic Income 205

A Proposal for Integrating the Unconditional Basic Income in a Coherent Form of Money Circulation

José H. Rocha

Universal Basic Income: The Brewing of a Storm 211

IV Basic Income in German-Speaking Countries   225
Das Bedingungslose Grundeinkommen im deutschsprachigen Raum

Ulrich Schachtschneider

Grundeinkommen: Ein gastliches Umfeld für Postwachstum?   227

Eine erste Annäherung an ein neues Forschungsfeld

Ronald Blaschke

Grundeinkommen: Positionen von Parteien und Zugänge von sozialen Bewegungen in Deutschland   239

Europäische Bürgerinitiative (EBI) Bedingungslose Grundeinkommen in der gesamten EU

Florian Wakolbinger, Elisabeth Dreer, Friedrich Schneider

Konsumfinanziertes BGE in Österreich   261

Finanzierungsbedarf und Preiswirkungen

Simon März

A Critical Analysis of a Proposed Basic Income Pilot Study in Germany   299

An Argument for Another UBI Pilot in Germany

Author's Biographies   339

Bernhard Neumärker, Jessica Schulz

Introduction: Financial Aspects of a UBI

An Insurmountable Obstacle or Disarmingly Simple?

> *"It is a beautiful, disarmingly simple idea."*
> *(Philippe Van Parijs, 1992: 3)*

Simple as the idea of an Unconditional Basic Income (UBI) may seem, presenting it in a public discussion is nevertheless a complex and difficult task. A monthly payment for every citizen that does not ask about one's assets, job, work motivation or other income and expenses. "Beautiful and disarmingly simple", writes Phillipe Van Parijs in his much-cited book, *Arguing for Basic Income*. Yet despite the widespread support for the idea, politicians, academics and journalists counter its simplicity with the question: who will pay for it?

In public debates on an Unconditional Basic Income, the question of financing is becoming increasingly dominant and is sometimes used as the disarming argument against the introduction of a UBI, which both Milton Friedman, with his related construct of the "negative income tax" (1962), and Van Parijs (1992) saw as inherent in the idea itself. Does financing really represent an insurmountable hurdle to implementing the idea of an Unconditional Basic Income? Is it so disarmingly simple in the end?

Friedmann has defused the financing question by arguing for an integrated tax-transfer mechanism known as the Negative Income Tax, which keeps the budget for basic income-equivalent payments relatively small from the outset by offsetting the transfer against the personal market income tax burden. He addressed the second long-standing question of whether basic income receipt would not make people work-shy with his much-discussed poverty gap, which aims to ensure that a fundamental incentive to earn income would always remain. However, as Van Parijs and others have pointed out, such an approach hardly produces the positive effects that one would expect from a basic income paid out without calculation and covering social participation.

With its contributions the FRIBIS Annual Conference 2021 reacted to the phenomenon that the financing of an Unconditional Basic Income is often considered to be impossible without the corresponding research or contextual background. Thus, the two-day conference presented financial aspects of an Unconditional Basic Income as the main topic in various international presentations and panels. The Freiburg Institute for Basic Income Studies (FRIBIS) offers a space for interdisciplinary and international discussion to the growing interest in basic income research in financial and monetary issues.

The aim of this volume is to make the presentations of the first FRIBIS annual conference available to a broader audience of professors, activists, students and all those interested in the UBI. FRIBIS sees itself as a competence network of international and multidisciplinary academics and activists with an institutionally innovative bridging function between research and actors, as well as interested parties from civil society. This mediating and bridging function becomes particularly clear when basic income is seen as a bottom-up strategy that also focuses on financing and monetary policy issues in dialogue between research institutions and society.

The first part of this conference volume examines Unconditional Basic Income from an economic perspective. While the first chapter provides an overview of key economic topics and debates at the heart of the basic income discourse, the second chapter deals with individual research directions and projects some of which are new to economic basic income research. In doing so, the implications of the research for civil discourse are always central to the discussion while questions about socially pressing topics and issues are also developed.

Thus, the first section of the book starts with one of the most discussed contexts of the basic income discourse: the question of labour productivity in the face of financial instability. In an analysis that involves the relationship between the financial sector and labour market, entitled The Natural Rate of Basic Income: Facilitating Financial Stability and Labour Productivity, **Alex Howlett** explains how an Unconditional Basic Income would free people from state regulation of labour choice and labour input while still maintaining productivity.

In the second paper, Universal Basic Income and Industrial Relations. A Theoretical Literature Survey by **Tobias Jäger**, the working subject and the labour market are at the core of the economic analysis. Jäger asks the question how an unconditional basic income could affect trade unions, gives a theoretical overview of central issues such as wage bargaining theories, and discusses an alternative concept to existing theoretical approaches via critical analysis with reference to Hirshman's exit and voice strategy.

The section concludes with a contribution by **Marcel Franke** and **Tobias Jäger**: How a Social Preference and Nash Bargaining May Lead to a Need for Transfer. The Impact of a Preference for Equal Reference Points in Nash Bargaining. Here, the optimal transfer of the social contract is examined with recourse to constitutional economics. From the point of view of social preferences for fairness, the Unconditional Basic Income is defined as an optimal transfer and analysed in the context of game-theoretical bargaining solutions.

In the second section, the first contribution, The Implications of UBI on Utility Functions and Tax Revenue: Towards Time Sovereignty and Consumption Taxation by **Bernhard Neumärker** and **Jette Weinel**, offers something new in the economic modelling of UBI by placing the individual utility function at the centre of the investigation. This is characterised here as consisting of multiplicative relationships and motives and thus offers an innovative basis for analysis compared to the motives negotiated as additively separable within the traditionally applied economic utility function between consumption and work. This change is justified by the gain in people's time sovereignty through an unconditional basic income. Finally, the authors contrast the effects of a basic income on consumption tax revenue with the consequences of the usual additive separable relationships, which differ considerably from previously assumed financing effects.

In the following contribution Basic Income as a just Social Contract: an experimental approach, **Lida Kuang** addresses the much-discussed question of an unconditional basic income as an ideal form of social justice. Based on John Rawls' theory of justice, Basic Income is analysed and experimentally investigated for the theory of a social contract. With the experimental approach, this analysis makes a new innovative contribution to constitutional social contract economics.

A concrete example of an implementation attempt of basic income is presented by **Thiago Monteiro de Souza** in his contribution Maricá Citizen's Basic Income. An Overview of the Pilot. Considering the geopolitical development of the Brazilian city, the basic income program in the city of Maricá is described and analysed in terms of the developments since its introduction in 2013. The interaction between the Covid 19 pandemic and its political, economic and social consequences are also discussed on the basis of the case analysis presented.

The last contribution of this section, entitled Foreign Aid Basic Income. Concept of Aid and a short Overview by **Tobias Jäger** introduces the topic of basic income as development aid. It focuses on the question of whether an Unconditional Basic Income could be financed through development aid. At the same time, Jäger provides an overview of the economics literature on the topic of development aid and basic income.

In the second part of the volume, the multi-perspective work and international nature of FRIBIS comes to the fore, offering a broad audience the opportunity to discover the basic income discourse from different research directions, disciplines and countries in several parallel sessions at the FRIBIS annual conference.

Section Three explores UBI from multidisciplinary perspectives. In the contributions, artistic, philosophical and legal discourses are linked to the idea of Unconditional Basic Income and each is analysed in a subject-specific way.

While **Leon Hartmann** in Universal Basic Income as a Discursive Formation of the Future. Sketch of a Discourse Analysis, views basic income as a narrative that can only be examined as such in a futuristic discourse structure, **José H. Rocha** attempts to bring Unconditional Basic Income into a legal framework in his conceptual analysis. In his contribution, Universal Basic Income and the Law: the Brewing of a Storm, he uses the Socratic method to contrast normative arguments with a potential implementation.

In The Enterprise Basic Income and its Proposal for Integrating Unconditional Basic Income in a coherent Form of Money Circulation, **Michael von der Lohe** devotes special attention to the activist approach within the basic income discourse. Following Joseph Beuys' famous dictum: Everyone is an artist, he presents the Unconditional Basic Income as a social sculpture, which defines all members of a society as cooperation partners of this sculpture and links the basic income to this cooperation and (co-)design of the social sculpture. Here a proposal for financing an unconditional basic income is based on the artistic discourse.

Section Four is devoted to the basic income discourse in the German-speaking world, so most of the contributions are written in German.

With Basic Income. A Hospitable Environment for Post-Growth? **Ulrich Schachtschneider** expands the discourse to include an ecological perspective. He examines the Unconditional Basic Income for its potential impact on a social, socio-ecological transformation. In the context of the conference on financial questions of basic income research, this contribution is mainly characterised by the fact that a socio-ecological analysis is linked to arguments of economic growth and the question of a post-growth economy.

Ronald Blaschke also argues from a social perspective in his contribution, Basic Income: the positions of political parties and approaches of social movements in Germany. European Citizens' Initiatives (ECI) Unconditional Basic Income throughout the EU. He deals directly with questions about the level of a basic income as a guarantee of participation. Here he presents the positions of various political parties on basic income and relates them to social movements in Germany.

In line with the main discourse, Consumer Financed Unconditional Basic Income in Austria. Financing Needs and Price Effects, from **Florian Wakolbinger**, **Elisabeth Dreer** and **Friedrich Schneider**, the authors discuss the financing of an UBI in Austria through a consumption and export tax. They present a model in which taxes are abolished and various scenarios for negotiation processes of wages and pensions are played out.

Simon März concludes this section with A Critical Analysis of the proposed Implementation of a Universal Basic Income Pilot Study from the NGO Expedition Grundeinkommen in Germany. It calls for another extensive Universal Basic Income pilot in Germany. The article gives an overview of the experiments with the unconditional basic income of the last sixty years, with a special focus on the transfer of results and findings of these experiments to an actual implementation policy. Based on this critical reflection, the organisation „Expedition Grundeinkommen" is introduced. It is planning to introduce an unconditional basic income in the first state model experiment in Berlin by democratic means via referendums, in which FRIBIS is significantly involved as an advisory institution. This contribution puts the narrative concept of Unconditional Basic Income developed by Leon Hartmann in Section Three and directed towards the future into current practice. It is also exemplary for this volume and the work of FRIBIS in building a bridge between research and social activism.

Overall, this volume provides initial insights into basic income issues that are dealt with at FRIBIS through systematic research and the incorporation of civil society challenges, thus contributing to the political, civil and academic discourse. In the coming years, further conferences and volumes on key topics of basic income research will follow.

I

Basic Income in Economic Discourse

Das Bedingungslose Grundeinkommen im ökonomischen Diskurs

Alex Howlett

The Natural Rate of Basic Income

Facilitating Financial Stability and Labor Productivity

Today's governments push money to consumers through the financial sector and the labor market. This generates financial instability and make-work. Basic income hands people money directly. Theoretically, there exists a level of basic income frees governments from having to interfere with the allocation with capital and labor. I call this the natural rate of basic income.

Any large-scale market-based economy requires that people have a source of money to spend on the economy's product. Basic income, an ongoing unconditional cash flow paid to every person, is a simple, efficient, straightforward money source. Today, we compensate for the absence of basic income by stimulating the financial sector to create jobs. This pushes money to people through wages. The resulting distribution of money is uneven and inconsistent.

Furthermore, by using the financial sector and the job market as money distribution tools, we hinder productive investment and interfere with labor allocation. The resulting investment occurs for a reason other than the development of productive capacity. The resulting jobs exist for a reason other than the product of the labor. The resulting wages are paid for a reason other than the incentive to work. In other words, our economic policy generates indirect make-work. The absence of basic income leaves us little other choice.

Basic income allows us to provide people money without interfering in the allocation of labor and other resources. The natural rate of basic income is what I call the level of basic income payout that obviates the need for make-work – indirect or otherwise.

The way we get people their money is broken. We can fix it by setting the basic income to its natural rate. Our challenge, then, is to discover the natural rate by feeling out the parameters of our economy. We must calibrate the basic income payout such that people are neither over- nor under-incentivized to sell their labor, and financial investment is neither overstimulated nor depressed.

1. Money and the Economy

An economy is any social system organized for the management and allocation of resources toward the production of goods and services. A government may allocate some resources directly, but money remains useful so long as some resources are left for the market to allocate through voluntary trade.

Markets use prices to balance supply against demand. People need a way to pay those prices to be able to buy goods and services. Money is whatever the market uses as its pricing and payments standard (Howlett, 2021a, pp. 1–2). People spend money to claim the economy's output.

Intuitively, we might assume that consumers come naturally endowed with useful labor that they can trade for money. But in a highly specialized large-scale economy, it is not generally true that jobs will naturally distribute money to consumers in a way that allows them to access the economy's full potential output. Absent a natural demand for labor that efficiently distributes money to consumers, we have conventionally used economic policy to create artificial labor demand.

Basic income is "a regular cash income paid to all, on an individual basis without means test or work requirement" (Van Parijs and Vanderborght, 2017, p. 1). The cash comes with no strings attached. A person need not do anything to earn or deserve it. As a direct source of money that bypasses the market, basic income allows consumers to spend money without selling labor. It thereby relieves the government from having to distort the labor market through artificial demand.

2. Wages as Incentive to Work

Much of people's work is not paid - for example, childcare, taking out the trash, eating, etc. Jobs exist for the remaining work that people will refuse to do without payment. Wages are the payments that provide an incentive for people to spend their time differently.

Because there will always be paid work, there will always be some amount of wages paid to consumers. It is therefore impossible for basic income to be the only source of money for all consumers.

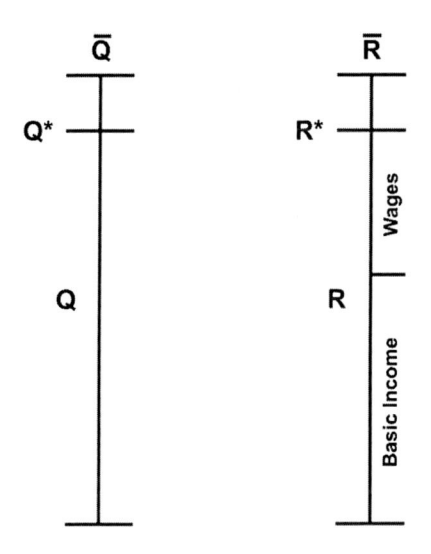

Figure 1: Proportion of Consumer Spending Originating in Wages

In Figure 1, Q is the quantity of output (goods and services) the economy produces in a period of time. Q* is the current output level and $\bar{Q}$ is the economy's productive capacity – the maximum possible level of output. R is the level of consumer spending in the economy. R* is the current consumer spending level and $\bar{R}$ is the maximum level of consumer spending the economy can sustain. Each level of consumer spending maps onto a certain level of economic output. Maximum consumer spending ($\bar{R}$) maps onto full economic output ($\bar{Q}$).

We can partition R* into the portion that comes from wages and the portion that comes from basic income. Conceptually, we can think of any money paid by the market - including income from capital ownership - as a kind of a wage. The lower the basic income, the greater the incentive for people to sell labor for money. At the natural rate of basic income, people are neither under-incentivized nor over-incentivized to sell labor.

3. Labor Versus Leisure

We typically use the term "leisure" to describe how people spend their time when not working. But it can be semantically tricky to draw a clear distinction between labor and leisure activities. Can we decide based on the level of enjoyment? How much exertion is required? How much, or whether, the activity pays?

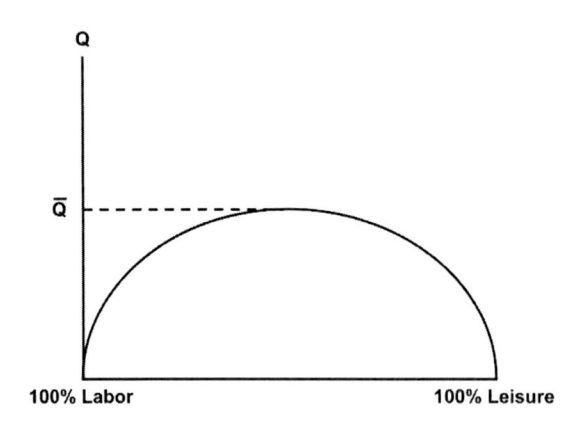

Figure 2: Allocating Time Between Labor and Leisure

This paper will use "leisure" as a label for people's unpaid time, regardless of how relaxing or enjoyable it is. Labor, then, means paying people to do something different. By this definition, people prefer to spend their time in leisure activities rather than labor activities. Otherwise, they would need no compensation. But leisure time need not be unproductive. Shifting people into paid work will not always boost economic output or make society better off.

A basic income higher than the natural rate leaves insufficient incentive for people to perform paid work. A basic income lower than the natural rate pulls people away from more useful unpaid work into less useful paid work.

In Figure 2, the horizontal axis is a continuum between 100% labor and 100% leisure. The vertical axis is the quantity of output (Q).

At either extreme, the economy produces nothing. Overwork depresses productivity. The labor-leisure balance that achieves maximum output $\bar{Q}$ corresponds to the natural rate of basic income.

The labor market is a market for people's time and effort. It can be difficult to classify that time and effort neatly into the binary categories of labor and leisure. Instead, we can think of everybody as having 24 hours in a day. That time is a resource. Those hours are allocated to various activities that fall somewhere on a labor-leisure continuum.

4. Productive Investment

Finance - that is, borrowing and lending - exists to support useful business activity and investment in future productive capacity. It contributes to present or future supply of economic output. An efficient financial sector never expands for the purpose of boosting demand.

Just as pushing money to consumers through jobs distorts the labor market, enabling extra private sector borrowing as an incentive to create these jobs distorts the financial sector.

Today's central banks do exactly that. They prop up consumer demand using expansionary monetary policy to boost employment and wages. This arrangement causes an unstable expansion of private credit that leaves the economy susceptible to financial collapse (Howlett, 2021b, pp. 5–6).

Basic income provides money directly – bypassing the financial sector and the labor market. The natural rate of basic income prevents both unstable credit conditions and overemployment.

Meanwhile, basic income facilitates productive investment by ensuring that consumers have the money to activate new productive capacity.

5. Real Purchasing Power

The natural rate of basic income represents an amount of real purchasing power. It derives from the quantity of actual goods and services that the market has the resources to produce for people. Changes in the price level (P) will not allow us to escape this resource constraint. In terms of the number of dollars people receive, a higher P may allow a higher natural rate of basic income, but this nominal increase in money will not translate into an increase in the quantity of goods and services that people can actually buy.

A nominal basic income above the natural rate causes a period of inflation until the inflation brings the real purchasing power of the basic income back down to its natural rate.

Any commitment to set the real rate of basic income above the natural rate will ultimately fail. Such a commitment represents a promise that consumers will be able to buy more output (goods and services) than the economy can produce. An attempt to meet this commitment will cause us to revise the nominal basic income payout forever upward. The result is hyperinflation.

A nominal basic income below the natural rate causes deflation, unless we compensate with other sources of consumer income. In today's world, we have a basic income of zero. We know that zero is below the natural rate of basic income because we currently compensate for insufficient basic income by propping up consumers with other income sources, such as wages and private-sector debt.

The natural rate of basic income works the same at any price level, or under inflation and deflation. For our present purposes, we can simplify our analysis by assuming that monetary policy holds P fixed at some level $\bar{P}$. With a fixed general level of consumer prices ($\bar{P}$), the same quantity of money buys the same quantity of output. The level of consumer spending (R) is economic output (Q) multiplied by $\bar{P}$ (Mehrling, 1997, p. 100).

$$R = \bar{P} Q$$
$$\bar{R} = \bar{P}\, \bar{Q}$$

In these equations, $\bar{P}$ is the fixed price level that maps every R onto a corresponding Q. $\bar{R}$ maps onto $\bar{Q}$.

6. The Consumer Slice

Consumers - that is, the people - derive the most benefit from the economy when their spending allows them both to activate the economy's full productive capacity and to claim the economy's full output. I call the cross-section of the economy that exists between consumers and producers the "consumer slice" of the economy. Within this slice, money flows from consumers to producers to claim a flow of goods and services moving in the opposite direction.

We can judge the performance of the economy based on how well it serves consumers. The consumer slice is where this happens. More consumer spending power – that is, access to money – allows more goods and services to flow to the people.

The actual production process occurs outside the consumer slice. The labor market and the financial sector exist outside the consumer slice. Basic income originates from outside the consumer slice. But what happens outside the consumer slice affects what happens within the consumer slice.

We can imagine the consumer slice as a pair of pipes carrying the equal and opposite flows of money and economic output between consumers and producers. The economy produces at full output ($\overline{Q}$) when the pipes are full and the basic income is at its natural rate.

7. Equilibrium Output

Figure 3 is an aggregate market diagram of the macroeconomy. The vertical axis is the price level (P) and the horizontal axis is the economic output (Q). It shows why the level of economic output can settle below the economy's productive capacity and how basic income can fix the problem.

$\overline{I}$ is the input price level: the general price level of inputs to the economy's production. $\overline{P}$ is the consumer price level: the general price level of the output of consumer goods and services produced by the economy. Producers pay $\overline{I}$ and receive $\overline{P}$. $\overline{P}$ must be above $\overline{I}$ for producers to gain a profit. $\overline{Q}$ represents full economic output. It is possible for output (Q) to reach equilibrium at a level that falls short of ($\overline{Q}$).

It is impossible for the real price level – that is the price level adjusted for inflation – to change. By definition, the real price level is fixed. Because the real price level cannot adjust to clear markets, output quantity must adjust instead. The two-aggregate demand (AD) curves each imply a different equilibrium level of economic output. The demand distribution represented by the shallower demand curve causes the economy to produce at full output.

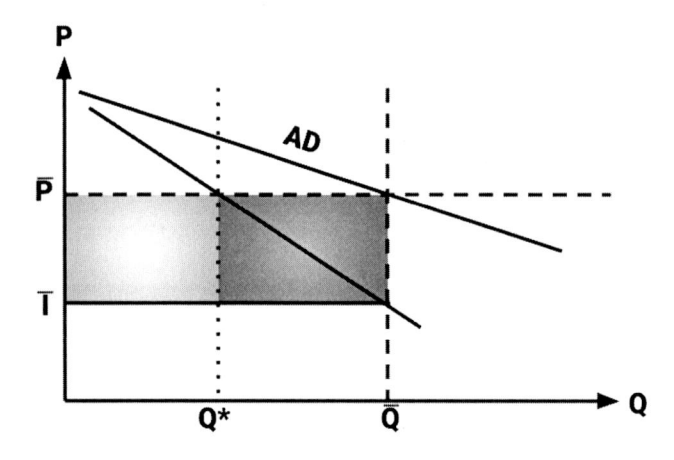

Figure 3: Aggregate Demand and Equilibrium Output

Individually, producers seek a combination of prices and quantities that earn them the most profit. In aggregate, they find equilibrium at the most profitable level of economic output (Q). To simplify exposition, the diagram assumes monopoly pricing, but the story is much the same if we add in competition.

For each demand curve, I have shaded the region bounded by the input price level ($\bar{I}$), the output price level ($\bar{P}$), and the quantity of output (Q). This area represents profit. Producers want to maximize this area. Each demand curve contains exactly one point that maximizes the area of the shaded rectangle. For the steeper demand curve, the most profitable point is at Q*.

Notice that the most profitable (P,Q) point along each demand curve occurs where the curve crosses the price level. This is no accident. We could draw a demand curve whose most profitable point fell at a different price level, but that would imply that the macroeconomy is not in equilibrium at the real price level. If some force keeps the demand curves fixed in real terms, the result is runaway inflation or deflation. The aggregate demand curves must adjust to re-establish equilibrium.

Because all price levels are equivalent, we gain nothing by pushing aggregate demand out of equilibrium with the price level. When demand settles back into equilibrium, the price level will again cross the aggregate demand curve at the most profitable (P,Q) point. Depending on the distribution of demand, any level of economic output up to $\bar{Q}$ is achievable at any nominal price level.

The shape of the aggregate demand (AD) curve ultimately determines the level of economic output (Q*). If AD is steeper, demand is less sensitive to changes in price (less elastic), and a lower Q* is profitable. If AD is shallower, demand is more elastic, and a higher Q* is profitable.

The absence of deflation or the presence of inflation imply neither that the economy is employing all of its resources nor that it is producing its output of goods and services to its full potential. The economy achieves full output ($\bar{Q}$) only if the most profitable point along the aggregate demand curve falls at the intersection of $\bar{P}$ and $\bar{Q}$. The flatter the distribution of consumer income, the flatter the aggregate demand curve. Basic income, on its own, represents a flat distribution of consumer income.

8. Monetary Policy

Central banks use monetary policy to manage instability in the financial sector, manage aggregate demand and stabilize the price level (P). However, policymakers are generally not thinking about changing the slope of the aggregate demand (AD) curve. Instead, they believe that propping up the price level also helps keep the economy close to full output ($\bar{Q}$) or "full employment." But, as we have seen, even at a fixed price level ($\bar{P}$), any level of equilibrium output (Q*) is possible up to ($\bar{Q}$).

Expansionary monetary policy works by allowing more credit expansion in the private financial sector. The distribution of consumer purchasing power generated by this credit expansion is unevenly skewed. And the central bank cannot control this. When monetary policy props up the price level (P), it steepens the AD curve. This pushes the equilibrium Q* below $\bar{Q}$.

Financial instability and price-level instability are not the same thing. Financial instability occurs when easy credit causes an excessive expansion of private debt that becomes more prone to default. The price level moves with any shift in the balance between the flow of consumer spending and the flow of goods and services they purchase with that money.

As a mechanism for distributing money to consumers, basic income is an alternative to easy credit. A higher basic income implies a monetary policy of tighter credit. Basic income at its natural rate flattens out the AD curve and allows the economy to activate its full productive potential ($\bar{Q}$) without requiring an excessive expansion of private credit and its concomitant financial instability.

9. Full Employment, Output or Access

Finite resources (e.g. materials and labor) exist and are available to produce the goods and services that people want and need. The economy provides the maximum possible benefit to the people when the only thing holding it back from doing more is the limited availability of resources.

While it is true that economic output is ultimately constrained by resource availability, it is not true that using up (fully employing) all of our available resources implies maximum economic output (Hazlitt, 1946, pp. 55–57). Unless we can promise that all resources are always employed to maximum efficiency, economic input does not automatically translate into economic output.

Labor is a resource. As with other resources, we can employ people's time more or less productively. On its own, employing more labor does not imply higher economic output. Specifically, to the extent that we employ workers for the purpose of providing them with money, those workers are not employed for the product of their labor. They are being employed unproductively.

"It would be far better, if that were the choice - which it isn't - to have maximum production with part of the population supported in idleness by undisguised relief than to provide "full employment" by so many forms of disguised make-work that production is disorganized. The progress of civilization has meant the reduction of employment, not its increase." (Hazlitt, 1946, 56)

By tying consumers' income to wages, we tie their access to goods and services to their employment. Economic output then becomes constrained by wage levels and employment levels. Even unproductive employment can lead to more output if it gives consumers more money to spend.

Basic income as a source of consumer purchasing power allows us to unbundle people's access to economic output from their employment as economic inputs. Basic income allows policymakers to pursue the simultaneous goals of maximum output, minimum employment, and maximum consumer access to the market.

10. Money as a Flow

It is tempting to adopt the assumption that there exists a certain quantity of money (money stock) in the economy that continues to circulate forever. Following this misguided assumption, the consumer slice becomes one segment in a perpetual money-flow circuit. The money stock then determines the level of spending (R) within the consumer slice. We can bring R up to $\bar{R}$ and Q* up to $\bar{Q}$ (See Figure 1) simply by ensuring that the money stock is the right size. Without some combination of economic growth and a tax to remove "excess" money from the economy, an ongoing basic income would cause sustained inflation.

This is not the real world. For the "money circulates" assumption to accurately describe the real world, it must be the case that nobody in the private sector accumulates money. Instead, money must always find its way back to the consumers who spent it so that they man spend it again (Menšík, 2014).

In the real world, money does not circulate perfectly. There are areas of the economy where money flows out faster than it flows in and vice versa. Importantly, these asymmetric and non-cyclical flows do not necessarily indicate any kind of defect in the economy, nor do they indicate a self-correcting disequilibrium state.

We can try to force the real world to follow a "money circulates" model by providing people jobs or actively redistributing existing money back to consumers. But we will never be fully successful. To plug the gap, we wind up forcing the financial sector to "print" our money through private credit expansion.

Rather than analyzing and managing some notion of a money stock, we can focus on directly optimizing the economy's money flow along with its equal and opposite flow of goods and services. The money that flows to consumers need not originate from producers. Just as goods and services have a source and a destination, so too can money. Basic income can be a source of money for the economy as a whole. (Howlett, 2020a)

11. The Market Versus the Government

Some resources are more efficiently allocated by the government, some by the market. It is beyond the scope of this paper to determine where best to draw the line. It can even make sense for the government to participate in resource allocation by trading in the market. The economy operates as a hybrid between private and public resource allocation.

The more resources that the government allocates directly, the fewer resources available to the market and the lower the natural rate of basic income. The government can increase the natural rate of basic income by using up fewer resources directly, and possibly by taxing or regulating activity that wastes resources, or by otherwise making more resources available.

If the government chooses to allocate all of the economy's resources - including labor - directly, then the economy has no need for money and there can be no basic income at any rate, natural or otherwise. Basic income becomes relevant only when the government leaves resources for the market to allocate. The market then requires that consumers have a source of purchasing power. Basic income can be that source up to the point where further money must be withheld to provide an incentive for people to sell their labor.

12. Resource Conservation

As we have seen, setting the basic income below its natural rate distorts the labor market and the financial sector away from efficiency. It also causes the economy to underproduce while we simultaneously overuse resources including labor. A low basic income forces us to employ our resources unproductively. It causes waste.

Nevertheless, even with basic income at its natural rate, though we may be using our resources efficiently in the short run, we may yet be using up resources at a rate that is unsustainable in the long run. It is possible for the natural rate of basic income to be incompatible with the level of resource conservation we desire.

Rather than setting the basic income below its natural rate, which only causes problems, we can adjust our fiscal policy to conserve resources. This has the effect of pushing down the natural rate of basic income.

Whether it be carbon, materials, or people's time, we can tax the excessive use of any resources we wish to conserve. If we wish to reduce overall economic activity, we can tax all sales of goods and services to consumers. These taxes make resource use more costly in general, and thereby reduce overall resource use. They also result in a lower productive capacity ($\overline{Q}$) and a lower natural rate of basic income.

By conserving resources through taxation and allowing the natural rate of basic income to fall, we avoid the negative effects of setting the basic income below its natural rate.

13. Local Versus National Basic Income

For local governments that operate below the level of the central bank, it is often not feasible to implement a basic income without other changes to fiscal policy. At the local level, the constraint on government spending is not resource availability so much as it is cash flow. A city perhaps has resources it can sell for cash, and debt it can issue in exchange for cash, but it ultimately still needs the cash, which is issued by the central bank.

The natural rate of basic income is the optimal level of basic income given no other changes to fiscal policy. This implies that the natural rate of basic income for a local government with a balanced budget is always whatever the current level of basic income happens to be. For a city without a basic income, the natural rate of basic income is zero.

As with a national basic income, it can nevertheless be useful to make fiscal adjustments - tax increases, reduced spending in other areas, etc. - that change the natural rate of basic income. At the local level, however, the macroeconomic effects of policy changes are insignificant enough that it is appropriate to think of tax revenue as funding government spending. Using taxes to fund a local basic income is really just a special case of using fiscal policy to move the natural rate.

Pushing around the natural rate of basic income solves fundamentally different problems than bringing basic income to its natural rate in the first place. At the level of the larger macroeconomy, bringing basic income to its natural rate prevents the central bank's monetary policy from leaning on the financial sector and the labor market from providing consumers their money. At the local level, this problem is mostly non-existent.

The low-hanging fruit for basic income is macroeconomic. Local governments are not doing monetary policy. Any government-supported job creation happens through the local government buying labor more or less directly, rather than through stimulating the financial sector. Basic income can still be worthwhile, but there are complicated trade-offs, and the choice is not always as clear as the macroeconomic policy choice between basic income and obviously broken monetary policy.

At the local level, it can be particularly hard to see the costs of basic income's absence. We can choose to make those costs explicit by instituting a basic income alongside a perfectly offsetting head tax. Alone, this leaves income distribution unchanged, but it reframes the absence of basic income as a tax on the poor, thereby bringing it into people's consciousness.

Fiscal trade-offs such as tax increases and spending cuts are useful to consider. The problem is that, even when thinking about basic income at the national level, people often start by asking about fiscal trade-offs associated with basic income without understanding that the way we get people their money is fundamentally broken to begin with. We can fix this problem by bringing basic income to its natural rate. In doing so, the only trade-off is between broken and fixed.

14. International Implications

The introduction of basic income by a country necessarily induces a shift in that country's monetary policy. But no country exists in an economic vacuum. We live in an interconnected global economy. Higher interest rates in one country will necessarily put pressure on the monetary policy of other countries as well as the exchange rates between currencies. The size of these effects will depend on many factors, including the size and global interconnectedness of the country introducing the basic income.

For example, the United States dollar is the international funding currency. When the United States raised interest rates in the early 1980s to stem domestic inflation, it caused a sovereign debt crisis in Mexico and other Latin American countries who could no longer afford to roll over their debt at the higher rates. (Ocampo, 2014)

If the United States were to unilaterally implement a domestic basic income, tighter international credit conditions will induce other countries to respond in some way, possibly following suit with basic incomes of their own to counter the effects of higher dollar interest rates.

Alternatively, the United States could simply decide to pay out a global basic income to every person in the world. This would further entrench the dollar's position as the international currency and the Federal Reserve's position as the central bank for the global monetary system.

There are many possible routes to a global basic income. Just as a national economy needs a source of money for consumers, so too does the global economy. The global economy has a certain productive capacity and also, therefore, a real level of consumer spending that it can sustain. Theoretically, there is a natural rate of basic income for the global economy.

15. Long-Run Equilibrium

There are some private-sector actors who are continually accumulating money - or, more precisely, financial assets. Some portion of the money that consumers spend does not circulate back to them. This alone forces us to provide consumers with a source of money beyond what the market supplies on its own. We are always in the process of replacing the money as it is being "accumulated away" from consumers. The most straightforward way to accomplish this is by issuing new money into the economy as a basic income.

The far less straightforward status quo is that consumers receive new money issued by the private financial sector and paid out through wages. The money then flows from consumers to producers as consumers buy goods and services. It accumulates in the pockets of the rich, making them richer and richer.

Because everyone's asset is someone else's liability, money issued by the private sector requires a corresponding growth in private-sector debt. The interlocking web of private debt obligations becomes increasingly brittle and unstable over time, making the economy more susceptible to financial collapse (Mehrling, 2011).

By originating consumers' money as a government-issued basic income, we solve some, but not all, of the problems with this status quo. Basic income can replace the growth of unstable private debt with growth of more stable public debt (national debt). But the rich still get richer in a basic income world.

This ongoing private-sector accumulation of money does not represent a stable long-run equilibrium. Eventually, a small number of rich people will have accumulated enough money to give them outsized power to cause significant problems in the economy, intentionally or not.

The solution to private-sector money accumulation is not obvious and could benefit from further research. Taxes are a popular suggestion for draining money from the economy, but taxes also cause incentive effects that may not align with our desired economic outcomes. Luxury taxes, in particular, can drain money from the economy while reducing resource waste. Another possibility would be for the government to enter the market as a producer selling goods and services to the people - especially rich people - as a way of draining their cash.

Basic income only solves the problem of where our money comes from. It does not address the problem of where our money goes.

16. Calibrating to the Natural Rate

The only way to discover our economy's natural rate of basic income is to gradually feel for it. We can start the basic income small and gradually increase the amount while we watch how the economy responds. As the basic income approaches its natural rate, the central bank will automatically tighten monetary policy. We should expect to see some businesses fail as tighter credit conditions prevent them from rolling over their funding (Mehrling, 2011). We should also expect to see changes in wage and employment structures as consumers receive a higher share of their income from outside the labor market.

When further increases in the basic income fail to provide any additional benefit, we will have reached the natural rate. Further increases would cause under-employment, under-investment, and inflation.

Once we have reached the natural rate, we can imagine policy administrators continuing to make adjustments to keep the basic income payout in line with the changing natural rate. Typically, this will involve increasing the payout as the natural rate grows to reflect productivity growth. I call this a policy of "calibrated basic income" (Howlett, 2020a).

As we calibrate the basic income, we can watch indicators such as interest rates, exchange rates, labor-market conditions, and economic output. Which economic indicators to use, and how best to use them remains an open research question. The technical aspects of calibrating basic income to its natural level are beyond the scope of this paper.

Absent a real shock to the economy's resource availability, we should expect the natural rate not only to grow, but to grow faster when policy administrators commit to matching the natural rate. Calibrating the basic income to its natural rate creates an incentive for productive investment. Productive capacity grows faster when investors know that consumers will have the money to activate new capacity.

For the purpose of resource conservation, we may instead choose to translate productivity increases into reduced resource usage. We can eschew output growth in favor of input shrinkage. The input shrinkage approach retains the incentive for productive investment. Regardless of the economy's size or rate of growth, producers compete for higher shares of the economy's total product.

17. Conclusion

Basic income is a simple solution to a simple problem: how to get people their money. For a given economy and a given fiscal position, there exists a single natural rate of basic income. The only way to boost the basic income beyond its current natural rate is to find a way to make resources more available to the market. This boosts the natural rate itself.

Only with an efficient money distribution mechanism can the market allocate resources for the maximum benefit of the people. But even before we discover the natural rate of basic income, we must accept that such a thing exists. The very concept helps us fix in our minds an idea of how to distribute money to consumers efficiently - an ideal to strive toward.

Hypothetically, we can achieve a world in which credit conditions are tight enough to prevent financial instability and wages merely provide an incentive for useful work. Such a world is a world with basic income at its natural rate. This world has no business cycles caused by the growth and collapse of asset bubbles. The elimination of "monetary make-work" affords people more freedom to spend their time in more fulfilling and productive ways.

There are problems that basic income does not solve. But fixing our broken money distribution system can help with a surprising number of problems that may, on the surface, seem unrelated to basic income. Furthermore, basic income at its natural rate removes a source of economic dysfunction that obscures our approach to addressing pressing problems such as immigration, financial crises, over-employment, poverty, crime, war and climate change.

There remain questions about how to discover the natural rate of basic income, how to calibrate basic income to its natural rate, and how to prevent the rich from becoming dangerously rich. But a fruitful exploration of these questions requires that we first accept the premise of a natural rate of basic income.

References

Hazlitt, H. (1946). Economics in One Lesson. Harper and Brothers

Howlett, A. (2020a). Introduction to Consumer Monetary Theory. Medium. https://medium.com/@alexhowlett/introduction-to-consumer-monetary-theory-78905b0606ca

Howlett, A. (2020b). The Economy Is a Giant Vending Machine. Medium. https://medium.com/discourse/the-economy-is-a-giant-vending-machine-20edc1348694

Howlett, A. (2021a). A Functional Approach to Money. Project Greshm. https://www.greshm.org/files/a-functional-approach-to-money.pdf

Howlett, A. (2021b). Basic Income and Financial Instability. Project Greshm. https://www.greshm.org/files/basic-income-and-financial-instability.pdf

Mehrling, P. G. (1997). The Money Interest and the Public Interest: American monetary thought, 1920–1970. Harvard University Press

Mehrling, P. G. (2011). The New Lombard Street: How the fed became the dealer of last resort. Princeton University Press

Menšík, J. (2014). The Origins of the Income Theory of Money. Review of Economic Perspectives, 14(4), 373–391.

Ocampo J. A. (2014) The Latin American Debt Crisis in Historical Perspective. In: Stiglitz, J.E., Heymann, D. (eds) Life After Debt (pp. 87–115). International Economic Association Series. Palgrave Macmillan

Van Parijs, P., & Vanderborght, Y. (2017). Basic Income: A Radical Proposal for a Free Society and a Sane Economy. Harvard University Press

Tobias Jäger

Basic Income and Industrial Relations

A Theoretical Literature Survey

The text is the first approach to the question of how a basic income affects trade unions. It gives a rough overview of existing wage bargaining theories. These theories are eye up for their suitability for UBI research. Afterward, Hirschman Exit and Voice Framework is presented and recommended as an alternative.

So far, most economic research on Basic Income has focused narrowly on financing and the labour supply. And in the public debate, the view that Basic Income makes people lazy and stops them working is not uncommon. To check the validity of these arguments, many researchers have investigated the reactions of the labour supply. Empirical studies based on so-called pilots, experiments and proxy data (gambling winners) provide mixed results. Research often stops at the econometric results without providing a deeper explanation of the results. So basic income research needs to take a hard look at economic models. Where these models are too simplistic, it must provide a stimulus for the extension of economic theory, or it will fail. Surprisingly, few people ask whether or how a basic income can change existing employment relationships, often claiming that Basic Income will lead to individual empowerment. There will be a minimum level for working conditions and no one will have to work under bad conditions. Such a development would hopefully also have a direct impact on existing employment relationships. Research on such issues has already achieved quite a bit, but not in a systematic way (see Gilbert, et al., 2019). This is why the work on this conference paper started with the way in which an unconditional basic income would affect industrial relations, i.e. employer and employee relationships. This is by nature a conflictual matter. Historically, the labour movement has played an important role in increasing democratisation and even today, when wage settlements are far more significant than general political programmes, labour struggles are an integral part of economic life.

Though the number of unionised workers has decreased significantly, their wage and quality rules still shape the labour market. This explains why trade unions are a lynchpin of our research. Trade unions, which in the past have expressed themselves critically towards basic income, fear a reduction of the welfare system (Mohr, et al., 2018) while activists for basic income believe that trade unions fear a loss of power. So both assumptions must be examined more closely. This conference paper is the author's first attempt to study the question in the light of economic theory. He has reviewed the literature to investigate ways in which it relates to Basic Income studies. Such research will hopefully help to close the gap between the labour movement and Basic Income activists.

The first chapter will provide a definition of trade unions. This will be followed by a review of the literature on trade unions and the economy. We will also give a rough overview of the way the literature has developed over the last century.

Chapter 3 will introduce the Exit and Voice framework, which goes back to Albert Hirschmann. Here exit as a category, behaviour and voice will be discussed in detail. This will be followed by an analysis of the interaction between basic income and Exit and Voice. Finally, in the summary, we will highlight the open questions and suggest ways to go further in Basic Income research.

1. Bargaining, Unions and Economic Science

As institutions, economics understand the "rule of the game" that drives economic outcomes (North, 1994). This is the common ground between such different schools as Industrial relations, Old Institutional Economics and New Institutional Economics. Here it is helpful to reactivate the term "industrial relation" for our purposes. John Dunlop describes industrial relations as a "web of rules" (Müller-Jentsch, 2004). At the centre of this web is the relationship between employer and employees, with all its manifestations (e.g., collective bargaining) (Kaufman, 2008). According to Dunlop the unions are one of the major actors when it comes to organizing this relationship (Müller-Jentsch, 2004). The author is concerned with the theoretical models involved in the introduction of a basic income and its consequences for trade unions, with a special focus on strikes, bargaining behaviour, union membership and the question whether a basic income is a threat or an opportunity for unions. Only the theoretical literature will be reviewed here. Please note that the rich empirical literature has not been systematically investigated. We shall start with a definition of a trade union. This is "an organization that represents the people who work in a particular industry, protects their rights, and discusses their pay and working conditions with employers". (Cambridge Dictionary)

At the macroeconomic level, the trade unions appear to play a key role in shifting the distribution between capital and labour, and between wage earners. Taking a critical stance, we can ask whether trade unions actually help to increase labour's share of the national income. Some economists maintain that only technological progress and demography are responsible here (Stansbury & Summers, 2020). This debate is not new; it has always been the subject of controversy (Dierwert, 1974). And as inequality increases, collective bargaining and trade unions are once again receiving more attention from economists (Jaumotte & Buitron, 2015) (Stansbury & Summers, 2018) (Stansbury & Summers, 2020) (Farber, et al., 2021). These papers find a link between the weakening of the unions and the increasing spread of factor incomes. Initial results show the importance of liberalisation of the labour market and applying political pressure (capital mobility, wage competitiveness) in weakening bargaining power (Keune, 2021). The reserved attitude of the trade unions, especially in Germany, is to be understood against the background of this development (Mohr, et al., 2018). Hence collective bargaining seems to have consequences not only for personal income but also for factor income. A change in industrial relations will probably impact the macro level, a dimension of the basic income debate that is often not taken into account.

This new attention cannot hide the fact that the topic has been ascribed little importance in the last thirty years. We can see cycles of rising articles. There was an upswing in the late 1930s/40s, then a steady levelling in the 1950s, followed by a decline in the 1960s and 1970s (Johnson, 1975). In the eighties, the topic picked up momentum, declining again in the mid-nineties. As we shall see later there is a huge theoretical gap between real trade unionism and economic doctrine. The theoretical approaches are extremely unsatisfactory in explaining nominal wage bargaining and union behaviour, where disregard for psychological causes and strategic communication play an important role (Usher, 2012). Beyond that, however, it is important to consider that collective bargaining has a conflict dimension at its core. Bargaining over the pieces of an apple means insecure ownership rights over the apple. It can also be said that the object of the wage rate and the conditions of employment are constantly, or at least periodically, up for disposition. From a business perspective this means that future dividends will be more uncertain. This conflict dimension has been stressed to the extreme by authors like Tugan-Baranowski, who saw social power as the only (or most important) factor when it comes to setting wages and factor income (Blümle, 1975).

Böhm-Barwerk in particular was opposed these views. In the end, it is an economic law that sets the real wages and nothing else. So neoclassic theories insist on the correctness of the marginal approach for wages as well. This is why the Neoclassical … stressed the monopolistic nature, seeing unions as a force for distortion (Drakopoulos & Katselidis, 2014). Not enough early neoclassical saw it as distortion they also denied that unions are in the field of economics science (Drakopoulos & Katselidis, 2014).

The first economists to deal in depth with trade unions were the so-called Old Institutional School. They considered the unions to be two-faced and saw them as both economic and political actors (Kaufman, 2002). Their methodological approach was strongly inductive and case study-oriented (Boyer & Smith, 2001), which meant there were no formal models. As a result, there was little exchange with the neoclassical authors (Boyer & Smith, 2001). It was only with the advent of John Hick's Theory of Wages (1932) that neoclassic became aware of this issue. From the 1940s onwards, we can see the rising numbers of trade unions models.

From our definition we can easily identify the two faces of the issue. One concentrates on rights and condition, the other on wages. This led to the emergence of two different traditions. The economic one is linked to John Dunlop's (1944) model while the political one goes back to Arthur Ross (1944). The first sees unionism as a method of price (quantitative) fixing and is sometimes called the monopole one. The second one, known as Sumner Slichter, "brings civil rights into the industry" (Kaufman, 2002). From a microeconomic point of view, the challenge in formalising such a model is to decide what exactly should be maximised. This is still a controversial issue (Oswald, 1985, p. 162). Dunlop argues for the wage bill while Ross is against it. The latter sees other preferences at work and mentions fairness, justice and personal ambition. Ross may have more in common with institutional economics and political science. In the middle of both is the industrial relations approach. (Kaufman, 2002, p. 118). In economic models unions are monopolists and maximize wage bills with regard to unemployment.

I will provide an overview of the existing literature in this chapter. For a better understanding, we shall first look at bargaining theory and then focus on the trade union models. After that we will look more closely at the real relationship between employer and employee.

2. Bargaining in the Economic Literature

Above we asked about the influence of Basic influence on employer and employee relationships. To answer this question, we will review the bargaining literature, with a special focus on nominal wage determination. The first step is to review the (collective) bargaining literature. Unfortunately, (collective) bargaining phenomena are a hard nut to crack for (neoclassical) economic theory.

By bargaining we understand the situation in which at least two people are entitled to something collectively but cannot appropriate or make use of it until they agree on how it is to be shared (Usher, 2012). Zeuthen characterizes bargaining as "a rational deliberation as to the most profitable behaviour in a situation of uncertainty" (Saraydar, 1965). Sixty years ago, Rothschild remarked that bargaining has no place in perfect competition theory (Rothschild, 1957, p. 282). Nevertheless, Frederik Zeuthen (1930) and John Hicks (1932) introduced the topic into the field of neoclassical economics. Zeuthen highlighted conflict risk as a factor (Blümle, 1975). Later Pen and Shackle contributed to this model. In each stage of the negation, both players compare, insisting on their own claim at the risk of causing a conflict (Sapsford, 1980). The player with a lower willingness to take risks will accept the other claim. Zeuthen does not explain how each player gets the probability of conflict (Sapsford, 1980). Nor does his model tell us much about exogen variables and their influence on bargaining.

We now move on to another model. Hicks, in his Theory of Wages, specifically in the seventh chapter, formulated a microeconomic intuition of how union/employer bargaining or, as he called it, "industrial disputes" works (Hicks, 1932).

2.1 Hicks' Bargaining Model

Hicks' attempts to answer the question whether unions can achieve higher wages. His model is in the tradition of bilateral monopolies. Here model unions optimize wage rates (Hicks, 1932). Hicks therefore constructs a schedule of wages and length of strike (Hicks, 1932). The weapon to achieve higher wages is a strike.

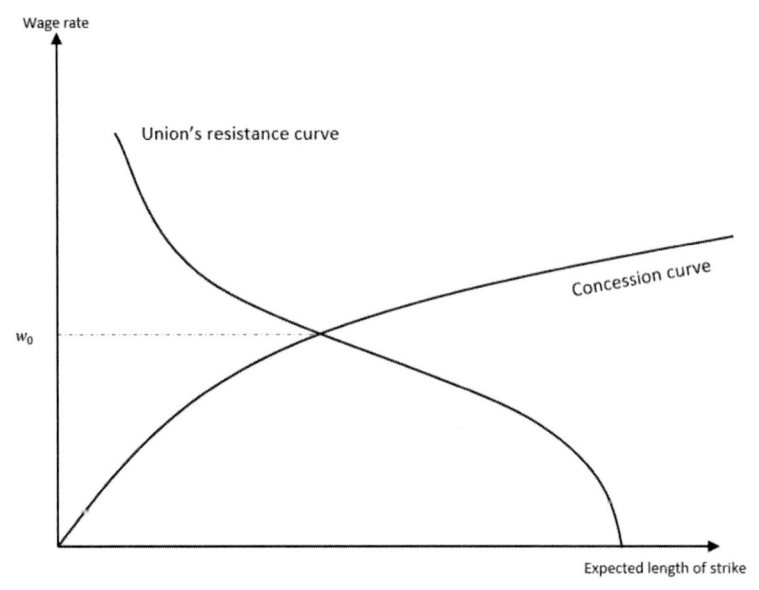

Hicks' bargaining Model. Own illustration following Hicks (1932)

Thus, he recognizes the conflict dimension of wage bargaining but doesn't mention it as a conflict. To increase the pressure on unions, the duration of strikes can be increased. Employers have the option to agree to higher wage rates or resist. For the employer, we can create a concession curve. Setting opposite to each period of strike the highest wage an employer will be willing to pay rather than endure a stoppage of that period. At this wage, the (expected) cost of the strike and the discounted expected cost of concession balance (Hicks, 1932). If resistance is cheaper than a concession, he will resist. Otherwise, he will meet the Union's claim. (Hicks, 1932) Figure 1 illustrates this point with the wage rate w_0. In reality both sides are unaware of the opposite curves. There is therefore room for negotiation tactics and skill (Blümle, 1975).

It should be clear that the concession curve must be finite. When the break-even point is reached, the entrepreneur will leave the market and close his factory (Hicks, 1932). Unions will have a strong incentive to strike if employers offer low wage rate growth. This can be observed bottom right in Figure 1. The strike duration is zero when employers satisfy all wage claims at the beginning of negotiations. This case doesn't show up in the graph. Strike duration increases as wage concessions diverge from wage expectations. This negatively sloped resistance curve intersects the x-axis at the strike length, which cannot be exceeded due to limited union funds. The resistance curve can be horizontal. This is the case when workers can resist a wage cut but are unable to push through wage increases (Hicks, 1932). If we assume perfect information, a strike will never occur. This is why Hicks allows for incomplete information on the union side (Sapsford, 1980). Only then can a strike happen.

In this model, the optimum (Hicks called it skilful negation) result of a negotiation occurs at a point where both would be willing to run the risk of a strike of the same duration rather than make further concessions (Bishop, 1964). While these models give us a feeling for bargaining, we cannot calculate a specific result (Blümle, 1975). More annoying is the fact that it tells us nothing about the Trade the non-market income on such a bargaining process. We can speculate that the resistance curve will take on another shape or shift. The duration of the strikes may increase because the strike funds are bigger. But the union might accept a lower wage before they strike if they achieve a utility level that is adequate. We do not know. Another weak point is the bilateral monopolies approach. The simplification of a monopoly approach also deprives us of the possibility to study the interaction between basic income and tariff-bound or non-tariff-bound sectors. We therefore need to search for other models. Harsanyi connects Zeuthen and Hicks with game theory (Bishop, 1964). He shows that the Zeuthen result is identical to a Nash Bargaining solution. This brings us to our next step.

Game theory deals with interactive decision-making, which is where two or more individuals make decisions that affect each other (Bonanno 2008). A bargaining situation is a game situation in the sense that the outcome of bargaining depends on both players' bargaining strategies (Muthoo, 1999). The Game theory goes back to Neumann and Morgenstern's (1951) theory of games and economic behaviour. Nash (1950) in particular made a significant contribution to the bargaining literature (Chatterjee, 2010). The literature makes a distinction between axiomatic and strategic bargaining models. Axiomatic theory is sometimes also called cooperative game theory. Such models are mostly concerned with an axiomatic characterization of bargaining solutions, such as the well-known Nash Bargaining Solution (NBS) (Nash, 1950) or the Raiffa solution- however discuss the process of reaching that solution. Much more important is the fact that cooperative models assume that agreement can be enforced without cost. (Chatterjee, 2010, p. 1) Strategic bargaining models or non-cooperative models allow statements to be made about the process itself. Such models can say something about the "tit-for-tat" motives and so they are more realistic (Chatterjee, 2010). Unfortunately, we can only take a brief look at the basic concept.

2.2 Cooperative Models and the Nash Bargaining Solution

A bargaining problem is characterized by a number of player's N and by the Pair (S, d). S is the Set of all feasible payoffs and stands for the disagreement point (Holler, et al., 2019). The object of study in cooperative bargaining theory is a (bargaining) rule. A bargaining rule describes, for each bargaining problem, the outcome that will be obtained as a result of the interaction between the negotiators. To make such a rule we need axioms. Axioms are assumptions that are taken to be true or desirable. Every bargaining rule develops from a series of axioms (Holler, et al., 2019). Nash describes his rule as an existing negotiation process and therefore interprets it in a positivist way (Kıbrıs, 2010). The real-world evaluation of such claims is weak (Chatterjee, 2010, p. 3) (Holler, et al., 2019). So, with time, a normative understanding of such rules has emerged (NBS) (Kıbrıs, 2010). For an application of the Nash bargaining solution, see Franke and Jäger in this conference volume.

Mathematically, we can express it as follows.

A (bargaining) rule F: B→R^N assigns each bargaining problem $(S, d) \in B$ to a feasible payoff profile $FS, d \in S$ (Kıbrıs, 2010).

John Nash establishes his famous solution from these four axioms (Holler, et al., 2019) (Kıbrıs, 2010).

1) Scale invariant

$F(\lambda(S), \lambda(d)) = \lambda(F(S, d))$, means that the result doesn't depend on standardisation of the arbitrary utility function (Holler, et al., 2019).

2) Symmetric

In simple terms, this means that the set of feasible payoff pairs is symmetric. The solution should give equal utilities to the two players (Chatterjee, 2010). The stronger case is anonymity and stipulates that no one has bargaining power (Kıbrıs, 2010).

3) Independence of irrelevant alternatives

Axiom 3 means that only conflict point d and the negotiation outcome themselves are relevant. The number of possible pay-offs functions doesn't matter. (Holler, et al., 2019) This assumption is empirically very weak. So, it is no surprise to discover that it is highly controversial. (Kıbrıs, 2010)

4) Pareto optimal

Pareto optimal mean it is not possible to make a player strictly better off without making the other player strictly worse off (Chatterjee, 2010).

Nash Bargain Solution:

$$N(S, d) = argmax \prod_{i=1}^{n}(x_i - d_i)x_i \in P(S, d)$$

The Nash solution means that maximizing the product of surplus utilities will archive a result that satisfies all four axioms (Kıbrıs, 2010). This makes the result unique and explains why the NBS is preferred by many economists to other bargaining rules. (Mas-Colell et al., 1995) For us, the Nash bargaining solution is of particular interest because it is widely used in bargaining literature. The axiomatic approach however does not have the same impact as theories on union bargaining (Kaufman, 2002). The Nash solution is about a fair bargaining settlement that is accepted by rational players. Fairness and efficiency (Pareto) are thus essential elements of Nash's solution. But this research agenda also has some very serious limitations. In the original set up strikes never occur (Franz, 2013). Below, Usher makes a harsh but not entirely unfounded verdict.

"Genuine bargaining is, almost by definition, indeterminate. A bargain is the resolution of a dispute. If bargainers can be relied upon to respect a notion of fairness, to agree on a fifty-fifty split of the pie, or to accept shares mandated by the Nash bargaining solution, then bargaining is just playacting, for there is no real dispute and nothing left to bargain about." (Usher, 2012, p. 28)

There are two critical points here. The first is connected with rationality. In an NBS something inefficient will never be reached (Chatterjee, 2010). We can also add the assumption of complete information. We can see with Hicks how important it was to relax this assumption in order to be able to explain that everybody can strike. A Basic Income can be modelled for example as a different form of threatening point. We will come back to this when we discuss the "outside option". The author is sceptical about the Nash bargaining research project as a description of reality. Nevertheless, it can help to clarify the different normative aspects. Kaufman notes that the impact of cooperating game theory on the field of union wage determination is limited (Kaufman, 2002). He mentions the three shortcomings of its behavioural foundations, neglect of the bargaining process, and lack of generating testable hypotheses. We move on to the non-cooperative models.

2.3 Non-Cooperative Models

Though cooperative bargaining theory has generated a large body of literature, its use for bargaining, especially wage bargaining is limited, especially when it comes to explaining strikes and unemployment cooperative models (Manzini, 1998). When in 1982 Rubenstein presented his model of "bargaining, using alternating offers", great optimism was associated with this approach. By taking into account the actual negotiation process, a better behavioural foundation was said to be ensured in a real bargaining situation (Kennan & Wilson, 1989). Let us demonstrate this in detail.

2.4 The Rubinstein Game

Rubinstein's game starts with two agents who make offers and counteroffers on how to share a pie (Manzini 1998, p.3). The assumption is that both players want more rather than less and don't want to delay. Any delay will harm both equally. Rubenstein proves that the game ends immediately. From a Bargaining Power perspective, we have the First Mover advantage (Manzini 1998). Binmore, Rubenstein and Wolinsky show that the solution of the Rubinstein game converges with the Nash bargaining solution depending on the parameters (Kaufman, 2002). In such a setting, the question arises: How does a basic income affect the "delay factor". We can try to explain this psychologically or in terms of material needs. Intuitively, at a moment when I receive a sufficiently large basic income, the "delay factor" swings significantly in favour of labour. The model doesn't tell us much about this issue. As before, there is no room for strikes or negotiation. Rubinstein's results failed for lack of more realistic modelling of the structure of wage negotiations (Manzini, 1998).

One way to get strikes in this kind of model is by considering incomplete information. Otherwise, they work with multiple equilibria and, with delay, arrive at a Pareto-optimal outcome. Multiple equilibria and the effects of non-market incomes are a wide and open field, which could provide some surprises for us, for example when not bargaining for a one-time payment but a flow of pay will arise with room for delay (Manzini, 1998). After a while the author understands that the question is "How do exit strategies influence wage bargaining?" Supporters of a basic income very often argue that a Basic Income can be an Exit strategy. In other words, there is a possibility of leaving the table. This is a variant of a so-called outside option. Within game theory, these outside options have been discussed several times and the Non-Cooperative Bargaining Theory with an outside-option appears to be the best starting point for modelling Basic Income theory. A wide range of papers have been written on this issue.

2.5 Conflict Dimension

The social and institutional settings of work have had conflict potential from the very beginning (Fernandez-Huerga, Garcia-Arias, & Salvador, 2017). This is often highlighted by Institutional and Marxian Economics (Bailly, 2016). One speciality is the critique of the view that labour is a commodity, which may also be fruitful for Basic Income research. The three traditional topics of the "radical school" all seem to be highly interesting for our purposes. They are work organization, labour force segmentation, work discipline and on-the-job effort. (Bailly, 2016). But in neo-classical tradition, there are also a number of papers about the unequal power between employee and employer (for more information see Card, 2022). Hicks and Zeuthen both understand the conflict potential but both models have only imagined conflict modelling, there is no harm at all (Usher, 2012). Usher correctly points out that there is no explanation for why bargaining breaks down and strikes occur (p.28). Another way to see it is as wage bargaining, a way of sharing "rent-seeking profit" with the Management. The idea of conflict as a part of rent-seeking activities goes back to Hirshleifer (Hirshleifer, 1989). As far as the author is aware, neither rent-seeking nor contest models are frequently used for questions relating to the labour market. Examples are (Rama, 1997) and (Guertzgen, 2009).

3. Theory of Trade Unions

If we widen our view, we also find models of trade unions without implicit bargaining. I call this model the Theory of Trade Unions though this is not quite correct. The focus of such a model often lies on the unemployment-wage question, which can be divided into two categories. One is the monopoly theory of unions, with the extension of the right-to-manage, the other is the efficient bargaining approach. Both have accused the unions of monopolistic behaviour. They maintain that the unions diminish the labour supply (quantity) or other speaking fix the wages (price). Unfortunately, none of these models allow for strikes so they cannot deal with the conflict aspect (Oswald, 1985). Before introducing both theories, the authors have another critique, one that, is highly important for Basic Income studies. The judgment when it comes to the unions is dependent on the market. In a world of perfect competition, we would come to a negative judgment. But when the labour market is imperfect, the picture is less clear. (Kaufman, 2005) All these models assume perfect competition without unions. But this is misleading. Nobel Prize winner David Card makes the point "the time has come to recognize that many firms have some wage-setting power" (Card, 2022). This should also be recognized by basic income researchers.

3.1 "Monopoly" – the "Right to Manage" Model

The monopoly model or "right to manage" starts with the assumption that there is only one Trade Union and one Employer (Franz, 2013). They assume that only union members will be hired and that the union must accept as a member any person hired by the employer. Anglo-Americans use the phrase "closed shop" for the first, while the second is referred to as the "union shop". In the USA, different laws apply at the state level. Whether such an agreement is legal is therefore strongly dependent on the location. For the next steps, we follow Oswald's description of the model (Oswald, 1985). If wages are negotiated between union and employer, we refer to the model as the "right to manage". If not, and the union can set the wage rate unilaterally, we have a monopoly model (p.169). Given the outcome of bargaining, the firm unilaterally sets the employment situation (Manning, 1994). The right to manage fits the facts more than monopoly setting though the results are very similar (Oswald, 1985).

Let's start with a union utility function, where n is employment, w is wage, m is a union member and fix, b is an unemployment benefit. Unions fix and optimize the wage. U is a concave utility function. (Franz, 2013).

$$u(.)' > 0 \text{ and } u(.)'' < 0.$$
$$\text{Union: } U = n * u(w) + (m - n)u(b)$$
$$\text{Firm: } pf(n)(\sigma + w)n$$

Firms maximize employment. The price is p, f is a concave production function, σ is an employment subsidy by the government.

$$f(.)' > 0 \text{ and } (.)'' < 0.$$

Back to the union utility, we implement subsidisation of employment and workers by the state. t is a marginal tax rate.

$$U = n * u(w(1-t) + s) + (m - n)u(b)$$

The main results are that if the unions set the wage over the competition level the employment will be lower. The equilibrium is inefficient. For us, more important than a rising unemployment benefit will be an increase in the desired wage and a worker's income subsidy lowers the union desired wages (Oswald, 1985). This renders the effect of the Basic Income ambiguous. The result is driven by the indifference curve/utility function. We need more research here. Union membership doesn't play any role (Oswald, 1985), which seems to be unrealistic. Membership can be suggested, as highlighted by Ross in a guideline for union behaviour (median voter theorem) (Kaufman, 2002). But it should also be realistic to assume that membership can be connected to bargaining power (Oswald, 1985).

3.2 Efficient Bargain Model

Another type of model was established by McDonald and Solow (1981) efficient bargain model, it is sometimes seen as a counterpoint to a pure monopoly model. The reason is that, unlike the previous model, it leads to efficient solutions. Again, the union and employer negotiate, again, in sole representation but now simultaneously on wages and employment (McDonald & Solow, 1981). This assumption is also criticised because in reality negotiations (directly) on employment levels rarely take place (Naylor, 2003). For the simplest case, we have (Oswald, 1985).

$$Firm: pf(n) - wn$$
$$Union: U = n * u(w) + (m - n)u(b)$$
$$Contract\ Curve: ((u(w) + u(b)))/(u'(w))) = w - pf^{\wedge\prime}(n)$$

The novelty of this approach was that the result is Pareto optimal (Naylor, 2003). Another interesting result is that Trade Unions can produce "overemployment". This result disappears when unions run an insurance system (Oswald, 1985). We cannot go into more detail here but before we go further, we want to look at what happens if we increase the reservation wage. Mathematically speaking, we derive the CC equation and get the following result:

$$\frac{\partial w}{\partial b} = \frac{-u'b}{[w - pf'(n)]U''(w)} > 0$$

This means that CC shifts to the left. In Graph 2 we can see that in the shift from c to c_1. Which goes hand in hand with an increased wage. This is not unexpected because we work with the same utility function. The opportunity for Basic Income research is to carefully examine utility functions and see how this changes outcomes. See, for example, Neumärker and Weinel in this publication. A basic income would have to be modulated in both models and its effect on the wage-employment ratio would have to be examined with different tax systems.

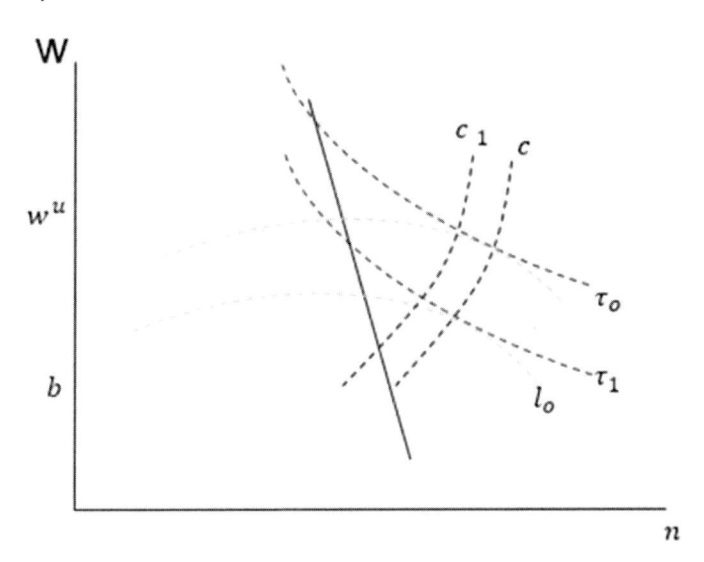

Efficient Bargain Model – Sources: Following (Oswald, 1985, p 170)

When comparing both models we have to consider that, if the unions don't care about employment, both models are identical (Manning, 1994). These models and all their followers have serious limitations but also some strengths. And some of them can explain certain empirical observations. But none of them explain the whole picture (Kaufman, 2002). What is more, the empirical verifiability of such models is still very difficult today (Oswald, 1985). The serious shortcomings that the theoretical framework of both models are that they are not robust (Manning, 1994). Changes in assumptions about the economic environment have overturned most of the results. Only the fact that union wages are higher than non-union wages seem stable Hence comes the harsh verdict that the Theory of Unions is very fragile and has failed (Drakopoulos & Katselidis, 2012).

3.3 Membership Models or Institutions Matter

Our search for wage bargaining models has been rather disappointing so far. Previously our model generalised such things as "close shops", a fixed level of union membership, monopolies and so on (Booth & Chatterji, 1995). But the "rule of the game" itself may vary from legislation to legislation and only a few observations can be generalised to all countries (Schnabel, 2013). Therefore, generalized assumptions do not describe the various legislation adequately. We can observe that the Union density between countries with different industrial relations differs greatly (Godechot & Salibekyan, 2019). If we don't find models that work well for wage bargaining, we may at least be able to find models that can explain Union density. Then we can also say something about the impact of Basic Income. Dunlop and Ross both argue about union behaviour with regard to their membership (Kaufman, 2002). Now we will take a short look at the data and then say something about the theory.

Claus Schnabel found four weak stylized facts (p.267). The union density and unionization do not converge in the Western world [1]. Union access to the working place is important for unions [2]. Unemployment reduces union growth and density. This relationship is the opposite in countries with the GHENT system, an arrangement in which unions are the sole providers of unemployment insurance. Such rules exist in Iceland, Denmark, Finland, Sweden and Belgium. In recent years, the first private unemployment insurance schemes have been introduced in some of these countries (Schnabel, 2013).

This can be observed in graph 3 (Source: Schnabel 2013, p. 257). Belgium and Finland are the countries with the lowest negative changes while Sweden and Denmark have negative changes but nevertheless the highest level of union density. Younger employees are less likely to unionize [4], but it is not clear if this changes with ageing or if it's a generational issue.

Table 1. Union density in 25 advanced countries.

	Union density (net membership/employment, %)						Change (% points)	
	1960	1970	1980	1990	2000	2010	1960–2010	1980–2010
AU	50.2	44.2	48.5	39.6	24.5	19.0 [a]	-31.2	-29.5
AT	67.9	62.8	56.7	46.9	36.6	28.1	-39.8	-28.6
BE	41.5	42.1	54.1	53.9	49.5	52.0 [a]	10.5	-2.1
CA	29.2	31.0	34.0	34.0	30.8	30.3 [a]	1.1	-3.7
CH	36.1	28.9	27.7	22.7	20.6	17.8 [a]	-18.3	-9.9
CL				18.2	13.5	14.3 [a]		
DE	34.7	32.0	34.9	31.2	24.6	18.6	-16.1	-16.3
DK	56.9	60.3	78.6	75.3	74.2	68.8 [a]	11.9	-9.8
ES			18.7	12.5	16.7	15.9 [a]		-2.8
FI	31.9	51.3	69.4	72.5	75.0	70.0	38.1	0.6
FR	19.6	21.7	18.3	9.9	8.0	7.6 [b]	-12.0	-10.7
GR			39.0	34.1	26.5	24.0 [b]		-15.0
IE	50.4	59.1	63.5	56.7	40.4	36.6 [a]	-13.8	-26.9
IT	24.7	37.0	49.6	38.8	34.8	35.1	10.5	-14.4
JP	32.9	35.1	31.1	26.1	21.5	18.5	-14.4	-12.7
LU		46.8	50.8	46.4	42.5	37.3 [b]		-13.5
NL	40.0	36.5	34.8	24.3	22.9	19.0 [a]	-21.0	-15.8
NO	60.0	56.8	58.3	58.5	54.4	54.4 [a]	-5.6	-3.9
NZ		56.5	69.1	48.8	22.4	21.4 [a]		-47.7
PT	100.0	100.0	54.8	28.0	21.6	19.3	-80.7	-35.5
SE	72.1	67.7	78.0	81.5	80.1	68.9	-3.2	-9.1
SG		25.4	22.8	14.4	16.1	17.6 [a]		-5.2
UK	40.4	44.8	50.7	39.3	30.5	27.5 [a]	-12.9	-23.2
US	30.9	27.4	22.3	15.5	12.8	11.4	-19.5	-11.0
cv[c], 18 countries	0.426	0.396	0.367	0.481	0.569	0.596		
cv[c], 24 countries			0.419	0.513	0.596	0.612		

[a] 2009; [b] 2008; [c] coefficient of variation.
Source: ICTWSS Database, version 3.0 (Visser, 2011); own calculations.

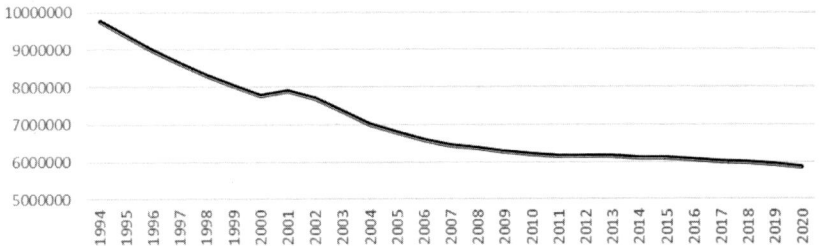

Members Deutsche Gewerkschaftsbund (1994 -2020)

Source: DGB, Membership Data

Demographic change and changing average firm size can be mentioned as exogen factors that hit union density hard (Schnabel, 2013). We should not necessarily believe that the negative union density trend will be ongoing.

As we see in Graph 4, for example, the DGB unions stabilized their numbers before Corona. If we look only at the membership, there is one weakness. From Graph 4 we might think that France has a very weak union movement, but membership doesn't necessarily mean a low participation rate. French unions can mobilize a lot more people for strikes and actions than they have members (Godechot & Salibekyan, 2019). We should keep this in mind.

Let us now look at models which can be helpful for further research. Endogenous membership models are a relatively new development (Kaufman, 2002). Here unions are confronted with a common "free-riding" problem (Olson, 1965). If unions are not able to solve the prison dilemma for each member. Then unions cannot organize enough members and will disappear. One way to solve this is with coercion (Olson, 1965). A weakened version of coercion would be "close shop". Neither are common in the western world. For the membership question, the industrial setting is an important determinate. We can distinguish three categories of membership models (Naylor, 2003). Firstly, dichotomous labour markets with one union and one non-union sector give the impression that wage bargaining determines the size of union membership as a result of a weighting of unemployment and wage preference from a median worker position (Naylor, 2003). However, it can be argued that different sectors, characterized by firm, size, capital/labour ratio, and production process may be related to membership density (Schnabel, 2013). Second, in line with our data above (Booth & Chatterji, 1995) and (Holmlund & Lundborg, 1999) create models that explain membership through a private good e.g. union unemployment insurance or legal advice. Their results suggest that the membership is independent of wage bargaining and in line with Olson's free-rider problem. Unions have to create incentives. The last category is that of Social Custom. George Aklerof defined this as "An Act whose utility to the agent performing it in some way depends on the beliefs or actions of other members of the community" (Naylor, 2003, p.78). In such a scenario the cost for collective action will be much lower. The free-riding problem will also disappear (Naylor, 2003). The data situation appears less clear here. While some authors assume there is a free-riding problem, others see no evidence of this in the data

(Booth & Bryan, 2004). Nor do they consider the problem to be exaggerated (Kaufman, 2005). But what we see clearly on this issue is that "institutions matter." That's why it will not be possible to find an answer that applies equally to all systems. In different settings, there will be different strategies from people and firms. How can Basic Income enter into this picture? The membership models from Booth & Chatterji and Holmlund & Lundborg can be used as starting point. Both are formal models that could potentially simulate a universal money transfer and its impact on membership. It is a frustration for basic income research that we have little knowledge of the dynamics from the employed, unemployed, and dropouts that we could incorporate into such models. In original, both work with a fixed labour supply. For the other two categories, we see that a basic income would initially give little reason to believe that membership numbers would decline as a result. The work culture would not change overnight and the impact of a basic income on wage agreements remains unclear. For more on this topic we follow Bruce E. Kaufman's suggestion and open our narrow microeconomic framework a little bit (Kaufman, 2002). The authors recognize that with Exit and Voice a helpful framework exists.

4 Exit and Voice

Let us now take a different approach to thinking about our questions. We have seen that the formal models can only unsatisfactorily explain the behaviour of trade unions. This makes them suboptimal when it comes to telling us about "potential" non-market income. In 1965, Mancur Olson wrote his famous theory of collective action. In line with neoclassical theory Olsen predicts that homo economics has no interest in participating in the creation of collective action. Ironically, as evidence to the contrary, there was a wave of movements and protests in the 1960s and 70s (Hirschmann, 1982). Due to his dissatisfaction with the collective action theory, Albert O. Hirschman wrote his famous book Exit-Voice and Loyalty (Almeida, 2021). As a result, he attracted not only friends but also many critics. Olson, and especially Tullock, rejected the book vehemently. Olson's significant contribution to the issue of collective action problems is not unimportant for our investigation (Olson, 1965). Hirschman argues that there is no question that free-riding is a threat to the existence of any organization (Voice). He asks how individuals react to divergences between the desired and the actual situation? For that Albert O Hirschman introduced, with Exit and Voice, two possible reactions. Voice means that this person starts to protest, articulating a complaint to the management. Voice can be a different type of action or protests, including mobilizing public opinion (Hirschmann, 1970).

By "exit", he means behaviour that one people leave the market. For his approach, he relaxes as the perfect competition assumption slightly. So it will happen that when a firm reduces the quality, what follows is a decline in revenue due to an exit of unhappy customers. The companies will move back to their old quality or he has to leave the market. (Hirschmann, 1970) This is the power of exit. Exit's border solution can be described as total "self-sufficiency." This renders the basic income superfluous or useless since society is based on the division of labour is abolished and so nothing can be bought with the money. Any form of paid work is a process that requires contact with others. We see that Exit is closely connected to the market system but can also be interpreted as a way to leave the market system. Exit seems more like a market instrument than a political tool. Nevertheless, it should not be ignored that "Exit" has a strong link to all liberal political and contract theories (Warren, 2011). Exit strategy establishes itself as a cornerstone in the (libertarian) pro-basic income argumentation also appear as a tool for democratizing (Warren, 2011) (Widerquist, 2013). The other side of the coin is "entry". It is frequently forgotten that exit and entry are closely linked. If I leave the market, it must be ensured that I can get back in. The problems one can get into if you fall out of a system can be observed in the housing market.

Birnbaum & DeWispelaer are correct when they mention that their exits strategy has not been subjected to a systematic economic analysis by basic income advocates (Birnbaum & Wispelaere, 2016) (Birnbaum & Wispelaere, 2021). We use the Exit and Voice for our question because it helps to understand the dimension of Basic Income's influence on Industrial relations. Further, it gives us an intuition of the connection between the labour movement and an exit option. Before dealing in detail with Voice and Exit we should make it clear that we keep away from a dichotomy between Exit and Voice. Both can be appropriate and interconnect responses to negative actions by others.

4.1 Exit

The term "voting with your feet" will be known to any economist. There is a tradition from Charles Tiebout to James M Buchanan that uses this principle as a public choice mechanism for the provision of the optimal size of the public good (Herzberg, 2018). With the knowledge of how important exit is for the market mechanism, it is not surprising that Buchanan with demogrant" is in favour of a Basic Income. Free market access is a basic assumption in every market model. It is usually briefly mentioned in the Theory of the Firm, e.g. (Jehle & Reny, 2010). Within the "Industrial Organization" field it plays a major role. Hirschmann uses the Exit-Option as a term for competition (Hirschmann, 1970). It should be indisputable that it is an important condition for competition. Most Basic Income advocates, especially those without savings, will agree that our society is characterised by the pressure to work. Such a view reflects a lack of competition. People cannot leave the job market and be forced to accept "bad jobs". If this is true, then the bargaining situation (at least for part of the labour market) cannot be equal. Accepting Exit as an important improvement in the world, together with Basic Income, is necessarily connected with the idea of the absence of freedom through unequal power. This should of course have an effect on the models we use.

Here I will briefly discuss what Economic 101 tells us about the labour supply and the labour market. It makes sense to look first at the labour supply. Let us start at the very beginning. Economics used to explain labour supply with the leisure-income model, which follows the theory of consumption. This is about the trade-off between leisure and consumption under the constraint of income and time (Franz, 2013).

The exit from the labour market can be interpreted as "job change/unemployment" or complete exit from the labour market (Wispelaere & Birnbaum, 2016). We measure job tenure, the unemployment rate and labour force participation. The labour force is usually definite:

$$\text{Labour force (LF)} = \text{Employment (E)} + \text{Unemployment (U)}$$

The labour force participation is now $\frac{LF}{Population}$. (Borjas, 2015)

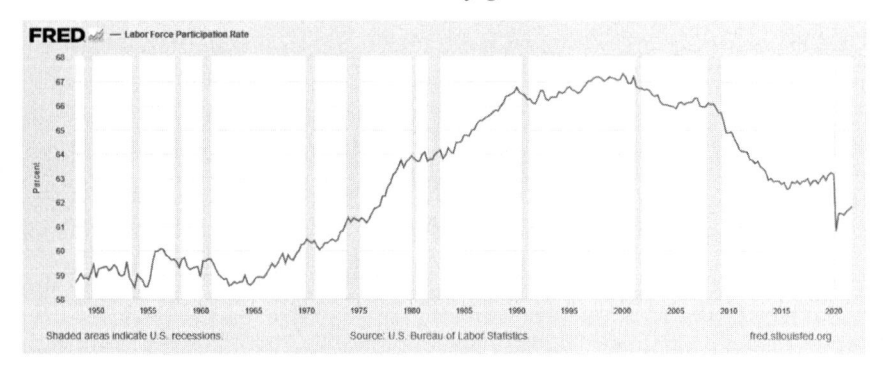

Labour Force Participation Rate. Source: FRED

Above we see labour force participation in the U.S. over a long period. There is a long positive trend that began in the 1960s and ended in the mid-1990s. This trend differs between women and men. Male labour force participation (LFP) decreased from 80% in 1900 to 67.5% in 2020 while women's participation increased from 20.6% (1990) to 58.6% (2010) (Borjas, 2015). According to the figures of the U.S. Bureau of Labor Statistics from 2010 to the present, there has been stagnation and a slight decline to 55.7% (2020).

But gender is not the only important factor. The different age groups also play an important role in the labour force participation rate. This is because, with a larger pension system, the number of older people who have to work is decreasing. Young people have also seen a change in their entry into the market via changes in the education system. In the US the education level correlates positively with labour market participation and each minority has its own characteristic labour supply (Borjas, 2015). For the long trend of the curve, rising real wages via technology change, demographics, and changes in cultural conditions have some explanatory power. As we see, recessions have almost negatively influenced Labour participation rates. Overall, there are long-term trends for which there are different reasons than for the short cycles. Since 2007 LFP has been declining stronger due to demographic factors (Cooper & Luengo-Prado, 2014). Nomadland by Jessica Bruder illuminates the cultural aspects of this development. It also shows the shadow sides of the exit strategy as a case of social withdrawal.

How do most economists explain labour force participation to their students? As mentioned above the use of the neoclassical model of labour-leisure. We will follow George Borja's textbook version (Borjas, 2015), starting with the individual decision level. We assume that leisure is a normal good. Individuals get satisfaction from consuming goods (C) and leisure (L). Therefore, we have a Utility function

$$U = f(C, L) \quad (1)$$

and for every Person there is a budget constraint following type

$$C = \text{wage per hour } (wh) + Non-Market\ Income\ (V).$$

To cancel hour h from the equation we can write $C = w(T - L) + V$ with $T = 24h$ then we can rewrite and get

$$C = (wT + V) - wL \quad (2).$$

From (1) we get the indifference Curve and (2) and the Budget Line so we can draw the following graph.

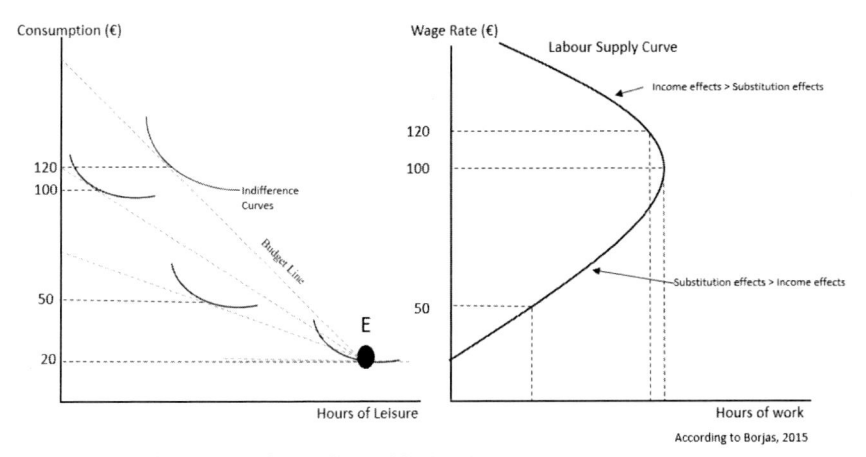

Individual labour supply. Source: Borjas 2015, p 44

There is a point E between a person being indifferent when it comes to non-working and starting to work. This point is given by the absolute value of the slope of the indifference curve given by the utility function at E. The reservation wage (here 20) seems a bit like an auxiliary construct. It arises from a person's preference for work (p.42). The reserve wage must not be interpreted as a minimum of vital income. If V, the non-market Income raising means that the Budget Constraint will shift to the right and we will archive a higher level of leisure with fewer working hours. The reservation wage also has to increase. As the reservation wage increases, we observe that leisure time will increase. However, only on the assumption that this is a normal good.

From this individual level, we can calculate a supply curve (right side). Below the 100 € line, an individual will be working more if the wage increases. In economic terms, we call this the substitution effect and it is higher than the income effect. Above the line, the income effect will be stronger and the individual will be working less. The degree to which labour supply will react to a change in wages has to do with the "elasticity of the labour supply". We defined this as

$$Elasticity\ of\ labour\ supply = \frac{(\%\ Change\ in\ hours\ of\ work)}{(\%\ Change\ in\ wage\ rate)}$$

Graphically we can observe this on the right side with the steepness of the Labour Supply Curve. Above and under the 100 line we see a reaction to wage change. At 100 there is no reaction to a change in wages. Expectations derived from this textbook model of work/leisure are not, or only partly, confirmed in empirical studies (Banerjee, et al., 2017) (Marinescu, 2018). The elasticity of the labour supply is hard to measure (Borjas, 2015). We can easily see that individuals can have a huge difference in their labour preferences. So, it is not easy to generalize results to other persons or groups. Basic Income means that we should aspect that the level is very important. Also so demography of the society in which the Basic Income will be introduced. After all, the general economic situation and the quality of jobs are equally important. What is certain is that the elasticity of the above supply is much more complicated than implied in Economic 101 (Krueger & Meyer, 2002). Getting a better understanding of the potential effects of a basic income on time allocation broadens Palermo-

Kuss and Neumärker the labour-income dichotomy on unpaid work (Palermo Kuss & Neumärker). This tradition can also be seen in Weinel and Neumärker in this publication. The fact that work is always modulated as a source of disutility has also been criticized by many (Fernandez-Huerga, Garcia-Arias, & Salvador, 2017). At the same time, the question of the voluntariness of taking up work can also be critically examined. In such a case, wages will be lower than optimum. A basic income would certainly have positive effects in such a scenario. Considering that the labour supply is dependent on many factors, a more detailed consideration of labour in economic theory is certainly one of the most productive aspects of basic income research.

4.2 Voice

Mainly because of voice, the Hirschmann approach has been used by political scientists and, sceptically, by economists. By assuming a transaction motive everywhere, the Public Choice approach becomes blind to the benefits of voice and participation (Verba, Schlozman, & Brady, 1995). Voice is defined as any attempt to change a situation (Hirschmann, 1970) and can be found in a wide range of activities. This might be a weakness of the approach because it is a vague concept and therefore hard to measure. While some activities have a clear conflict potential, such as protests and strikes, sending a protest letter can also be seen as a way of sharing information but is not conflictual at all. Hirschmann himself recognized this connection to the early writings of Arrows (Hirschmann, 1980). Interestingly, Hirschmann mentions two conflict strategies, boycotts and strikes, on the edge between Exit and Voice (Hirschmann, 1970) although these were not originally intended for the labour market. We have to bear in mind that Hirschman originally argued with quality disappointments and not with salary issues (Godechot & Salibekyan, 2019). Nonetheless, there is a body of literature in labour market research that has made use of the concepts of exit and voice (Freeman, 1980). Freeman maintains in his work (as seen above) that trade unions are monopolies. This he judged negatively. At the same time, he identifies an Exit and Voice channel where he sees the positive sides of trade unions (Freeman & Medoff, 1985). Nevertheless, it is questionable of whether you can separate the bargaining power from the power to introduce better labour standards (Kaufman, 2005). But unionization doesn't capture all forms of voices (Godechot & Salibekyan, 2019). Most exit-voice labour market literature follows this voice equal union simplification (Freeman & Medoff, 1985; Freeman R. B., 1980). Because it makes it a little bit easier to get an intuition of Voice. But between the two-way communication between employer and employee, there is not necessarily a formal institution (Hirschmann, 1970). This leads us to a psychological argument. Belatedly, we come to a point that we have hardly considered so far, namely the motivation for and through paid work. If we expand the concept of work, we can concede that satisfaction is obtained in paid work itself. This opens up new perspectives especially from an economic point of view, which previous models could not depict. Three basic requirements are often mentioned for human development: competence, autonomy, and relationships. Max-Neef maintains that the satisfaction of these needs necessarily involves interaction with other people (Max-Neef, 1991). Satisfaction is thus strongly related to the process (in our case, the work process) and not just to the fact of work in and of itself (Fernandez-Huerga, Garcia-Arias, & Salvador, 2017). "It's not only whether but also how that counts". The possibility to shape the work processes remains a central need of people, no matter what the institutional setting. This clearly demonstrates the additional rationality of "voice". The act of helping to shape work processes is satisfying in itself. Participating in politics and bargaining is more unstable than the preference for certain goods (Hirschmann, 1980). Interestingly, initial studies seem to show that poor working conditions lead to a voice strategy and low wages lead to an exit strategy. (Godechot & Salibekyan, 2019).

In a well-worked market, the cost of exit should be zero. Voice always costs something however. Organisational efforts to organize are always accompanied by costs (Olson, 1965). It is correct to assume that the cost is less if we consider voice as a self-fulfilling activity (Hirschmann, 1980) How a basic income affects the possibility of participation is being investigated by the FRIBIS Participation Team. If, for example, a basic income reduces the fear of losing one's job, trade union activity in a company may increase rather than decrease. In such a case, the basic interest in the work is there but one is not satisfied with the working conditions. At the moment we do not know how basic income (a true exit option) influences voice as a mechanism. But this could be a field for experimental and theoretical economic studies.

Voice can be seen as a residual of Exit or as an alternative (Hirschmann, 1970) Economics is very familiar with research to "exit as a decision". But with voice, it is much more complicated. It is hard directly to observe. They work via proxies, such as unions' activity and the impact on turnover. Voice seems to be something like an art (p.43).

4.3 Interaction between Basic Income, Exit and Voice

One example of interaction between Voice and Exit is the impact of unions on job turnover. The theory goes that unions help workers to articulate grievances, forcing the management has to change to react. As a result, the job turnover rate decreased (Freeman & Medoff, 1985). The empirical literature mostly agrees that unionization reduces quiets (Kaufman, 2005) (Freeman, 1980). Job satisfaction is more of a puzzle however. Here the empirical situation has been confusing until now (Freeman & Medoff, 1985). How will basic income affect the exit and voice mechanism? Can we derive some hypotheses from our previous considerations?

4.4 Basic Income and Bargaining Power

With Birnbaum & DeWispelaer we can distinguish three different scenarios for three basic income scenarios. "Incomplete Exit", "Exit a poor job" and "Exit the labour market". Incomplete Exit means little more than reducing working hours while "Exit a poor job" means leaving your company. Here you are willing to work for others or be self-employed but not under certain conditions. "Dropping out of the labour market" means that someone is not willing to work for others (or at least not for money) (Birnbaum & Wispelaere, 2016).

Assuming that the Basic Income is high enough, we should see some reaction to the labour supply. If the labour supply decreases, companies have to increase the wages. This mass exit will increase the bargaining power of the remaining workers. If we increase the level of education, then we should expect an increase in bargaining power at the bottom and decreasing wages in the top occupations.

So far bargaining power has only been a product of supply and demand (Lindblom, 1948). Other aspects of bargaining power are not so clear. The costs of conflict on the part of the employees may be reduced (e.g. by strikes). On the other hand, the standard of living cannot be lowered arbitrarily and one therefore remains dependent on a certain salary. Besides, basic income can also be used by the employer as an argument for a lower salary. The position of the workers would possibly be presented greedily and this would hurt their position in the negotiations.

Exit as a Threat in a Bargaining situation is another example of the close connection between exit and voice because we use the exit option to get a better solution on the job. As when striking, the individual doesn't want to leave completely but uses the threat to push the other side towards a better agreement. Leaving the labour market is not as easy as leaving the market for consumer goods. In reality, exit is connected with costs. Search and Sunk costs. Without an alternative income or adequate savings there is a danger that Exit won't be a reliable threat. Without a reliable threat (one that is not high enough) a basic income scheme can develop closely understand the connection between labour market conditions and exit strategies. Otherwise, there is a risk of a deep split inside the society between those who have access to good jobs and those who receive a basic income and unskilled jobs and cannot help themselves out of this situation.

It is open whether "Exit as a Threat" works under today's labour market as it did with UBI. As an outside option today, we can see different jobs (state of the labour market) or social policies (support for the unemployed). "Exit Threat" should be much more effective under full employment than with a high unemployment rate. (Highly skilled workers are a special case) (Kalecki, 1943), (Chamayou, 2019)). Again, an exit threat doesn't automatically mean exit. This makes empirical research complicated. We know that trade unions change or have an impact on exit behaviour (Freeman & Medoff, 1985). But we don't know how this is connected with "Exit as Threat". Historically, times with full employment were times with high bargaining power on the worker side (Chamayou, 2019).

5. Conclusion and Further Research

The impact of a basic income on the labour market is one of the most discussed issues in the basic income debate. To get definitive answers to our questions, we will probably have to wait until a country as a whole is ready to implement a Universal Basic Income. Nevertheless, I argue that basic income research needs to engage intensively with a broad range of economic models. Only then can it make a substantial contribution between different basic income advocates or sceptics and basic income supporters. At the same time, it will serve as an innovator by putting (economic) science models to the test. Without doubt, Basic Income research is at the beginning of its journey. I have tried to systematize the economic theory on labour market relations, scanning it basic income approaches. Unfortunately, however I could not go into much depth because I was not able to take into account the numerous pieces of literature on the topic of monopsony that have appeared in the last few years. All I could do was briefly mention the contest models. Nevertheless, I view the attempts to expand or improve the labour supply theory as promising. (See Weinel and Neumärker.) Further, in the field of game theory, non-cooperation bargaining as a repeated game with outside options seems to be the best way. If empowerment is the focus of research, urgent care should be taken to ensure that what is being addressed here also appears in the model (power imbalance). This brings us to another point, namely that it is necessary to critically question assumptions without completely abandoning the model framework. The extent to which basic income influences the organization of work seems to me to depend on three aspects: 1) the type of work activity and 2) the organization of work (large company, small company, self-employed...) and external circumstances (personal type including health, age and social type, level of unemployment, laws....). Basic Income can be an Exit strategy but this depends heavily on the exogenous circumcises. This dynamic still needs more research.

References

Almeida, d. G. (2021). Against a voiceless world: Albert O. Hirschman's political economics as an alternative to public choice. Iberian Journal of the History of Economic Thought, 8(1).

Bailly, F. (2016). The Radical School and the Economics of Education. Journal of the History of Economic Thought, 38(3).

Banerjee, A., Niehaus, P., & Suri, T. (2019). Universal Basic Income in the Developing World. Annual Review of Economics, pp. 959-983.

Birnbaum, S., & Wispelaere, D. J. (2021). Exit strategy or exit trap? Basic income and the 'power to say no' in the age of precarious employment. Socio-Economic Review, 19(3), pp. 909–927.

Birnbaum, S., & Wispelaere, J. D. (2016). Basic Income in the Capitalist Economy: The Mirage of "Exit" from Employment. Basic Income Studies, 11(1), pp. 61–74.

Bishop, L. R. (1964). A Zeuthen-Hicks Theory of Bargaining. Econometrica, 32(3), pp. 410-417.

Blümle, G. (1975). Theorie der Einkommensverteilung: Eine Einführung. Berlin Heidelberg New York: Springer Verlag.

Booth, A. L., & Bryan, L. M. (2004). The Union Membership Wage-Premium Puzzle: Is There a Free Rider Problem? ILR Review, 57(3), pp. 402-421.

Booth, L. A., & Chatterji, M. (1995). Union Meembership and Wage Bargaining when Membership is not Cumpulsory. The economic Journal, 105(429), pp. 345-360.

Borjas, J. G. (2015). Labour Economics (7 ed.). 2 Penn Plaza, New York, NY 10121: McGraw-Hill Education.

Card, D. (2022). Who set your wages ? NBER WORKING PAPER SERIES, 1-31.

Chamayou, G. (2019). Die unregierbare Gesellschaft. Eine Genealogie des autoritären Liberalismus. Berlin: Suhrkamp.

Chatterjee, K. (2010). Non-Cooperative Bargaining Theory. In D. M. Kilgour, & C. Eden (Eds.), Handbook of Group Decision and Negotiation. Switzerland: Springer Nature .

Cooper, D., & Luengo-Prado, M. J. (2014). Labor Market Exit and Re-Entry: Is the United States Poised for a Rebound in the Labor Force Participation Rate? Current Plicy perspectives 14-2 - Federal Reserv Bank of Boston, pp. 1-24.

Dierwert, E. W. (1974, September). The Effects of Unionization on wages and employment: A General equilibirum analysis. Economic Inquiry, 12(3).

Drakopoulos, S., & Katselidis, I. (2012). The Development of Trade Union Theory and Mainstream Economic Methodology. Journal of Economic Issues, 48(4), pp. 1133-1149.

Farber, H. S., Herbst, D., Kuziemko, I., & Naidu, S. (2021, April 09). Unions and Inequality over the Twentieth Century: New Evidence from Survey Data*. The Quarterly Journal of Economics, Volume 136, Issue 3, , pp. 1325–1385.

Fernandez-Huerga, E., Garcia-Arias, J., & Salvador, A. (2017). Labour supply: toward the construction of an alternative conception from post Keynesian and institutional economics. Journal of Post Keynesin Economics, p. 1.24.

Franz, W. (2013). Arbeitsmarktökonomik. Wiesbaden: Springer.

Freeman, B. R. (1980). The Exit and Voice Tradeoff in the labor Market: Unioism, Job Tensure, Quits, and Separations. The Quarterly Journal of Economic, pp. 643-672.

Freeman, B. R., & Medoff, L. J. (1985). What Do Unions Do? New York: Basic Books.

Gilbert, R., Huws, U., & Gurnmin, Y. (2019). Employment Market Effects of Basic Income. In M. Torry (Ed.), The Palgrave International Handbook of Basic Income (pp. 47-69).

Godechot, O., & Salibekyan, Z. (2019, 425-449,). Should we Clash or Should I go? The impact of low Wage and Poor Working Conditions on Exit-Voice Trade.Off. Labour, 33(4).

Guertzgen, N. (2009). Rent-Sharing and Collective Bargaining Coverage: Evidence from Linked Employer–Employee Data. The Scandinavian Journal of Economics, 111(2), pp. 323-349.

Herzberg, R. (2018). Votes, Vetoes, Voice, and Exit: Constitutional Protections in the Work of James M. Buchanan and Vincent Ostrom: A Theorist of Political Economy and Social Philosophy. In E. R. Wagner (Ed.), James M.

Buchanan: A Theorist of Political Economy and Social Philosophy (pp. 467 - 286). Palgrave Macmillan .

Hicks, R. J. (1932). Theory of Wages (II ed.). London: Macmillan.

Hirschmann, O. A. (1970). Exit, Voice, and Loyalty: Responses to Decline in Firms, Organizations, and States. Cambridge, MA: Harvard University Press.

Hirschmann, O. A. (1980). Exit, Voice and Loyalty: Further Reflections and a Survey of recent Contributions. The Milbank Memorial Fnd Quartley. Health and Society, pp. 430-453.

Hirschmann, O. A. (1982). Shifting Involvements. Private Interest and Public Action . Princeton NJ: Princeton University Press.

Hirshleifer, J. (1989). Conflict and Rent-Seeking Success Functions, Ratio vs. Difference Models of Relative Success. Public Choice,(63), pp. 101-112.

Holler, J. M., Illing, G., & Napel, S. (2019). Einführung in die Spieltheorie. Springer.

Holmlund, B., & Lundborg, P. (1999). Wage abrgaining, union membership, and the organization of unemployment insurance. Labour Economics(6), pp. 397-415.

Jaumotte, F., & Buitron, C. O. (2015). Inequality and Labour Market Institutions. IMF Staff Discussion Note, pp. 1-31.

Jehle, G., & Reny, P. J. (2010). Advanced Microeconomic (3 ed.). Financial Times/ Prentice Hall.

Johnson, E. G. (1975). Economic Analysis of Trade Unionism. The American Economic Review, 65(2), pp. 23-28.

Kalecki, M. (1943). Political Aspects of Full Employment. Political Quarterly, pp. 1-9.

Kaufman, E. B. (2002). Models of Union Wage Determination: What Have we Learned Since Dunlop and Ross? Industrial Relation, 1, pp. 110-157.

Kaufman, E. B. (2005). What Do Unions Do? - Evaluation and Commentary. Journal of Labor Research, XXVI(4), pp. 555-584.

Kaufman, E. B. (2008, June). Paradigms in Industrial Relations: Original, Modern and Versions In-between. British Journal of Industrial Relations (46 (2)), pp. 314–339.

Kennan, J., & Wilson, R. (1989). Strategic Bargaining Models and Interpretation of Strike Data. Journal of Applied Econometrics (4), 87-130.

Keune, M. (2021). Inquality between capital and labour and among wage-earners: the role of collective bargaining and trade unions. Transfer, 27(1), pp. 29-46.

Kıbrıs, Ö. (2010). Negotiation as a Cooperative Game. In Handbook of Group Decision and Negotiation. Springer Nature.

Külp, B. (1994). Verteilung Theorie und Politik (3 ed.). Stuttgart: Gustav Fischer Verlag.

Lindblom, E. C. (1948). "Bargaining Power" In Price and Wage determination. The Quarterly Journal of Economics, pp. 396-417.

Manning, A. (1994). How robust is the microeconomic Theory of the Trade Union? Journal of labour Economic, 3.

Manzini, P. (1998). Game Theoretic Models of Wage Bargaining. Journal of Economic Survey, 12(1), 1-41.

Marinescu, I. (2018). No Strings Attached: The Behavioral Effects of U.S. Unconditional Cash Transfer Programs. NBER Working Paper Series, pp. 1-20.

Max-Neef, M. A. (1991). Human scale development: conception, application and further A Note on Methodology . Apex Press.

McDonald, M. I., & Solow, M. R. (1981). Wage Bargaining and Employment. The American Economic Review, 71(5), pp. 896-908.

Mohr, K., Smolenski, T., & Bothfeld, S. (2018). Bedingungsloses Grundeinkommen. (I. M.-V. Gesellschaftspolitik, Ed.) Arbeitspapier.

Müller-Jentsch, W. (2004). Theoretical Approaches to Industrial Relations. In B. E. Kaufmann (Ed.), Theoretical perspectives on Work and the employment relationship. Chicago: Industrial Relations Research Association.

Muthoo, A. (1999). Bargaining Theory with Applications. Cambridge: Cambridge University Press.

Naylor, R. (2003). Economic models of union behaviour. In J. T. Addison, & C. Schnabel (Eds.), International Handbook of Trade Unions (pp. 44-85). Edward Elgar.

Olson, M. (1965). The Logic of Collective Action ((Revised ed.) ed.). Harvard University Press.

Oswald, J. A. (1985, Jun). The Economic Theory of Trade Unions: An Introductory Survey. The Scandinavian Journal of Economics, 87(2), pp. 160-193.

Palermo Kuss, A. H., & Neumärker, K. J. (n.d.). Modelling the Time Allocation Effects of Basic Income. Basic Income Studies, 13(2), pp. 1-15.

Rama, M. (1997). Imperfect Rent Dissipation with Unionized Labor. Public Choice, 93, pp. 55-75.

Rothschild, W. K. (1957). Approaches to the Theory of Bargaining. In J. T. Dunlop (Ed.), The Theory of Wage Determination. Palgrave Macmillan UK.

Salvo, L. (2006). Gewerkschaften und Wohlfahrtsstaat: Das Gent System. WSI Mitteilungen(2 / 2006).

Sapsford, D. (1980). The Theory of Bargaining: A Selective Survey with Particular Reference to Union-Employer Negotiations and the Occurrence of Strikes,. Papers ME134, Economic and Social Research Institute, 1-43.

Saraydar, E. (1965, Oct). Zeuthen's Theory of Bargaining: A Note. Econometrica, 33(4), pp. 801-814.

Schnabel, C. (2013). Union membership and density: Some (not so) stylized facts and challenges. European Journal of Industrial Relations, pp. 255-273.

Stansbury, A., & Summers, L. H. (2018). Productivity and Pay: Is the Link Broken? Peterson Institute for International Economics Working Paper (No. 18-5), pp. 1-51.

Stansbury, A., & Summers, L. H. (2020). The Declining Worker Power Hypothesis: An explanation for the recent evolution of the American economy. NBER Working Papers(27193,), pp. 1-139.

Usher, D. (2012). Bargaining unexplained. Public Choice, 151, pp. 23-41.

Verba, S., Schlozman, L. K., & Brady, E. H. (1995). Voice and Equality: Civic Voluntarism in American Politics. Harvard University Press.

Warren, E. M. (2011). Voting with Your Feet: Exit-based Empowerment in Democratic Theory. The American Political Science Review, 4, pp. 683-701.

Widerquist, K. (2013). Independence, Propertylessness, and Basic Income. New York: Palgrave Macmillan, New York.

Wispelaere, D. J., & Birnbaum, S. (2016, August). Basic Income in the Capitalist Economy: The Mirage of "Exit" from Employment. Basic Income Studies, 11(1).

Marcel Franke, Tobias Jäger

Nash Bargaining with a Social Preference

A Preference for Equal Reference Points in Bargaining

Constitutional economics considers alternative sets of rules to reflect the interests of the individuals in the constitution. This article adds to this direction by investigating a preference for the negotiation conditions of the constitution itself. If the reference points in a bargaining situation represent inhuman conditions, we may call it a slave contract. By assuming a preference for inequality aversion in the status quo slave contracts may be ruled out endogenously. Additionally, we interpret the resulting incentives for Pareto-optimal transfer as an unconditional basic income.

1. Introduction

A private contract in a developed society is a regulated and enforced agreement (Schwartz & Scott, 2003). In the case of only two parties being affected, the unanimous agreement serves the betterment of both. Otherwise, one party would not agree, and the contract would not take place. This condition ensures efficiency in private contracts (Laffont, 2000).

In contrast, a social contract concerns multiple parties and focuses on communal improvements, not just the advantage of an individual (Homann, 1997, p. 16). This brings its difficulties, however (Olson M. L., 1965). So, the interests of all people must be considered if Pareto-efficiency is to be guaranteed (Buchanan J. M., 1962). This can be ensured by the provision of a veto right when designing the social contract (Buchanan J. M., 1999b, p. 465f). Anyone who has ever tried to reach a unanimous decision on a complex or contentious issue in a larger group will know that reaching an agreement is not easy. In the case of a social contract, this problem is also present (Buchanan & Tullock, 1999a, p. 62f). Here it requires equally strong forces to make individuals cooperate. Traditionally, the alternative to an agreement is the unattractive status quo, which Hobbes described as the "war of all against all" (Hobbes 1841, p. 64).

An agreement forced by a war challenges the legitimacy of a social contract. Born of the hardship of such anarchy, the value of such an agreement is questionable and may be affected by retention of the social contract after overcoming the hardship. However, a socially sustainable social contract requires such security against renegotiation (Neumärker K. J., 2017). Finally, there is no external body that could preserve the contract should there be interest in renegotiation. Individuals first create an entity empowered to legislate and adjudicate only through the social contract (Brennan & Buchanan, 2000a, p. 31f).

This point is illustrated by the example of the slave contract in the desert, where there are two individuals in a water-scarce environment. One of the individuals has a supply of water and the other is suffering from thirst. A "contract of sale" for water may be beneficial to both in this situation. And given the desperate situation of the thirsty individual, he will agree to any contract that can avert the imminent danger of dying, including a slave contract. Once this danger is averted, however, there is no incentive beyond moral obligations or external enforcement to fulfill the duties as a slave. So the slave contract is broken or renegotiated by the slave. It is the same with the social contract. Weatherman imagines the political difficulties in the context of slavery and the law in the USA (Weatherman, 1985).

Due to forming the first authority via the social contract, the issue of absence of an external authority to enforce the social contract occurs. Thus, the social contract must be self-enforcing (Neumärker K. J., 2017). The same applies to international agreements (Franke & Neumärker, 2022). There are different mechanisms, such as social norms, which demonstrate how this can succeed among humans (Young, 2008). How a threat point and morality lead to enforcement of the social contract can be identified in the above example. These factors are required to be stable over time to keep the enforcement running.

These two factors are examined for their implications in this article. For this purpose, a social preference for equality in the bargaining situation is integrated with the Nash bargaining solution (Nash Jr., 1950).

The article is organized as follows: Section 2 presents the concepts, assumptions, and model building blocks used, namely anarchy, the social contract, social preferences, and bargaining theory, in particular the Nash bargaining solution. The model is developed in section 3 and implications are presented and discussed in section 4. Section 5 offers the conclusion.

2. Related Literature

This section presents the literature relevant to the conducted study. It relates to the fundamental concepts that are relevant to the bargaining situation, the contractarian endeavor, and social preferences. These three strands of literature connect to provide an interesting insight from modelling a social preference specific to contractarian bargaining in the Nash bargaining solution.

The origin of the idea is straightforward. Olson (1993) argues that it is more realistic that roving bandits establish the government (Olson M., 1993). This inspired Neumärker (2003) to set up and analyze this scenario from a positive contractarian perspective (Neumärker K. J., 2003). Franke (2021) suggests interpreting constitutional formation as a bargaining situation in which different interests are to be given unanimous consent (Franke M., 2021). The model developed in this paper may be considered the continuation of this idea in the direction of endogenous forces that work towards the actual implementation of such a constitution. A specific social preference will therefore be assumed.

Accordingly, the following section begins with a short introduction to bargaining theory, especially to the Nash bargaining solution the model applies. An introduction on how the status quo leads to the contractarian endeavor, unanimity, and the veil of uncertainty follows. A passage about social preferences in economics and the issue of enforcing social contracts completes this section.

2.1 Bargaining Theory and the Nash Bargaining Solution

The book Theory of games and economic behavior by Von Neumann and Morgenstern (1951) provides the foundation for game theoretic thinking (Von Neumann & Morgenstern, 1953). They focus on the possibility of coalitions and thus cooperative solutions and Nash (1951) introduces non-cooperative solutions (Nash, 1951). In non-cooperative bargaining, enforcement is only possible within the game. Thus these solutions must be self-enforcing (Neumärker K. J., 2017). This differs from the cooperative approach, where the issue of enforcement is often neglected and considered to be exogenously solved (Chatterjee, 2020, p. 2), (Holler, Illing, & Napel, 2019, p. 6).

This paper builds on the cooperative bargaining solution by Nash (1950) (Nash Jr., 1950). This seems fitting in the context of Buchanan's (1990) exchange paradigm for the contractarian research program, which argues that "economics involves inquiry into cooperative arrangements for human interaction" (Buchanan J. M., 1990, p. 9f). However, since the non-cooperative strand developed subsequently, connections to the earlier approaches are frequent (Chatterjee, 2020).

The Nash bargaining solution, which is used as the model in this paper, may be considered a reference outcome of bargaining between rational players. This is due to the assumptions of full information and the model being static. Further, it must be assumed that the players act on their threat point of returning to the status quo and the contract gets somehow enforced (Nash, 1953, p. 130). For example, the Rubinstein Model (1987) is an important complement to the Nash bargaining solution (Kıbrıs, 2020, p. 18), (Sutton, 1986). Rubinstein developed a sequential bargaining model including a time preference (Rubinstein, 1987). Along with other connections of actual games to the Nash bargaining solution, for example, (Nash, 1953), Binmore et. al. (1986) show that the solution of the Rubinstein game converges on the Nash bargaining solution depending on the parameters (Binmore, Rubinstein, & Wolinsky, 1986).

Also, the possibility of interpretation of the Nash bargaining solution as a bargaining convention is possible. Here, any argument against the Nash bargaining solution is shot down by the lower expected utility due to the higher probability of rejection and thus the status quo payoff taking place. This is one possible explanation for why the Nash bargaining solution should be of relevance (Muthoo, 1999, pp. 33-35). The application of the Nash bargaining solution, sometimes referred to as the "Nash program", is continuously being worked on (Kıbrıs, 2020, p. 18). Additionally, variations on the assumption of complete information have been investigated (Harsanyi & Selten, 1972), (Feltovich & Swierzbinski, 2011).

Another interesting continuation for social contracting is the characteristic of maximizing the product of the individual utilities, which lead to the formulation of the Nash social welfare function (Kaneko & Nakamura, 1979). See the comment on social welfare functions in the sub-section on social preferences below.

In this paper, the Nash bargaining solution offers a solid foundation for the integration of a specific social preference. The results may be limited to the character of a stylized fact. Nevertheless, the extensive Nash program yields the necessary background to carry the results over into actual bargaining situations. Since the cooperative approach deals with the distribution of a surplus, it typically incorporates a reference point. This is called the status quo and will be discussed in the following sub-section.

2.2 The Status Quo

Contractarian constitutionalism investigates the functioning of the constitution. Its aim is to explain what the best actions are, based on the interests of the individuals. Thus the contractarian-constitutionalist enterprise keeps a lookout for cooperative solutions to the benefit of all participants (Vanberg V. J., 2004, p. 155). Buchanan (1962) argues that the "constitutional" limits are the relevant region for the application of welfare economics (Buchanan J. M., 1962, p. 343). The use of Pareto-improvement allows us to compare two states to some degree. It either ranks the states into Pareto-better and Pareto-worse states or displays indifference between two states. The latter raises the question of choosing between the alternatives in the face of indifference. Franke (2021) suggests approaching the question of choosing between competing contract proposals by modelling the contractarian stage as a bargaining situation (Franke M., 2021).

A second possibility when dealing with this question is provided by the constitutional reform literature. The assumption that there is already some constitution in place provides rules for the selection of the reform, e.g. majority voting. This allows for the selection between options that the Pareto-criterion may not be able to produce a complete ranking order (Suzumura, 1981). Nevertheless, this solution adheres to a path dependency since the current constitution is relevant for the selection of its improvement.

Thus the search for an adequate starting point began: a societal origin much as the arrival of Friday on Robinson Crusoe's Island. Political philosophers outlined anarchy to be such a starting point. On the one hand, there is the Hobbesian jungle: a "solitary, poor, nasty, brutish and short" life (Hobbes T., 1839, p. 113). People are in urgent need to end the "war, as is of all men against all men" (Hobbes T., 1841, p. 64). Thus they would agree to limit their unlimited liberty in anarchy mutually to stop others from harming their lives and stealing the fruits of their work (Nozick, 1974). Locke, by contrast, describes a world in which everyone is entitled to natural resources (Locke, 1689, p. 195f). The harsh anarchy following Hobbes's description allows for an easy justification of improvement by a social contract. The Lockean version sets up for a more demanding initial situation, which is much harder to improve. However, an improvement here provides new possibilities: change in a wealthy situation is more likely to be able to deal with the problem of distribution. Whereas the constitution used to escape the Hobbesian jungle is required to settle the conflicts and some property rights, including their enforcement, first. In this way Buchanan (2000) describes the way of improvement via a constitution as follows.

The status quo represented by point D allows for an improvement in the utilities U of individuals A and B, used as indices here. This leads to the first constitution in point C, which aims at pacification. It provides the fundamental and most urgent public goods in defense of the citizens' life and basic goods. Property and contract rights are included, allowing for the reliable economic provision of basic goods. According to the libertarian tradition, this is the minimal state that suffices as a legitimate government (Nozick, 1974) and pacifies the Hobbesian jungle.

It is further possible to extend the government to improve an already provision of public goods and merit goods (Blankart, 2017, pp. 47-65). Their efficient private provision systematically fails, while for the society their consumption is demanded. Thus, an extension of the minimal state towards a productive state in point E may be worthwhile.

In addition, the difference in wellbeing in the status quo of the different agents is essential for the bargaining result (Franke M. , 2021, p. 13), (Neumärker K. J., 1995, p. 51), (Mueller, 2003, p. 63), (Buchanan J. M., 1999c, pp. 69-95), (Alesina & Drazen, 1991). This point may become neglected in a sufficiently bad Hobbesian jungle that forces the individuals into a contractarian solution. However, anarchy as a reference point may have different forms, as shown by Hirshleifer (1995) in analyses of the stability of an anarchy (Hirshleifer, 1995). Classical contractarian ideas will be introduced in the next section.

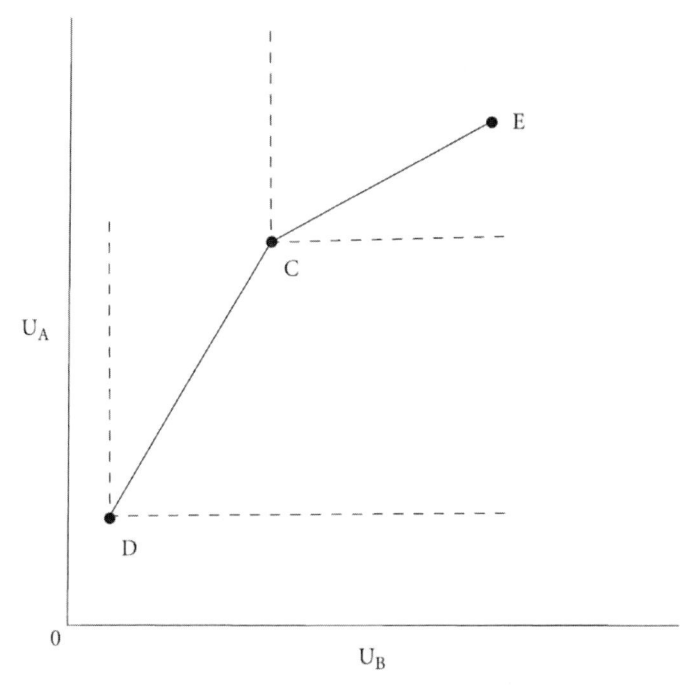

Figure 1: From Anarchy to a constitution, Source: (Brennan & Buchanan, 2000a, p. 39)

2.3 Social Contract

The field of contractarianism is rooted in the ideas of prominent authors of the enlightenment. John Locke (1689) and Thomas Hobbes are the most prominent in the economic tradition here. For Locke, the consent of individuals is capable of forming a society: "For if the consent of the majority shall not, in reason, be received as the act of the whole, and conclude every individual, nothing but the consent of every individual can make anything to be the act of the whole" (Locke, 1689, p. 281). Hobbes, by contrast, focuses more on the urgent need of founding a state. He describes the natural state as the liberty to make use of the own power as one likes. Nevertheless, to stop others from harmful actions he proposes the formation of a government that is powerful enough to enforce the required boundaries to natural liberty (Hobbes T., 2001, pp. 118-128). Thus the prominent "Leviathan" is formed. A government that obtains all the power of the citizens to end the war of all against all and provides national defense as well as a property right system (Hobbes T., 2001, p. 155).

Although not as prominent in the economic tradition, Immanuel Kant and Jean-Jacques Rousseau provide prominent original contractarian proposals. Kant proposes the categorical imperative "d.i. ich soll niemals anders verfahren, als so, daß ich auch wollen könne, meine Maxime solle ein allgemeines Gesetz werden" (translation: "i.e. I shall never act otherwise but in such a way that I also want my maxim to be common law") (Kant, 1785, p. 28). Here the contractarian agreement does not take place between individuals. The contractarian dimension is integrated as an individual criterion to judge one's own action if one were to try to reconstruct it in economic terms. In Kant's text, this reasoning is a priori demanded by rationality (Kant, 1785, pp. 44-48). Thus, the criterion takes place in the individuals out of moral reasoning, or a priori as a result of logic itself.

Rousseau justifies the government in terms of the benefits generated. These must be mutual due to the natural equality of human beings (Rousseau, 1762, p. 22). This even includes the decision over life and death, including the death sentence (Rousseau, 1762, p. 24f). The status quo Rousseau refers to is the alternative to a social contract. I.e., some form of harsh anarchy. Hence even soldiers' entries can be legitimate if they lead to death, as the alternative has no more to offer (Rousseau, 1762, p. 23f). The attempt to form a government also demands subsidiarity to allow for constructive shaping of the society (Rousseau, 1762, pp. 27-29).

Other endeavors have followed in the present age, the most prominent being John Rawls's A Theory of Justice (Rawls, 1971). Rawls claims that under the sufficient uncertainty of a veil of ignorance individuals would agree on two principles. The first is "an equal right to the most extensive scheme of equal basic liberties" while in the second, "inequalities are to be arranged so that they are both (a) reasonably expected to be to everyone's advantage, and (b) attached to positions and offices. This is the prominent difference principle and states that inequalities must serve the least advantaged. In continuation of these principles, Van Parijs (1997) suggests basic equal positive liberty via a UBI (Van Parijs, 1997). In addition, the libertarian justification of a minimal state by Nozick (1974) and the suggestion by Buchanan (1999) are also widely acknowledged (Nozick, 1974), (Buchanan J. M., 1999c). These abstract "neo contractarian" approaches may be perceived as a continuation of the original contractarian approaches mentioned above. Rawls emphasizes equal rights in the natural state, utilizing the veil of ignorance to get rid of special interests. Rousseau also starts with the equality of individuals and argues against special interests in generating the social contract. Buchanan's approach follows Hobbes attempt of pacifying the anarchy via a social contract and creating a government this way (Buchanan J. M., 1999c, p. 76f). Nozick starts with an encompassing set of natural rights, as Locke does, which are intended to be enforced by a government (Koller, 1987, pp. 17-30). These approaches have also received criticism due to obstacles in applying them (Gordon, 1976). Nevertheless, they have left their indelible stamp on political-economic thinking, especially the contractarian approaches.

Several reviews have been written and many ideas have been developed based on the contractarian idea (Boucher, 1994). Ken Binmore has tried to endogenize the contractarian endeavor in an evolutionary approach. He explains the contractarian solution as an equilibrium in the game of life (Binmore, 2005). As a stabilizing factor for such an "empathy equilibrium" empathic preferences are assumed (Binmore, 2005, p. 175). David Gauthier justifies a social contract with the aim of utility maximization (Gauthier, 1987). To overcome the issue of opportunistic bargaining, his agents act according to justice, which "is the disposition not to take advantage of one's fellows, not to seek free goods or to impose uncompensated costs" if others act in the same way (Gauthier, 1987, p. 113). In sociology Karl-Otto Apel and Jürgen Habermas have developed the discourse ethics approach. This approach may follow the contractarian objective in identifying consensus via communication (Seiler, 2014). At least its core idea is not too far from this paper's aim in modelling the social contract negotiation as Nash-bargaining. Nevertheless, one criterion for a private contract is the consent of all parties involved. The following section deals with the approval of a social contract.

2.4 Unanimity

Constitutional design is usually not an explanation of history. Vanberg (2016) names the original, hypothetical, and implicit contracts as possible interpretations of the contractarian endeavor (Vanberg V. J., 2016, pp. 2-6). The original is the historical account. However, there are more reasonable conclusions than peaceful bargaining over a constitution out of anarchy, such as bandits hired for protection (Olson M., 1993), (Neumärker K. J., 2011b). Current constitutions have emerged out of a long process, by established governments, or revolutions (Arato, 1995). The hypothetical contract aims at identifying possible consent (Homann, 1997, p. 16). "The purpose of the contractarian exercise is not explanatory in this sense. It is, by contrast, justificatory in that it offers a basis for normative evaluation" (Buchanan J. M., 1999b, p. 466f). Finally, the implicit contract justifies a running set of rules by people voluntarily remaining under this regime. This interpretation may only be valid if the choice is given, which again, depends on the alternatives and the procedure of rule formation (Barnett, 2003).

Even if the hypothetical contract and its aim of legitimation are accepted, the value of this legitimation still depends on the voting rule used. Trying to find the appropriate rule endogenously leads to the issue of never identifying an appropriate first voting rule (Buchanan & Tullock, 1999a, p. 6). Thus, the unanimity rule may be appropriate to protect the interests of everyone (Brennan & Buchanan, 2000b, p. 27f). In Buchanan's (1999) words: "Only the unanimity rule will ensure that all external effects will be eliminated by collectivization." (Buchanan J. M., 1999c, p. 70). Buchanan follows Wicksell's description of the problem that either a minority gets protected or the majority rules and can do what is good for itself (Wicksell, 1896, p. 111), (Buchanan J. M., 1999a, pp. 140-142). This idea may be transferred to the individual level when deciding on the voting rule. If in the majority, would the individual rather have protection or the power to rule? (Buchanan & Tullock, 1999a, pp. 56-58). In constitutional questions, the right to interception may be appropriate considering the high costs of being overruled (Buchanan J. M., 1999b, p. 370f). One prominent argument against the unanimity rule is the high transaction costs (Buchanan & Tullock, 1999a, pp. 218-220). Nevertheless, due to rent-seeking, the costs of other voting rules may also entail additional costs (Spindler, 1990). Due to his tradeoff the empiric question of the appropriate constitutional rule for decision making with respect to economic costs remains unanswered (Crain & Tollison, 1977). Further, Buchanan (1962) suggests that the unanimity criterion be the appropriate enforcement of Pareto-improvements on a constitutional level (Buchanan J. M., 1962). Additionally, non-unanimous voting rules are coercive since self-interest demands voting for the taxation of someone else rather than oneself (Block & DiLorenzo, 2000). Finally, the question of an appropriate voting rule is intertwined with the stability of the constitution (Barbera & Jackson, 2004).

These arguments render a unanimous agreement appealing. Modelling the consent of all parties is a fruitful starting point since it treats all players equally and ignores coalitions. Further, it applies to private contracting, which by default requires unanimous agreement. To reduce the drawbacks of a higher probability of remaining in the status quo, Rawls suggested reducing partiality via a veil. This is explained in the next section.

2.5 Rawls' Veil

Rawls' (1971) approach calls attention to the issue of partiality (Rawls, 1971, pp. 11 and 118-123). To isolate the notions of justice, special interests must be put aside. So Rawls assumes a veil of ignorance that allows only rough planning. Enforcing special interests is not possible, simply because the special attributes and positions in society are not assigned or not known yet. This allows for an impartial discussion of the fundamental rules in society. Neumärker (1995) classifies the veil according to its characteristics of completeness and perfectness. A veil with high completeness disguises the knowledge about economic mechanisms and the results of social interaction before the social contract gets enacted and the veil is lifted. This unpredictability allows the Rawlsian veil of ignorance to isolate social preferences. In contrast, the perfection of a veil of uncertainty conceals the individual position in the future society. This lack of knowledge can be understood as a form of uncertainty, which allows for expected utility maximization (Neumärker K. J., 1995, p. 43f). The interpretation of Rawl's "difference principle" as emerges under the veil of uncertainty instead of the veil of ignorance allows for economic reconstruction. For individuals to put a large value on the worst-off position, they must be very risk-averse (Harsanyi J. C., 1953). Harsanyi (1955) replied by providing a concept of an individual utility function considering risk-neutral individuals (Harsanyi J. C., 1955). Frohlich and Oppenheimer (1978) checked these approaches empirically and found a solution in-between to be the voting result on average (Frohlich N., Oppenheimer, Smith, & Young, 1978). This result turned out to be robust in the follow-up studies (Frohlich & Oppenheimer, 1992), (Wolf & Lenger, 2011), (Lenger, Wolf, & Goldschmidt, 2020).

This paper does not explicitly assume a veil. The purpose is to provide a positive study of the effects of a specific social preference on bargaining. The positive nature of this study does not require the details of a veil, whether realistic or not. The level of abstraction concerning the details of the social contract proposals does not require specification of whether a veil exists and what properties it may have, at least to a certain extent. Individuals are required to have expectations of utility from contract proposals. Thus a complete veil of ignorance would be problematic as it does not allow for any planning. And bargaining without expectations about the impact of the solutions is not reasonable. However, there are arguments for a thick veil as well. These are covered in the literature on incomplete contracts and unforeseen contingencies (Rosen, 1985), (Hart & Moore, 1999), (Schmitz, 2001).

2.6 Social Preferences and the Social Contract

"Homo economicus" is the dominant behavior model in economics (Kirchgässner, 2013). It is a basic starting point and adds to an analysis of a reliable reference case. In this paper the model has been modified to apply to arguments of social preferences too (Meckling, 1976), (Lindenberg, 1985).

Nevertheless, not only the technical assumptions required for fruitful model building but also the human motives for behavior are violated by human beings. Prominent studies have dealt with, and several approaches are still dealing with these deviations. For example, Tversky and Kahneman (1974) in their prominent studies about bounded rationality (Tversky & Kahneman, 1974). Vanberg

(1994) deals with incomplete information and changing utility functions (Vanberg V. J., 1994, pp. 41-59). In this paper, the homo economicus serves as a useful modeling tool to investigate the impact of a specific social preference.

Social preferences are discussed in the predecessors of classic economics. A. Smith emphasized feelings and benevolence as the basis of virtues as a motivation of human behavior (Smith, 1976). And these considerations are common from an anthropological point of view (Homann, 2003, p. 2). There are several approaches to social preferences (Konow, 2003). Not only positive but also negative social preferences have been integrated into economic theory (Brennan G., 1973a), (Neumärker K. J., 2011a). Empirical approaches, especially in lab experiments, have identified systematic deviations from self-interest assumptions (Fong, 2001), (Clark, 1998), (Levitt & List, 2007).

Welfare economics is a prominent continuation of moral theory in economics. It follows the utilitarian concept by J. Bentham, who tried to develop a measurement that would allow for the comparison and aggregation of happiness among different beings – and was not limited to human beings (Bentham, 1781). This approach was very appealing since, if it worked, it would be able to solve the question of what the best action is based on the aggregation principles, even in the long run. However, economists developed this approach further just to identify insuperable problems inherent to the approach. This is the issue of measuring happiness objectively on an individual basis. The aggregation is scientifically impossible (Buchanan J. M., 1999b, p. 191). And even if these problems had been solved via the required cardinal utility measurement, basing a decision on the happiness aggregate is largely dependent on the aggregation method, which is exogenous and therefore not solvable within this approach (Boadway & Bruce, 1984), (Buchanan J. M., 1999b, p. 284). Kaldor (1939) and Hicks (1939) therefore suggested applying Pareto-efficiency based on potential redistribution. The trick here is that a betterment through compensation payments would be possible but does not have to be implemented (Kaldor, 1939), (Hicks, 1939). However, the application of the recommendation for action turned out to be problematic. In reality people, rather than a benevolent dictator, would need to be incentivized to implement the best action. Otherwise, they would follow their own needs instead of the demands of the welfare of others (Olson M., 1993).

This differentiates the contractarian endeavor from the welfarist tradition. Here individuals are the only source of action and the only source of value in society (Vanberg V., 1986). Some external evaluation along social welfare indicators is simply irrelevant if it is not integrated into the goals of the actual people in society (Brennan & Buchanan, 2000b, pp. 25-27). This leads to Buchanan's formulation of the constitutional efficiency check: "If a presumed or apparent nonoptimal rule cannot be changed through an agreement among members of the group, the hypothesis stating that the rule is nonoptimal is effectively refuted." (Buchanan J. M., 1962, p. 353).

The moral may be justified by the possibility of agreeing on it (Thoma, 2015). Social preferences were also built into Nash bargaining (Barkaoui & Dragicevic, 2016). However, the use of a social preference that is only plausible in the context of a social contract solution, namely a benefit due to equality of the negotiating partners in the initial situation, has not yet made its way in as a special case, to the knowledge of the authors. The closely related preference of a general inequality aversion (Fehr & Schmidt, 1999), on the other hand, does not provide any special insight into the model of the Nash bargaining solution, as will be shown below. This may be the reason for its absence from the literature so far.

Social contract theory deals with the social contract as an instrument for the betterment (however defined) of the members of society, as presented above. Another dimension represents the creation of justice through binding rules and their enforcement using a social contract (Vanberg V. J., 2004). Both approaches are about achieving a goal through the social contract (Blankart, 2017, pp. 67-74).

However, a scenario in which a social contract was given to achieve the goals of society itself, in the sense of a unanimous social contract, is not known historically nor is it plausible. Therefore, the purpose of social contract theory has always been to invoke purposes other than the one stated (Vanberg V. J., 2016, pp. 2-6). Conversely, this article examines the scenario in which a negotiator's preference exerts influence on the negotiation outcome and design. The results of this investigation indicate how such a negotiator's preference could affect a bargaining outcome. This preference could also apply to the enforcement of a social contract.

Thus, the original solution for the transmission of the power necessary to enforce the social contract, according to Hobbes, is: "Jeder muß alle seine Macht oder Kraft einem oder mehreren Menschen übertragen, wodurch der Willen aller gleichsam auf einen Punkt vereinigt wird, so daß dieser eine Mensch oder diese eine Gesellschafft eines jeden einzelnen Stellvertreter werde und ein jeder die Handlung jener so betrachte, als habe er sie selbst getan, weil sie sich dem Willen und Urteil jener freiwillig unterworfen habe" (Translation: "Each person must transfer all his energy and strength to one or more men, so that the will of all is united, as it were, to one point, so that this one man or this one society becomes the representative of each, and each considers the action of the as if he had performed it himself because they have voluntarily submitted to their will and judgment") (Hobbes T. , 2001, p. 153). This transfer occurs of one's own free will, given the insight of the necessity for the social contract to escape the alternative, namely, anarchy. However, it is not apparent how a society of homines economici would make a permanent transmission of their power to a ruling body. This is an open question both factually in terms of the mere transmission of their weapons, property and labor, as well as in relation to the incentive compatibility in each case and over time.

Historically, it is more plausible that rulers have incentives in the management of their spheres of influence. With a revenue-enhancing incentive structure, the subject ruled can be motivated to engage in productive activity, which means a corresponding increase in revenue for the ruler. Such an incentive structure includes predictability and protected property rights (Olson M., 1993). This scenario can also be illuminated from a social contract perspective, for instance, when a protective community obliges a bandit to be its guardian (Neumärker K. J., 2011b). The idea of a community of protection to secure property rights also prompts the most liberal approaches to the justification of a minimal state (Nozick, 1974).

Meanwhile, economic social contract theory has been concerned with the way in which a Leviathan would and could act and be constrained in the face of its omnipotence (Neumärker K. J., 1995). Rawls was aware of this problem and foreshadows the need for a preference contributing to enforcement (Rawls, 1971, pp. 293-301). Likewise, business economics is concerned with the fact that functioning contractual relationships cannot be explained without forces such as trust, a joint history, and solidarity unless external enforcement of each detail is available (Blois, 1999).

The social preference studied in this paper can be interpreted as heuristic in this sense. Thus, inequality between negotiators in the bargaining situation leads to unequal threat points of withholding consent. However, it is precisely this veto power by unanimity that legitimizes the social contract and thus makes it valuable to maintain once it is agreed upon (Chan, 2000). Even a preference for negotiation on an equal footing would then no longer be as far-fetched as it might initially have seemed. This is especially true since the agreement to the contract must be permanent (Block & DiLorenzo, 2000).

The popular understanding of justice to comply with the contract (Blankart, 2017, pp. 67-74), sets the foundation on which the rule of law stands (Homann, 1997, p. 16f). However, a corresponding understanding of justice leaves the question of the legitimacy of the content of the contract unanswered. Thus, adhesion contracts, slave contracts, and forced contracting are unanimously conceivable as social contracts (Buchanan J. M., 1999c, p. 77f), even if their stability can be disputed (Hobbes T., 1841, p. 95f). However, they are nevertheless normatively critical (Locke, 1689, pp. 212-214), (Buchanan J. M., 1995). Again, the question arises as to how such an evaluation can be incorporated into an investigation. Homines economici are incapable of doing this. A social preference that considers inequality in contracting to be bad represents the first approach in this direction.

The argument that contracts must be observed is also only given weight by a normatively valuable conclusion of a contract. Homines economici do not take this argument into account and therefore break contracts at will. So a social preference for a legitimate conclusion of a contract can be used to illustrate an incentive to comply with contractual rules.

In the following section, a social preference is therefore incorporated into Nash bargaining. It demonstrates that such a social preference can establish convergence and stabilization of threat points in the initial situation. Closer threat points lead to meeting as equals, to which a higher degree of legitimacy can commonly be attributed. The value of this legitimacy is in its role as the starting point of equality (Rawls, 1958, p. 165f). More consistent threat points may also reduce the problem of renegotiation.

3. The Model

This section presents the Nash bargaining solution (Nash Jr., 1950) alongside the presentation by Kıbrıs (2020) (Kıbrıs, 2020). An investigation of social preference in this framework is also deliberated. The technical assumptions are only discussed as needed and can be found both in the articles by Nash (1950) and examples in Kıbrıs (2020).

Social contract negotiation is about agreeing to one of many possible social contracts S by all parties in order to escape from the reference point of anarchy d.

Such a situation is already very close to the representation of a bargaining problem (S, a). a_h is the payoff in the status quo and $h \in [i, j]$ is the index for the two INDIVIDUALS, indicated by the indices i and j. The set of possible agreements on a social contract S is represented in a simplified way by the design parameter s∈S. This indicates the influence INDIVIDUAL j has on the bargaining solution in comparison to INDIVIDUAL i. A lower (higher) s means that INDIVIDUAL i (INDIVIDUAL j) can influence the bargaining outcome towards his or her interests.

S contains only Pareto-optimal social contracts in the representation used here. This pre-sorting, which requires the sorting out of Pareto-inferior contracts, allows the representation of the bargaining space by a one-dimensional parameter s, without neglecting the complexity of the social contract proposals. Nash (1950) solves this issue by reducing it to the monetary value (Nash Jr., 1950, p. 161f). The gain of one INDIVIDUAL necessarily leads to the loss of the other when comparing contracts from the set of Pareto-optimal social contracts. Otherwise, one of the contracts would be a Pareto-improvement of the other. However, this then Pareto-inferior contract was previously sorted out (Franke M., 2021, pp. 22-24). Thus, the negotiation can be represented as determining the value of s. This differs from Nash's (1950) account, where part of the outcome was the identification of a Pareto-optimal agreement point. Another difference here is that the status quo is not incorporated into S. This necessitates the explicit assumption that the agreement space is also constrained to be better than the status quo values (Neumärker K. J., 1995, p. 51)

$$U_h(s) > U_h(a_h) \forall s \in S.$$

U stands for the utility function of the respective INDIVIDUAL indicated by the index. This assumption replaces the usual assumption that there is at least one better agreement option than the status quo. The payoff in the absence of an agreement is the retention in the status quo a_h.

For simple presentation, let the utility of missing out on a bargaining solution U_h (a_i) be d_i let it equal to a_i:

$$d_i = U_i(a_i) = a_i.$$

For INDIVIDUAL j respectively:
$$d_j = U_j(a_j) = a_j.$$

The utility functions considering the bargaining solution are represented by s:

$$U_i(s) = 1 - s,$$

and

$$U_j(s) = 1 - s,$$

Note that the maximum utility of INDIVIDUAL i is normalized to 1. For the applied ordinal representation such a normalization serves the presentation without adding limitations. The Nash bargaining solution is

$$N(S,d) = argmax\ s \in S\left[\left(U_i(s) - U_i(a_i)\right)\left(U_j(s) - U_j(a_j)\right)\right].$$

Substitution of the definitions of the utility functions yields

$$N(S,d) = argmax\ x\left[(1 - s - d_i)(s - d_j)\right].$$

Calculation results in the bargaining solution of the bargaining game without social preferences s^*

$$s^* = 0.5(-d_i + d_j + 1).$$

The respective utilities of the bargaining solution are

Nash Bargaining with a Social Preference

$$U_i(s^*) = 1 - 0.5(-d_i + d_j + 1),$$

and

$$U_j(s^*) = 0.5(-d_i + d_j + 1).$$

This is the reference case in which there is no social preference. The indirect utility functions are linear equations in d_i and d_j, which therefore do not have a global extremum except for the corner solution.

Now, assume that there is a benefit from agreeing on a social contract. This depends negatively on the inequality in the bargaining situation. Let this be the sum of the squared deviations of the anarchy payoffs

$$P = (a_i - a_j)^2.$$

This inequality aversion in the initial situation now enters negatively into the utility function V_h. Let the weight of this preference be parameterized by k_h>0. For k_h=0∀h the reference case occurs again. Thus,

$$V_h(s, a_i, a_j) = U_h(s) - k_h P$$

The solution in the two-person case thus results from

$$N(S, d) = argmax\ x[(1 - s - k_i P - d_i)(s - k_j P - d_j)]$$

A general preference for equality in endowments, such as suggested by Fehr and Schmidt (1999), may also be considered. This may apply even in anarchy without a contract. Nevertheless, this does not affect the Nash Bargaining Solution. To show this let

$$d_h = a_h - k_h P$$

Insertion in formula (13) reveals that these do not result in any change compared to the reference case in formula (7)

$$N(S, d) = argmax\ x\big[(1 - s - k_i P - (a_i - k_i P))(s - k_j P - (a_j - k_j P))\big] = argmax\ x[(1 - s - a_i)(s - a_j)].$$

Furthermore, again

$$d_h = a_h$$

This gives the bargaining solution for the case with social preferences

$$s^{**} = 0.5(-d_i + d_j + k_i P - k_j P + 1).$$

From this follows that an unequal distribution of social preferences shifts the bargaining outcome to the disadvantage of the preference holder.

Thus the indirect utility calculus of the expected outcome of the negotiation is calculated as

$$V_i(s^{**}) = 1 - 0.5(-d_i + d_j + k_i P - k_j P + 1) - k_i P,$$

and

$$V_j(s^{**}) = 0.5(-d_i + d_j + k_i P - k_j P + 1) - k_j P.$$

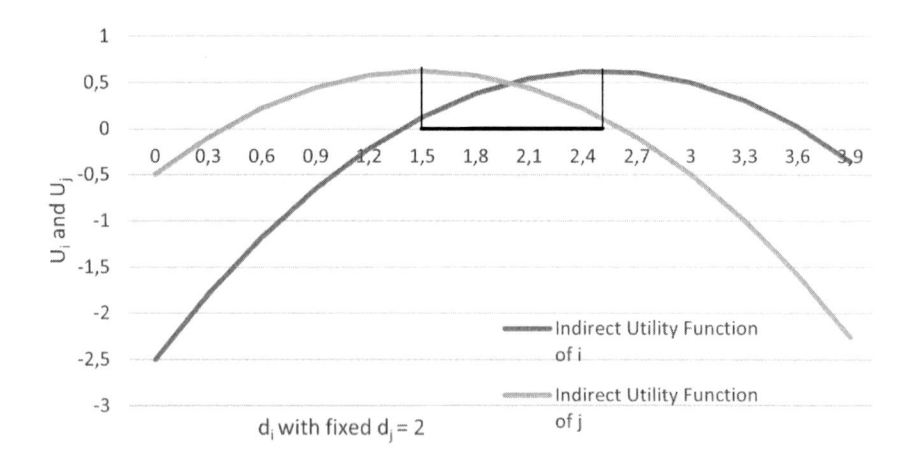

Figure 2: Indirect utility functions and transfer incentives

Nash Bargaining with a Social Preference

Substituting formula (3) and formula (11) reveals quadratic indirect utility functions in a_i und a_j due to P. This has a maximum at

$$V_i^*(s^{**}) = 0.125 \left(\frac{1}{k_i + k_j} + 4 \right),$$

for

$$a_i^*(a_j, k_i, k_j) = a_j + \frac{0.5}{k_i + k_j}.$$

Notably, both INDIVIDUALS lower the difference to be compensated for by the same factor t

$$t = \frac{0.5}{k_i + k_j}.$$

Thus for INDIVIDUAL j the maximum is

(1) $V_j^*(s^{**}) = 0.125(2t + 4)$,

for

(2) $a_j^*(a_i, k_i, k_j) = a_i + t.$

Hence the localization of social preference does not matter for utility maximization. This is due to $k_i + k_j$ always occurring together in this calculus so that only their sum matters.

Transforming formula (23) as lower bound allows formulating the interval

$$a_i \in [a_j - t, a_j + t],$$

in which a negotiated settlement takes place without individuals having an interest in paying a transfer.

Figure 2 provides an example with fixed $a_j = 2$, and $k_i = k_i = 0.5$. The quadratic shape of the indirect utility functions generates a global maximum in utility for both symmetric individuals at $V_h^*(s^{**}) = 0.625$. For i this is straight forward $a_i^*(a_j, k_i, k_j) = a_i^*(2, 0.5, 0.5) = 2.5$. And for j, since $a_j = 2$ is fix, this is $a_j^*(a_i, k_i, k_j) = a_j^*(a_i, 0.5, 0.5) = 2$ results in $a_i = 1.5$, which generates maximum utility for j if $a_j = 2$.

The horizontal area between the two maxima marked by the black line indicates the area of the bargaining solution taking place without any incentives for redistribution. This can be seen by the incline of the indirect utility functions. In this area the indirect utility of i is rising, while the indirect utility of j is declining in a_i with fixed $a_j=2$. Thus, a move to the right is beneficial for i while it is harmful for j. This is a classic bargaining situation.

Nevertheless, for the area to the left and the right of this interval, there is a common interest in moving towards the interval in the middle. Once again, the incline shows the incentives. To the left of the interval, both indirect utility functions are rising. Thus, a movement to the right is better for both, indicating a Pareto-improvement. On the right side of the interval both indirect utility functions are declining, indicating a movement to the left to be a Pareto-improvement. In the following, we will describe these movements into the middle as a possibility for transfer payments.

The transfer payment is half the difference between the respective boundary of the interval and the actual value of the status quo a_j. The transfer amounts to only half of this difference because, for a difference to be compensated, a transfer costs the payer and benefits the receiver of the transfer. Thus, every unit of transfer lowers the difference by double the amount of its value.

The transfer payment above the upper bound by INDIVIDUAL i to INDIVIDUAL j is

$$2T = a_i - (a_j + t).$$

By rearranging the transfer amount in the area above the upper bound can be seen.

$$T = 0.5a_i - 0.5a_j - 0.5t.$$

The transfer payment in the area below the lower bound gets paid by INDIVIDUAL j to INDIVIDUAL i, and thus denoted as a negative cash flow, is

$$-2T = a_j - t - a_i$$

By rearranging the transfer amount in the area below the lower bound can be seen.

$$T = \begin{cases} 0.5a_i - 0.5a_j - t \text{ for } a_i < a_j - t \\ 0 \text{ for } a_j - t \leq a_i \leq a_j + t \\ -0.5a_j + 0.5a_i + t \text{ for } a_j + t < a_i \end{cases}.$$

This allows for the complete formulation of the transfer to be predicted as

The derivation of T with respect to the social preferences k_h is

$$\frac{\delta T}{\delta k_i} = \frac{\delta T}{\delta k_j} = \begin{cases} \dfrac{0.5}{(k_i + k_j)^2} \text{ for } a_i < a_j - t \\ 0 \text{ for } a_j - t \leq a_i \leq a_j + t \\ -\dfrac{0.5}{(k_i + k_j)^2} \text{ for } a_j + t < a_i \end{cases}.$$

This reveals that an increase in the inequality preference increases the transfer potential since there is a positive derivative in the corresponding range.

4. Discussion

This section discusses the interpretation of the results. It starts with a critical remark on the interpretation. It is then argued that these findings would recommend universal basic income for constitutional contracting.

The transfer in this model is never actually paid, which is why its effect can be questioned. This is due to two factors that simplify the model, but which make the transfer payment a reality in a more realistic scenario.

The Nash bargaining solution represents the bargaining outcome of fully informed and fully rational individuals who know who their fellow players are. This results in an agreement that is reliable and foreseeable by all (Nash Jr., 1950, p. 158). Thus, remaining in anarchy with a zero probability of occurrence is effectively not represented in the individuals' calculus. The costs arising from the transfer only enter the calculation with zero probability and are therefore not considered dynamically here.

Secondly, the model simplifies the negotiation process. The bargaining is built into the expectations of the negotiators. At least a realistic bargaining situation between human beings was not modelled in this paper. In fact, despite social preference, the homo economicus described here finds it difficult to engage in true communication. After all, he already knows everything. And his promises mean nothing to him, which everyone also knows and expects. So, why should they get involved in the act of negotiation at all (Harsanyi J. C., 1962)? However, this view leads to an immediate solution without any negotiation period since it delivers an immediate betterment. As a result, the duration of the transfer payment during the bargaining in the anarchy is zero and thus the transfer is in principle irrelevant. Nevertheless, the bargaining solution can be affected.

These two simplifications of the model do not allow us to contrast the costs of the transfer payment with the benefits. Nevertheless, this model argues that there is a potential for a transfer. However, the question of whether this justifies the cost to transfer payers is a broader question that would require an adjustment of at least one of the two points above in further research.

Additionally, this approach needs to be applied with sufficient uncertainty about the end of the cooperation due to circumstances, expectations, and an infinite time horizon. Otherwise, backward induction may suggest cooperation not to take place due to the incentives to defect in the last round. This problem carries over to the second last round and so on. (Abreu & Pearce, 1991). For a social contract, the time horizon is sufficiently long and the end of the contract sufficiently uncertain.

The specific social preference attached to the equality in the status quo of the bargaining situation does not apply to bargaining situations in general, however. In most private transactions the seller does not care about the situation of the buyer, and vice versa, especially in those situations where the partners are anonymous. Nevertheless, some sellers may try to provide affordable goods, especially to poor people. This behavior may lead related situations as the model describes. Nevertheless, the point is that for the whole status quo to matter, the bargaining situation needs to be able to change the status quo. So a social contract must be set up to change the circumstances of life in a society.

Applying the results of the model to the contractarian approach, as introduced in section two, makes an argument for some basic rights and basic goods to end up with something in the direction of Rawls's conclusion for the content of a social contract (Rawls, 1971, p. 53). For the sake of bargaining on an equal footing, there are incentives in society to provide something as an appropriate status quo for everyone, as shown. This requires the assumption of social preference to be existent in society. Nevertheless, our results suggest that only the extent and the sum of these preferences in society is relevant, not their distribution. It should be noted that the exclusion of people from the bargaining stage would be problematic in this model (Buchanan J. M., 1999c, p. 78).

Thus providing basic rights and access to basic goods to the worse off in society make the status quo more equal. One may consider such provision an unconditional basic income if one ignores the issue of no monetary system being developed in this situation. Van Parijs (2004) includes the following points when defining an unconditional basic income (Van Parijs, 2004):

"An Income Paid in Cash" (Ibid., p.8)
"Paid by a Political Community" (Ibid., p. 9)
"To All Its Members" (Ibid., p. 10)
"On an Individual Basis" (Ibid., p. 11)
"Without a Means Test" (Ibid., p. 12)
"Without Work Requirement" (Ibid., p. 15)

These criteria provide a reasonable summary. Of course, without a government, there is no financial system, no property rights, and no enforcement of contracts. Very different in detail from "An Income Paid in Cash". Nevertheless, it is "Paid by a Political Community" that is formed by engaging in the bargaining process with social preferences in mind. It is not paid "To All Its Members". Instead, it can be interpreted as negative income tax (Friedman, 1982, pp. 157-161). Its net effect with the aim of redistribution "Without Work Requirement" corresponds to the suggested result of the model. As shown, the amount of the transfer needs to be relative to the status quo of the better bargaining partner. Whether it is paid "On an Individual Basis" may depend on assumptions about the social preference. If it is aimed at an individual level, this may be the implication. Nevertheless, the preference may aim at families, tribes, or nations, which would go along with the respective implications for the basis of the transfer. The presented model suggests the well-being in the status quo to be more equal than in modern societies, which would also consider the wealth distribution. A transfer based on this would probably go against the "Without Means Test" aspect of a universal basic income. This seems to be a huge difference to the universal basic income proposal by Van Parijs (2004) at the first glance. However, in the setting of constitutional design, there are no property rights and people live in a conflict equilibrium as set out in section two. Thus, at least in the interpretation on an individual basis, there cannot be too much of a difference in wealth between the people since defending this wealth would be difficult and hoarding wealth would generate incentives for people to steal (Franke M., 2021, p. 12), (Hirshleifer, 1991).

This implies that our results suggest something as close to a universal basic income as possible without a previous social contract to enable fair bargaining over a social contract. It should be noted that this suggestion goes in the direction of sequential reform instead of a big bang implementation of a social contract. Nevertheless, it is in line with Buchanan's (1999) statement: "Behind a sufficiently thick veil of uncertainty and/or ignorance, contractual agreement on rules that allow for some in-period fiscal transfers seems clear to be possible. The precise features of a constitutionally approved transfer structure cannot, of course, be derived independently because of the restriction of evaluative judgment to the process of the constitutional agreement" (Buchanan J. M., 1999b, p. 466).

5. Conclusion

This paper shows that a preference for equality in the starting position of negotiation has the potential to restrict the bargaining range to a tolerated area of inequality. Outside this range, one individual at a time has an incentive to support the other with a transfer. Under favorable circumstances, such as low uncertainty and high agreement potential, a transfer can thus be expected in the case of unequal starting conditions and the need for negotiation on an equal footing.

For the transfer, it is irrelevant how the social preference is distributed. All preferences enter the Nash bargaining solution and influence the tolerated inequality. This allows an individual who is deterred by the inequality of the initial situation to better represent his interests in the negotiation in such a way that, even for a purely selfish negotiator $k_i=0$, the transfer can produce an overcompensating negotiating advantage.

The results suggest that when striving for cooperation among equal partners, it may be effective for all parties to strive for equality of the partners through a transfer payment. For the interpretation of bargaining over a social contract, it has been shown that the suggested transfer is close to a universal basic income. This may be appropriate content for a first constitution to build more sophisticated reforms on.

The model above is a good starting point on which to further develop the research on this special preference. This can be done in numerous ways. First, the artificial Nash bargaining solution can be substituted by a game from the Nash program, including dynamic games and incomplete information. This would make the explicit modelling for n-player games in combination with the free-rider problem more interesting. Further, the inequality aversion may vary. Finally, it may be possible to make an empirical guess at the existence and structure of such a social preference.

Abbreviations

*	Index indicates the Nash bargaining solution without social preferences
**	Index indicates the Nash bargaining solution considering the social preference
a	Default payoff in the status quo
C	Basic constitution in Buchanan's Anarchy to a constitution
d	Utility of the default payoff, for the most time set to d(a)=a

D   Anarchy in Buchanan's Anarchy to a constitution
E   Developed constitution Buchanan's Anarchy to a constitution
h   Index for the individuals, h∈{1,2}
i   Index for one individual
j   Index for the other individual
k   Parameter for the intensity of the social preference
N   Nash-Bargaining-Lösung zur Bestimmung von s^* and s^(**)
P   The social preference
s   Resembles the bargaining solution in one parameter s∈S. The higher, the better for j. The lower, the better for i.
S   Set of possible Pareto-optimal social contracts
t   Tolerated inequality in the status quo. This defines the area where the bargaining solution takes, $t=(0.5)/k_i + k_j$
T   Transfer from i to j
U   Utility function without social preference, i.e., k=0
V   Utility function containing the social preference P with the intensity k

Author Contributions

Conceptualization M.F. and T.J.; formal analysis, M.F.; investigation, M.F.; writing—original draft preparation, M.F.; writing—review and editing M.F. and T.J.; visualization, M.F.

References

Abreu, D., & Pearce, D. (1991). A Perspective on Renegotiation in Repeated Games. In Game Equilibrium Models II (pp. 44–55). Springer Berlin Heidelberg. doi:10.1007/978-3-662-07365-0_4

Alesina, A., & Drazen, A. (1991). Why are Stabilizations Delayed? The American Economic Review, 81, 1170–1188.

Arato, A. (1995). Forms of constitution making and theories of democracy. Cardozo L. Rev., 17, 191.

Barbera, S., & Jackson, M. O. (2004). Choosing How to Choose: Self-Stable Majority Rules and Constitutions. The Quarterly Journal of Economics, 119, 1011–1048. Retrieved from http://www.jstor.org/stable/25098708

Barkaoui, A., & Dragicevic, A. Z. (2016, 8). Nash bargaining and renegotiation with social preferences: case of the roundwood log supply contracts in the French timber market. Forest Policy and Economics, 69, 90–100. doi:10.1016/j.forpol.2016.04.007

Barnett, R. E. (2003). Constitutional legitimacy. Colum. L. Rev., 103, 111–148.

Bentham, J. (1781). An Introduction to the Principles of Morals and Legislation. Kitchener 2000: Batoche Books.

Binmore, K. (2005, 5). Natural Justice. Oxford University Press. doi:10.1093/acprof:oso/9780195178111.001.0001

Binmore, K., Rubinstein, A., & Wolinsky, A. (1986). The Nash Bargaining Solution in Economic Modelling. The RAND Journal of Economics, 17, 176–188. Retrieved from http://www.jstor.org/stable/2555382

Blankart, C. B. (2017). Öffentliche Finanzen in der Demokratie. Verlag Franz Vahlen GmbH. doi:10.15358/9783800653485

Block, W., & DiLorenzo, T. J. (2000). Is Voluntary Government Possible? A Critique of Constitutional Economics. Journal of Institutional and Theoretical Economics (JITE) / Zeitschrift für die gesamte Staatswissenschaft, 156, 567–582. Retrieved from http://www.jstor.org/stable/40752232

Blois, K. J. (1999, 3). Trust in Business to Business Relationships: An Evaluation of its Status. Journal of Management Studies, 36, 197–215. doi:10.1111/1467-6486.00133

Boadway, R. W., & Bruce, N. (1984). Welfare economics. B. Blackwell New York.

Boucher, D. (1994). The social contract from Hobbes to Rawls. London: Routledge.

Brennan, G. (1973a). Pareto desirable redistribution: The non-altruistic dimension. Public Choice, 14, 43–67.

Brennan, G., & Buchanan, J. M. (2000a). The Power to Tax: Analytical Foundations of a Fiscal Constitution. Library of Economics and Liberty. Retrieved from <http://www.econlib.org/library/Buchanan/buchCv9c2.html>

Brennan, G., & Buchanan, J. M. (2000b). The Reason of Rules: Constituional Political Economy. Library of Economics and Liberty. Retrieved from <http://www.econlib.org/library/Buchanan/buchCv10.html>

Buchanan, J. M. (1962). The Relevance of Pareto Optimality. The Journal of Conflict Resolution, 6, 341–354. doi:https://doi.org/10.1177/002200276200600405

Buchanan, J. M. (1990). The Domain of Constitutional Economics. Constitutional Political Economy, 1, 1–18.

Buchanan, J. M. (1995, 4). Individual Rights, Emergent Social States, and Behavioral Feasibility. Rationality and Society, 7, 141–150. doi:10.1177/1043463195007002002

Buchanan, J. M. (1999a). The Demand and Supply of Public Goods. Library of Economics and Liberty. Retrieved from <http://www.econlib.org/library/Buchanan/buchCv5c2.html>

Buchanan, J. M. (1999b). The Logical Foundations of Constitutional Liberty. Indianapolis: Liberty Fund Inc.

Buchanan, J. M. (1999c). The Limits of Liberty: Between Anarchy and Leviathan. Library of Economics and Liberty. Retrieved from <http://www.econlib.org/library/Buchanan/buchCv7.html>

Buchanan, J. M., & Tullock, G. (1999a). The Calculus of Consent: Logical Foundations of Constitutional Democracy (Vol. 3). Indianapolis: Liberty Fund Inc.

Chan, J. (2000, 1). Legitimacy, Unanimity, and Perfectionism. Philosophy $\less$html{_}ent glyph="@amp\mathsemicolon$" ascii="{\&}amp$\mathsemicolon$"/$\greater$ Public Affairs, 29, 5–42. doi:10.1111/j.1088-4963.2000.00005.x

Chatterjee, K. (2020). Non-Cooperative Bargaining Theory. In Handbook of Group Decision and Negotiation (pp. 1–13). Springer International Publishing. doi:10.1007/978-3-030-12051-1_9-1

Clark, J. (1998). Fairness in Public Good Provision: An Investigation of Preferences for Equality and Proportionality. The Canadian Journal of Economics / Revue canadienne d'Economique, 31, 708–729. Retrieved from http://www.jstor.org/stable/136209

Crain, W. M., & Tollison, R. D. (1977, 1). Legislative Size and Voting Rules. The Journal of Legal Studies, 6, 235–240. doi:10.1086/467569

Fehr, E., & Schmidt, K. M. (1999). A theory of fairness, competition, and cooperationn. The quarterly journal of economics, 114, 817–868.

Feltovich, N., & Swierzbinski, J. (2011, 5). The role of strategic uncertainty in games: An experimental study of cheap talk and contracts in the Nash demand game. European Economic Review, 55, 554–574. doi:10.1016/j.euroecorev.2010.07.001

Fong, C. (2001, 11). Social preferences, self-interest, and the demand for redistribution. Journal of Public Economics, 82, 225–246. doi:10.1016/s0047-2727(00)00141-9

Franke, M. (2021). Eine Verhandlung zur Selektion der konstitutionenökonomischen Lösung. Constitutional Economic Network Papers.

Franke, M., & Neumärker, B. K. (2022, 2). A Climate Alliance through Transfer: Transfer Design in an Economic Conflict Model. World, 3, 112–125. doi:10.3390/world3010006

Friedman, M. (1982). Capitalism and Freedom (Phoenix Books). University Of Chicago Press. Retrieved from https://www.amazon.com/Capitalism-Freedom-Phoenix-Milton-Friedman/dp/0226264017?SubscriptionId=AKIAIOBINVZYXZQZ2U3A&tag=chimbori05-20&linkCode=xm2&camp=2025&creative=165953&creativeASIN=0226264017

Frohlich, N., & Oppenheimer, J. (1992). Choosing justice: an experimental approach to ethical theory. Berkeley, CA: University of California Press.

Frohlich, N., Oppenheimer, J. A., Smith, J., & Young, O. R. (1978). A Test of Downsian Voter Rationality: 1964 Presidential Voting. The American Political Science Review, 72, 178–197.

Gauthier, D. (1987, 5). Morals by Agreement. Oxford University Press. doi:10.1093/0198249926.001.0001

Gordon, S. (1976). The New Contractarians. Journal of Political Economy, 84, 573–590.

Harsanyi, J. C. (1953). Cardinal Utility in Welfare Economics and in the Theory of Risk–Taking. Journal of Political Economy, 61, 434–435.

Harsanyi, J. C. (1955). Cardinal Welfare, Individualistic Ethics, and Interpersonal Comparisons of Utility. The Journal of Political Economy, 63, 309–321.

Harsanyi, J. C. (1962). Bargaining in Ignorance of the Opponent's Utility Function. The Journal of Conflict Resolution, 6, 29–38. doi:doi.org/10.1177/002200276200600104

Harsanyi, J. C., & Selten, R. (1972, 1). A Generalized Nash Solution for Two-Person Bargaining Games with Incomplete Information. Management Science, 18, 80–106. doi:10.1287/mnsc.18.5.80

Hart, O., & Moore, J. (1999, 1). Foundations of Incomplete Contracts. Review of Economic Studies, 66, 115–138. doi:10.1111/1467-937x.00080

Hicks, J. R. (1939). The Foundations of Welfare Economics. The Economic Journal, 49, 696–712. Retrieved from http://www.jstor.org/stable/2225023

Hirshleifer, J. (1991). The Paradox of Power. Economics and Politics, 3, 177–200.

Hirshleifer, J. (1995). Anarchy and its Breakdown. Journal of Political Economy, 103, 26–52.

Hobbes, T. (1839). The English Works of Thomas Hobbes of Malmesbury by Sir William Molesworth, Bart. Vol.3. London: John Bohn.

Hobbes, T. (1841). The English Works of Thomas Hobbes of Malmesbury by Sir William Molesworth, Bart. Vol.2. London: John Bohn.

Hobbes, T. (2001, 2 28). Leviathan. Reclam Philipp Jun. Retrieved from https://www.ebook.de/de/product/1338298/thomas_hobbes_leviathan.html

Holler, M. J., Illing, G., & Napel, S. (2019). Einführung in die Spieltheorie. Springer Berlin Heidelberg. doi:10.1007/978-3-642-31963-1

Homann, K. (1997). Sinn und Grenze der ökonomischen Methodein der Wirtschaftsethik. In D. A. Dabrowski (Ed.), Wirtschaftsethik und Moralkonomik : Normen, soziale Ordnung und der Beitrag der Ökonomik. Berlin Germany: Duncker & Humblot.

Homann, K. (2003). Braucht die Wirtschaftsethik eine "moralische Motivation". Lutherstadt Wittenberg: Wittenberg Center for Global Ethics.

Kaldor, N. (1939). Welfare Propositions of Economics and Interpersonal Comparisons of Utility. The Economic Journal, 49, 549–552. Retrieved from http://www.jstor.org/stable/2224835

Kaneko, M., & Nakamura, K. (1979). The Nash Social Welfare Function. Econometrica, 47, 423–435. Retrieved from http://www.jstor.org/stable/1914191

Kant, I. (1785). Grundlegung zur Metaphysik der Sitten. Digitale Bibliothek Band 2: Philosophie. Retrieved from https://silo.tips/download/grundlegung-zur-metaphysik-der-sitten-5

Kıbrıs, Ö. (2020). Negotiation as a Cooperative Game. In Handbook of Group Decision and Negotiation (pp. 1–24). Springer International Publishing. doi:10.1007/978-3-030-12051-1_10-1

Kirchgässner, G. (2013). Homo oeconomicus das ökonomische Modell individuellen Verhaltens und seine Anwendung in den Wirtschafts- und Sozialwissenschaften. Tübingen: Mohr Siebeck.

Koller, P. (1987). Neue Theorien des Sozialkontrakts. Duncker & Humblot. doi:10.3790/978-3-428-46208-7

Konow, J. (2003, 11). Which Is the Fairest One of All? A Positive Analysis of Justice Theories. Journal of Economic Literature, 41, 1188–1239. doi:10.1257/002205103771800013

Laffont, J.-J. (2000). Incentives and Political Economy. Oxford: Oxford University Press.

Lenger, A., Wolf, S., & Goldschmidt, N. (2020, 12). Choosing inequality: how economic security fosters competitive regimes. The Journal of Economic Inequality, 19, 315–346. doi:10.1007/s10888-020-09472-5

Levitt, S. D., & List, J. A. (2007, 4). What Do Laboratory Experiments Measuring Social Preferences Reveal About the Real World? Journal of Economic Perspectives, 21, 153–174. doi:10.1257/jep.21.2.153

Lindenberg, S. (1985). An Assessment of the New Political Economy: Its Potential for the Social Sciences and for Sociology in Particular. Sociological Theory, 3, 99–114. Retrieved from http://www.jstor.org/stable/202177

Locke, J. (1689). Two Treatises of Government (6. Reprinted ed.). London: A. Millar et al.

Meckling, W. H. (1976, 12). Values and the Choice of the Model of the Individual in the Social Sciences. Swiss Journal of Economics and Statistics (SJES), 112, 545-560. Retrieved from https://ideas.repec.org/a/ses/arsjes/1976-iv-1.html

Mueller, D. C. (2003). Public Choice III. Cambridge: Cambridge University Press.

Muthoo, A. (1999). Bargaining theory with applications. Cambridge University Press.

Nash Jr., J. F. (1950). The Bargaining Problem. The Econometric Society, 18, 155–162.

Nash, J. (1951). Non-Cooperative Games. Annals of Mathematics, 54, 286–295. Retrieved from http://www.jstor.org/stable/1969529

Nash, J. (1953). Two-Person Cooperative Games. Econometrica, 21, 128–140. Retrieved from http://www.jstor.org/stable/1906951

Neumärker, K. J. (1995). Finanzverfassung und Staatsgewalt in der Demokratie. Frankfurt am Main: Peter Lang GmbH.

Neumärker, K. J. (2003). Die politische Ökonomie der privaten Bereitstellung öffentlicher Grüter. Frankfurt am Main: C. Folkers, Peter Lang.

Neumärker, K. J. (2011a). Missgunst, Neid und Feindseligkeit: negative soziale Präferenzen aus konfliktökonomischer Sicht. In Konflikt, Macht und Gewalt aus politökonomischer Perspektive.

Neumärker, K. J. (2011b). Konflikt, Macht und Gewalt aus politökonomischer Perspektive. Metropolis-Verlag.

Neumärker, K. J. (2017). Ordnungspolitik, Neuer Ordoliberalismus und Mainstream Economics. WISU, 46, 830–840.

Nozick, R. (1974). Anarchy, state, and utopia (Vol. 5038). New York: Basic Books.

Olson, M. (1993, 9). Dictatorship, Democracy, and Development. American Political Science Review, 87, 567–576. doi:10.2307/2938736

Olson, M. L. (1965). The Logic of Collective Action. Cambridge: Harvard University Press.

Rawls, J. (1958). Justice as Fairness. The Philosophical Review, 67, 164-194.

Rawls, J. (1971). A Theory of Justice: Revised Edition. Cambridge, Massachusetts: Harvard University Press.

Rosen, S. (1985). Implicit Contracts: A Survey. Journal of Economic Literature, 23, 1144–1175. Retrieved from http://www.jstor.org/stable/2725461

Rousseau, J. –J. (1762). Der Gesellschaftsvertrag oder Grundlagen des Staatsrechts. In F. Roepke (Ed.). Amsterdam Leipzig.

Rubinstein, A. (1987). A sequential strategic theory of bargaining. Advances in Economic Theory: Fifth World Congress, 5.

Schmitz, P. W. (2001, 1). The Hold-Up Problem and Incomplete Contracts: A Survey of Recent Topics in Contract Theory. Bulletin of Economic Research, 53, 1–17. doi:10.1111/1467-8586.00114

Schwartz, A., & Scott, R. E. (2003). Contract theory and the limits of contract law. Yale LJ, 113, 541–619.

Seiler, C. (2014). I Diskursethik (Habermas). In Die Diskursethik im Spannungsfeld von Systemtheorie und Differenzphilosophie (pp. 31–52). Springer Fachmedien Wiesbaden. doi:10.1007/978-3-658-08756-2_1

Smith, A. (1976). The Theory of Moral Sentiments. (D. D. Raphael, & A. L. Macfie, Eds.) Oxford University Press.

Spindler, Z. A. (1990, 9). Constitutional design for a rent-seeking society: Voting rule choice. Constitutional Political Economy, 1, 73–82. doi:10.1007/bf02393241

Sutton, J. (1986). Non-Cooperative Bargaining Theory: An Introduction. The Review of Economic Studies, 53, 709–724. Retrieved from http://www.jstor.org/stable/2297715

Suzumura, K. (1981, 12). On pareto-efficiency and the no-envy concept of equity. Journal of Economic Theory, 25, 367–379. doi:10.1016/0022-0531(81)90037-5

Thoma, J. (2015, 4). Bargaining and the impartiality of the social contract. Philosophical Studies, 172, 3335–3355. doi:10.1007/s11098-015-0472-7

Tversky, A., & Kahneman, D. (1974). Judgement under Uncertainty: Heristics and Biases. Science, 185, 1124–1131.

Van Parijs, P. (1997, 11). Real Freedom for All. Oxford University Press. doi:10.1093/0198293577.001.0001

Van Parijs, P. (2004). Basic income: a simple and powerful idea for the twenty-first century. Politics & Society, 32, 7–39.

Vanberg, V. (1986, 11). Individual Choice and Institutional Constraints. Analyse & Kritik, 8, 113–149. doi:10.1515/auk-1986-0201

Vanberg, V. J. (1994, 12). Rules and Choice in Economics. Routledge. doi:10.4324/9780203422588

Vanberg, V. J. (2004). The Status Quo in Contractarian–Constitutionalist Perspective. Constitutional Political Economy, 15, 153–170.

Vanberg, V. J. (2016). Social Contract vs. Invisible Hand: Agreeing to Solve Social Dilemmas. Freiburger Diskussionspapiere zur Ordnungsökonomik, 16, 1–29.

Von Neumann, J., & Morgenstern, O. (1953). Theory of Games and Economics Behavior (3 ed.). Princeton: Princeton University Press.

Weatherman, D. V. (1985). James Buchanan on Slavery and Secession. Presidential Studies Quarterly, 15, 796–805. Retrieved from http://www.jstor.org/stable/27550278

Wicksell, K. (1896). Finanztheoretische Untersuchungen nebst Darstellung und Kritik des Steuerwesens Schwedens. Jena: Verlag von Gustav Fischer.

Wolf, S., & Lenger, A. (2011). Choosing Inequality An Experimental Analysis of the Impact of Social Immobility on the Democratic Election of Distributive Rules. Constitutional Economic Network Papers.

Young, H. P. (2008). Social Norms. In S. N. Durlauf, & L. E. Blume (Eds.), The New Palgrave Dictionary of Economics (2nd ed.).

II

Basic Income: Models and Experiments

Das Bedingungslose Grundeinkommen: Modelle und Experimente

Bernhard Neumärker, Jette Weinel

The Implications of a UBI on Utility Functions and Tax Revenue

Towards Time Sovereignty and Consumption Taxation

Economic modelling of the UBI does not account for how the individual's utility calculation changes as a result of the unconditional transfer. In this paper we aim to overcome this blind spot by characterizing a utility function adapted to a UBI. We argue that, while an additively separable relationship between consumption and labor is the basis of the mainstream fiscal thinking in theory and practice, the utility calculation of an individual socialized by the UBI is reflected in a multiplicative relationship. This change is due to the time sovereignty, that individuals gain through an unconditional basic income and which in turn enables them to be self-determined, creative, and intrinsically motivated. In the second part we then consider the consequences of the UBI utility function on tax revenue. Therefore, we examine the consumption tax revenue curve with an UBI (multiplicative preferences) and a means-tested welfare system (additive separable preferences).

1. Introduction

This paper aims to investigate the implications of an unconditional basic income on the representation of utility in economics and the consequences for the consumption tax revenue curve. Arthur B. Laffer is said to have first articulated the classical hump-shaped form of the tax revenue curve at a business dinner in 1974 (Wanniski, 1978). However, according to more recent research by Trabandt and Uhlig (2011, 2013), this curve does not necessarily apply to consumption tax. Hiraga and Nutahara (2016, 2018, 2019 a & b, 2021) confirm this view by showing that the Laffer curve is sensitive to the utility function. Based on the multiplicative utility function by King and Rebelo (1999, Eq. 6.7; see also King, Rebelo & Plosser, 1988 a & b), the tax revenue curve of consumption tax increases monotonically (Trabandt & Uhlig, 2011, Hiraga & Nutahara, 2019). These findings are particularly interesting for two reasons within the context of the Unconditional Basic Income (UBI). First, the multiplicative relationship between consumption and labor in the King and Rebelo utility function (KR utility function) is crucial for the representation of the utility calculus of an individual receiving the UBI, and a switch from a workfare system like the German Hartz IV to a basic income system implies a switch from additive separability between consumption and work effort to a multiplicative relationship. To some extent this indicates an endogenous utility function, depending on the social policy. Second, several UBI models mainly rely on financing through consumption taxation (Werner, 2006; Werner (ed.), 2012; Wakolbinger, Dreer, Schneider & Neumärker, 2020; Wigger, 2012). It seems remarkable that we can add to this discussion the specific consumption tax revenue effect of UBI based directly on the utility side rather than on the traditional arguments from the production side. Our results indicate that only the consumption tax shows the monotonic revenue effect, which makes this tax base the most relevant for financing UBI.

Firstly, the concept of utility and rationality in economics is rooted in utilitarianism. Yet, for Utilitarian philosophy, 'utility' was a primitive term (Kapteyn, 1985). Bentham (1823, p.3) roughly defined as follows: "By utility is meant that property in any object, whereby it tends to produce benefit, advantage, pleasure, good or happiness [...]". However, in economics the conception of utility and rationality is as controversial as it is fundamental (Blume & Easley, 2008). Utility is defined in terms of preferences and these are based on a few axioms. This reduction to axioms allows the mathematical representation of an individual's behavior. The utility function is then to be understood as an instrument to summarize the most fundamental preference relations (Jehle & Reny, 2011). By contrast, the principal-agent theory shows the conventional utility relationship between consumption and work for workers and their labor contract straightforward. It illustrates how we think individuals behave in the labor market. Accordingly, the agent and the principal face a conflict of interest. This is because the principal hires the agent to complete a task, but the agent himself acts on her own best interest which is contrary to the principal's best interest. In a state of asymmetric information moral hazard occurs (Frey & Bohnet, 1994). When modelling the agent's utility, it is therefore modelled as an additively separable function. Here the agent divides his or her time between work, which provides a livelihood, and consumption. But s/he shows the well-known disutility of effort because s/he dislikes her work and suffer as a result while working. The disutility of effort is the main driver of labor supply in the traditional household supply and aggregated labor market supply function and results in a utility function in which utility derives from consumption minus work suffering multiplied by labor. The rigorous and non-sensitive application of these assumptions about utility calculus and labor market participation have important fiscal and policy implications.

But the UBI fundamentally breaks with this approach. With the idea of an unconditional basic income for every citizen in a society being based on the understanding that humans have intrinsic motivation, prefer time sovereignty as an essential part of liberty to conventional simple consumer sovereignty, and strive to be a productive part of society (Liebermann, 2012), it breaks with the principal-agent approach for the labor market. The unconditional transfer, which ensures socioeconomic participation, enables people to be sovereign with respect to time in a new sense. This means that the individual is now no longer obliged to take on work and suffer in order to secure a livelihood. Rather, it is about being free and self-determined in one's decisions when it comes to work. For instance, someone who wants to pursue further schooling, education, and training or take on care work is now empowered to do so without worrying about their livelihood, stigmatization or bureaucratically burdensome applications. An agent or worker no longer has to rely completely on a heteronomous labor relationship. On the production side, in a principal-agent model, for example, this work adjustment effect can be integrated in the household budget constraint (we do this as well) or the agent's participation constraint, demonstrating the impact of the UBI (labor market or agency contract) exit option and the incentive compatibility effects on production (e.g, Davies, Franke, Kuang, Neumärker, 2022).

When someone receives such a transfer, it will automatically cause a change in the calculation of utility. The utility function with respect to the UBI considers not only the time sovereignty of individuals but also the resulting intrinsic motivation to work. We therefore argue that a distinction must be made between the preference relation of an agent who is socialized in a means-tested social security system and one who receives a UBI.

Secondly, the discussion around the UBI seems to be driven mainly by two questions: how such an unconditional transfer can be financed and how the labor supply will adjust. Milton Friedman (1962, 1980) made an early attempt, at least implicitly, to respond by arguing that his UBI version of a "Negative Income Tax" leave the citizens with a poverty gap, thus ensuring incentives to enter the labor market and to supply labor time, and a "net version" of UBI making the public budget relatively small by calculating the transfer immediately against the individual (income) tax payments.

The focus is on the fiscal challenge here. When it comes to social security systems, it is, for obvious reasons, essential to consider the transfer and the tax system as a whole. Although there are a number of UBI proposals, we have chosen to consider a rather abstract version of the UBI rather than a detailed proposal in this paper since the primary focus is on the basic approach. The implementation of a UBI makes a change in the tax system seem reasonable as it would replace a means tested social security system. In their models UBI proponents repeatedly refer to consumption tax as being of particular relevance. Several economists (e.g., Mirrlees et al., 2010) point out that the advantages of the consumption tax lie in the efficiency of tax revenue and the relatively low distortion of labor market decisions. Wakolbinger et al. (2020) add to this and argue along the lines of an inverted Atkinson-Stiglitz theorem that consumption taxation should be responsible for efficient taxation while from the negative income tax the basic transfer, i.e., the gross UBI payment, would be left for regulating issues of justice. Hardorp (2012) puts the emphasis on international fairness and the natural avoidance of multiple taxation of earned income and the exclusive taxation of domestic consumption. This is also criticized for its regressive effect however (Keen & Lockwood, 2010; Keen, 2007). To preserve the progressive tax effect, Hardorp (2012) argues for a differentiation in tax rates between basic life consumption and conspicuous consumption. Wakolbinger et al. (2020), on the other hand, call for the necessity of a replacement of all direct and indirect taxes by a consumption tax. They show that the transfer and tax system (consumption tax financed UBI) has no inherent regressive effect overall due to the indirect progressive effects of the UBI. Given the results by Trabandt/Uhlig (2011) and Hiraga/Nutahara (2019) and the significance of the consumption tax in the UBI context, we will focus on this in our approach.

From our point of view, the issue of time sovereignty, integrated formally via the multiplicative utility function, implies nothing less than a paradigm shift in deliberating on labor, leisure, volunteerism, and care work, as well as the function of work, labor, and the labor market by the shift from additive separability to multiplicative utility. After a short exploration of this issue (Section 2), the remaining paper will focus on the modeling of a utility function that takes both time sovereignty as well as extrinsic and intrinsic motivation into account (Section 3). We will then develop the implications in terms of the fiscal returns to the UBI. In this regard, the paper is closely related to the work of Hiraga and Nutahara (2019 a, b), who used a neoclassical model to investigate the sensitivity of the Laffer curve with respect to the utility function (Section 4). In section 5, we supplement our theoretical investigation with a numerical example of the model with additive separable utility function versus multiplicative function to demonstrate the respective effects on tax revenues and relevance of the consumption tax Laffer curve. Section 6 concludes by presenting an outlook on subsequent research.

2. The Paradigm Shift in Time Sovereignty

The UBI-induced shift from additive separability to multiplicative linkage represents not only a change in utility pattern but also challenges the reasoning that our systems of basic security and social insurance, as well as social policy design as a whole, are based on, namely, a very restrictive and incomplete concept of work and labor. When reviewing a number of studies on Negative Income Tax experiments, Widerquist (2019, 304 ff.) reports implicitly that the authors interested in testing labor market effects have interpreted the results under the additive separability assumption with the consequence of presenting simple labor-time-reduction effects. Beside the fact that applying a deficient labor incentives and work ethics approach is a general critique of UBI proponents (see, e.g., Standing 2017, Van Parijs & Vanderborght 2017, Torry, 2019), the refinement of the utility function is, to our knowledge, the first contribution that shows that, in a rigorous logical setting, the critique implies the analytical shift in the utility function we propose. If this shift can be construed as a change in work ethic, we do not know, but that this shift requires a paradigm shift in social policy and labor market design, we take for granted. The facets of work we have in mind, not yet well developed explicitly in the utility function due to our abstract modelling, as voluntary and unpaid work, creative leisure time, and low or unpaid care work, are components of a multiplicative linkage rather than an additive separable connection. The traditional and, from our point of view, outdated viewpoint of consumer sovereignty based on the logic of additive separable utility in which only consumption of goods financed by disutility-generating labor income and traded in markets or provided by governments can be a part sovereign decision-making, has to be replaced by time sovereignty as the multiplicative effects generating societal and social policy norm. The pure disutility of work-effort logic must be dropped from economic theory and social policy. The conventional means-testing system of social welfare states is built on additive separability and old-fashioned consumer sovereignty, and is therefore not a forward-looking concept. In addition to this paradigm shift, there is also the transition from paternalistic capitalism to post paternalistic capitalism, in which transfer donors do not have the right nor the moral obligation to demand certain outcomes, such as a return to labor market efforts. The enforcement of return-to-labor market efforts in a means testing system is based on the assumption that the re-entry into the labor market necessarily indicates disutility to the recipient. With a UBI, the citizen is emancipated from this paternalistic threat and given his or her full time sovereignty. The individual utility relation may become multiplicative. As long as we spread the story of the "lazy citizen" we still believe at least in a subliminal way in additive separability, which is not what UBI is about. Subliminally, this points to the wrong socialization and thinking for an upcoming social policy instrument such as the UBI. On the contrary, UBI can direct and extricate, and thus "socialize" society towards the freedom of time sovereignty. Hence, it is a way to transfer the individual planning under additive separability into optimization and policy design under multiplicative preference relations. This and nothing less is the normative background of our elaboration of the understanding of utility.

3. The Understanding of Utility

In this section, we will examine the implications of the paradigm shift for the utility function. As the utility function is the most fundamental way of visualizing an individual's preference relation, time is divided into time spent consuming and time spent working. A common utility function, which is a version to the famous principal agent theory applied in labor or management relationships, is given by the following additive separable preferences.

$$U^{AS} = \frac{c^{1-\eta}}{1-\eta} - \kappa \frac{n^{1+\lambda}}{1+\lambda} \quad (1)$$

Labor, n, is rewarded with a certain wage which in turn enables the individual to consume c. Let $1/\lambda$ denote the constant labor supply elasticity and η the constant relative risk aversion. It is assumed that the individual dislikes labor and therefor suffers to a certain extent, $\varkappa$. This assumption is fundamental from the economics point of view and has important policy implications. As labor is always associated with some form of suffering, the individual cannot derive positive utility from working (Murdock, 2002). This kind of logic is very common in economics, politics, and society as it follows the well-known principal-agent model, where the agent is assumed to be willing to perform work solely through extrinsic incentives (Holstrom, 1979). It is questionable however whether this still fits in with our times, as we observe rapid changes on the labor market. Prendergast (2008), for example, argues that, as jobs become more specialized, monitoring for the principal (employer) becomes increasingly impossible or disproportionately costly. This trend of increasing and cross-branch specialization of professions is rooted in globalization and digitalization, thus causing extensive changes in the German labor market (Vogel-Ludwig & Kriechel, 2013). Spermann (2016) argues that a further consequence is the disappearance of a large number of jobs, primarily those with relatively low monitoring costs. Education is therefore becoming increasingly important with regard to the high demands of the labor market (Weber, 2017). Some economists therefore point to the positive effects of considering intrinsic motivation, particularly in specialized jobs that are difficult to monitor, in order to minimize the monitoring costs of the employer (Murdock, 2002, Prendergast, 2008).

Pasma (2010) defines an activity as intrinsically motivated if it is characterized by self-fulfillment, a sense of calling, ambition, and the achievement of goals. Kreps (1997) emphasizes the nature of the work, pointing out that task variety, creativity, and the quality of the work are central to an agent's intrinsic motivation. For Harter (1981) intrinsic motivation occurs whenever one successfully masters a challenging task and thus becomes aware of one's own abilities. Spinath and Steinmayer (2008) define it as follows: An individual who finds pleasure in a task or activity for reasons that lie in the activity itself and not in its consequences is intrinsically motivated. Thus they follow Frey (1994, Frey & Reto, 2000) who refers to the psychologist Deci (1971). When an activity is motivated by external contributions, one speaks of extrinsic motivation. It should be noted, however, that these incentives do not necessarily have to be monetary in nature. They can be material or non-material, with non-material incentives being understood to include recognition, or popularity (Frey, 1994). However, since the welfare state and the social security system are also based on the principal-agent theory, accounting for intrinsic motivation in the labor market requires changes in the design of the welfare state.

Unconditional basic income, on the other hand, is based on fundamentally different assumptions about the individual's desire to work. Intrinsic motivation and time sovereignty confer positive utility on work. It cannot be separated from consumption utility, as is the case with the additive separable utility function. Inspired by the utility function developed by King and Rebelo (1999) and the work of Trabandt and Uhlig (2011, 2013) and Hiraga and Nutahara (2019), we have formulated a function that models the preference relation of an individual socialized by the UBI.

Thus we consider the following equation,

$$U(c,n) = \frac{1}{1-\eta}\{c^{1-\eta}[1-(\kappa-\rho)(1-\eta)n^{1+\lambda}]^{\eta} - 1\} \quad (2)$$

$$\kappa > 0, \rho > 0, \eta > 0, \eta \neq 1, (\kappa - \rho) > 0.$$

The function inherits the multiplicative link between labor and consumption, the constant labor supply elasticity $1/\lambda$, and the constant relative risk aversion η of the initial function by King and Rebelo (1999, Eq. 6.7). However, a crucial difference arises from the implementation of intrinsic motivation through the parameter ϱ. The condition $(\kappa - \rho) > 0$ implies that the representative individual suffers from the disutility of labor and yet enjoys an intrinsic value of labor after all. The reason for this is that, in this model, for the representative person who receives a UBI, there is neither a job from which he or she exclusively suffers nor one in which he or she exclusively enjoys.

The perception of time and the implementation of intrinsic values in the preference relation is equally crucial (although both motives go hand in hand). If the regular and unconditional transfer covering the socioeconomic subsistence minimum influences the preferences of an individual, it is too short-sighted to consider only the intrinsic factor in the utility function. If we were to continue to assume an additively separable relationship here, it would not be possible to model the behavioral change enabled by the UBI. It is the emancipatory character of the UBI that causes a change in the relationship between work and consumption, enabling people to participate autonomously on the labor market and position themselves according to their true preferences. Once your socioeconomic participation is secured, you are free to choose how to use your time. This time sovereignty that the UBI provides is reflected in our interpretation of the utility function by the multiplicative link between consumption and work.

King and Rebelo (1999) argue that the multiplicative linkage of consumption and labor is closer to the evidence than the additive one and that it better reflects the variations in consumption and labor. In our view, this does not contradict our interpretation of the multiplicative relationship. Even in a UBI society, being gainfully employed is associated with a higher income and thus with better consumption opportunities. But the fact of not being gainfully employed but investing time in one's own qualification or doing unpaid work, for example, is no longer associated with financial hardship. If the strength of the multiplicative relationship lies in the possibility of considering both the extensive and intensive margin, this corresponds to the labor market participation of individuals receiving a UBI. This has been demonstrated in numerous studies (e.g., Marx & Peeters, 2008; Specianova, 2018; and Palermo & Neumärker, 2019).

4. The Simple Model

To examine our theory, we study the implications of the additive separable utility function and the UBI utility function in a simple static economy by Hiraga and Nutahara (2019) with a representative household.

The Production function is given by,

$$y = n, \qquad (3)$$

where n is the only input. The Resource constraint is given by,

$$y = c + g. \qquad (4)$$

g is for public consumption. The public budget constraint is

$$T = s + g. \qquad (5)$$

The unconditional transfer to households (UBI) is given by s. Since we are particularly interested in the tax revenue of consumption taxation, we exclude any other taxes in our baseline model. Thus the total tax revenue is

$$T = \tau^c c. \qquad (6)$$

The wage and the consumption tax rate are given by w and τ^c. The household budget constraint is then

$$(1 + \tau^c)c \leq wn + s. \qquad (7)$$

We differentiate between the additive-separable utility function, (1), as representation for means tested social security system,

$$U^{AS}(c,n) = \frac{c^{1-\eta}}{1-\eta} - \kappa \frac{n^{1+\lambda}}{1+\lambda},$$

and the UBI utility function (2), which is given by,

$$U^{UBI}(c,n) = \frac{1}{1-\eta}\{c^{1-\eta}[1-(\kappa-\rho)(1-\eta)n^{1+\lambda}]^{\eta} - 1\}$$

$$for\ \eta > 0, \eta \neq 1, (\kappa - \rho) > 0.$$

To derive the consumption tax revenue curve, we apply the following conditions (as in Hiraga and Nutahara, 2016, 2018, 2019 a & b, 2021).

The household's consumption/labor choice is given by

$$-\frac{U_n}{U_c} = RPL. \tag{8}$$

While the relative price of leisure, RPL, is

$$RPL \equiv \frac{1}{(1+\tau^c)} \times w. \tag{9}$$

The equilibrium elasticity of consumption with respect to the consumption tax (τ^c) is

$$\left|\frac{dc/c}{d\tau^c/\tau^c}\right| = \left|\frac{dRPL/RPL}{d\tau^c/\tau^c}\right| \times (-\frac{cU_{cc}}{U_c} + \frac{nU_{nn}}{U_n} + \frac{cU_{cn}}{U_n} - \frac{nU_{cn}}{U_c})^{-1}, \tag{10}$$

where the elasticity of the relative price of leisure, RPL, with respect to τ^c is given by

$$\left|\frac{dRPL/RPL}{d\tau^c/\tau^c}\right| = \frac{\tau^c}{1+\tau^c}. \tag{11}$$

Hiraga and Nutahara (2018) have also shown that a necessary condition for the consumption Laffer curve to be humped shaped

$$\frac{dc/c}{d\tau^c/\tau^c} < -1 \qquad (12)$$

holds.

Scheme I:

The total tax revenue is used for an unconditional transfer to households, so that s=T holds. The preferences of the individual are given by the additive separable utility function, U^AS.

In this case, the consumption labor supply condition is given by

$$\frac{1}{(1+\tau^c)} \times w = \kappa n^\lambda c^\eta. \qquad (13)$$

Solving this condition for c with (3) = (4) yields to

$$c = [\kappa(1+\tau^c)]^{-1/(\eta+\lambda)}. \qquad (14)$$

Hence, the total tax revenue is

$$T = \tau^c[\kappa(1+\tau^c)]^{-1/(\eta+\lambda)} \qquad (15)$$

and

$$\frac{\partial T}{\partial \tau^c} = \frac{(\lambda+\eta-1)\tau^c + \lambda + \eta}{(\lambda+\eta)(\tau^c+1)(\kappa(\tau^c+1))^{1/(\lambda+\eta)}}. \qquad (16)$$

It follows from the above, that the elasticity of consumption to the consumption tax rate is

$$\left|\frac{dc/c}{d\tau^c/\tau^c}\right| = \frac{1}{\eta+\lambda} \times \frac{\tau^c}{1+\tau^c}. \tag{17}$$

Proposition 1 states the necessary conditions for a humped-shaped consumption tax revenue curve.

Proposition 1: For the additive separable utility function, U^AS, the consumption tax revenue curve is humped shaped iff η+λ<1 holds. The revenue is maximized at τ^c=(η+λ)/(1-η-λ) (Hiraga & Nutahara, 2016).

Proof: See Appendix A.

Scheme II.

Let us assume the UBI utility function. The total tax revenue is again used as the unconditional transfer to households, such that s=T holds. The individual's optimization condition for consumption and labor is given by:

$$\frac{1}{(1+\tau^c)} \times w = \eta(\lambda+1)\left(\frac{c(\kappa-\rho)n^\lambda}{1-(\kappa-\rho)(1-\eta)n^{\lambda+1}}\right). \tag{18}$$

Since there is no public consumption in this baseline model because the total tax revenue is used as an unconditional transfer to households (g=0), c equals n. Hence, solving this condition for c leads to the following

$$c = [(\kappa-\rho)(\eta((\tau^c+1)\lambda+\tau^c)+1)]^{-1/(1+\lambda)}. \tag{19}$$

Total tax revenue is given by the tax rate times the consumption

122   Bernhard Neumärker, Jette Weinel

$$T = \tau^c \times [(\kappa - \rho)(\eta((\tau^c + 1)\lambda + \tau^c) + 1)]^{-1/(1+\lambda)}. \qquad (20)$$

The derivative of the tax revenue is

$$\frac{\partial T}{\partial \tau^c} = \frac{\eta\lambda(\tau^c + 1) + 1}{(\eta((\lambda + 1)\tau^c + \lambda) + 1)((\kappa - \rho)(\eta((\lambda + 1)\tau^c + \lambda) + 1))^{1/(\lambda+1)}}. \qquad (21)$$

In the case of the UBI utility function we observe the following

$$-\frac{cU_{cc}}{U_c} = \eta,$$

$$\frac{nU_{nn}}{U_n} = \frac{n^{\lambda+1}(\eta - 1)(\eta(\lambda + 1) - 1)(\kappa - \rho) + \lambda}{n^{\lambda+1}(\eta - 1)(\kappa - \rho) + 1},$$

$$\frac{cU_{cn}}{U_n} = 1 - \eta,$$

$$-\frac{nU_{cn}}{U_c} = \frac{n^{\lambda+1}(\kappa - \rho)(1 - n^{\lambda+1}(\kappa - \rho)(\eta - 1))^{\eta-1}(1 - \eta)\eta(\lambda + 1)}{(1 - n^{\lambda+1}(\kappa - \rho)(1 - \eta))^{\eta}}.$$

This implies

$$\frac{dc/c}{d\tau^c/\tau^c}$$

$$= \frac{\tau^c}{(1 + \tau^c)} \times \left(\frac{n^{\lambda+1}(\eta - 1)(\eta(\lambda + 1) - 1)(\kappa - \rho) + \lambda}{n^{\lambda+1}(\eta - 1)(\kappa - \rho) + 1}\right. \qquad (22)$$

$$+ \frac{n^{\lambda+1}(\kappa - \rho)(1 - n^{\lambda+1}(\kappa - \rho)(\eta - 1))^{\eta-1}(1 - \eta)\eta(\lambda + 1)}{(1 - n^{\lambda+1}(\kappa - \rho)(1 - \eta))^{\eta}} + 1\right)^{-1}.$$

Hence, the elasticity of consumption to the consumption tax rate is given by

$$\left|\frac{dc/c}{d\tau^c/\tau^c}\right|$$
$$= \frac{\tau^c}{(1+\tau^c)} \times \left(\frac{n^{\lambda+1}(\eta-1)(\eta(\lambda+1)-1)(\kappa-\rho)+\lambda}{n^{\lambda+1}(\eta-1)(\kappa-\rho)+1}\right. \tag{23}$$
$$\left. + \frac{n^{\lambda+1}(\kappa-\rho)(1-n^{\lambda+1}(\kappa-\rho)(\eta-1))^{\eta-1}(1-\eta)\eta(\lambda+1)}{(1-n^{\lambda+1}(\kappa-\rho)(1-\eta))^\eta} + 1\right)^{-1}.$$

Proposition 2 states the necessary conditions for a monotonically increasing consumption tax revenue curve.

Proposition 2: Suppose the utility function is multiplicative and accounts for time sovereignty as well as intrinsic motivation, in the form of U^{UBI}. The consumption tax revenue curve is monotonically increasing and not humped shaped if $\lambda > 0$.

Proof.

$$\left|\frac{dc/c}{d\tau^c/\tau^c}\right| = \frac{\tau^c}{(1+\tau^c)} \times \left(\frac{n^{\lambda+1}(\eta-1)(\eta(\lambda+1)-1)(\kappa-\rho)+\lambda}{n^{\lambda+1}(\eta-1)(\kappa-\rho)+1}\right.$$
$$\left. + \frac{n^{\lambda+1}(\kappa-\rho)(1-n^{\lambda+1}(\kappa-\rho)(\eta-1))^{\eta-1}(1-\eta)\eta(\lambda+1)}{(1-n^{\lambda+1}(\kappa-\rho)(1-\eta))^\eta}\right.$$
$$\left. + 1\right)^{-1},$$

for $\lambda > 0$ and $\tau^c > 0$.

If $\tau^c = 0$, then $\left|\frac{dc/c}{d\tau^c/\tau^c}\right| = 0$. If τ^c is increasing, then $\left|\frac{dc/c}{d\tau^c/\tau^c}\right|$ increases.

5. A Numerical Example

Next, we provide a simple numerical example of the model with the additive separable utility function, equation (1), and the multiplicative function, equation (2). Note that for the consumption tax revenue curve to be humped shaped in the case of the additive separable preferences, $\eta + \lambda < 1$ must hold. A review of the literature provides a wide variety for supporting estimates of η and λ (e.g., Prescott, 1986, Trabandt & Uhlig, 2011 or Chetty, 2006). For our numerical example to be consistent we set η and λ such that $\eta + \lambda < 1$ holds for both utility functions. The constant relative risk aversion, η, is set at 0.71. This is consistent with the estimated average risk aversion of Chetty (2006), which, however, is based on a relatively small estimate of labor supply elasticity. Yet, the behavior towards risk is not relevant here as this is a static model without uncertainty or frictions. But η can be understood "[…] as an index of the curvature of the utility function" (Hiraga & Nutahara, 2019, p. 13).

The labor supply elasticity is given by $1/\lambda$, λ is set to 0.1, which is in line with Christiano et al. (2010), who estimated the parameter for the US economy. This elasticity is commonly interpreted as the Frisch elasticity of labor supply (Trabandt & Uhlig, 2011, Shimer, 2009), proposed by Frisch (1932, 1959) and crucial for the multiplicative preferences of King and Rebelo (1999, Trabandt & Uhlig, 2011).

Literature on estimates of intrinsic motivation and the weight of labor in the labor market in a UBI context, on the other hand, is lacking to our knowledge. This is not surprising since we cannot observe this empirically at the moment. However, Cappellari and Turati (2004) studied the motivation of volunteering labor supply in Italy. Based on questionnaires from 1998 of approximately 1400 employees of a public utility company, they provided related estimates of intrinsic and motivation for supplying work voluntarily. For the estimate of the weight of labor, we are referring to Trabandt and Uhlig (2011), who estimated κ for the US and Europe. Thus, we set $\rho \approx 0.8$ and $\kappa = 3.46$. The difference between the intrinsic value of labor and labor suffering, $(\kappa - \rho)$, is thus 2.7 in our numerical example. The condition $(\kappa - \rho) > 0$ for the multiplicative utility function holds.

The consumption tax rate is set at 0.19, like the standard value-added tax for goods and services in Germany (see the note on consumption tax rates at the end of the paper).

Supposing the additive separable utility function, we observe the following. The total tax revenue equals the consumption tax revenue in this model. The partial derivative of the total revenue with respect to the consumption tax rate for the numerical example is given by,

$$\frac{\partial T}{\partial \tau^c} = \frac{(0.1 + 0.71 - 1)0.19 + 0.1 + 0.71}{(0.1 + 0.71)(0.19 + 1)(3.46(0.19 + 1))^{1/(0.1+0.71)}} \approx 0.134 > 0$$

The tax revenue is maximized at

$$\tau^c = \frac{\eta + \lambda}{1 - \eta - \lambda} = \frac{0.71 + 0.1}{1 - 0.71 - 0.1} \approx 4.263.$$

The elasticity of consumption to the consumption tax rate for the additive separable utility function is given by

$$\left| \frac{dc/c}{d\tau^c/\tau^c} \right| = \frac{1}{0.71 + 0.1} \times \frac{0.19}{1 + 0.19} \approx 0.196.$$

The results of the numerical example for the additive separable utility function confirm that the tax revenue curve is increasing. However, the tax revenue is maximized at a certain tax rate τ^c. The key parameters to this result are the labor supply elasticity $1/\lambda$ and η as they determine whether we are observing the classical humped shaped Laffer curve (Hiraga & Nutahara, 2016).

The numerical example for the multiplicative utility function, on the other hand, provides the following results. The partial derivative of the total tax revenue with respect to the consumption tax rate is given by

$$\frac{\partial T}{\partial \tau^c}$$
$$= \frac{0.71 \times 0.1(0.19 + 1) + 1}{(0.71(1.1 \times 0.81) + 1)((3.46 - 0.8)(0.71(1.1 \times 0.19 + 0.1) + 1))^{1/(1.1)}}$$
$$\approx 0.228 > 0.$$

The elasticity for the numerical example of consumption to the consumption tax rate for multiplicative UBI utility function is given by

$$\left|\frac{dc/c}{d\tau^c/\tau^c}\right|$$

$$= \frac{0.19}{(1+0.19)} \times \left(\frac{0.343^{1.1}(0.71-1)(0.781-1)(3.46-0.8)+0.1}{0.343^{1.1}(0.71-1)(3.46-0.8)+1}\right.$$
$$\left. + \frac{0.343^{1.1}(3.5-0.8)(1-0.343^{1.1}(3.46-0.8)(0.71-1))^{-0.29}(1-0.71)0.781}{(1-0.343^{1.1}(3.46-0.8)(1-0.71))^{0.71}}\right.$$
$$\left. + 1\right)^{-1} \approx 0.112.$$

In the case of the multiplicative function the result of our example suggests that the curve of the total tax revenue is increasing. Other than the additive function, there is no consumption tax rate at which the tax revenue is maximized. Both elasticities of consumption with respect to the consumption tax rate are smaller than one for this numerical example. Note, however, that for the additive separable function, the elasticity of consumption with respect to the consumption tax rate may be greater than one if the parameter values are relatively high (cf. Hiraga & Nutahara, 2016). We have shown in Scheme II that the elasticity of consumption to the consumption tax rate for the UBI utility function cannot be humped shaped if $\tau^c > 0$.

The numerical example is provided to illustrate and compare the modeling results for both functions. The relevance of such examples or calculations based on a simple model does not lie in their supposed transferability, nor is that the aim of these models. It is rather about showing that a theoretical approach can also be formulated analytically in a consistent form relevant for a UBI regime.

6. Closing Remarks and Outlook

This paper contributes to the economic theoretical base of UBI and shows that main UBI issues such as time sovereignty, intrinsic motivation, endogenous fiscal capacity effects, and consumption tax earmarking can be examined and specified in a neoclassical setting. New conclusions can be presented. We begin by arguing why we believe that the additive utility function is the basis of current fiscal thinking and optimization, while the multiplicative function with an intrinsic factor represents a UBI regime. We derive this argument from economic theory and support it with a simple model. Finally, we conclude that introducing

UBI and calculating the fiscal feasibility of a certain level of UBI with a Laffer Curve which is still based on an additive separable utility function of the conventional workfare world (see, e.g., Piketty & Saez, 2013, and Cahuc, Carcillo & Zylberberg, 2014) will lead to the wrong conclusions. The impact of UBI on utility measured in our approach by the change from additive separability to multiplicative utility with intrinsic and time-sovereign value changes the fiscal scope of financing UBI. It has been demonstrated here by the effect that a hump-shaped Laffer curve turns into a monotonic one, thus increasing tax revenue function. We expect that the fiscal capacity will be much higher due to the "UBI utility effect" on tax revenue, especially in the case of high tax rates. It would certainly be of interest to calculate these revenue differences.

A next step would be to identify the fiscal rules (e.g., adding income/wage taxation, mixed public budget with public infrastructure expenditures, explicit tax earmarking, such as consumption tax for UBI and income/wage tax for public infrastructure compared with mixed financing, social dividend instead of fixed UBI payment) which could present the highest possible UBI or maintain a certain UBI level, and what this level could be in relation to national income and the total public budget. Another interesting possibility would be to expand the model explicitly towards voluntary unpaid work, or, a social contract investigation for the endogenous choice and constitutional regulation of the level of UBI and its financing as suggested in Atkinson (1995) and Davies, Franke, Kuang and Neumärker (2022).

References

Atkinson, A.B., 1995. Public Economics in Action. The basic income / flat tax proposal. Oxford et al.: Clarendon Press.

Bentham, J., 1823. An Introduction to the Principles of Morals and Legislation. Utility Theory. A Book of Readings.

Blume, L. E., Easley, D., 2008. Rationality. Palgrave Macmillan (ed.), The New Palgrave Dictionary of Economics. 2nd edition.

Cappellari, L., Turati, G., 2004. Volunteer labour supply: The role of workers' motivation. Annals of Public and Cooperative Economics 75:4.

Cahuc, P., Carcillo, S., Zylberberg, A. (2014). Labor economics, 2nd Ed., MIT Press: Cambridge, Mass. & London.

Chetty, R., 2006. A New Method of Estimating Risk Aversion. The American Economic Review. Vol. 96 (5), 1821-1834.

Christiano, L.J., Trabandt, M., and Walentin, K., 2010. DSGE models for monetary policy analysis. Benjamin M. Friedman and Michael Woodford (Eds.), Handbook of Monetary Economics 3(3), 285–367.

Davies, C., Franke, M., Kuang, L., and Neumärker, B., 2022. A Contractarian View on Homann's Ethical Approach: The Vision of "New Ordoliberalism", CEN Discussion Paper, University of Freiburg.

Deci, 1972. Intrinsic Motivation, Extrinsic Reinforcement, and Inequity. Journal of Personality and Social Psychology 22 (1), 113-120.

Deci, E. L., Ryan, R. M. 1985. Intrinsic motivation and determination in human behavior. New York: Plenum.

Frey, B. S., 1994. How intrinsic motivation is crowded out and in. Rationality and Society 6, 334-352.

Frey, B. S., 1997. On the relationship between intrinsic and extrinsic work motivation. International Journal pd Industrial Organization 15(1997), 427-439.

Frey, B. S., Bohnet, I., 1994. Die Ökonomie zwischen extrinsischer und intrinsischer Motivation. Homo Oeconomicus, Vol. 11, 1-19.

Frey, B., Reto, J., 2000. Motivation Crowding Theory. Journal of Economic Surveys, 15 (5), 589-611.

Friedman, M., 1962. Capitalism and Freedom, University of Chicago Press.

Friedman, M., Friedman, R., 1980. Free to Choose: A Personal Statement, Harcourt.

Frisch, R., 1932. New Methods of Measuring Marginal Utility. Beiträge zur ökonomischen Theorie, Verlag von J. C. B. Mohr.

Frisch, R., 1959. A complete scheme of computing all direct and cross demand elasticities in a model with many sectors. Econometrica, 27 (2), 177-196.

Hardorp, B., 2012. Steuerreform und Transfereinkommen – stellen wir uns den sozialen wie ökonomischen Aufgaben Deutschlands in Europa? Das

Grundeinkommen, Publisher: Werner, G. W., Eichhorn, W. & Friedrich, L., in Scientific Publishing.

Harter, S., 1981. A model of mastery motivation in children: Individual differences and developmental change. Aspects on the development of competence: The Minnesota Symposia on Child Psychology, Vol. 14, 215-255.

Hiraga, K., Nutahara, K., 2016. When is the Laffer curve for consumption tax hump-shaped? CIGS Working Paper Series 16-002E, The Canon Institute for Global Studies.

Hiraga, K., Nutahara, K., 2018. Why is the shape of the Laffer curve for consumption tax different from that for labor income tax? CIGS Working Paper Series No. 18-004E. The Canon Institute for Global Studies.

Hiraga, K., Nutahara, K., 2019. Fragility in modeling consumption tax revenue. CIGS Working Paper Series No. 19-003E. The Canon Institute for Global Studies. a.

Hiraga, K., Nutahara, K., 2019. Appendices: Fragility in modeling consumption tax revenue. [https://cigs.canon/article/uploads/pdf/workingpapers/190226_nutahara_appendix.pdf]. b.

Hiraga, K., Nutahara, K., 2021. Can the Laffer curve for consumption tax be hump-shaped? [https://ssrn.com/abstract=3995917].

Holmström, B., 1979. Moral Hazard and Observability. Bell Journal of Economics, 10, 74-91.

Imai, S., Kean, M. P., 2004. Intertemporal Labor Supply and Human Capital Accumulation. International Economic Review, 45 (2), 601-641.

Jehle, G. A., Reny, P. J., 2011. Advanced Microeconomic Theory. Third Edition. Pearson Education Limited

Kapteyn, A., 1985. Utility and Economics. De Economist, 133, 1-20.

Keen, M., 2007. VAT attacks!. International Tax and Public Finance, 14:4, 365-381.

Keen, M. & Lockwood, B., 2010. The value added tax: Its causes and consequences. Journal of Development Economics, Vol. 92:2, 138-151.

King, R.S., Rebelo, S.T., 1999. Resuscitating real business cycles. Handbook of Macroeconomics, vol. 1B. Elsevier, Amsterdam, 927-1007.

King, R.S., Plosser, C.I., Rebelo, S.T., 1988. Production, Growth and Business Cycles. I The Basic Neoclassical Model. Journal of Monetary Economics, 21, 195-232. A.

King, R.S., Plosser, C.I., Rebelo, S.T., 1988. Production, Growth and Business Cycles. II New Directions. Journal of Monetary Economics, 21, 309-341. B.

King, R.S., Plosser, C.I., Rebelo, S.T., 2001. Production, Growth and Business Cycles: Technical Appendix.

Kreps, D., 1997. Intrinsic Motivation and Extrinsic Incentives. American Economic Review, 87, 370-377.

Liebermann, S., 2012. Das Menschenbild des Grundeinkommens – Wunschvorstellung oder Wirklichkeit? Das Grundeinkommen, Scientific Publishing.

Mirrlees, J., Adam, S., Besley, T., Blumdell, R., Bond, S., Chote, R., Gammie, M., Johnson, P., Myles, G. & Poterba, J., 2010. Tax by Design. The Mirrlees Review. Conclusions and Recommendations for Reform. Institute for Fiscal Studies, Oxford.

Murdock, K., 2002. Intrinsic Motivation and Optimal Incentive Contracts. The RAND Journal of Economics, 33 (4), 650-671.

Palermo, A., Neumärker, B., 2018. Modelling the time Allocation Effect of basic income. Basic Income Studies, 10.1515

Pasma, C., 2010. Working through the work disincentive. Basic Income Studies, 5, 442.

Piketty, T., Saez, E., 2013. Optimal Labor Income Taxation, in: Handbook of Public Economics, Volume 5, Elsevier, 391-474.

Prendergast, C., 2008. Work incentives, Motivation, and Identity. American Economic Review, 98 (2), 201-205

Prescott, E. C., 1986. Theory Ahead of Business Cycle Measurement. Federal Reserve Bank of Minneapolis Quarterly Review, 10.

Rauh, C., Santos, M.R., 2022. How do transfers and universal basic income impact the labor market and inequality? Cambridge Working Papers in Economics, 2208. Janeway Institute Working Papers, 2022/05.

Shimer, R., 2009. Convergence in Macroeconomics: the labor wedge. American Economic Journal: Macroeconomics 1(1), 280-297.

Spermann, A., 2016. Industrie 4.0 = Mehr Roboter = das Ende von Routineobs?. Wirtschafts-politische Blätter 63, 335-346.

Spinath, B., Steinmayer, R., 2008. Longitudinal Analysis of Intrinsic Motivation and Competence Beliefs: Is There a Relation Over Time? Child Development, 79 (5), 1555-1569.

Standing, G., 2017. Basic income, and how we can make it happen. London: Pelican.

Trabandt, M., Uhlig, H., 2009. How far are we from the slippery slope? The Laffer curve revisited. National Bureau of Economic Research Working Paper 15343.

Trabandt, M., Uhlig, H., 2011. The Laffer curve revisited. Journal of Monetary Economics 58, 305-327.

Torry, M. (Ed.), 2019: The Palgrave International Handbook of Basic Income. Cham: Palgrave Macmillan.

Van Parijs, P, and Vanderborght. Y., 2017: Basic income. A radical proposal for a free society and a sane economy. Cambridge, Mass. & London: Harvard University Press

Vogel-Ludwig, K., Kriechel, B., 2013. Arbeitsmarkt 2030 – Eine strategische Vorausschau auf die Entwicklung von Angebot und Nachfrage in Deutschland. On behalf of the Federal Ministry of Labor and Social Affairs.

Wakolbinger, F., Dreer, E., Schneider, F., Neumärker, B., 2020. Konsumsteuer finanziertes BGE in Deutschland. FRBIS Discussion Paper Series, No. 01-2020.

Weber, E., 2017. Vollbeschäftigung. Fern, aber erreichbar. Ifo Schnelldienst 16/2017, 3-5.

Werner, G. W., 2006. Ein Grund für die Zukunft. Das Grundeinkommen. Ed.: Freies Geistesleben, Stuttgart.

Werner, G. W., 2012. Das Grundeinkommen. Publisher: Werner, G. W., Eichhorn, W. & Friedrich, L., in Scientific Publishing.

Widerquist, K., 2019. The Negative Income Tax Experiments of the 1970s, in: Torry, M. (Ed.), The Palgrave International Handbook of Basic Income. Cham: Palgrave Macmillan, 303-318.

Wigger, B. U., 2012. Konsumsteuer in der Demokratie. Das Grundeinkommen, in Scientific Publishing.

Wanniski, J., 1978. Taxes, revenues, and the Laffer curve. The Public Interest 50, 3-15.

Notes

On the various UBI modeling options for Germany, see also https://www.grundeinkommen.de/wp-content/uploads/2017/12/17-10-Übersicht-Modelle.pdf, https://fuereinander.jetzt/sites/default/files/Vergleich%20BGE%20Modelle%20Österreich%20%284Modelle%29.pdf [last checked: 5.30.22]

On the Consumption tax rates in the European Union, see https://europa.eu/youreurope/business/taxation/vat/vat-rules-rates/index_de.htm [last checked: 5.30.22]

Appendix

First, note that the standard assumptions for utility functions hold.

Additive separable Utility function:

$U_c > 0, U_{cc} < 0, U_n < 0, U_{nn} < 0$

UBI Utility function:

$U_c > 0, U_{cc} < 0, U_n < 0, U_{nn} \leq 0$

Proof of Proposition 1:

$$-\frac{cU_{cc}}{U_c} = \eta, \frac{nU_{nn}}{U_n} = \lambda, \frac{cU_{cn}}{U_n} = 0, -\frac{nU_{cn}}{U_c} = 0$$

$$dc/c\, d\tau c/\, \tau c = 1\eta + \lambda \times \tau c1 + \tau c$$

$$\left|\frac{dc/c}{d\tau^c/\tau^c}\right| = \frac{1}{(\eta + \lambda)} \times \frac{\tau^c}{(1 + \tau^c)}$$

If $\eta + \lambda \neq 1$, then

$$\left|\frac{dc/c}{d\tau^c/\tau^c}\right| - 1 = \left(\frac{1-\eta-\lambda}{\eta+\lambda}\right)\left(\frac{1}{1+\tau^c}\right)\left(\tau^c - \frac{\eta+\lambda}{1-\eta-\lambda}\right)$$

Assume $\eta + \lambda > 1$, then $\left|\frac{dc/c}{d\tau^c/\tau^c}\right| \leq 1$.

Assume $\eta + \lambda < 1$ and $\tau^c \leq \frac{\eta+\lambda}{1-\eta-\lambda}$, then $\left|\frac{dc/c}{d\tau^c/\tau^c}\right| \leq 1$.

If $\tau^c > \frac{\eta+\lambda}{1-\eta-\lambda}$, then $\left|\frac{dc/c}{d\tau^c/\tau^c}\right| > 1$.

If $\eta + \lambda = 1$, then

$$\left|\frac{dc/c}{d\tau^c/\tau^c}\right| - 1 = \frac{1}{(\eta+\lambda)} \times \frac{1}{(1+\tau^c)}\left((1-\eta-\lambda)\tau^c - (\eta+\lambda)\right) < 0$$

See also Hiraga and Nutahara (2016) for a detailed supporting explanation of this result.

Lida Kuang

Basic Income as a Just Social Contract

An Experimental Approach

As John Rawls claims, an institution will be reformed or abolished if it is not just and the entitlements secured by justice are not "subject to political bargaining or to the calculus of social interests" (Rawls, 1971, p.4). The relevance and comparability of basic income to the Rawlsian theory of justice has been mentioned in many articles. This paper will experimentally test whether basic income can serve as a preferred form of social justice compared to the Rawlsian principle and the market economy under an approximated environment of the veil of ignorance. It will also discuss differences in treating UBI as a policy and an institution.

1. Introduction

The universal basic income is a payment to all community member without mean test or work requirement (van Parijs, 2004, p.8). Its benefits include enhancing the social welfare and protection system, increasing employment and motivation to work, and enhancing citizens' well-being and self-respect. This once seemingly unattainable form of welfare has been replicated by an increasing number of pilot experiments, even on a trial basis at national level in Finland from 2017 to 2018. However, experiments that provide basic income to only a small, targeted group of people over a period of time have their limitations. For example, when basic income is given out gratuitously in an experiment, participants do not perceive that their welfare set-up has been changed and the results of the experiment are not necessarily linear with the results in the real world (Merrill et al. 2022, pp.10-11).

If we want the universal basic income (UBI) to be a long-term institution instead of just a policy, the stability and substantiality of its implementation should be the first things we need to consider. It is obviously that we cannot run basic income without an appropriate tax reform or proper trade-off between it and the existing welfare system. However, the financing of basic income and its feasibility and potential negative impact on incentive to work are not the most difficult obstacles that eventually lead to its failure. Constitutionalisation can be considered as a solution to maintain its stability, but it is not the most reliable way because the influence of basic income will be lost since different political and judicial powers interpret it differently. Therefore, besides the "entitlement" (de Wispelaere &Morales, 2016, p.521), we should treat basic income as a form of justice within the social contract.

As John Rawls claims, an institution will be reformed or abolished if it is not just, the entitlements secured by justice are not "subject to political bargaining or to the calculus of social interests" (Rawls, 1971, p.4). The relevance and comparability of basic income to the Rawlsian theory of justice has been mentioned in many articles (see for example Midtgaard 2009; Sirsch 2021; Farrelly 1999; Torisky 1993; Mori 2019)). This paper will experimentally test whether basic income can serve as a preferred social justice compared to the Rawlsian principle and the market economy under an approximated environment of the veil of ignorance. It will also discuss the difference between treating UBI as a policy and an institution, and a significant inherent characteristic that may interfere with their choice according to Fleurbaey's rejection (Fleurbaey, 2018, pp.32-33).

2. Rawlsian Social Justice and UBI

Among the discussions of justice theory in the past century, the ideas brought up by John Rawls cannot be ignored. Rawls generated this field by modifying the traditional social contracts therefore Locke, Rousseau and Kant, introducing an elaborate, novel argument for a particular theory of distributive justice as an alternative to the utilitarian view.

The Rawlsian principle of justice concerns the basic structure of society and the allocation of basic rights and obligations and the determination of the distribution of the benefits from social cooperation (Rawls, 1971, p.6). Rawls attempts to apply this to inequalities arising from different social status, including being born with a different status, perhaps knowing that such inequalities are inevitable. Hence, unlike the traditional social contract concerns about entering

Basic Income as a Just Social Contract 137

a society or establishing a form of government, Rawls interprets the principle of justice as "the object of original agreement in the basic structure of society". It can be accepted by "free and rational persons in an initial position of equality" (p.11).

The original position is a method of reasoning and a fair situation as a "hypothetical situation of equal liberty" (Rawls, 1971, p.11). One of the most distinctive features is its assumption under the veil of ignorance where "no one knows his place in society, his class position or social status, nor does anyone know his fortune in the distribution of natural assets and abilities, his intelligence, strength, and the like". Besides, "the parties do not know their conceptions of the good or their special psychological propensities." (p.11). As an appropriate status quo, the original position ensures "no one is advantaged or disadvantaged in the choice of principles by the outcome of natural chance or the contingency of social circumstances" (p.11) and "fundamental agreements reached in it are fair". In short, this assumtion can remove as many factors as possible that would interfere with the choice of justice, so that the choice can be justified by itself (Wenar 2021)

After determining the circumstances of justice, Rawls assumes that the principles would have been chosen initially under a veil of ignorance. "First, each person should have an equal right to the most extensive scheme of equal basic liberties compatible with a similar scheme of liberties for others. Second, social and economic inequalities are to be arranged so that they are both (a) reasonably expected to be to everyone's advantage and (b) attached to positions and offices open to all (Rawls, 1971, p.53). But why would people choose the Rawlsian principle of justice in the original position under the veil of ignorance? In brief, Rawls thinks it is because behind the veil of ignorance, everyone is afraid of being the worst-off one when s/he loses much that is important to them." (p.134). On the other hand, he overlooks that aversion to risk is not important "there are many considerations in favor of the difference principle in which the aversion to risk plays no role at all." (p.63)

A number of experiments (Traub et al. 2005); Schildberg-Hörisch 2010; M. Weber 2017; Sarkar, S., Chakraborty 2019; Amiel and Cowell 1992)) examine the Rawlsian assumption in the laboratory, the most enlightening of which directed by Fronlich and Oppenheimer. They summarise Rawlsian assumption as follows: "(1) individuals will always reach unanimous agreement; (2) individuals will always choose the same principle ;(3) the principle that will be chosen is to maximize the welfare of the worst off" (Frohlich et.al, 1987, p.4). Their experiments showed that although participants could reach a unanimous agreement, they would not choose a principle dedicated to improving the worst-off member as Rawls envisaged; instead, a principle of "maximize the average with a floor constraint" was favoured.

Not coincidentally, Fleurbaey further addresses the factors that are likely to cause the Rawlsian principle of justice to deviate from its original assumptions. To begin with, Fleurbaey does not agree that the aversion to risk is irrelevant under the veil of ignorance in decision-making. Instead, the individual's risk preference plays an important role. If a risk-loving individual assumes that he will not be the worst-off in the society, a principle which benefits the worst-off member more should be chosen by him. This consequence is leaving the Rawlsian principle of justice becomes invalid here. Secondly, Fleurbaey does not think that "people would always choose the same principle" can be "not far off the mark" (Frohlich et.al, 1987, p.5)." He concludes that the choice would not be inconsistent when the individuals make a decision for others. The choice a person makes is related to the role he has in the decision. Furthermore, these decisions will demonstrate especially stronger inequality-aversion for others (Fleurbaey, 2018, pp.32-33). Of these factors that may affect the original assumption under the veil of ignorance, the experimental design will place a premium on his view about risk aversion by inferring participants' risk tolerance.

This paper favours the concept of justice as fairness proposed by Rawls, although its corresponding criteria for a fair distribution is difficult to be preferred, at least in the laboratory. Therefore, this paper would like to propose the universal basic income(UBI) as an alternative hypothesis for the social contract under the veil of ignorance. UBI is a monthly payment from the community to every citizen without mean tests or other requirements (van Parijs, 2004, p.8), and it would be referred as a way of distribution in the experiment setting. The main idea is that, if all citizens were guaranteed a minimum welfare income, their fundamental rights and liberties would also be protected, especially for the worst-off group in society. To some extent, this fits Rawls' definition of justice as he claims that just social cooperation should lead citizens to decent lives (Wenar 2021).

Validating the UBI as a social contract under the veil of ignorance can be justified in such a setting. In the theoretical discussion of the UBI and the Rawlsian principle of justice, there are articles both for and against. For example, Sirsch (2021) discusses how an UBI can be a part of the ideal liberal-egalitarian welfare system and what the trade-off is with the currently existing welfare system. He argues that although UBI is not ideal for taking on the welfare system on its own and should be integrated with other welfare systems, we are sufficiently committed to pursuing it to bring us closer to it (pp.230-231). Midtigaard (2009) mentions the application of the Rawlsian criterion to refer to the stability of basic income. He argues the basic income should be granted conditionally rather than unconditionally because the concept of justice should not be too demanding in the interests of stability. But basic income is still the most logical institutional outcome of our basic concern for justice (p.15). But in Farrelly's article (1999), for example, he developed three Rawlsian objections from leisure, citizenship and self-respect which may throw doubts on the proposal of a UBI. He argues that although the proposal of UBI raises an important issue that a market society must address, which is that one's purchasing power and talents contribute significantly to one's freedom, this is not sufficient to achieve Rawlsian justice from institutional arrangements which are necessary to shape the basic structure of society (pp.292-294).This view also inspired the design of the experiment in this paper, in which, in addition to the UBI and Rawlsian principles, the logic of market economy has been added as the principle of merit for participants to choose from.

3. The Approach

The goal of this experimental design is to ascertain the availability of basic income as a social contract in the approximation of a veiled situation by comparing it to the Rawlsian and merit principles. When conducting distributive experiments relies on the veil of ignorance, the laboratory is typically open to the participants, for there is a very important assumption that unanimity can always be reached after discussion. This, however, was not viable during the Corona pandemic due to health and safety concerns. The analysis of this experiment cannot be given solely through a survey, nor statements and Likert-scales. We mainly want to use the method of reasoning as a veil of ignorance that enables the participants to choose the preferred social contract. Thus an experiment is designed that requires decision-making but is entirely online, with each participant required to complete a seven-page questionnaire.

3.1 Procedures

The three sections comprise a two-stage experiment. First, we include some simple questions in the introductory section to estimate the risk tolerance of the participants. The participants then move on to stage 1 of the experiment, where they choose a principle to receive the welfare payment as a policy. Stage 2 involves establishing an environment in which all players behave as impartial observers, selecting a welfare system as an institution for others.

3.2.1 Risk Attitude Self-Assessment

Generally, risk tolerance determines an investor's trade-off between expected return and return variance (Elton et al. 2013, p.224). In other words, one's risk tolerance reflects one's perception of it. If a greater tolerance is detected, the more risk an investor is expected to take willingly. In the financial industry, psychometric questionnaires are frequently viewed as a way to assess risk tolerance, which can result in a fair measure of accuracy (Davies, 2017, p.19).

To take a cue from this approach, two simple questions from real financial agencies (Edward Jones 2019; The Voya Financial Service 2016) were extracted because our risk tolerance self-assessment is intended to be as brief as the experiment's initial component. The questions have been rewritten and illustrated to improve readability and visual stimulus for all participants.

The section on the measurement of risk tolerance, despite being brief, is critical to the experiment's success. Some literature (Wong and Carducci 2013; Sahm 2007; Hanna and Chen 1997; Weber and Klement 2018) points out that risk tolerance is relatively stable for individuals although it changes significantly across races, countries etc. Individually, it may vary with the time horizon and subjective circumstances. But this experiment did not have a follow up session, so it is assumed that risk tolerance as measured by the psychometric assessment presented should be valid.

3.2.2 Stage 1

Stage 1 is designed to investigate the participant's attitude towards distribution of welfare payment with involvement under the veil of ignorance, thus the participants are asked to make the distributional judgments intuitively for themselves. In addition, participants have not been told their exact original position to approximate the veiled situation at greatest extent.

While an individual's risk tolerance is stable, one's behavioural risk attitude is "unstable, context dependent, myopic, present biased and procyclical" (p4, Davies 2017). There are not many articles that have discussed the effect of behavioural risk tolerance on questionnaire-based experiments, so in order to investigate whether there are differences in the results, participants are divided into two groups in stage 1. Participants in group A (non-risk scenario) would have an initial wealth set as {20,60,100}, whereas those in group B (risky scenario) would have an initial wealth value of [20,100]. An interval can be seen as a significantly riskier piece of information because it indicates that a participant has a larger likelihood of not becoming the "worst-off" in group B. It's curious to see the choice from the participants with low risk tolerance here. In other experiments that have compared the effect of how much information is disclosed on distributional judgment, for example, in Traub et al.'s experiment, participants demonstrated less inequality-averse in their "risk scenario" (where participants have received more information)" than in the "ignorance scenario"(Traub et al. 2005).

Participants are then asked to choose the fairest principle of four to accept a welfare payment. All principals were described in textual form and participants were asked to use their intuition to make the choice. They were not informed of any possible consequences by their choice and the welfare payment would cost some participants a portion of their wealth.

All principles and consequences are listed in the following table:

Original position		The Principle		(Possible) Consequence	
Group A	Group B	N.	Description	Group A	Group B
{20,60,100}	[20,100]	1	It should be given some less to richer participant (from first distribution), some more to poorer participant.	{40,60,95}	[40,80]
{20,60,100}	[20,100]	2	It should be equally given to every participant.	{20,60,100}	[20,100]
{20,60,100}	[20,100]	3	It should depend on scores in a math quiz	{15,60,105}	[15,105]
{20,60,100}	[20,100]	4	It should make everyone eventually receive the same	{60}	[60]

Table 1: Summary of scenarios in experiment

Principle 1 and 4 have been applied the Rawlsian principle, they improved the situation of the "worst-off" and the range in the group would become smaller. The concept of principle 2 is the basic income though distributing the welfare payment equally to everyone. Principle 3 is based on merit and the range would become larger after its application. It makes sense because when one from the "best-off" group also gets a good score, his or her wealth would be further increased. Thus, the choice from each participant can be used to deduce people's attitude towards distribution under the veil of ignorance.

After choosing the fairest principle according to them, the questionnaire also out asked some short questions containing views on whether everyone should contribute the same to the welfare system receive the same welfare payment, etc. These will be used as explanatory variables in the analysis part.

3.2.3 Stage 2

In stage 2, the participants are confronted with a scenario in which they need to choose a welfare system for the citizens of an imaginary country, Yama. This country is assumed to have only five income levels, ranging from high to low (4500, 3700, 3000, 2200, 1500) in local Yama currency. The income level means that no matter what work a citizen relies on for their income, it always falls into one of five income levels. The Yama government has recently decided to reform their welfare system but has been unable to reach unanimous agreement on how this should be and hence wishes to refer to the idea of impartial observers. The role of participants now switches to that of impartial observers choosing for Yama citizens.

Table 2 explains the main ideas of five different systems (S 1,2,3,4 and 5) proposed for the reform. For the sake of simplicity, we will refer to "welfare" in the table as a welfare payment in the questionnaire as stage 1. The principles applied to these income systems share the same three categories as stage 1: Merit (S5), Rawlsian (S2, S3) and Basic income (S1,S4): the principle of merit allows the best-off in S5 to continue to enjoy the highest welfare payment.

Level		Income		Tax	Welfare	Final		Tax	Welfare	Final
1	S0	4500	S1	15%	447	4272	S2	34%	0	2980
2		3700		15%	447	3592		19%	0	2980
3		3000		15%	447	2997		1%	0	2980
4		2200		15%	447	2317		0%	780	2980
5		1500		15%	447	1722		0%	1480	2980
		$\sigma_{income} \approx 1061$		$\sigma_{final\ income\ S1} \approx 902$				$\sigma_{final\ income\ S2} = 0$		

Level		Tax	Wel-fare	Final		Tax	Welfare	Final		Tax	Welfare	Final
1	S3	23%	1035	3465	S4	23%	447	3935	S5	23%	503	3990
2		18%	666	3211		18%	447	3500		18%	391	3444
3		12%	360	2908		12%	447	3087		12%	268	2908
4		8%	174	2428		8%	447	2473		8%	177	2203
5		0%	0	2014		3%	447	1906		3%	61	1520
		$\sigma_{final\ income\ S3} \approx 525$				$\sigma_{final\ income\ S4} \approx 722$				$\sigma_{final\ income\ S5} \approx 876$		

Table 2: Summary of income schemes in stage 2

The situation of the worst-off extent in S2 and S3 would be improved to the most among all five income schemes, thus the Rawlsian principle is met; in S1 and S2 each citizen would receive the same welfare as the form of basic income.

The major difference between the design of Stage 1 and Stage 1 is that the participants are now aware that these principles of justice will be applied to institutional design. They are no longer intended as a one-off policy but are here as a reform implicated in tax reform. This is more complex in reality because of the trade-offs with the existing welfare system etc. When considering people's preferences for the social contract, it is not sufficient to use people's choice of a single welfare payment, so the stage 2 design is used to supplement the overall experiment. Last but not the least, one of the Fleurbaey rejections to results under the veil of ignorance would deviate from Rawlsian assumption is the involvement of participants, who would probably demonstrate more inequality aversion towards others. In a situation where the choice is made for others, the focus of our observation is on whether basic income, as a means of providing the same welfare payment to everyone, would be chosen by more people.

4. The Results

A total of 103 volunteers participated in the questionnaire survey, 40.78% of them female. Participants needed about 10 minutes to fill out the questionnaire and received no monetary payoff. The behavior pattern of a participant who is recognised to have higher risk tolerance (referred to as risk-loving participants) would be highlighted in the following analysis.

We start with the general figure of the stage 1 where the participants need to choose how to receive the welfare payment for themselves. At this stage the participants are assigned to two different groups randomly. Based on the hypothesis, the environment of group B contains more information than group A, is considered as risky scenario. As we can see in table 3, according to the simple statistical results, in both risky scenario and non-risky scenario, more than half of the participants are willing to follow the original Rawlsian assumption by choosing a principle in which the welfare payment can improve the welfare of the worst-off: 55% in a non-risky scenario and 56% in a risky scenario.

Group A: Non Risky Scenario

	Merit	Basic Income	Rawlsian	Total
Risk-loving	0,11	0,47	0,42	1
Not R-loving	0,24	0,12	0,64	1
Total	0.18	0.27	0.55	1

Group B: Risky Scenario

	Merit	Basic Income	Rawlsian	Total
Risk-loving	0,31	0,24	0,45	1
Not R-loving	0,17	0,17	0,67	1
Total	0.24	0.20	0.56	1

Table 3: Simple statistics of risk and non-risk-loving choices in stage 1

The pattern of selection of basic income varies considerably between the two scenarios. To be more specfic, in which participants who were inferred to be risk-loving in the non-risky scenario were far more enthusiastic about basic income than other principles in the same scenario. The results were twice as high when compared to the same participants in the risky scenario.

Overall, among the participants who did not choose the Rawlsian principle, the risk-loving group account for the majority. We can preliminarily infer that risk appetite can interfere with the choice under the veil of ignorance.

	Rawlsian			Merit			Basic Income		
	Non-risky	Non-risky	All	Non-risky	Non-risky	All	Non-risky	Non-risky	All
male	-0.0526	0.767	-0.465	0.0906	-0.690	0.438	-0.0563	-0.406	0.253
	(-0.19)	(1.50)	(-1.31)	(0.30)	(-1.23)	(1.11)	(-0.18)	(-0.69)	(0.62)
risk loving	-0.556**	-0.740	-0.653*	0.132	-0.519	0.797*	0.614**	1.366**	0.0744
	(-2.18)	(-1.59)	(-1.72)	(0.47)	(-0.90)	(1.80)	(2.12)	(2.27)	(0.17)
unanimous	0.171	0.136	0.0232	-0.192	0.230	-0.713	-0.0569	-0.349	0.674
	(0.65)	(0.30)	(0.06)	(-0.65)	(0.41)	(-1.64)	(-0.20)	(-0.57)	(1.56)
same welfare	-0.0165	-0.580	0.103	-0.363	-0.0846	-0.459	0.387	1.073	0.365
	(-0.05)	(-0.99)	(0.24)	(-0.98)	(-0.12)	(-0.91)	(1.06)	(1.37)	(0.72)
same edu.	0.126	-0.312	0.556	0.395	0.468	0.311	-0.536	-0.127	-1.112*
	(0.36)	(-0.57)	(1.13)	(0.99)	(0.65)	(0.57)	(-1.38)	(-0.20)	(-1.83)
same contr.	-0.425	-0.196	-0.431	-0.151	-0.550	-0.0479	0.684*	0.746	0.630
	(-1.27)	(-0.33)	(-0.99)	(-0.41)	(-0.73)	(-0.10)	(1.82)	(0.98)	(1.20)
_cons	0.485*	0.453	0.622*	-0.761*	-0.302	-0.975*	-1.286***	-2.013**	-1.382***
	(1.73)	(0.81)	(1.80)	(-2.44)	(-0.48)	(-2.46)	(-3.87)	(-2.53)	(-3.25)
	103	44	59	103	44	59	103	44	59

Table 4: Simple probit regression in stage 1

Statistics in parentheses, $^* p < 0.1$, $^{**} p < 0.05$, $^{***} p < 0.01$

Here begins the more analytical part of the experiment. This paper will mainly use the simple probit model to analyse the choices of participants in an environment approximates to the veil of ignorance. Assuming that the standard errors are distributed normally, the maximum likelihood of choosing each principle of distribution can be estimated by the following probit regression model:

$$Pr(Y = 1|X) = \Phi(\beta_0 + \beta_1 riskloving + \beta_2 x_2 + \beta_3 x_3 + \ldots + \beta_k x_k)$$

In table 4 (page 137), the result of risk loving as an explanatory variable is very significant. In general, under the veil of ignorance, a participant who is relatively risk-loving will tend not to choose the Rawlsian principle for distribution. Moreover, this situation is clearer in the risky scenario than in the non-risky scenario. On the contrary, if the Rawlsian principle has not been chosen, the risk-loving participants would prefer basic income as their way to receive the payment. Although this result appears more frequently in the non-risky scenario, it is still surprising.

In stage 2, participants were asked to select a welfare system for others to see if involvement would interfere with the choice under the veil of ignorance. Compared to stage 1, the results for stage 2 are more evenly split, with more than half of the participants choosing the Rawlsian principle. For participants who are not risk-loving, basic income may be an alternative to the Rawlsian principle as shows table 5.

Stage 2: Choice of Welfare System for Others

	Merit	Basic Income	Rawlsian	Total
Risk-loving	0,19	0,29	0,52	1
Not Risk-lov.	0,15	0,35	0,51	1
Total	0,17	0,32	0,51	1

Table 5: Simple statistics of risk and non-risk-loving choices in stage

	Rawlsian		Merit		Basic Income	
	R others	R for others	M others	M for others	BI others	BI for others
male	0.0592	-0.248	-0.250	-0.684*	0.0890	0.179
	(0.22)	(-0.77)	(-0.78)	(-1.73)	(0.30)	(0.60)
riskloving	0.0531	0.631**	0.169	0.340	-0.148	-0.221
	(0.21)	(2.13)	(0.54)	(0.89)	(-0.55)	(-0.81)
unanimous	-0.422	-0.0980	0.114	0.762*	0.370	0.347
	(-1.63)	(-0.33)	(0.35)	(1.82)	(1.35)	(1.22)
same_welfare	-0.142	0.0215	0.0850	0.583	0.0773	-0.0877
	(-0.44)	(0.06)	(0.22)	(1.35)	(0.22)	(-0.25)
same_edu.	-0.170	-0.154	-0.0583	-0.558	0.219	0.345
	(-0.50)	(-0.40)	(-0.14)	(-1.17)	(0.61)	(0.93)
same_contr.	0.0522	0.808**	-0.811*	-0.659	0.457	0.278
	(0.16)	(2.15)	(-1.92)	(-1.40)	(1.34)	(0.79)
_cons	0.308	-1.275***	-0.709**	-1.371***	-1.005**	-1.050***
	(1.12)	(-3.78)	(-2.22)	(-3.34)	(-3.28)	(-3.35)
N	103	103	103	103	103	103

Table 6: Simple probit regression in stage 2

The analytical results established in table 6 from stage 2 are neither not as significant as stage 1. There is a positive and significant effect which states for the relatively risk-loving participants: they are more likely to choose a Rawlsian principle when they choose for others. This result is consistent with Fleurbaey rejection. However, it is very unfortunate that most of the explanatory variables cannot be used for more illustration.

5. Discussion

The biggest finding in the experimental results is that, under the assumption of a veil of ignorance, if a risk-loving participant did not choose the Rawsian principle to receive a welfare payment, basic income is likely to be his preference.

However, when necessary to compare the principles within institutional designs, the chosen pattern was not significant. This result is relatively pessimistic for the proposal of this paper. If we want to treat UBI as a just institution for society as Rawls claims social justice should provide a standard for the distributive aspects of the basic structure of society (Rawls 1971).

There are several possible improvements for the experiment: firstly, the explanatory variables designed for regression in stage 2 were not good enough. There should be more explanatory variables that represent the inherent traits of the participants rather than their views. Secondly, the number of people coming back to answer was insufficient for such a two-stage questionnaire with subgroups. Thirdly, I personally think that the most important thing to improve is a monetary payoff, which is essential for experiments which require participants to choose by decision-making. A monetary payoff would allow participants to be more aware of the consequences of their choices. In the previously mentioned experiment conducted by Fronlich and Oppenheimer (1987), they included the monetary payoffs to partly encourage a unanimous agreement, followed by many laboratory experiments regarding distribution. Although it has been found that some participants would seek to maximise their revenue in the laboratory and this leads to the divergence of the utility function set by the conductor (Veszteg et al. 2018), I think this is very applicable to this experiment. If this option can be added, stage 1 of the experiment can be improved by deleting the setting of diverse risky scenarios because increasing returns is a simpler, more direct way to stimulate risk-seeking behaviour among participants. This should allow us to better compare the behaviour of risk-takers with that of non-risk-takers.

So why do we keep talking about the behaviour of risk lovers? Put it another way, we are discussing the stability of a basic income. Political stability has been discussed intensively, and now we are looking at the issue of reception from the citizen's point of view. Our original concern was that for a risk taker, one might not be willing to accept the welfare that was equal for everyone, but from the results of the experiment it appears that basic income as a welfare payment is optional and acceptable, even for them. However, once the results from the experiment contradict Rawls' original assumptions, it's likely that all other chosen principles are biased since participants are framed to choose solely between the given options. But we can think of basic income as a complement to a just institution and a just society.

Acknowledgements

The original work for this paper was derived from the seminar "social justice and basic income" held during the University of Freiburg's Summer Term 2020. I would like to express my gratitude to Wenyao Li for his assistance and suggestion for the original paper, as well as his permission for the adaptation.

References

Amiel, Yoram, and Frank A. Cowell. 1992. "Measurement of Income Inequality. Experimental Test by Questionnaire." Journal of Public Economics 47(1).

Davies, Greg B. 2017. "New Vistas in Risk Profiling." Research Foundation Briefs 3(5). https://www.cfainstitute.org/en/research/foundation/2017/new-vistas-in-risk-profiling?s_cid=ppc_RF_Google_Search_NewVistasinRiskProfiling (March 2, 2022).

Edward Jones. 2019. "Risk Tolerance Questionnaire." chrome-extension://efaidnbmnnnibpcajpcglclefindmkaj/viewer.html?pdfurl=https%3A%2F%2Fwww.edwardjones.com%2Fsites%2Fdefault%2Ffiles%2Facquiadam%2F2021-02%2Frisk-tolerance-questionnaire.pdf&clen=129248&chunk=true (March 2, 2022).

Elton, E. J., M. J. Gruber, S. J. Brown, and W. N. Goetzmann. 2013. 53 Wiley Modern Portfolio Theory and Investments Analysis. 9th Ed.

Farrelly, Colin. 1999. "Justice and a Citizens' Basic Income." Journal of Applied Philosophy 16(3).

Fleurbaey, Marc. 2018. "Welfare Economics, Risk and Uncertainty." Canadian Journal of Economics 51(1).

Frohlich, Normam, Joe A Oppenheimer, and Cheryl L. Eavey. 1987. "Laboratory Results on Rawls's Distributive Justice." British Journal of Political Science 17(1).

Hanna, Sherman, and Peng Chen. 1997. "Subjective and Objective Risk Tolerance: Implications for Optimal Portfolios." Journal of Financial Counseling and Planning 8(2).

Merrill, Roberto, Catarina Neves, and Bru Laín. 2022. Basic Income Experiments A Critical Examination of Their Goals, Contexts, and Methods. 1st ed. Springer International Publishing.

Midtgaard, Søren F. 2009. "Rawlsian Stability and Basic Income." Basic Income Studies 3(2).

Mori, Luca. 2019. "Basic Income and Ideas of Justice." Iride 32(2): 351–62.

van Parijs, Philippe. 2004. "Basic Income: A Simple and Powerful Idea for the Twenty-First Century." In Politics and Society.

Rawls, John. 1971. A Theory of Justice. Original. Cambridge, Massachusetts: Harvard University Press. https://www.hup.harvard.edu/catalog.php?isbn=9780674017726 (February 7, 2021).

Sahm, Claudia R. 2007. "How Much Does Risk Tolerance Change? Stability of Risk Preference." Finance and Economics Discussion Series. http://hrsonline.isr.umich.edu.

Sarkar, S., Chakraborty, S. 2019. "Stakeholder Fairness under an Induced 'Veil of Ignorance': Findings from a Laboratory Experiment." International Journal of Strategic Decision Science 10(1): 65–81.

Schildberg-Hörisch, Hannah. 2010. "Is the Veil of Ignorance Only a Concept about Risk? An Experiment." Journal of Public Economics 94(11–12): 1062–66.

Sirsch, Jürgen. 2021. "Should Liberal-Egalitarians Support a Basic Income? An Examination of the Effectiveness and Stability of Ideal Welfare Regimes." Moral Philosophy and Politics 8(2).

The Voya Financial Service. 2016. "Risk Tolerance — Portfolio Financial Services." https://www.itsyourportfolio.com/risk-tolerance-2016 (March 2, 2022).

Traub, Stefan, Christian Seidl, Ulrich Schmidt, and Maria Vittoria Levati. 2005. "Friedman, Harsanyi, Rawls, Boulding - Or Somebody Else? An Experimental Investigation of Distributive Justice." Social Choice and Welfare 24(2).

Veszteg, Róbert F., and Yukihiko Funaki. 2018. "Monetary Payoffs and Utility in Laboratory Experiments." Journal of Economic Psychology 65.

Weber, Elke, and Joachim Klement. 2018. "Risk Tolerance and Circumstances." SSRN Electronic Journal.

Weber, Matthias. 2017. "Choosing Voting Systems Behind the Veil of Ignorance: A Two-Tier Voting Experiment." SSRN Electronic Journal.

Wenar, Leif. 2021. "John Rawls." In The Stanford Encyclopedia of Philosophy, ed. Edward N. Zalta. https://plato.stanford.edu/archives/sum2021/entries/rawls/ (March 17, 2022).

de Wispelaere, Jurgen, and Leticia Morales. 2016. "The Stability of Basic Income: A Constitutional Solution for a Political Problem?" In Journal of Public Policy.

Wong, Alan, and Bernardo Carducci. 2013. "Does Personality Affect Personal Financial Risk Tolerance Behavior?" IUP Journal of Applied Finance 19(3): 5–18. http://capella.summon.serialssolutions.com/2.0.0/link/0/eLvHCXMwY2BQSEu2MEt-JNLRMMktNsgDWECZp5qlJyebJqWZJlmaWSZaos7kMpbBhAUjUwkpEcDGdkp8MGiHXNwQWm6BNluam9gWFuqA7o0Bzq7ALNFDHPVB WDiHOVkyE3r6QYmtkbmkG2pYOLL1Blz34GjjDR2WAFaqlCfjORtCxNrqg1gdGIQ2uedwEGGYRZe2AeE6.

Thiago Monteiro de Souza

Maricá Citizen's Basic Income

An Overview of the Pilot

This paper aims to analyse the citizen's Basic Income set up in the city of Maricá and point out which possible debates may arise from this experience. To achieve this end, the geopolitical aspects of the Brazilian city are highlighted. The genesis of the Basic Income program is described, as is its development since its establishment in 2013. Its importance during the Covid-19 Pandemic is also taken into consideration. Multiple discussions will thus be proposed from this case analysis, namely the lessons that may be preliminarily drawn from the pilot regarding its social, economic and political aspects.

1. Introduction

In the present century, several governments around the world have set up Unconditional Basic Income (UBI) pilot projects in order to test their viability. One of the biggest ongoing ones is the Citizen's Basic Income in the city of Maricá.

Implemented in 2013, the pilot has been gradually enhanced since its creation. It started as a monthly transfer of 85 Mumbucas (equivalent to 85 Reais, the Brazilian currency) to approximately 14 thousand households (Dektar et al., 2020). Nowadays, the transfer amounts to 170 Mumbucas (M$) and it targets individuals, no longer households.

This paper aims to describe the policy in Maricá, since its genesis until the Covid-19 Pandemic. To achieve this end, geopolitical aspects of the Brazilian city have been highlighted. The impact of the Covid-19 Pandemic on the program is also considered. Some implications and outcomes of this Basic Income are also brought up and opened to debate. The main goal of the analysis is to show how the aforementioned policy can enrich the debate surrounding the Unconditional Basic Income.

2. Brazil UBI Conjuncture

This section aims to describe Brazilian history regarding cash transfer policies. It will help to explain the origins of the Maricá Basic income policy after decades of developments of social policies.

The federal constitution of 1988 played an important role in the development of social programs in Brazil. At the outset of the constitutional text, the fundamental objectives of the Federative Brazilian Republic are set. Among them, the eradication of poverty and the need to decrease social inequalities are highlighted. Further on, in the 21st article, social security is recognized as a right to be enforced by the federal administration. Also, according to the 23rd article, all three public spheres (federation, state and county) must be held accountable for fighting against poverty in order to achieve social integration. This scenario was of vital importance for the creation of programs such as the Bolsa Família.

According to Ana Fonseca (2013), executive secretary of the Bolsa Família program in the year of its creation, the core of the Brazilian cash transfer policies was the law presented by the former senator, Eduardo Suplicy, which proposed an Unconditional Basic Income in Brazil in 1991. In addition, two important laws were passed in the same decade: The Estatuto da Criança e do Adolescente and Lei Orgânica de Assistência Social (loosely translated as The Statute of the child and the adolescent and Organic Law of Social Assistance), were central in this matter. Later on, during the administration of President Fernando Henrique Cardoso (1995-2002), several assistance programs were created, such as the Bolsa Alimentação and the Bolsa Escola (Loosely translated as Food Grant and School Grant).

During the 1990's, inspired by Senator Suplicy's proposal, several cities adopted cash transfer policies. Campinas, Ribeirão Preto and even the capital city, Brasília, introduced financial aid to fight famine and poverty. Since the mentors of the policies acknowledged that it was common for poor children to drop out of school to assist their families financially, these aid programs required the assisted families to have their children attend schools. Such programs also stipulated a minimum amount of residence time of the family in the city to become eligible for the benefit (Campello et al., 2013).

In this conjuncture, the Bolsa Família program was officially created in 2003. At the outset the program presented (and has continued to maintain these characteristics throughout its existence) three conditionalities for the beneficiaries: (i) school attendance by the children of those families in the public schools in which they were enrolled; (ii) regular medical check-ups, with special attention to pregnant women; (iii) and a monthly per capita family income up to the limit of the poverty line. (This was up to 178 Reais at the termination of the program, in 2021).

Although there were criticisms of such conditionalities, they turned out to be impactful in the attempt to improve educational and health indices in Brazil. Extensive studies demonstrate how the Bolsa Família was impacting those areas (Júnior et al., 2013; Craveiro and De Aquino Ximenes, 2013, Campello et al., 2013). Also, it is worth noting that these same studies point to the enormous success of the program, which is recognized worldwide as one of the largest and most successful conditional income transfer policies.

The main effects of the Bolsa Família program in relation to its beneficiaries can be summarized as follows (Souza, 2021): (i) progressive increase in the number of beneficiaries covered; (ii) transformation of the Brazilian voting map; (iii) increase in medical follow-up of the vulnerable population and decrease in infant mortality; (iv) educational boom; (v) reduction of extreme poverty, poverty and vulnerable groups; (vi) growth of employment rates for the working-age population and more specifically female work, concomitant to a drop in child labor; (vii) decrease in fertility rates; (viii) greater access to infrastructure services such as electricity, water, sewage and garbage collection; (ix) increase in the purchasing power of the beneficiaries; and (x) the growth of small urban businesses.

The PBF achievements may be deemed unique. Not only are they globally recognized but they also represent a significant example of successful cash transfer policy in the world (Souza, 2021). Its achievements are globally recognized and it was, until the very end, a significant example of successful cash transfer policy in the world (Campelo et al., 2013). This made the BF possibly the biggest effort in Brazil to face up to the historical inequality and poverty of the country.

A key event in the Brazilian sociopolitical scenario that heavily influenced the field of assistance policies was the discovery of several oil reserves along the coast of the country (Postali e Nishijima, 2011). Some cities had a huge increase in their revenues, which opened up space for new public policies to be financed (ibid.). One of these cities, the city of Maricá, is the main focus of the present paper. Its municipality used the new oil profits to finance one of the largest current UBI policies.

The next section includes some important information about Maricá and the implementation of its Citizen's Basic Income.

3. The Citizen Basic Income in Maricá

The city of Maricá is located in the Rio de Janeiro state, close to Rio de Janeiro city. As far as socioeconomic aspects are concerned, Maricá has a population of 157.789 residents (IBGE, 2018), a GDP (gross domestic product) of R$ 26,9 billion (ibid.) and GDP per capita of R$ 171.003,42 (ibid.). The poverty rate is 4,88% (ibid., 2010), while the extreme poverty rate is 1,47% (ibid.), and the gini index is 0,49 (ibid.). In 2019, 72,3% of the city's revenue came from oil profits (Dektar, 2020). The Worker's Party, the main left-wing Brazilian party in the last decades, has governed the city since 2009.

The former major, Washington Quaquá, who was elected in 2008 and took office in 2009, was responsible for the implementation of the Citizen Basic Income in the city of Maricá. From the profits of the recently discovered oil reserves on the city's shore, Quaquá was able to implement a whole range of public services, thus increasing the city's welfare protection. Fabiano Horta succeeded Quaquá in 2014.

Regarding the Basic Income program itself, it is possible to see a gradual development. Before its implementation, the first act of the city hall was to promulgate Law 2.448, creating the "Programa Municipal de Economia Solidária, Combate à Pobreza e Desenvolvimento Econômico e Social de Maricá" (Municipal Program of Solidarity Economy, Fight Against Poverty and Economic and Social Development of Maricá). This program was the foundation of all social policies that would emerge in the following years in the city. Soon afterwards the Mumbuca bank was created in order to centralize the financing of the program and institute the digital currency, also called Mumbuca, through which the payment would be made. This currency equals the value of the official Brazilian counterpart, the Real (R$), but it is only accepted within the Maricá city limits. The local shops that accept Mumbuca pay a 2% tax in order to convert it to Real. The revenues from this taxation finances loans to the city's residents, stimulating the growth of local entrepreneurs.

Finally, in December 2013, the first payment of 85 Mumbucas was made to 14.000 households. In order to be eligible for the benefit, these families needed to be enrolled in the "Brazilian Unified Register" of social assistance, that is, the household needed to earn up to 3 minimum wages as their total monthly income. Additionally, the recipients had to have resided in the city of Maricá for at least three years.

Two years after the start of the program, the program was enhanced. In 2015, families started receiving 10 additional Mumbucas in the Basic Income transfer. Again, two years after that, in 2017, there was another increase in the payment. The transfer of 95 Mumbucas was then 130 M$.

In 2019 another big change was announced. The payment stopped being targeted to families/households and began to be paid to individuals, which significantly increased the total amount transferred to the city's residents. In December of the same year, the official data from the program showed that the Basic Income was reaching 42,5 thousand individuals (approximately 27% of the population).

During the COVID-19 pandemic, there was a significant effort to assist the citizens of Maricá and the transfer was raised to 300 (three hundred) Mumbucas. The 13-month salary (also known as the Christmas bonus) was also paid in advance to help the beneficiaries. Informal workers were eligible to receive a monthly payment of R$ 1.045 (one minimum wage at the time) for three months. The government also provided food baskets to more than 24.000 families whose children were enrolled in public schools in Maricá between the months of April and June 2020 and offered R$ 20 million in interest-free loans in order to help small businesses.

This conjuncture of heavy assistance during the pandemic is one more example of how the Marica local government devotes significant attention towards the economic security of its population. Nonetheless, this is something made possible by increasing oil profits, as discussed previously. In any case, the significant effort of the Maricá municipality, especially when compared to the Brazilian scenario, both national and regional, is worth mentioning.

Besides the Basic Income, the former major, Washington Quaqua, and his successor, Fabiano Horta, introduced the following benefits: (i) scholarships and saving accounts for public school students; (ii) financial support for studies in private higher education institutions; (iii) free public transport system within the city limits; (iv) a basic income of 300 Mumbucas per month for indigenous residents; (v) "Feiras Livres Solidárias" (Free Solidary Fairs) and "Hortas Comunitárias" (Communal Vegetable Garden); (vi) the Mumbuca Futuro Program for students; (vii) the construction of an Industrial Park and a university campus (Dektar el al., 2020).

Of these policies, the one that is most worth highlighting is the Mumbuca Futuro, which is directed at young students enrolled in public schools so that they can learn and develop critical thinking with regard to financing and labor, and engage in socioeconomic debates. The students that take part in the program have to attend a series of extra classes in order to qualify for an extra benefit of 50 Mumbucas. In the event that they are approved during the school year, they get an additional 1.200 Mumbucas, so they can also learn how to manage their money. As it is a long-term project, it is still too early to see the results. However, it can be deemed a thriving, innovative and exciting measure on the part of the city hall.

Another point that is worth noting is that in 2017 the government of Maricá created a sovereign wealth fund which aims to perpetuate all the social policies that have been created over the last years. Due to a series of issues, such as decrease of oil consumption in a green economy horizon, the oil profits may be somewhat uncertain in the future. For this reason, one may argue that wealth fund will be vital for the sustainability of the micro-welfare state of Maricá.

Having described the functioning of the pilot, the following sections lean on debates that may arise from the concrete case of Maricá Citizen Basic Income.

4. Lessons to be Learned from Maricá Citizen Basic Income

Although the example of Maricá is one of resounding success so far (Dektar, 2020), it is undeniable that this success is facilitated by two primary factors: (i) it is a small town and (ii) its revenues have grown exponentially in recent years.

The size of Marica makes the implementation of public policies easier. If it was a national policy in a large country with several regional differences, the process would be much more complex and difficult. Thus, when it comes to national Basic Income plans, it is crucial that regional idiosyncrasies are taken carefully into consideration so as to make the isonomic distribution of benefits as well as the implementation of public policies more feasible.

In addition, it is important to reiterate that the City of Maricá would not have been able to implement such a wide range of public services without the oil royalties. Other municipalities in the state of Rio de Janeiro aim to implement a basic income in a way similar to Maricá but this process is significantly harder due to the lack of resources (Postali e Nishijima, 2011).

In this sense, it is urgent to think about public policies and basic income projects that are fundable regardless of resources from extractive and non-renewable activities. Although it is commendable for the city of Maricá to allocate much of its revenue to social assistance, this should not be considered as a model for the rest of Brazil, or the world, as it will not be possible to reproduce in many cases (Da Silva et al., 2020).

It is also necessary to address the way in which the federalist issue in Brazil renders the case of Maricá even more complex. There is a clash in the Brazilian political field due to the division of oil royalties. (This theme is widely addressed in Najjar et al. (2019). The amount that will be allocated exclusively to the municipality of Maricá is uncertain and is currently being modified by decisions by the Brazilian legislative and judicial powers.

The federative issue can be viewed from two perspectives: (i) a regionalist perspective, defending the right of the municipality of Maricá and the State of Rio de Janeiro to have access to most royalties or (ii) a more national perspective, claiming an equal division of royalties among all Brazilian territories.

The federative pact of Brazil presupposes a relative division, granting a specific part of the profits to the state and the municipality where the extraction takes place. However, the way these profits are shared among Brazilian localities is at the heart of an ongoing dispute between federal entities in the legal-political field. The percentage of division among the entities of the federation has been modified several times in recent decades (Najjar et al., 2019) and the future remains uncertain.

In addition to uncertainty regarding the royalties, there is also the environmental-political issue, which is concerned with oil exploration in the future. As for all the environmental problems on the horizon, it is urgent that fossil fuel consumption be decreased. In this conjuncture, it is dangerous therefore to rely on oil extraction to finance public policies.

Nevertheless, the city of Maricá is aware of this risk. One initiative that comes to mind is the creation of an independent fund with the intention to perpetuate and make the social programs sustainable in the long run. Eventually, it is only fair to argue that the dependence on this oil exploration will come to an end.

Ideally, according to the classical Basic Income literature (Widerquist et al., 2013), an Unconditional Basic Income project should be financed by an isonomic system of income taxing. As it turns out, however, for economic and political reasons, such a taxation system is still far from becoming a reality in the Brazilian case (Souza, 2021). Besides, the effort needs to start from the federal government, not the state or municipal government. Therefore, bearing in mind that the Brazilian taxation system and the fight against poverty and inequality are largely the competence of the Brazilian federal sphere, the criticism of the financing of Maricá public policies is not a demerit. As a matter of fact, it is significantly positive that the municipality allocates its resources to social policies, especially in a Brazilian context, where many municipalities with more abundant revenues than Maricá do not make the same effort to fight poverty and inequality (Najjar et al., 2019).

On a different but correlated note, another point of enormous interest related to the case of Maricá is the success in creating a digital currency to put the transfer of the RBI into practice. In a global context of progressive strengthening of digital currencies, this could be a welcome facilitator in the implementation of Basic Income projects around the world.

The commercial establishments that accept Mumbucas as payment can exchange it to Real (the Brazilian official currency). The only snag is that they are obliged to pay a 2% tax in this conversion, which allows the government to be able to make loans and finance projects for the citizens of Maricá. In addition, it is important to emphasize the fact that Mumbuca is only accepted within the city limits, so as to prevent capital evasion but also to strengthen the internal economy of the city, creating opportunities for small businesses to flourish. This conjuncture of factors (public investment added to the non-evasion of capital) is extremely positive for the city to develop socioeconomically.

Investment in human capital is something to be emphasized as well. Maricá has earmarked a reasonable portion of its revenues for the financing of quality public services, such as school and health. Moreover, an industrial park and a university campus are currently being built in the city, which will increase job offers and public university places. This reality provides a much greater atmosphere of security, enabling the city to develop economically. Besides, it even encourages foreign investments in the region. When it comes to human capital, Mumbuca Futuro is once again worth mentioning since it was also a bold measure that, if well executed and successful, can add much to the development of the city.

It can be seen from these findings that Maricá has been able to combine public investment with economic growth. The COVID-19 pandemic is a remarkable instance in this case, given that the citizens of the city were in a relatively high economic security situation compared to other Brazilian realities. The city human development indexes have also shown constant growth (IBGE, 2020), evidencing the success of public policies.

Finally, it is necessary to point out two last topics in this section. They focus more specifically on the theme of Basic Income itself. First, it is vital to remember that Brazil is a strongly inequal country, with high rates of poverty. This is a crucial social factor that needs to be taken into account when planning a Basic Income policy and would make it problematic to set up a UBI for all citizens at once. Van Parijs (2003) recognizes that, in poorer and inequal countries, starting a non-universal basic income program can be a good way to begin a process of plain implementation. In order to achieve a level of economic equality that enables a universal and unconditional Basic Income project for all citizens, it should be necessary to correct historical inequalities present in Brazil. However, to name one shortcoming, unless the program meets these goals, the poverty trap might be an issue. Therefore, it is important for the program to expand gradually in order to encompass more and more citizens, until it becomes a proper universal basic income.

The second factor worth highlighting has to do with how the Citizen Income of Maricá functioned in coordination with a wide range of public services (health, education, transportation, to name but a few). The discussion on "universal public servicing versus UBI" (Standing, 2019) comes up regularly in academia (Vanderborght, 2006). In addition, there are several political groups that are sceptical of the idea of the Basic Income as it could mean the end of the welfare state. In countries such as Belgium, the Netherlands and Canada, where there is a wide range of social protection services, this is a justifiable concern (ibid.). In countries like Brazil, where the state as a service provider has not developed the same way as in other nations, the discussion becomes more complex. There are those who advocate the implementation of a Basic Income as a priority, regardless of the development of the public service network (Suplicy, 2006), while others argue that one should invest in public services and, only later, introduce a Basic Income (Lavinas, 2018).

The case of Maricá is significant within the realm of this discussion because it is a clear and concrete instance of how the government has been successful in combining both fronts: the growth of the public service network and investment in a Basic Income. The strategy of the city has been to use both fronts in a symbiotic way so that many citizens, such as students from Mumbuca Futuro and pregnant women, use public services and enrol in social programs and thus become eligible for more benefits. This does not exclude a degree of independence between the UBI and public services, but it is important to bear in mind that there is a coordinated effort between both aspects. The next few years will be fundamental to understand whether the method adopted by Maricá has been successful from a socioeconomic point of view. Nonetheless, the preliminary results have proved encouraging.

As previously mentioned, the positive effects and the proper functioning of Maricá social programs became even more evident during the COVID-19 pandemic (Silva et al., 2020). Many countries around the globe have faced difficulties in granting emergency aid to their citizens because of registration problems (ibid.). These money transfers were made in a conditioned and arbitrary manner, which generated much controversy. Two examples worth mentioning are the Portuguese and Italian cases. In both instances the age criteria had to be met in order for the money to be transferred. Maricá, on the other hand, was leveraged due to a previous well-developed and solid registration system and the fact that the Citizen Income project was already in operation as of 2013 (Dektar, 2020). This suggests the need for a global basic income program (even though regional specificities must be respected), so that individuals in times of crisis, such as the COVID-19, are financially secure. Society must evolve to a point where it should no longer be necessary to enter the labor market to earn the existential minimum. In that respect, Maricá, in spite of its unique characteristics and being at the starting point of an ideal UBI, has much to offer the academic debate as well as the political-economic environment.

5. Final Remarks

Based on what has been discussed in this paper so far, it may be argued that the Marica project is a fertile area of study when it comes to future analyses of UBI policies. Even though it is a small and very specific case, it has a lot to teach academia and the political community. The digital currency, the coordination with public services and the creation of the sovereign fund were actions that seem to be fundamental to the policy's success.

The Maricá Basic Income program has a vast growth potential. It has reached a level of great importance within the city, and it can be considered a great achievement. This successful policy significantly influenced the Brazilian elections of 2020, when several candidates from other municipalities in Rio de Janeiro brought in their proposals projects, inspired by the Maricá UBI.

Consequently, the horizon in the state of Rio de Janeiro state reveals exciting perspectives regarding UBI pilots. These will be vital in order to make the Basic Income proposal more feasible in the Brazilian conjuncture, showing a distinct perspective from the literature and pilots from more equal countries, such as those in Europe. The exchange of experiences between both perspectives can be symbiotic and vital to strengthen a UBI proposal as it approaches the entire globe.

References

Brasil. Constituição (1988). Constituição da República Federativa do Brasil. Brasília, DF: Senado Federal: Centro Gráfico, 1988.

Brasil. Lei nº 10.835/04, de 8 de janeiro de 2004. Institui a Renda Básica de Cidadania e dá outras previdências. Diário Oficial [da República Federativa do Brasil], Brasília, DF, v. 134, n. 248, 8 jan. 2004. Seção I, p. 1677-7042.

Campello, T.; Neri, M.C. (2013). Programa Bolsa Família: uma década de inclusão e cidadania.

Carvalho, L. (2018). Valsa brasileira: do boom ao caos econômico. Editora Todavia SA.

Craveiro, C. B. A.; De Aquino Ximenes, D. (2013). Dez anos do Programa Bolsa Família: desafios e perspectivas para a universalização da educação básica no Brasil. BOLSA FAMÍLIA, p. 109.

Da Silva, J.L.; Da Silva, R.C.; Waltenberg, F. (2020). Resposta à crise da Covid-19 no município de Maricá: Análise preliminar comparativa com medidas tomadas no Brasil e no mundo. Texto para discussão, p. 154-2020.

Da Silva, J.L.; Da Silva, R.C.; Freitas, F.; Waltenberg, F. (2020). Políticas socioeconômicas de reação à crise da Covid-19 no município de Maricá, Rio de Janeiro.

Dektar, M. (2020). Informações sobre políticas socioeconômicas de Maricá e sua avaliação/Information on Maricá's socioeconomic policies and their evaluation.

Fonseca, A., Fagnani, E. (2013). Políticas sociais, desenvolvimento e cidadania. São Paulo, Fundação Perseu Abramo.

Júnior, H.M.M.; Jaime, P.C.; De Lima, A.M.C. (2013). O papel do setor saúde no Programa Bolsa Família: histórico, resultados e desafios para o Sistema Único de Saúde. BOLSA FAMÍLIA, p. 93.

Lavinas, L. (2015). Latin America: anti-poverty schemes instead of social protection. Contemporary Readings in Law and Social Justice, v. 7, n. 1, p. 112-171.

_____. (2018). Renda Básica de Cidadania: apolítica social do século XXI? Lições para o Brasil. Friedrich Ebert Stiftung, Brasil.

Pereira, A.S., Siqueira, D.Z.C, Senra, L.T., Costa, N.M. (2020). As políticas públicas de economia solidária no município de Maricá/RJ. 2020.

Najjar, J.N.V.; Da Silva Vicente, D.; Morgan, K.V. (2019). Federalismo cooperativo, financiamento da educação e royalties do petróleo. Revista Contemporânea de Educação, v. 14, n. 31, p. 13-32.

Postali, F.A.S.; Nishijima, M. (2011). Distribuição das rendas do petróleo e indicadores de desenvolvimento municipal no Brasil nos anos 2000S. Estudos Econômicos (São Paulo), v. 41, p. 463-485.

Souza, T. (2021). THE BOLSA FAMÍLIA CASE: a road to the unconditional basic income. Portugal, Lisboa, 107 páginas.

Standing, G. (2020). Battling eight giants: Basic income now. Bloomsbury Publishing.

_____. (2008). How cash transfers promote the case for basic income. Basic Income Studies, v. 3, n. 1.

Suplicy, E. M. (2006). Renda Básica de Cidadania: a resposta dada pelo vento. Porto Alegre: L&PM.

Van Parijs, P., Vanderborght, Y. (2017). Basic Income: A radical proposal for a free society and a sane economy. Cambridge, MA: Harvard University Press.

Van Parijs, P. (2013). The universal basic income: Why utopian thinking matters, and how sociologists can contribute to it. Politics & Society, 41(2), 171-182.

Vanderborght, Y. (2006). Why trade unions oppose basic income. Basic Income Studies, v. 1, n. 1.

Widerquist, K., Noguera, J. A., Vanderborght, Y., & De Wispelaere, J. (2013). Basic Income. Chichester: Wiley.

Tobias Jäger

Foreign Aid Basic Income

The Concept of Aid and a Short Overview

Basic Income in developing countries sounds unrealistic, where low tax revenue and low state capacity render it unthinkable. Considering the high sums involved in development aid, the question arises whether a basic income financed by development aid is feasible. This paper gives an overview of foreign Aid. I illuminate rules, patterns, and use of aid. At the same time, it provides a small survey of the economic literature on the subject.

1. Introduction

This contribution contains a summary of the author's thoughts on his work as coordinator of the FRIBIS WEF-FABI (Water-Energy-Food - Foreign Aid Basic Income) team. The paper contains aspects of the content of a presentation at our last conference but takes it further. While team goals will not be elaborated on, it is nevertheless important for me to briefly introduce the team framework and mention some of the difficulties that have arisen previously. The WEF-FABI started as a research meeting to discuss the issue of Water-Energy-Food from the perspective of environmental resilience, with basic income and its possibilities as a social resilience tool. All members agree that is important to consider both these resilience concepts. The challenges lie in the transdisciplinary approach and the novelty of discussing them together. Finding a common language is thus a permanent challenge. As the focus is on the Global South, it goes without saying that people from the Global South should be involved. At the heart of this project is the desire to implement a bottom-up approach and Basic Income is bottom-up from the start. It is a tool to empower citizens regardless of their nationality, religion, and class. Such a project sounds unrealistic in fragile or less developed countries utopian, where low tax revenue and low state capacity render it unthinkable. Considering the high sums involved in development aid, the question arises whether a basic income financed by development aid is actually feasible. So could it be modified gradually to be financed by domestic taxes? Can a Foreign Aid Basic Income make a positive contribution to a country's development? And does such a foreign-funded system differ from a domestic one? There are many questions to be answered here. This article takes the first step in this direction by taking a closer look at Foreign Aid and will proceed as follows: The next chapter gives a short, intuitive description of Foreign Aid Basic Income followed by an overview of the history of Foreign Aid. The paper then gives an overview of flows and the amount of Foreign Aid. Where it comes from and flows to. Chapter 3 presents an overview of economic theories and highlights empirical results. Finally, the conclusion will provide a summary from a Basic Income perspective.

2. Intuition of FABI

In January 2008, in the small town of Otjivero-Omitara, a basic income of 100 Namibian dollars started to be paid to every person under sixty. The project was financed by a private sponsor, namely the churches (Haarmann & Haarmann, 2005). This observation led to the consideration of a basic income being considered a development project funded via Aid.

Based on our observations during Covid-19 we have generated a considerable amount of new data and evidence on the behaviour of people when it comes to cash transfers. We now have data from 984 social assistance implementation 475 was conditional or unconditional cash transfer schemes (Gentilini, et al., 2021). Clearly, analysing this data and including the conclusion to policy measures will be very work-intensive.

The other Side of FABI is also important. Here we need a better understanding of how we can fund a Basic Income, especially in developing countries.

These countries, especially the so-called fragile states, tend to suffer from volatile government revenues. Often their social budgets are significantly lower than those of their peer groups. Moreover, during and after crises most developing countries are stressed by many funding gaps (Harvey, et al., 2007). To help such countries we could plausibly finance part of the funding from foreign aid and the other part from domestic revenues (Banerjee, et al., 2019). This should be interesting for the donors because they can finance people's needs directly, thus minimising project costs and corruption. Otherwise, some technocrats might lose influence and become sceptical (Banerjee, et al., 2019). Many questions remain unanswered, and the first step is to better understand what we refer to as "foreign aid".

3. Overview of Foreign Aid

Foreign aid is closely linked to the "idea of development", making it an integral part of controversial debates. Heated disputes are common in the sciences, politics, and in the broader discussion around modernization and humanitarianism. We will draw attention to some of these debates within the economic disciplines in the chapter entitled "Empirical Evidence". Foreign Aid can be seen as a policy tool or economic instrument and is the subject of discussion in many works in the field of International Relations as well as in the field of economics. To reach a balanced understanding both views need to be considered ... (Morgenthau, 1962). Diplomacy works with concessional agreements and tends to (material and immaterial) exchanges (Cohen, 2007). In this respect Aid is always a political tool used to establish, maintain and restore an international political system. (Markovits, et al., 2019). According to Hans Morgenthau, only humanitarian aid, such as that following natural disasters, is per se non-political but it too can have a political effect (Morgenthau, 1962). When it comes to such thinking, foreign aid is a soft tool and historically it goes back to the time of colonial and imperialist power (Führer, 1996). It existed in the ancient world between Romans and the periphery as well as in ancient China (Markovits, et al., 2019). Nevertheless, it is not uncommon for theorists to begin the "history of aid" with the Marshall Plan (Edwards, 2014). Given its success, more and more countries have established their AID agencies (Ali & Zeb, 2016), making it necessary for the donor countries to coordinate and institutionalize Foreign Aid. At the same time, efforts have been made to distribute the costs of development aid fairly (Hynes & Scott, 2013). Until 1955 about 90% of the aid from the developed countries was provided by the USA, the UK, and France (Therien, 2002). But in 1960 the Development Assistance Group (DAG) was founded and later renamed the Development Assistance Committee (Führer, 1996). Today, it is part of the OECD and operates under the name OECD-

DAC. The organization for Economic Co-operation and Development (OECD) has 38 member states and its aim is to stimulate economic progress and trade. The roots of the organization go back to the administration of the Marshall Plan. Within this organisation, the DAC's goal is to monitor flow, set international standards and exchange good practices (OECD, 2015). The DAC regularly holds so-called "high-level" and "senior-level meetings" to discuss and regulate co-operation. The main goal of the meetings is to coordinate the donor-recipient relationship. We can trace the origins back to the UN Millennium Declaration (2000), which articulates one goal as "a global partnership for development". In 2002 followed the Monterrey Consensus, which has become the main reference for international development cooperation. Monterrey deals with financing for development. One year later the first high-level forum was organized in Rome, followed in 2005 by the High-Level Forum on Aid Effectiveness. The result was the important "Paris Declaration on Aid Effectiveness" (Klingebiel, 2011). The declaration established five principles

1) Ownership
2) Alignment
3) Harmonisation
4) Result-orientation
5) Mutual accountability

The goal in Paris was to increase aid effectiveness and was followed in 2008 by the signing of the Accra Agenda for Action agreement. This summit can be seen as a rapprochement of the North/South countries (Hackenesch & Grimm, 2011). The Accra Agenda deepened and strengthened the Paris implementation. The declaration was expanded slightly given the South-South cooperation (Hackenesch & Grimm, 2011). The last of these high-level meetings, in 2012, emphasized the importance of the above five points in the so-called Busan Agreement. Busan was overshadowed by the tensions between the old and new donor countries (Hackenesch & Grimm, 2011), which explains why the agreement was a strong compromise. It did not so much deepen as broaden the development context.

Definition of ODA 1972 - 2018

Those flows to countries and territories on the DAC List of ODA Recipients and to multilateral institutions which are: provided by official agencies, including state and local governments, or by their executive agencies; and each transaction of which:
a) is administered with the promotion of the economic development and welfare of developing countries as its main objective; and
b) is concessional in character and conveys a grant element of at least 25 per cent (calculated at a rate of discount of 10 per cent).

Definition of ODA 2018

ODA flows are defined as those flows to countries and territories on the DAC List of ODA Recipients and to multilateral development institutions which are: provided by official agencies, including state and local governments, or by their executive agencies; and each transaction of which:
- is administered with the promotion of the economic development and welfare of developing countries as its main objective; and
- is concessional in character. In DAC statistics, this implies
  A grant element of at least (see note 4)
  - 45 per cent in the case of bilateral loans to the official sector of LDCs and other LICs (calculated at a rate of discount of 9 per cent).
  - 15 per cent in the case of bilateral loans to the official sector of LMICs (calculated at a rate of discount of 7 per cent).
  - 10 per cent in the case of bilateral loans to the official sector of UMICs (calculated at a rate of discount of 6 per cent).
  - 10 per cent in the case of loans to multilateral institutions (see note 1) (calculated at a rate of discount of 5 per cent for global institutions and multilateral development banks, and 6 per cent for other organisations, including sub-regional organisations) (see notes 2 and 3).

Source: (OECD, 2022)

With the establishment of the Global Partnership for Effective Development Co-operation (GPEPC), the final chapter of the institutional architecture of international development assistance has been opened so far. This culminated in the Mexico Conference, where the result was seen as a setback (Fues, 2014). With the GPEPC, the private sector and especially the philanthropists, will be given greater consideration. Following this brief overview of the institutional framework, we return to the definition itself.

Before 1972 there was no overall definition of Foreign Aid. The economist Rosenstein-Rodan highlighted the importance of making a difference between Aid and Foreign capital inflow (Ali & Zeb, 2016) while others argued for more differentiation based on goals and objectives (Morgenthau, 1962). In the early years of the DAC there was much debate about the exact definition. The point of interest was whether "loans" and Export Credit should count for Foreign Aid or not (Scott, 2015). In 1972 a big step forward was made with a unity definition. This was a milestone that helped to clarify what exactly foreign aid is and how it is measured (Führer, 1996). Over 46 years later we saw the first update after long debates. The background for this update aimed to better measure private sector support. At the same time, a changeover was made from a flow concept to an equivalent calculation (Obrovsky & Riegler, 2019).

The motive for the flow of money is at the heart of the title "Economic development and the welfare of developing countries" (see Graph 1). Note that Aid can come in the form of a gift or as a very low-interest loan. Aid may be provided bilaterally, direct from donor to recipient, or through a multilateral development agency (OECD, 2022). We can also see from the definition how closely it is linked to development economics. The latter is not a static field however but has its own dynamics like any other science. Since 1945 the "idea of what development is" and "how we can achieve it" has changed more than once (Alacevich & Boianovsky, 2018). To what extent the change in development theory has altered and influenced the work of development aid is an exciting field that unfortunately cannot be explored further here. Furthermore, it can be argued that the practice of development cooperation has established itself as an independent field so that the connections to development economics are not so close anymore. One negative side of this is that it is now difficult to transfer knowledge between both sectors (Collier & Dollar, 2002). Interestingly, no overtly political aspects appear in the definition. A normative level is provided by the phrase "welfare of the developing countries", which is of course very vague. From this definition it is clear that military spending and export credits have completely disappeared from the ODA statistics. Also excluded are peacekeeping programs, nuclear energy, and cultural programs (OECD, 2022). There are still loans but, to quote Rodan-Rodenstein, "which normal markets do not provide" (Ali & Zeb, 2016). The actual counting of what and when is recognised as Foreign Aid was not made easier by the definition reform (Obrovsky & Riegler, 2019). Critical voices about OECD-DAC definitional power note that the modern multipolar world needs a new kind of organization (Bräutigam, 2011). Such criticism mirrors the increasing influence of the non-membership states (e.g., India, Brazil, and China). These can be split into three categories 1) emerging donor states (Poland, CZ, Israel and Hungary) and 2) South-South Cooperation, like Brazil, India and the Gulf states. (Zimmermann & Smith, 2011) Twenty non-DAC countries reported statistics to the OECD in 2022. But their other, big donor countries, including China, India, and Brazil, did not. The South-South countries in particular have a strong mistrust of some of the DAC rules (Zimmermann & Smith, 2011) and hold back on the transmission of data. For researchers, lack of transparency and the unavailability of data makes it difficult to make reliable statements in this respect. China's One Belt One Road, in particular, is the focus of much media coverage. And aid funds and business relationships become even more blurred when it comes to non-DAC nations. (Bräutigam, 2011). In 2019, the OECD estimated China's Foreign Aid at around $4.4 billion, with India's at $3 billion (Ahmad, et al., 2020).

One area that has not been well documented in the official statistics is donations by civil societies and the commitment of the churches. This area is therefore not taken into account in this paper even though its volume is quite considerable.

In 2020 we saw the first data from a new international statistical measure, the Total Official Support for Sustainable Development (TOSSD) (Ahmad, et al., 2020). TOSSD is designed to monitor all official resources flowing into developing countries but also focuses on private resources mobilized through official means. The Idea of TOSSD is also to contribute to international Public Goods visible (e.g., climate mitigation).

3.1 ODA Data

Thus far we have tried to clarify our understanding of Foreign Aid. Now we want to talk about where it comes from and where it goes. In 1970 every member committed themselves to the 0,7 ODA to GNI rule (Gross National Income) (Ahmad, et al., 2020). Gross National Income measures the total amount of money earned by domestic recipients and businesses (GDP) + earnings received from foreign sources. This means that each country should contribute 0.7% of its GNI to aid development.

Indeed, only the United States and Switzerland failed to commit to the target. In addition, there is a target of allowing the least developed countries (LDC) to achieve at least between 0.15 and 0.2 ODA/GNI (VENRO, 2021). In 2020 the total ODA provided was USD 161.2 billion (Wilcks, et al., 2020). With the agreement of a Millennium Development goal in 2000, a booming period of ODA began (Ahmad, et al., 2020). In the early 2010s we see, with a lag, the financial crisis impact ODA. Nevertheless, the total amount returned to its former growth level in the late 2010s.

The figure on page 169 shows eight countries and the DAC country's average ODA Flow in percentage of GNI. This time the series is measured with the old definition. In the middle at the top, we can observe that the DAC average is far from the 0,7 target. In 2020 seven countries (DK, GER, LUX, NOR, SWE, UK, and Turkey) reached the target (Wilcks, et al., 2020). On average, only 0,31 was achieved and this remained more or less constant over time. Only the Nordic countries have a history of higher AID figures. Germany pays a little over the average but is lower than 0.7 %. Around 2015, with the migration crisis, Germany starts to increase its Foreign Aid contribution. Below we can see that in 2020 Germany achieved 0.7 % for the first time. France's contribution is visibly cyclical.

In 2020 France paid 0.53, which is equivalent to 13.5 billion US-dollars. In absolute terms, the situation is somewhat different however. With $34.5 billion (2020), the USA is the largest single donor. Germany is in second place with 28.3 billion, followed by the United Kingdom with 17.8 billion. In third place is Japan with 15.4 billion US Dollars. France and Sweden occupy 5th and 6th place.

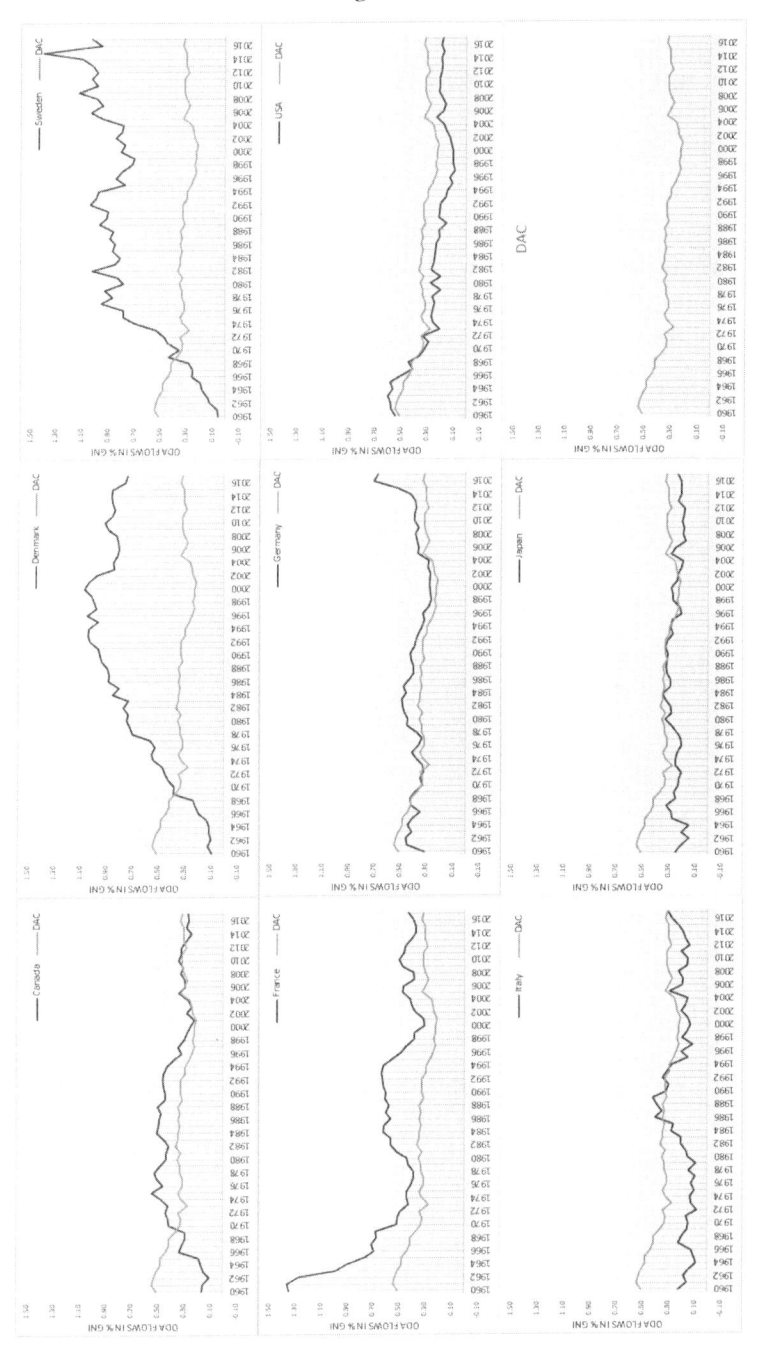

Graph 2: ODA flows basis, % of gross national income, 1960 – 2017 – Source: (OECD, 2022)

Non-DAC members provided 13.15 billion USD. 75% was contributed by Turkey, Saudi Arabia, and the UAE (Wilcks, et al., 2020). Their focus is primarily on Yemen and Syria (OECD, 2022). Another sector where continuity is increasing is that of philanthropic donors. In 2020, the OECD collected data from thirty such foundations. Among them are well-known names that go back to individuals such as the Melinda and Bill Gates and Buffet families. Other foundations are directly linked to companies such as the Mastercard Foundation or the Citi Foundation. A total of 8.954 billion US dollars was raised by private donors with the Bill & Melinda Gates Foundation contributing around half of this amount. This data collection is still relatively new and it is difficult to estimate what has not yet been collected in this area.

In graph 3, in the row after the name, we see the individual distribution in millions of U.S. dollars.

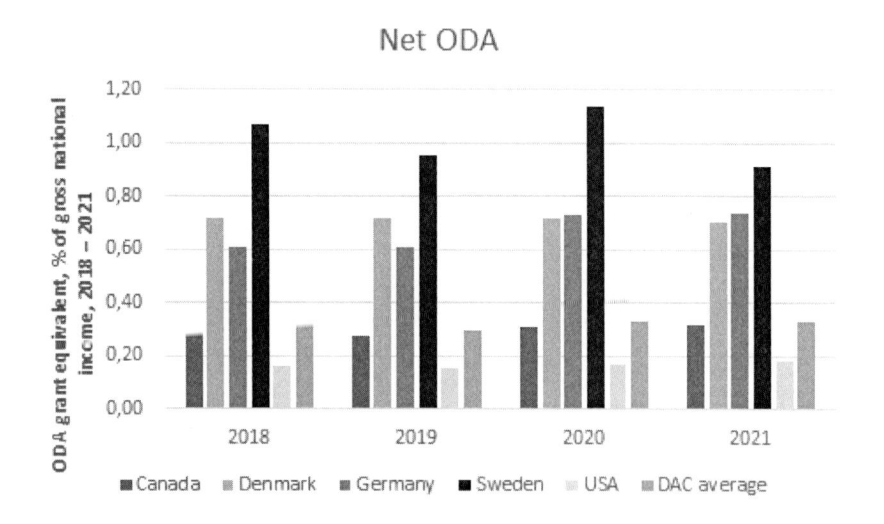

Graph 3: NET 2018-2020 – Source: (OECD, Net ODA (indicator) 2022)

3.2 Where the Money Comes from

Foundation	Assets in Mio. USD	Foundation	Assets in Mio. USD
Arcadia Fund	55,0	John D. & Cath. T. MacArthur F.	109,0
Arcus Foundation	15,1	La Caixa Banking Found.	41,1
BBVA Microfinance Found.	1314,7	Laudes Foundation	45,5
Bernard van Leer Found.	14,2	LEGO Foundation	44,4
Bill & Melinda Gates Found.	4108,5	Margaret A. Cargill Found.	44,1
Bloomberg Family Found.	142,9	Mastercard Found.	298,2
Carnegie Corporation of New York	23,9	MAVA Found.	39,7
Charity Projects Ltd (Comic Relief)	46,2	Mc Knight Found	8,7
Children's Investment Fund F.	253,4	MetLife Found.	14,0
Citi Foundation	26,92	Michael & Susan Dell Found.	35,3
Conrad N. Hilton Found.	42,26	Oak Foundation	136,2
David & Lucile Packard Found.	119,8	Omidyar Network Fund, Inc.	58,9
Ford Foundation	193,9	Rockefeller Foundation	110,5
Gatsby Charitable Found.	18,8	Susan T. Buffett Found.	296,6
Gordon and Betty Moore Found.	48,1	Wellcome Trust	326,9
Grameen Crédit Agricole Found.	45,4	William & Flora Hewlett Found.	123,3
H&M Foundation	16,55	World Diabetes Found.	16,6
Howard G. Buffett Foundation	155,5	United Postcode Lotteries, Total	353,0
IKEA Foundation	192,4	Dutch Postcode Lottery	237,9
Jacobs Foundation	17,3	Norwegian Postcode Lottery	2,0
Swedish Postcode Lottery	55,7	Peoples Postcode Lottery	57,2

Table 1: Philanthropic Foundations and their Foundation Assets – Source: OECD, 2022

With the Gates Foundation and BBVA Microfinance Foundation, we have two foundations with over a billion individual donations. In principle, ODA contributions are stable and rarely affected by economic cycles, especially GDP (Ahmad, et al., 2020). In addition, in the past other countries have stepped in when there were shortfalls (Wilcks, et al., 2020). We see that the recession as a result of Covid 19 has not yet harmed revenues overall. So far we have had an overview of where the money comes from. Now let's take a closer look at where it goes.

3.3 Where the Money Goes to

The geographical distribution is highly concentrated. As can be seen from graph 5 on page 172, most of the money goes to Sub-Saharan Africa (50bn US Dollar). In 2019, the Far East Asia category had the lowest allocations, at $256 million. South America, with 3.6 billion dollars, is also not well endowed, especially when you consider the population size. The country with the most Net ODA recipients in 2019 is Nigeria (5) with a very stable donor-recipient relationship. Yemen's ODA accelerates with the War. In 2019 Yemen received 3,7 bn. Before the return of the Taliban, Afghanistan was also one of the top recipients; it is to be expected that these figures will drop significantly.

Graph 5: ODA, Geographical Distribution (Source: OECD, 2022)

Bangladesh increased significantly from 2,44bn (2013) to 4,3bn (2019). With 4,6bn US Dollars in 2019, Ethiopia gets the biggest amount of all countries. It also has a very stable donor-recipient relationship. We know which countries and regions the ODA flow to but we know nothing about the sectors to which the money flows. Chart 6 shows some sectors in more detail but omits others. This means that the absolute figure cannot be added up and compared to the total line. As we can see, Social Infrastructure & Services are the main target for money. At this point at the latest, Covid has made it clear how important it is to have a well-functioning health care system and a viable social safety net.

Geographical distribution of total net ODA
constant prices Million 2019 USD

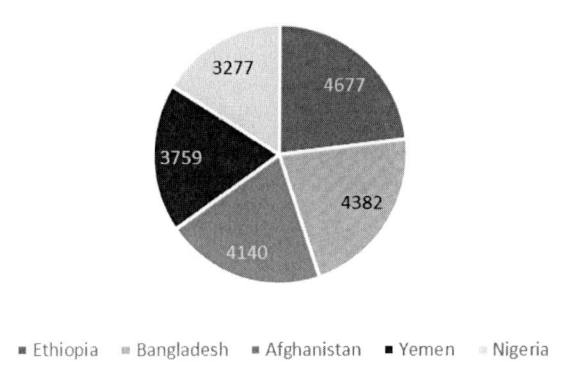

■ Ethiopia   ■ Bangladesh   ■ Afghanistan   ■ Yemen   ■ Nigeria

Graph 6: Top Five recipients total net ODA in 2019 – Source: OECD, 2022

Nevertheless, the trend of focusing on these sectors in particular has been underway for some time now (Ahmad, et al., 2020). We will see exactly what this means later. But for now, we will concentrate on the other sectors.

Under Economic Infrastructure & Services we mainly understand transportation, energy, and the banking sector. The latter in particular has received higher sums. In previous years there was stronger growth here but now we are seeing a sideways movement. The production sector refers to Agriculture, Manufactory, Mining, and Tourism. The latter sector is by far the smallest, which is of course also due to its commercial origins. The Humanitarian Aid sector has the biggest growth rates and involves every kind of emergency and distress relief in cash or kind. Some Aid organisations are multi-sector so it difficult to pin them down to one sector. In this section, you will find environment payments. Omitted from the chart above are areas such as General Program Assistances (3,9bn US Dollar), Acting related to debt, Unallocated/Unspecified. The amounts in parentheses refer to 2020. The social sector is particularly interesting for us, of course. If we open the black box "Social Infrastructure & services", we observe the following. In graph 7 the black line is the total amount drawn to the right scale.

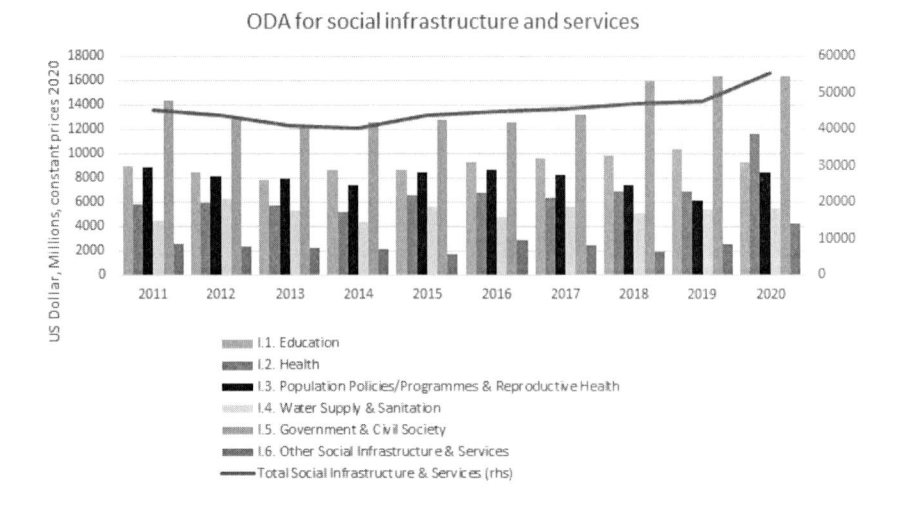

Graph 7: Total ODA by sectors – Source: OECD, 2022

Government and Civil Society (GCS) can be further divided. It includes public finance management, democratic participation, public procurement, and so on. GCS is by far the largest sub-sector in the sector. Over the last decade the education sector has been heavily funded but has now lost significant funding due to Corona. The Population Policies Sector has had very high allocations historically. However, there is a downward trend. Closely linked to this sector is, of course, health. This sector has seen enormous growth, especially as a result of Corona, with private donors participating very strongly. Before Corona the health sector had its up and downs, oscillating at around 6bn US dollars. The same pattern can be found in the water and sanitation sector.

The smallest of the subsectors listed is the "other social infrastructure. Nevertheless, this is one of the most interesting from the point of view of a basic income as it includes the category "social protection" (727 million US dollars in 2019), multisector aid for basic needs (430 million US dollars in 2019) and employment creation (463 million US dollars in 2019). So we can summarize the weight of social protection as a percentage of the total ODA: it is very small (Ortiz, et al., 2019). Nevertheless, we should treat these numbers with caution. The methodology will allocate payments to other categories to prevent double bookings (McCord, et al., 2021).

ODA for social infrastructure and services

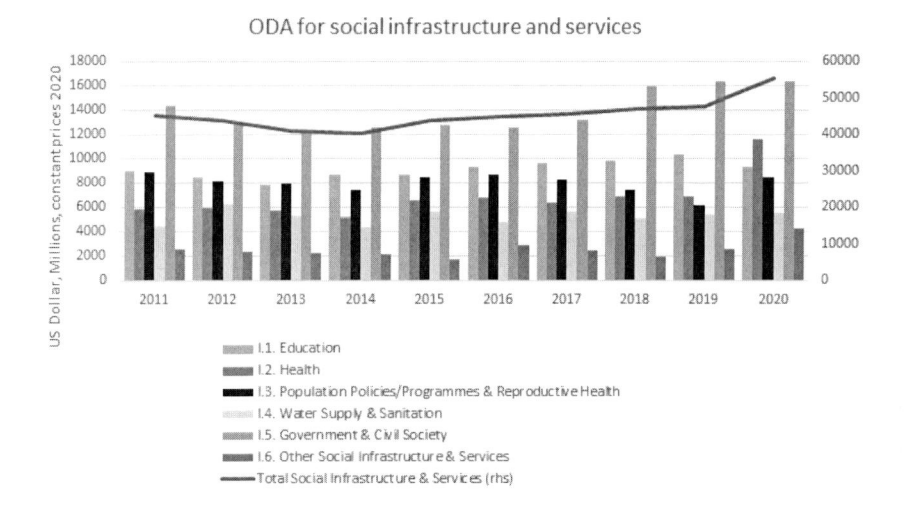

Graph 8 – ODA by Social Infrastructure and Services

At the same time, a very narrow definition of "social protection" is used. Humanitarian aid has often been the primary source of social protection, particularly in fragile states (Harvey, et al., 2007).

4. Overview of Economic Literature

In a debate with much media coverage, the economists William Easterly (Easterly, 2006) and Dambisa Moyo (Moyo, 2010) sharply criticize Foreign Aid, blaming it for mismanagement and supporting corrupt governments. Nevertheless, Jeffrey Sachs and Joseph Stiglitz write in favour of AID and development projects. From an academic point of you we can split Foreign Aid into two categories 1) effects of foreign aid on the receiving and 2) determinants of foreign Aid (Alesina & Dollar, 2000). The most controversial aspect of this discussion is on Aid effectiveness. A mass of research papers on this topic exists. To investigate aid effectiveness, researchers investigate the macroeconomic impact of foreign aid on the economic development of poor countries (Quibria, 2014). The body of research was built around in a cross-country regression framework (p.75). This literature follows cycles with pro-Aid arguments and is followed by another paper with counter-founding (Rajan & Subramanian, 2008). One problem with the empirical methods is dealing with the endogeneity of Aid (Galiani, et al., 2017). Other critical aspects are lags (Brückner, 2011). Then there is the problem with the underlying heterogeneity of countries included, which might tarnish positive effects (Askarov & Doucouliagos, 2015). Until today the result of the aid-growth regression framework is unclear with only a few robust results (Quibria, 2014). In a meta-analysis of 50 influential papers, we can observe this mixed result. 38 percent found that aid effectiveness is conditional when it comes to development; 27% find it is effective and 35% find it ineffective (Asatullaeva, et al., 2021). Regardless of the no-effect literature, Collier and Hoeffler have stressed the important role of Aid in the process of rebuilding and peacebuilding (Quibria, 2014). It is important to keep in mind the heterogeneity of aid motives (Bourguignon & Sundberg, 2007). This can also be seen in the aid effectiveness debate, where silent growth or even more unspecific development is often used as a target variable. What is important is that there is no consent on how and if aid works (Asatullaeva, et al., 2021). Burnside and Dollar argue if the policy is good (e.g., sound finance, inflation...), then aid works (Addison, et al., 2017). There is a scientific agreement that Aid has a diminishing return (Collier and Dollar, 2001). However, the marginal productivity of the aid is variable and depends on the inefficient initial situation (p.1497). Aid can hurt the domestic economy by reducing its manufacturing sector. That can happen through pervert incentives for the government and via overvaluation (Dutch disease) (Rajan & Subramanian, 2008). But Dutch disease can be contained by policy (Addison, et al., 2017). Counterintuitive results show that AID does not influence policy reforms (Alesina & Dollar, 2000). Surprisingly, the World Bank and other organizations do not react to such results. To get out of this impasse, there has been a move towards stronger micro and local studies for some years now. The focus is not on the average effect in aggregated data but on the specific case. This development is sometimes referred to as the "experimental turn" and is closely linked to the economists Abhijit Banerjee and Esther Duflo.

The second question relates to Aid allocation and determinants. There is economic evidence that the pattern of Aid giving is dictated by political and strategic considerations (Alesina & Dollar, 2000). Thus former colonial empires still tend to give preference to their former colonies (Drazen, 2000), which is not surprising. If you take IR or historical literature into account, there has never been any doubt about this point. Cross-country studies have made a very simplistic assumption that aid would always and fundamentally be used to fight poverty. IR Scholars see aid as a tool that donor countries use to pursue their interests (Markovits, et al., 2019). At the same time, the great potential for abuse is also described. From this perspective arises a whole series of literature that I call the "political economy of Foreign Aid".

What are the theories behind the idea that aid has an impact on growth or that aid inevitably impacts on the political economy of a donor country? How can we explain the donor-recipient relationship? In this sector, I will give a short introduction to these questions.

On the Macro level, there are two classical growth models. The neoclassical Solow model was little used in the field of development economics, where Harrod-Domar was more common. The original business cycles model was widely used in the developing economy. From the Macro perspective, the influence of Aid on saving and investment is important. In classical growth theory investment and shortfall of capital (fewer savings) is one of the biggest problems of low-income countries (Paul, 2006). Foreign Aid should help to overcome this bottleneck. Otherwise, some argue, aid can displace national savings. (Addison, et al., 2017) This can be interpreted as a narrow perspective because saving and investment are the tools for economic development, not the end (Quibria, 2014).

Beyond these growth models there are studies, especially in the field of new institutional economics, which ask why aid still does not work. Three points, in particular, are considered here. First are non-economic incentives for the recipient, secondly incentives in donor organizations to give aid strategically and not productivity, and finally misuse by recipients (Drazen, 2000). The first and third aspects have been highlighted by literature on the domestic political process (Paul, 2006). Famous models in this tradition are (Becker, 1983) and (Boone, 1996). Boon highlights the importance of the political regime for aid effectiveness. This model can be seen in the tradition of Bauer and Friedman, both vehement critics of foreign Aid. They argue that only elites will benefit from Aid (Boone, 1996). The main thrust of the argument can be described as donor-financing changes the incentive of the recipient government (Drazen, 2000).

That can also be modulated via rent-seeking competition (Paul, 2006). Aid increases the prize and sets pervert incentives (p.4). Boon's work inspired a whole series of empirical papers whose results, however, are mixed. The literature that addresses the second point in more detail comes from (Burnside & Dollar, 2000), (Alesina & Dollar, 2000), and (Lundborg, 1998). This occurs when aid is used to initiate policy reforms that strengthen property rights, for example. These policies are not harmful. However, as described in the previous chapter, the evidence that aid leads to lasting political change appears to be rather weak. And even if it helps, there remains a certain paternalism. But that can't be discussed here.

To better understand the donor-recipient relationship, some economists use the principal-agent theorem (Paul, 2006). The principal-agent theory examines economic relationships in which a principal tells an agent to do something. Classically, three problems are discussed, namely, hidden information, hidden action, and moral hazard. The starting point for such research programs is Azam & Laffront, 2003, who create an international public good "consumption of the poor in the South" (Paul, 2006). The Government of the North (donor) is fully altruistic and averse to poverty, which only occurs in the South. The South governments are rich people and they have different preferences for poor people. (Azam & Laffront, 2003) In such a setting the optimal aid contract must take account of the strategic behaviour of the south government (Paul, 2006). Unconditional Aid doesn't work here (Azam & Laffront, 2003). Subsequently, some authors have set out to improve this simple model. For more, see (Paul, 2006).

Then there are papers that ask about the financing modalities. Here the donors can finance the budget directly or finance projects (Paul, 2006). Cordella & Dell' Ariccia found that "while project aid is preferable when recipients have little own resources and developmental preferences far apart from those of the donor, budget support is preferable when recipients have relatively large own resources and preferences relatively close to those of the donor". (Cordella & Dell'Ariccia, 2007, p. 1273). As long as growth is the goal, Cordella and Ulku argue that grants are always better than loans when governments are burdened by high debt and bad policies (Paul, 2006). Which of course reduces the incentive to reform the institutions. To some extent this also contradicts the other results. Another study found that misaligned interests and informational asymmetries influence the shares of aid given as budget and project aid (Dreher, et al., 2016). They conclude "when recipients' local knowledge is more important than the donors' information, their discretion in the choice of reforms (delegation) should be increased. Conversely, there should be less freedom in designing reforms (centralization) when the donors' information is more relevant" (p.21).

5. Conclusion

Research on a possible Foreign Aid Basic Income in developing countries has, in my opinion, the task of closely examining and analysing both the expenditure and the revenue side. In this paper, I have taken a rough look at the Foreign Aid phenomenon. For future work, two different institutional levels play a special role 1) the political system in the target "developing country" and 2) the system of international foreign aid. Future work needs to look more closely at how "Foreign Aid Basic Income" fits into the OECD framework and where it differs drastically. In a second step, we need to look at how both levels can best be linked with each other when it comes to basic income.

The next steps are to check OECD data for trade-offs between social protection and other expenditures. The principal-agent literature can help make the aid-disbursement mechanisms smart and corruption poor. For this purpose, the models must be examined in more detail.

References

Addison, T., Morrissey, O. & Tarp, F., 2017. The Macroeconomic of Aid: Overview. The Journal of Devlopment Studies, 53(7), pp. 987-997.

Ahmad, Y. et al., 2020. Six decades of ODA: insights and outlook in the COVID-19 crisis. Development Co-operation Profiles.

Alacevich, M. & Boianovsky, M., 2018. Writing the History of Development Economics. History of Polticial Economy, pp. 1-14.

Alesina, A. & Dollar, D., 2000. Who gives Foreign Aid to Whom and Why? Journal of Economic Growth, Band 5, pp. 33-63.

Ali, M. & Zeb, A., 2016. Foreign Aid: Origin, Evolution and its Effectivness in Poverty alleviation. The Dialogue, XI(I).

Asatullaeva, Z., Aghdam, R. F. Z., Ahmad, N. & Tashpulatova, L., 2021. papers, The impact of foreign aid on economic development: A systematic literature review and content analysis of the top 50 most influential. Int. Dev., Issue 33, p. 717– 751.

Askarov, Z. & Doucouliagos, H., 2015. Development Aid and Grwoth in Transition Countries. World Development, Band 66, pp. 383-399.

Azam, J.-P. & Laffront, J.-J., 2003. Contracting for Aid. Journal of Development Economics, Band 70, pp. 25-58.

Banerjee, A., Niehaus, P. & Suri, T., 2019. Universal Basic Income in the Developing World. Annual Review of Economics, pp. 959-983.

Barro, R. J., 1990. Government spending in a simple model of endogenous growth. Journal of Political Economy, 98(S5), pp. 103-125.

Becker, G. S., 1983. A Theory of Competition Among Pressure Groups for Political Influence. The Quarterly Journal of Economics, pp. 371-400.

Boone, P., 1996. Politics and the effectiveness of foreign aid. European Economic Review, Band Issue 2, pp. 289-329.

Bourguignon, F. & Sundberg, M., 2007. Aid Effectiveness-Opening the Black Box. The American Economic Review, 97(2), pp. 316-321.

Bräutigam, D., 2011. Aid "with Chinese Characteristics: Chinese foreign Aid and Development Finance meet the OECD-DAC AID regime. Journal of International Development, Band 23, pp. 752-764.

Brückner, M., 2011. On the simultaneity problem in the aid and grwoth debate. Journal of Applied Econometrics, Issue 28, pp. 126-150.

Burnside, C. & Dollar, D., 2000. Aid, Policies, and Growth. The American Economic Review, 90(4), pp. 847-868.

Cohen, R., 2007. 'The Great Tradition: The Spread of Diplomacy in the Ancient World'. Diplomacy & Statecraft, 12(1), pp. 23-38.

Collier, P. & Dollar, D., 2002. Aid allcoation and poverty reduction. European Economic Review, pp. 1475-1500.

Cordella, T. & Dell'Ariccia, G., 2007. Budget Support Versus Project Aid: A Theoretical Appraisal. The Economic Journal, 117(523), p. 1260–1279.

Drazen, A., 2000. Political Economy in Macroeconomics. Princeton, New Jersey: Princeton University Press.

Dreher, A., Langlotz, S. & Marchesi, S., 2016. Information Transmission and Ownership Consolidation in Aid Programs. CEPR Discussion Paper, pp. 1-45.

Easterly, W., 2006. The White Man's Burden: Why the West's Efforts to Aid the Rest Have Done So Much Ill and So Little Good. s.l.:Pinguin.

Edwards, S., 2014. Economic Development and the effectiveness of Foreign Aid: A historical perspective. NBER working Paper 20685, pp. 1-47.

Fues, T., 2014. Nicht erwiederte Liebe: Was bleibt vom ersten Global-Partnership-Treffen? Die aktuelle Kolumne.

Führer, H., 1996. The Story of Official Development assistance, Paris: https://www.oecd.org/dac/1896816.pdf.

Galiani, S., Knack, S., Xu, C. L. & Zou, B., 2017. The effect of aid in growth: evidence from a Quasi-experiment. Journal of Economic Growth, Band 22, pp. 1-33.

Gentilini, U., Almenfi, M., Orton, I. & Dale, P., 2021. Social Protection and Jobs Response to Covid.19: A Real-time Review of Country Measures. World Bank, Washington, DC. © World Bank.

Haarmann, C. & Haarmann, D., 2005. The Basic Income Grant in Namibia Resource Book, Windhoek: Desk for Social Development of the Evangelical Lutheran Church.

Hackenesch, C. & Grimm, S., 2011. Busan und die "Neuen Aktuere": Der steinige weg zu einem gemeinsamen Verständnis von wirksamer Entwicklungspolitik. Die neueste Kolumne.

Harvey, P., Holmes, R., Rachel, S. & Martin, E., 2007. Social Protection in Fragile States, s.l.: Overseas Developmen Institute.

Hynes, W. & Scott, S., 2013. The Evolution of Official Development Assistance: Achievements, Criticisms and a Way Forward. OECD Development Co-operation WorkingPapers, No. 12.

Klingbeil, S. & Leiderer, S., 2011. Aid effectiveness der zwei Geschwindigkeiten. Die aktuelle Kolumne.

Klingebiel, S., 2011. Der Gipfel von Busan: Neue Ansätze der Entwicklungshilfe. Die aktuelle Kolumne.

Lundborg, P., 1998. Exchange, Foreign Aid and International Support as a Gift. Economics and Politics, 10(2), pp. 127-142.

Markovits, D., Strange, A. & Tingley, D., 2019. Foreign Aid and the Status Quo: Evidence from Pre-Marshall Plan Aid. The Chinese Journal of International Politics, 12(4), p. 585–613.

McCord, A., Cherrier, C., Both, N. & Bastagli, F., 2021. Official development assistance financing for social protection lessons from the Covid-19 response. ODI Working Paper.

Morgenthau, H., 1962. A Political Theory of Foreign Aid. The American Political Science Review, 56(2), pp. 301-309.

Moyo, D., 2010. Dead Aid: Why Aid Is Not Working and How There Is a Better Way for Africa. s.l.:Penguin.

Obrovsky, M. & Riegler, H., 2019. Die quantitative Seite der Entwicklungszusammenarbeit: politisches Wunschkonzert oder solide statistische Messung? Policy Note, Issue 31/2019.

OECD, 2015. Development Co-operation by Countries Beyond the DAC, s.l.: OECD Development Co-operation Directorate.

OECD, 2022. Net ODA (indicator).

OECD, 2022. Official development assistance – definition and coverage. [Online]
Available at: https://www.oecd.org/dac/financing-sustainable-development/development-finance-standards/officialdevelopmentassistancedefinitionandcoverage.htm

Ortiz, I. et al., 2019. Fiscal Space for Social Protection. A Handbook for Assessing Financing Options. ILO: s.n.

Paul, E., 2006. A Survey of the Theoretical Economic Literature on Foreign Aid. Asian-Pacific Economc Literature, pp. 1-16.

Quibria, M., 2014. Aid effectiveness: research, policy and unresovled issues. Development Studies Research, 1(1), pp. 76-87.

Rajan, G. R. & Subramanian, A., 2008. Aid and Grwoth: What does the cross-country evidence really show ? Review of Economics and Statistics, Band 4, pp. 643-665.

Scott, S., 2015. The accidental birth of "official development assistance". OECD Development Co-operation Working Papers.

Therien, J.-P., 2002. Debating foreign aid: right versus left. Third World Quarterly, 23(3), p. 449–466.

VENRO, 2021. VENRO Report: OECD DAC peer, Berlin: VENRO.

Wilcks, J., Pelechà Aigües, N. & Bosch, E., 2020. Development co-operation funding: Highlights from the complete and final 2019 ODA statistics. Development Co-operation Profiles.

Zimmermann, F. & Smith, K., 2011. New partnerships in development co-operation. OECD Journal: General Papers, Issue 2010/1.

III

Basic Income:
Multidisciplinary perspectives

Das Bedingungslose Grundeinkommen aus multidisziplinären Perspektiven

Leon Hartmann

Universal Basic Income as a Discursive Formation of the Future

Sketch of a Discourse Analysis

This paper attempts to present some possible approaches to an analysis of the current discourse on unconditional basic income (UBI). The starting point is the fundamental observation that the UBI, as an unrealised concept, can discursively only be negotiated within a futuristic temporal structure. The study draws on post-structuralist discourse-analytical and semiological methods of Michel Foucault, Roland Barthes and Gilles Deleuze. An attempt is made to describe regularities and central signs within contemporary discursive practices, which make it possible to work out different 'families of statements' that make up the discursive formation.

1. Introduction

When reflecting on the title of this paper, one might ask: What are 'discourses of the future' and why should the universal or unconditional basic income (in short UBI) constitute such a discourse? A pre-emptive answer to this question can be given by noting that the UBI – apart from some currently running pilot projects – has not been realised in Germany. The public statements that make up the UBI discourse are essentially future-oriented. There is much discussion about the UBI, but little about what distinguishes this discourse in its specific characteristics. This paper aims to give an insight into possible ways of describing the genuine structures of this discourse on the future of our society. This orientation towards the future in its relation to the present defines this discourse and sets it apart from others. Statements come together from all political camps in this discursive formation, yet the most diverse statements find their common ground in this relation to time. But the questions arise – which the French philosopher Michel Foucault also posed in Archaeology of Knowledge (1969):

How can these plural collections of the most diverse statements be grouped into one field and analysed without systemizing them towards coherence and uniformity? How can an analysis do justice to the ruptures, discontinuities, and complexities within a discourse? Following the theoretical lead of Michel Foucault, Roland Barthes and Gilles Deleuze, I would like to give a brief overview of my analysis of the UBI discourse. I will mainly refer to the German-speaking debate, which nevertheless contains many of the widespread discursive practices. To conduct an investigation that is as unbiased as possible, it seems reasonable to follow Foucault in his basic methodological stance: not to assume an external meaning, purpose or origin of a discourse – like Habermas's 'communicative rationality' (see Habermas, 1979), for example –, but to describe a discourse on the basis of its inherent practices. According to Foucault, it is only within these practices that the regularities of a discourse are constituted. To determine these regularities while doing justice to the heterogeneity of the statements, two attempts to investigate this subject will be combined. Firstly, the question which rules can be used to describe these different statements as part of one discourse will be answered. Secondly, by examining the boundaries between certain discursive groups or 'families' of statements, an attempt will be made to describe the ruptures in the discourse. Within the heterogeneous collection of diverse statements in the overall discourse, these 'families' allow for the categorisation of certain statements by similarities and common rules of discursive practice. I will limit myself to a few selected statements and conduct my analysis in three steps. First, I present the method of my investigation, starting from Foucault. Then I describe the relationship between future and present which defines the UBI discourse. Finally, I describe two groups of statements within the overall discourse that can be distinguished by their precise temporal arrangement of present and future.

2. The Archaeological Rules of a Discourse

Foucault asks the question: What is a discourse? But he does this not by determining a guiding principle, but by granting each discourse – each "discursive formation", as he calls it – its own fundamental rules to be investigated:

"We shall call discourse a group of statements in so far as they belong to the same discursive formation; [...] it is made up of a limited number of statements for which a group of conditions of existence can be defined." (Foucault, 1989, 131)

A discourse gets its unity from the fact that the most diverse statements constitute themselves according to the same basic rules and distribute themselves within the discursive formation, thus forming common discursive practices. In his 1970 text on Foucault, Deleuze also describes these rules as a common "distribution curve" (Deleuze, 1988, 4) on which the individual statements are arranged despite their heterogeneous distribution and stand in a relationship to one another. Foucault calls his method to describe these rules "archaeology" and writes:

"Archaeology tries to define not the thoughts, representations, images, themes, preoccupations that are concealed or revealed in discourses; but those discourses themselves, those discourses as practices obeying certain rules." (Foucault, 1989, 155)

Archaeology is directed at the discourse itself, and thereby at the immanent relations and rules constituted by it. This question of what these archaeological rules of the UBI discourse are brings me to the second step of my analysis.

3. Future and Present in the UBI Discourse

The archaeological future is on everyone's lips. Even the introductory question posed by the former Prime Minister of Thuringia and CDU politician, Dieter Althaus, in his 2007 article points to this archaeological level: "We politicians like to raise the hope that everything will be all right, and that everything can basically stay as it is. Is that really true?" (Althaus, 2017, 16; translation LH) Doubt about the persistence of the status quo and the consequent anticipation of future 'challenges' becomes a condition for social change towards a successful future: "It is also not enough to just point out the challenges without offering a concrete solution. With my proposal of a Solidary Citizen's Income [in German: "Solidarisches Bürgergeld"], I have a concept that provides answers." (Ibid.) The "Solidary Citizen's Income", which Althaus describes as "an unconditional basic income" (ibid.), is presented as an answer to the approaching future. This shows that the archaeological regularity of the orientation towards the future is often accompanied by an interpretation of the present that defines it primarily in terms of its rapid change. Although coming from an opposed political camp, Gregor Gysi, the former parliamentary group leader of the Left Party, speaks in his contribution from 2017 – on an archaeological level – similarly about the UBI. He also addresses the UBI as something futuristic, however, in a critical-ironic utopian rhetoric: "What a grandiose utopia! Everyone would be entitled to a basic, unconditional income" (Gysi, 2017, 49; translation LH). Even though on the surface of discursive practices the statements are in a hegemonic struggle, they follow the same implicit rules: a certain relation between UBI and future. This utopian or dystopian rhetoric which determines large parts of the discourse also reveals the archaeological level. By examining the different ways by which statements deal with the UBI-future, it is possible to identify the basic archaeological rules that disperse individual statements within the discourse.

However, within this multiplicity of statements, "group[s] of statements" (Foucault, 1989, 131) or, as Deleuze calls them, "famil[ies] of statements" (Deleuze, 1988, 6) can still be identified, which makes it possible to describe ruptures within the discourse. All statements establish a certain relationship between the present and the future and thus follow the archaeological rules which determine the entire discourse. Still different 'families of statements' can be described in terms of the precise way the present and the future are related. Based on the fundamental rules, these families again establish their own additional rules according to which the individual statements are grouped by their argumentative methods.

4. Families of Statements in the UBI Discourse

This distinction occurs primarily through the fact that certain statements judge certain objects differently and position them differently in the temporal order. Considering the semiological theory of Roland Barthes, it can also be said that they form different signs, which then form statements. As Barthes writes in

Mythologies from 1957, meaning is only created through the interplay of "signifier" and "signified" in a "sign": "[T]here are, therefore, the signifier, the signified and the sign, which is the associative total of the first two terms", whereby the signified is that which the signifier "signif[ies]", to get "meaning" (Barthes, 1991, 111 f.). Finally, a "signified can have several signifiers" (ibid., 118). Thus, an object can be named by several expressions, or several signifiers can signify a signified or be combined with the same signified to form a sign. While, for example, the signifier – the term 'justice' – remains the same in the individual statements and families of statements, it all depends on what meaning it receives through the composition with the signified. It is precisely this meaning that differs and thus forms a way of distinguishing families of statements from one another. A particularly central sign in the UBI discourse is that of 'justice'.

The first family includes statements that classify 'justice' as not given in the present but as attainable with a UBI-future. Thus, the rule of this family of statements is that the future is a derivation from the interpretation of a deficient present. This classification then guides the naming, in other words, which signifiers are linked to the signified 'justice'.

Many examples can be listed that, even though differing, could nevertheless be classified in the same family. For example, the contributions by Adrienne Goehler, former president of the Hamburg University of Fine Arts and Senator for Science, Research and Culture of the State of Berlin, Jakob Augstein, editor-in-chief of the left-leaning newspaper Der Freitag, Daniel Binswanger, editor at the Swiss Tages-Anzeiger, and Götz W. Werner, founder and supervisory board member of the drugstore chain dm (see Goehler, 2017, 42–48; Augstein, 2017, 20–22; Werner, 2017, 210–219). But even Althaus's vision of the future, drafted in 2007 – the "Solidary Citizen's Income" – draws its basis from the problematisation of the present welfare state: "Child poverty, old-age poverty, earned income that no longer provides a livelihood, and the development towards a two-class medical system strengthen mistrust in the existence of the social security systems." (Althaus, 2017, 16) Althaus then expands his interpretation of reality to include the problems of the democratic system: "And what is even worse, the acceptance of the free democratic basic order suffers as a result." (Ibid.) This interpretation of the present crisis marks a social change that needs to be addressed and that is 'answered' by the future model of the Solidary Citizen's Income, which, would – as an UBI – provide basic existential security. Althaus uses the phenomena of poverty to make a diagnosis of social injustice and the crisis of the basic social order. The implicit sign of social injustice, also represented by the phrase "two-class medicine", is constituted with the signifiers "child poverty, old-age poverty" and a "gainful employment income" that does not provide a livelihood (ibid.). These signifiers are now linked to a sign by connecting them to the signified of social injustice. According to Barthes' conception, these signifiers are supposed to 'mean' 'social injustice'. The very name of the UBI model as 'Solidary Citizen's Income', points to the fact that it is introduced as a counter-model to the diagnosis of social injustice, which is evaluated as social unsolidarity. Thus, the UBI simultaneously becomes a signifier for future justice.

The second family of statements includes statements that regard 'justice' as already given in the present and threatened by a future with UBI. The rule of this family of statements is that the positively evaluated present is a derivative of a dystopian interpretation of the future. This family of statements includes, for example, contributions by Norbert Blüm, former Federal Minister of Labour and Social Affairs, Heinrich Alt, former member of the board of the Federal Employment Agency, Rainer Hank, economic journalist at the Frankfurter Allgemeine Sonntagszeitung and Katja Gentinetta, former deputy director of the think tank Avenir Suisse and a political philosopher and consultant (see Blüm, 2017, 26–32; Alt, 2017, 11–15; Hank, 2017, 53–55; Gentinetta, 2017, 38–41). As an example, I would like to use Gregor Gysi's statement again, in which he connects the signifier UBI with the signified of an 'egalitarianism' that would undermine the necessary needs test for welfare state payments:

"The unconditional basic income is not only antisocial because it is paid to all citizens, whether they are rich or poor, but it is also antisocial because it would extend to welfare recipients in an egalitarian way. Statutory pensioners, the unemployed, recipients of sickness benefits – they would all receive the same basic income according to the watering can principle [Gießkannenprinzip]. The basic income would not be fair because it does not promote those who actually need it but treats everyone equally." (Gysi 2017, p. 50 f.)

The UBI 'means' 'egalitarianism' and thus, also, a lack of 'justice', which in Gysi's case is also expressed by the adjective "antisocial" ["unsozial"]. The UBI is seen as a deficient future in which utopia degenerates into dystopia, as is clear in Gysi's statement when he ironically begins his article with the exclamation already quoted above: "What a grandiose utopia! Everyone would be entitled to an unconditional basic income". Immediately afterwards he doubts the possibility of realising the UBI and predicts the future abolition of social benefits in connection with the UBI: "There would be no more state pension, no more unemployment benefit, no more sickness benefit – and thus no more necessary differentiations." (Gysi 2017, 49 f.) The interpretation of the present is thus determined by its incompatibility with a future UBI. The UBI thus becomes a signifier for the signified "injustice" in exact contrast to the first family of statements.

5. Conclusion

The UBI discourse structures its discursive practices primarily through the temporal order of present and future. Each of the statements that has a voice in this discourse must operate within this temporal order. As an archaeological rule, the temporal order guides the dispersion structure of all statements. But ruptures can also be observed within this order, which can be examined by describing different families of statements. These follow their own rules, which, nevertheless, are only variants of the rules that determine the entire discourse. Two families of statements can be distinguished: while the first equates the present with unjust social conditions and sees the solution for these conditions in an UBI, the second family of statements points in the opposite direction: the future with an UBI would destroy precisely the just conditions that already exist in the present. The heterogeneity of these statements and their interpretation of the present and the future reveals that the discourse is determined less by objective truths and realities than by very diverse interpretations, all of which claim to be truthful to reality.

References

Alt, H. (2017): Gegen die Menschenwürde. In: Kovce, P. (Ed.): Soziale Zukunft. Das bedingungslose Grundeinkommen. Die Debatte. Stuttgart: Verlag Freies Geistesleben, 11–15.

Althaus, D. (2017): Mut zur Revolution. In: Kovce, P. (Ed.): Soziale Zukunft. Das bedingungslose Grundeinkommen. Die Debatte. Stuttgart: Verlag Freies Geistesleben, 16–19.

Augstein, J. (2017): Fairness ist Zufall. In: Kovce, P. (Ed.): Soziale Zukunft. Das bedingungslose Grundeinkommen. Die Debatte. Stuttgart: Verlag Freies Geistesleben, 20–22.

Barthes, R. (1991): Mythologies. Translated by Annette Lavers, New York: Farrar, Straus & Giroux.

Blüm, N. (2017): Wahnsinn mit Methode. In: Kovce, P. (Ed.): Soziale Zukunft. Das bedingungslose Grundeinkommen. Die Debatte. Stuttgart: Verlag Freies Geistesleben, 26–32.

Deleuze, G. (1988): Foucault. Translated and edited by Sean Hand, Minneapolis / London.

Foucault, M. (1989): Archaeology of Knowledge. Translated by A. M. Sheridan Smith, London/New York: Routledge.

Gentinetta, K. (2017): Freiheit für alle – Verantwortung für alle anderen. In: Kovce, P. (Ed.): Soziale Zukunft. Das bedingungslose Grundeinkommen. Die Debatte. Stuttgart: Verlag Freies Geistesleben, 38–41.

Goehler, A. (2017): Freiheit, Gleichheit, Grundeinkommen! In: Kovce, P. (Ed.): Soziale Zukunft. Das bedingungslose Grundeinkommen. Die Debatte. Stuttgart: Verlag Freies Geistesleben, 42–48.

Gysi, G. (2017): Weder gleich noch gerecht. In: Kovce, P. (Ed.): Soziale Zukunft. Das bedingungslose Grundeinkommen. Die Debatte. Stuttgart: Verlag Freies Geistesleben, 49–52.

Habermas, J.: Communication and the Evolution of Society. Translated and with an Introduction by Thomas McCarthy. Boston: Beacon Press.

Hank, R. (2017): Elend der Fülle. In: Kovce, P. (Ed.): Soziale Zukunft. Das bedingungslose Grundeinkommen. Die Debatte. Stuttgart: Verlag Freies Geistesleben, Stuttgart, 53–55.

Werner, G. W. (2017): Ist der Mensch Mittel oder Zweck? In: Kovce, P. (Ed.): Soziale Zukunft. Das bedingungslose Grundeinkommen. Die Debatte. Stuttgart: Verlag Freies Geistesleben, Stuttgart, 210–219.

Michael von der Lohe

The Enterprise Basic Income

A Proposal for Integrating the Unconditional Basic Income in a Coherent Form of Money Circulation

The Basic Income Company presented in the following text is the basic company of the Social Sculpture (Joseph Beuys). In it, all people are co-operators and therefore receive an income. The enterprise idea to be worked out by all is the unconditionality. A proposal for financing the income for all co-operators is described.

The Enterprise Basic Income is announced by an NGO in Germany. It is called OMNIBUS for Direct Democracy in Germany and it is working on the introduction of nationwide referenda. Its foundation is the idea of the expanded concept of art, which was found and described by the artist Joseph Beuys, who's most famous sentance is: "Every human beeing is an artist."

The idea of the expanded concept of art tells us, that everything can be seen and done with an artistic gesture, not only in the well-known classical parts of art, like painting, sculpture, literature, theatre, music, ... but in everything we do in daily life.

What makes an artist? An artist never delegates his responsibility, he always takes it on himself. He is looking for the right measure, the right proportion, the coherent form. The artist feels the need of creating something, which he does not know how it will look like in the end. The piece of art tells him during the process how it wants to occur. The artist has to keep himself open and empty from habits during the process. If someone mingles the ego into the process, no art will arise, no coherent form emerges.

Everything can be seen and done under the gesture of art. The greatest work of art, we can realize only with every human being together, is the Social Sculpture. It is a living piece of art, which changes constantly, but nevertheless stays a piece of art at any time.

The Unconditional Basic Income is part of the Social Sculpture. It gives us the possibilty to be the artist we want to be and the opportunity to work for bringing up the Social Sculpture.

What does Corporation or Enterprise or Company Basic Income mean?

$$\Sigma \text{ credits} = \Sigma \text{ income} = \Sigma \text{ prices}$$

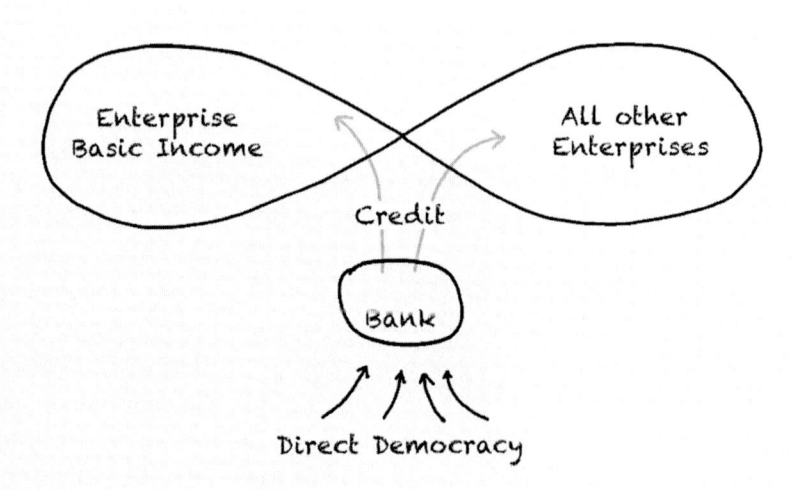

```
     Enterprise                    All other
     Basic Income                  Enterprises
                    Credit
                    Bank
              Direct Democracy
```

© OMNIBUS FÜR DIREKTE DEMOKRATIE – Kurl Wilhelmi

What is the Idea of any Company? Someone has an idea that he cannot realise alone. Therefore, he needs other people with special skills to work together. In order to be able to do this, they need an income with which they can satisfy their daily needs. After all, they cannot be self-sufficient at the same time. This is how we work worldwide in a division of labor. Properly thought, we all need our income from the beginning. At the beginning of life, at the beginning of the month. The thought of being paid for work done is absurd in the world based on the division of labor. I would already have starved to death before I had finished my work.

$$\Sigma \text{ credits} = \Sigma \text{ income} = \Sigma \text{ prices}$$

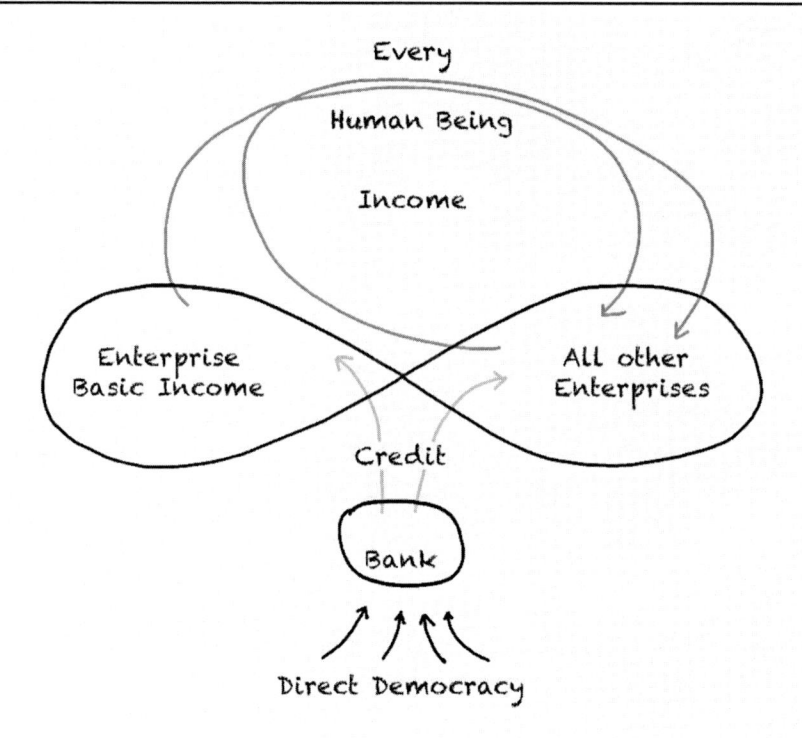

```
                          Every
                       Human Being
                         Income

          Enterprise                   All other
          Basic Income                 Enterprises

                          Credit

                          Bank

                     Direct Democracy
```

© OMNIBUS FÜR DIREKTE DEMOKRATIE – Kurt Wilhelmi

Also, the capital of a company is not the available money, but the skills of the people who work together in it.

The Enterprise Basic Income is the basic company of the Social Sculpture. Every human beeing is co-artist in this company. It allows us to work in freedom for the realisation of living together with every being in a harmonius way. The idea of the company is to realize unconditionality in cooperation.

$$\Sigma \text{ credits} = \Sigma \text{ income} = \Sigma \text{ prices}$$

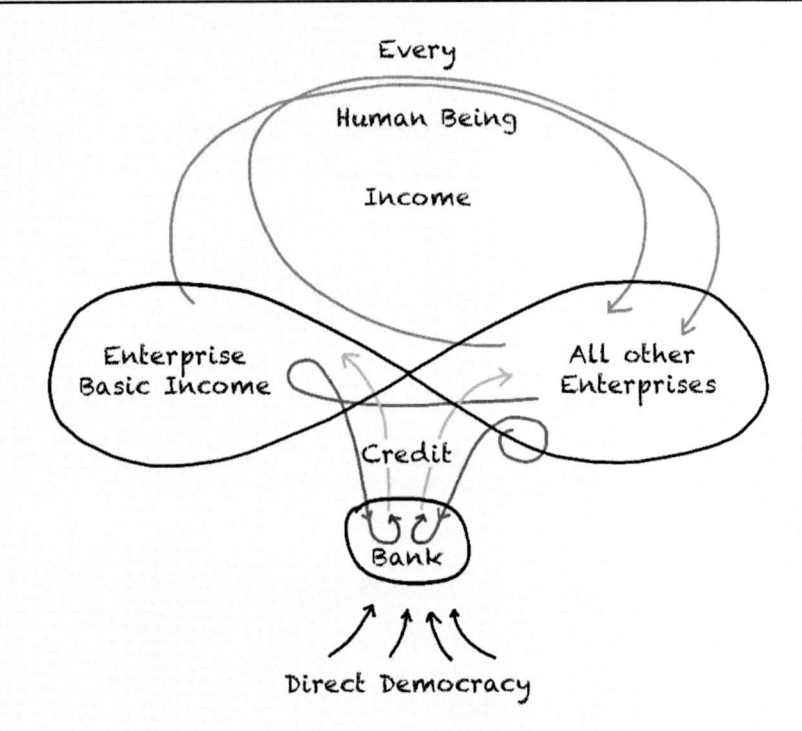

[Diagram: "Every Human Being Income" encompassing "Enterprise Basic Income" and "All other Enterprises", with "Credit" from "Bank", and "Direct Democracy" below.]

© OMNIBUS FÜR DIREKTE DEMOKRATIE – Kurt Wilhelmi

We will only get a truly unconditional basic income if we work for it. That means: Working through the daily and always new and lively unconditional interest for each other.

And: Finally, work it out through a joint decision in a referendum. We artists take the responsibilty for our lives. It is also the task of this corporation to answer the question how to be financed in a coherent way:

1. In the modern economy, based on the division of labour, companies are financed through credit – „aterial" money. The basic income corporation/ company/enterprise should receive credit for everyone. With a referendum, we create the legal basis for this: The bank is instructed to create fresh money regularly for the crediting of the basic income enterprise.

2. With this money, the company pays out basic income to all its employees - that is: every person – the amount must be large enough to enable the work for the Social Sculpture, without additional further obligations. All the credits become income and allow everyone to purchase produced goods and services to satisfy the personal needs.

3. By selling their goods and services, the companies generate money with which the loans taken out can be paid off again. In order for the basic income corporation to be able to pay off its loans regularly it is supplied with refluxing money from all other companies. Important: In this part of the process the money, flowing back to the place where it was created, changes his character. It is now „venous" money. In the Bank it changes its character again to „aterial" money. Money is circulating.

Postludium

The development of this financing is well founded in the work of Wilhelm Schmundt, who described the „archetype" of the money cycle in the sixties of the twentieth century.

„The revolution in the realm of thought will bring about an evolution of society towards the humane. If it were sufficiently brought into public consciousness and made - where this can be achieved - a part of school and university education, it would be far more far-reaching than anything that can be achieved by external reforming and curing of symptoms of the sick social organism." (Schmundt, W., Erkenntnisübungen zur Dreigliederung des Sozialen Organismus, Klappentext, Achberger Verlag,1982)

José H. Rocha

Universal Basic Income and Law: The Brewing of a Storm

This paper seeks to present the Universal Basic Income concept as a possible future legally recognized concept. While working on its definition and cross-sectorial logic, using the Socratic Method, my interest in reflecting on this "new field" was awakened.

1. Introduction

In addition to introducing some readers to a little-known term and idea not yet present in Positive Law, my intention here is to introduce a set of questions that, for those who believe that "by failing to prepare, we are preparing to fail" (1), are necessary for a way that legal science might have to implement legislative solutions and do so effectively.

The institution of a legal figure is usually preceded by being instituted in legislation in other legal systems, thus having inputs from comparative law. The Universal Basic Income, or Unconditional Basic Income, or just Basic Income, is a concept that was not designed in Portugal, nor in the Portuguese-speaking (Lusophony), nor in the context of the European Union. For want of a better explanation, it is an Anglo-Saxon design by Thomas Paine, proposed primarily as a response to the agricultural and industrial revolution (King and Marangos, 2006). However, the lack of an application, tout court, means that most of the studies and investigations into the topic have been in the fields of philosophy, political science, economics, sociology and psychology.

The above does not mean that there have been no considerations of legal relevance in this field (2); there are some studies that may have argumentative utility and scientific value that is vital for a rigorous and complete conception. Nor does this mean that Law, as a science whose function is the study of the normative-principological structures that bind society, cannot (and should not) receive knowledge obtained from the scientific methods that have been indicated, particularly Political Philosophy, to determine the framework and thinking of Economics to contemplate the lines of sustainability necessary for the management of any scarce good (or rather, any good subject to scarcity), of Sociology and Psychology, in particular in their connection to social and other policies, such as criminology, to support criminal policy.

Nowadays there are more than a handful of idealists, intellectuals and researchers who propose, in various forms and formulas, a Basic Income as a solution to problems such as extreme poverty, hunger, lack of housing, failures or loopholes in social security, the problem of automation and robotization in the productive sectors, the distribution and redistribution of wealth between social classes, gender, race, age, careers. Others focus on psychological problems such as the study of the "psychology of scarcity", clinic depression, nutrition and food problems, the problems of marginalized societies, including those with criminal tendencies, or simply trying to solve the dimension of the State machine to "deal with" previous problems and their dimension and stagnating bureaucracies of quick and efficient responses (Management Science), which can mean a growing political will for practical implementation of that kind of legal solution of sufficient response since its lack implies not only the failure to achieve the noble objectives announced but also the violation of the structural principles of Law, Justice and Legal Security.

Daniel Nettle asks, "Why, if Universal Basic Income seems like such a good idea, which has been cognitively available for a long time, when so many intelligent people have postulated and accepted it as desirable, is there no developed society in the face of the World where it has been fully implemented?". He then provides his own answer, "partially because democratic governments, and societies in general, are weak at implementing deep, structuring reforms, finding it simpler instead to "smooth out" and "tune out" the system. Only political outsiders would dare to propose structural change – they have less to lose" (Nettle, 2018, p.167).

To quote Elon Musk, one of the foremost visionaries and successful entrepreneurs in the first two decades of the 21st century, in an interview: "There is a good chance that we will end up with a Universal Basic scheme, or similar solution, due to automation (…) Yes, I'm not sure what else we could do. I think that would be the case (implying a tone of inevitability)" (3), which, though not an argument from authority, will at least give a glimpse that the study of this issue may take time but will, "inevitably", be useful and necessary.

The time has come to begin, hopefully, to design not only the legal framework, namely the legal-constitutional one, of the law figure, but also to begin to problematize, highlight and prioritize issues that involve the positivization and execution, at all levels, of a Basic Income.

We will start, succinctly by defining Basic Income, saying where it has repercussions in the legal fields and why we consider it a transversal issue. All this for the sole purpose of projecting our concerns onto the reader – now made aware of the risk – to ask several questions that we have grouped together as best we can.

2. Defining Basic Income

Entering into what is the substance of the topic at hand reflects the need to give mass and significance to the concept of a Basic Income. As we do not, for now, intend to filter, a lot of what should be thought when listening to or reading about UBI, we will serve as curators of various forms of definition, not to be confused with various UBI formula that can be implemented.

We start at the "Ocidental Praia Lusitana", by considering the notion adopted by the definition of the Associação pelo Rendimento Básico Incondicional Portugal, which reads: the "Basic Unconditional Income is a benefit attributed to each citizen, regardless of their financial, family or professional situation, and sufficient to allow a life with dignity" (4). This implies that the benefit is in cash not kind, and that it is dense enough to instruct the idea of Universal Basic Income (for this entity Unconditional Basic Income, praeter opus option), and linked, by definition, to the idea of dignity, in the sense of human dignity.

In addition, we have another associative form, this one with a German base and a community impetus (the European Union), the UBI4ALL Association, for whom in "general the UBI European network agrees that the Unconditional Basic Income is defined by four aspects: sufficient to live on and to participate in cultural and social life; individual; seen as a human right and without conditions and free of obligations" (5). In this definition we note the legal classification as a human right in the prevailing nomenclature in Portugal, as a fundamental right or legal position (to include the version of liberty or guarantee), which involves a vision that "promotes" or sees importance in the legal form that a Universal Basic Income will be implemented in. Legal language also dominates the expressions "without conditions" and "free of obligations" but leaves us with some "antibodies" because they correspond to expressions that will be, in our understanding, incompatible with what is really intended, as the possibility of a definition, as given, might be unattainable because of the consequences of such inaccuracies, which is definitely not the intention.

A third aspect in the literature that is undoubtedly a good starting point for a well-founded understanding of Universal Basic Income comes from our translation of Gentilini, Grosh, Rigolini and Yemtsov. "In principle, social assistance systems can be traced back to three characteristics or dimensions: the type of transfer they operate in; what conditions they involve and if and how they are targeted. (…) A Universal Basic Income (…) is the combination of three choices, i.e., a transfer provided universally, and unconditionally and in cash. Within this framework the Universal Basic Income proposals may still differ in a range of important parameters such as the size and frequency of the transfer, age of eligibility and whether citizens or residents are covered.

Outlining the three general design parameters gives us a framework to gauge whether present and past experiences can be classified as a Universal Basic Income program. (…) We propose the definition of the Universal Basic Income based on these central design choices, i.e., an income that is paid to everyone, unconditionally and in cash – with other important characteristics being debatable, such as frequency (e.g. monthly or yearly) and whether children and non-citizens should have access" (Gentilini, 2020, p.20 ff.).

A fourth contribution to our conceptual search is Daniel Nettle's definition, in which a "Universal Basic Income (UBI) is a regular financial payment made to all eligible adults, regardless of whether they work or not, regardless of their means (or wealth), and without any other condition. Receiving it is a fundamental right or entitlement that is inherent to being a member of (or belonging to) a social structure. People can be assured that it will arrive, at present and in the future. It may not be a fortune, but ideally it should be enough so that no one ever has to be cold or go hungry (Nettle, 2018). Going back to the idea of fundamental rights and offering here two strong examples of "surmountable" issues that serve as a "quantifier" of the Universal Basic Income, that is, that serve to prevent someone from ever being cold and hungry and therefore must be sufficient in its value so that, receiving it, no one will ever have to be cold or hungry again.

The hypothesis of a Universal Basic Income as a solution may be problematic in several areas, meanwhile providing definitions and results of interest for the further understanding of this idea. For example, in a small Scottish study that seeks to link mental health to Universal Basic Income, a UBI is given as "a regular cash payment that everyone receives without regard to their circumstances. It is a proposal for a political measure considered around the world, with an interest reinforced by the Covid-19 crisis, where it was considered as an emergency and recovery measure. If the amount is sufficient and implemented universally and worldwide, the Universal Basic Income has the capacity to totally eliminate (extreme) poverty" (Smith, et al., 2021). Interestingly this definition shows UBI as an emergency measure, understood both as a response to a difficult situation whose attribution is preventive of unpredictable situations and as a recovery measure with the aim of strengthening the "social fabric" and allowing development and growth to compensate for the pandemic crisis situation.

Another area where Universal Basic Income is relevant is the climate issue, perhaps due to the order of magnitude inherent in the need for a paradigm shifter inherent to the response that the climate issue involves. In an extremely pragmatic way, Hein Marais defines as a set of principles (an expression used in a loose way), a Universal Basic Income grant as "something that is paid as a universal basic financial grant (i.e. to each an identical amount; it is something paid to individuals and not to households and it is unconditional, so the recipient can use it however he or she sees fit. It is something that is not targeted, nor does it involve proof of necessity (means-tested). Ideally, the amount is sufficient to cover basic needs and allow the individual to participate actively in society" (Marais, 2018).

Finally, in the academic development of nature conservation and the climate issue in relation to Universal Basic Income, the authors Mumbunan, Maitri, Tazkiana, Prajoso, Sihite and Nabella, using the BIEN (Basic Income on the

Earth Network), describe UBI as a "periodic cash payment distributed unconditionally to all individuals, without needing to and without having to work to gain access (…). The aforementioned characteristics help to clarify what a Basic Income is. However, in practice some of these features can, or should, be adjusted to reflect the context. This is true for the Basic Income for Nature and Climate conservation in Tanah Papua, the focus of our report. Thus we will focus on the distinctive features of a Basic Income which in context relate to (i) universality (ii) what is a "basic" (sufficient) income in a Basic Income (iii) regularity of payment, and (iv) unconditionality (Mumbunan, et al., 2021).

Our view of Universal Basic Income, as outlined in the various forms presented by us, will then be examined in terms of various ramifications of the Law.

3. The Transversal Question of Transversality

Equipped with one, or several, sometimes unscrutinized, definitions of Universal Basic Income, we can focus on the question of transversality, which is linked to whichever we are dealing with, be it a right, freedom or guarantee (that is, status positivus, status negativus or status processualis) that creates, economically, a position that affects transversally how the individual intervenes in society and how politically organized society is structured in the face of this new reality, as has not happened since the creation of the welfare state with the Bismarck and Beveridge systems, the way in which the State intervenes as a social regulator changes (Queiroz, 2006). Very much in line with what has been the progress of the so-called regulatory state, a system that contains a Basic Income would have to change some intervention paradigms, primarily administrative ones, becoming potentially less involved in each case but instead taking on the role of a supervisor who interconnects information, unofficially, in order to provide the necessary conditions for the development of citizens in society.

Of course, even in this somewhat utopian vision, there is still much to be legally regulated and socially addressed. A large number of important policy options are involved and these have very relevant implications for the "ultimate" design of the Basic Income. But if they are worthy of the name Universal or Unconditional Basic Income, they must all have a paradigm shifter in social functioning. The question of money is a transversal question by nature, not going into matters of other scientific orders, if money serves as a basis of exchange and if there is a need to attribute value to what is scarce, money serves to mediate need and utility of goods with scarcity. However, to manage, from the Latin ad mannus trahere (Caupers, 2013), means to bring into the hands, in the sense of "taking the reins". This means that the public administration brings to its hands what concerns the community, the res publica, and therefore, more than at any other time in history, it also manages scarcity to some extent, crossing its logic of acting where there is a notorious urgency, even more so in a democratic state of law that has social state obligations, with the lasting connotations that are associated with these terminologies.

Thus transversality is evident and necessary in many areas of Law to make adjustments and review coercive institutes and formulations (because of the Law, or Moral needs, and because of establishing Coercivity and/or Effectiveness). At the same time, the question is transversal in various areas of the same type of regulation, or a better type of regulation, can be achieved in a society "endowed" with a Universal or Unconditional Basic Income.

Certainly, because of its implications (even for the staunchest "denialists" of the effects of the various scientific experiments around the globe), for its elements, for the objectives it "proposes" and for the human ambition that accompanies its proponents, one cannot escape the prediction of situations on a scale equivalent to the weighting of the social effect. This is true regardless of which "model" or version of Basic Income is in question. Especially because, if disconnected from any political ideologies, or just moved by the moral imperative that states that a basic set of principles that are enough to distinguish between a positive and a negative, and each one from a neutral, and from these apply one or several mechanisms of practical evaluation theh same answer would emerge. Even so, in a system as complex as current human society, we would have to obtain a vast set of anticipatory and preparatory predictions of behavior to be legally regulated.

4. Main Questions

It is therefore time to "purge" some of our many issues in this domain. Far from the usual comfort of investigation where a handful of problems are raised and as many answers as problems are pointed out. Here we will only ask questions, framing them, without the due certainty of the frame used in the question, only with the certainty of the doubt-framed.

Before proceeding to this exercise of questioning, we emphasize that all questions are posed in relation to their legal dimension, not that this can be dissociated from the social, economic-psychological and sociological issues of the main issue, but that the positioning has, as it has an overlapping effect on the question, of the need to amend legislation or the interpretation of legal norms in the face of this new figure that requires a transversal readjustment in the scale of what the Right to Environmental Protection deserved and deserves but, notoriously and unfortunately, never had. It should also be emphasized that many of the questions may have a relatively simple "yes" or "no" answer, but nevertheless the expression "and on what terms" is tacitly included in these cases.

Thus we begin with questions related to the place of treatment and the way in which the questions are dealt with. Should Universal Basic Income necessarily be treated by amending the Constitution of the Portuguese Republic, via Constitutional Revision, and is this constitutionally possible; should and can it be dealt with at the European Union level, for a European Universal Basic Income (6); is it a different Social Security formula, a Preventive Social Security, and therefore should it be dealt with legislatively with the Law of reinforced value in this area, Social Security Basis Law, or does it simply require an ordinary legislative change; whether we can guarantee its essential elements, especially those that are temporally permeable. If we are to create a legal definition of Basic Income and its elements, we must create a principled framework. If we have to legislate, how are we going to limit the legal framework to the correct expression of a new institution like a Universal or Unconditional Basic Income? If it enters the spirit of the system, what kind of legal concerns do we have to implement a Universal or Unconditional Basic Income that fulfills the intended intentions? How will implementing these norms enable a Basic Income to be regulated and will they be able to be regulated in terms of jurimetrics. If the Universal or Unconditional Basic Income can, in the European context and in the Portuguese legal and constitutional order, be taken both in its "right" and "left" versions, in its "liberal" and substitutive versions and in its "conservative" versions, by complementing the existing programs (7).

So, we start with questions related to its connection to justice and the legal security of the matter, questions of the idea of law, that is, whether the UBI is a right to a benefit of money or rather a guarantee of freedom and economic liberation; whether the UBI results from the very principle of human dignity. How fair is it that this Universal Basic Income is financed, particularly on intergenerational terms; how should the "cost" of a UBI be borne and by whom? When should it be assigned temporally; where does it begin; does it have an end (for example retirement)? Is it fair that it is annual, if it's annual, monthly if it's monthly, weekly if it's weekly, etc. How should it be linked to citizenship, if necessary to obtain the exercise of civic, military or other services, or if it is linked to pure nationality, naturalization and residence? If there is a possibility that its non-attribution may result in unjustified discrimination based on citizenship or nationality; if a UBI will make a difference (positive and/or negative) when accessing rights such as access to justice and the courts, to housing, health services, education, culture, sport and healthy lifestyles, in equality of opportunity and non-discrimination; freedom of conscience, religion, free expression and political freedoms, implementation of environmental policies and the conservation of nature and the environment; whether the necessary and different coverage of the stages of childhood, youth, end of life and physical and psychological disabilities will be ensured; whether to replace or change the type of natality measures; whether it will face the exponential growth and technological development; whether it will have an effect on territorial cohesion and on the excessive Portuguese demographic and economic centralization; If the State's wealth redistribution function is fully "satisfied" with the institution of a Universal or Unconditional Basic Income; at what point does income cease to be basic, or (only) sufficient, and to what extent can a ceiling be created and not just a base for the Universal or Unconditional Basic Income.

We move on to questions related to the Administration and Management of this possible public interest by Administrative Law, i.e. if the UBI will imply the distribution of income directly by the State (the central administration), or if it should be by a different administrative entity of the State and if it is enough to be an indirect administration or if, for reasons of political permeability, it has to be an independent administrative entity (autonomous administration); to know how it should be implemented, that is, what transitional issues have to be considered, the benefits replaced, workers in public functions that are no longer needed, what are the needs of new human and technical resources of the public administration involved and other transitional issues; how to ensure that services are effectively being provided to citizens, namely issues related to computer hackers and the value that the data of "any" citizen takes on; how to carry out the necessary updates or accounting of the amounts to be provided; how will this value be calculated, its indexing, budgeting; whether there will be situations in which, administratively or by court order, the provision or delivery of the provision may be suspended; whether the administration of a specific Unconditional or Universal Basic Income can be left to the management of third parties, for the permanently or temporarily disabled; the object and purposes of the public administration linked to certain benefits are changed, mainly those linked to social benefits and employment and professional training. It involves the power to create and manage individual bank accounts by the Public Administration. What are the implications for Public Administration in the control of immigration and the acquisition of citizenship?

We move on to issues related to the administration and management of this possible public interest by financial and tax law, that is: how is it financed, "logistically" or operationally; how is the Basic Income accounted for and whether it is accounted for personal income taxation purposes; whether the initial exemption, deductible expenses and the Singular People Income Tax (IRS) will be maintained. How and when can the tax execution of a specific Basic Income be admitted? If the availability implies changes in taxation, whether in rates or taxes, in order to impact or moderate uses and consumption (or other quasi-fiscal issues); whether it implies the maintenance of other property tax exemptions; the need for fiscal transparency regimes and special taxation regimes changes, such as "quick-wearing" professions; whether there is a possibility of taxing "robots" (as a new legal fiction) to finance Universal or UBI;

We move on to questions related to labor, business, union and compensation law in general, i.e: if the Universal Basic Income creates the uselessness of the specialization of Labor Law and Union Law; whether a Basic Income can and should affect the minimum wage, or the minimum hourly rate; the presumption of the existence of an employment contract for an indefinite period is changed, and the need for exhaustive causes of employment contracts with a term or resolute condition ends; the obligations and rules of rest periods, vacations, working hours, possibilities of paid absences, as well as a set of prerogatives specific to some sectors and special and general careers of the public service, are changed; limited and unlimited forms of liability of the partners in a commercial partnership are changed; workers' personal liability for non-compliance with rules that generate mere social ordering offenses is added; trade union and labor organization rights are changed, namely, the need/utility of collective bargaining agreements; possibilities of maintaining employment relationships are changed to exercise union positions; the need and form of compensation for political positions changes; the need and form of lifetime compensation for judicial magistracy positions is changed; the need and form of compensation for military exercise positions is changed; and the need or proportion of "life annuities" linked to the exercise of sovereign functions, and the implementation or deregulation of other instruments of "independence and impartiality" through economic means will be maintained; whether the need and proportion of incentives for the inclusion of people with disabilities is maintained, such as quotas and guarantees of access to public tenders in the public service;

We move on to issues related to Criminal Law and Criminal Policy, i.e. whether a UBI has effects equivalent to the general and special, positive and negative prevention measures; If the provision of a UBI affects the type of crimes committed because there is not the same type of economic scarcity, because of an increase in the individual's capacity to distance him- or herself from continuous situations that are criminal such as sexual abuse, domestic violence, pimping. It is possible, for example, due to the need to create (concentrated) social housing, to combat the intergenerational perpetuation of marginal valuations; whether it should be maintained, in the execution of the sentence, in the provision of the Universal or Unconditional Basic Income; whether a Basic Income must, during a period of imprisonment, be transferred to the prison system to offset its cost; whether it is possible to apply the penalty of deprivation of economic liberty, that is, to withdraw part or all of the Basic Income; whether an Unconditional or Universal Basic Income can be withheld as a coercive measure; if, with the implementation of the Basic Income, it is necessary to aggravate or mitigate penal frameworks, such as issues related to the acquisition of nationality, and create new types of crime related, for example, to the non-declaration of death for enrichment or deviation of a person's Basic Income or the crime of false indication of residence in national territory; if the Universal or Unconditional Basic Income does not create the need to punish more severely in illicit acts of mere social order.

We move on to questions related to Civil Law and Civil Procedural Law and current life, asking if the right to a Basic Income can be the subject of a legal transaction; if it can be partially or totally the subject of guarantee rights; if the Basic Income can be used as a basis for installment payment of bank loans; if Universal Basic Income can be fully executed, or partially. Can you by judicial sentence only garnish the existing installments or also the future ones; can it be considered unseizable or unpawnable, and whether other forms of income can be derived from unseizable income; If the Basic Income is an income that has a common use for married couples, what about unmarried ones; whether Universal or Unconditional Basic Income can generate succession consequences; should it be inherited; whether the Basic Income can be used as a general guarantee of personal obligations as a rule, or only by means of a contract clause stipulation to that effect; whether creditors can go on accumulating unsatisfied credits, knowing that they have a "guaranteed" income, or if they have to effect the credits so as not to alter the dynamics of interest in the general satisfaction of credits;

We could go on ad aeternum and ad nauseam.

Finally, to end the "storm" of questions raised by explaining the subtitle of this essay. What we tried to do here was to promote a sequence of legal works de jure condendo, creating our "storm" of problems in the hope of giving weight to the popular expression that "Depois da Tempestade, vem a Bonança", meaning "After the storm comes the calm.", that is, that after issues have been raised and dealt with, peace and security will come. So if there is room for the implementation of a Universal Basic Income, the transition will be peaceful and fruitful (8).

Notes

(1) Quoting Benjamin Franklin, in the quote that he popularized in 1970, in a Publication of the "Minneapolis Tribune", Retrieved from https://quoteinvestigator.com/2018/07/08/plan/
(2) As an example, in Portugal, Brito, Miguel Nogueira de. (2019). Rendimento Básico: Uma perspetiva constitucional, in Estudos em homenagem ao Conselheiro Presidente Joaquim de Sousa Ribeiro, Lisboa: Almedina. Pp. 171-216.
(3) As translated by us and with our parenthesis, for Elon Musk´s statement as broadcasted by CNBC, retrieved from https://bigthink.com/the-present/why-elon-musk-thinks-well-have-universal-basic-income/
(4) As defined by the Institution website RBI - O que é? - Rendimento Básico Incondicional (rendimentobasico.pt)
(5) As defined by the Institution website https://ubi4all.eu
(6) Mentioned in the popular initiative with the European Parliament, ECI.EU, now extinct for not completing the minimum signatures by the deadline.
(7) To better understand this question in detail, because it does not have an expression in Portugal in the ideological political right, vide Nettle, Daniel. (2018). Getting your head around the Universal Basic Income, in Hanging on to the Edges: Essays on Science, Society and the Academic Life, Open Book Publishers. Pp. 163 - 180, pp. 179 e 180.
(8) "Depois da tempestade, vem a bonança" is a Portuguese saying that means that after a troubled situation comes a calm and good period, the "Bonança", establishing a parallel with Sea navigation. In Sea, after the storms, periods of calm follow, and then you can navigate with ease.

References

Brito, Miguel Nogueira de. (2019). Rendimento Básico: Uma perspetiva constitucional, in Estudos em homenagem ao Conselheiro Presidente Joaquim de Sousa Ribeiro, Lisboa: Almedina. Pp. 171-216.

Caupers, João. (2013). Introdução ao Direito Administrativo. 11ª Ed. Lisboa: Âncora Editora.

Gentilini, Ugo; Grosh, Margaret; Rigolini, Jamele; Yemtsov, Ruslan. (2020). Exploring Universal Basic Income, A Guide to Navigating Concepts, Evidence, and Practices. The International Bank for Reconstruction and Development/The World Bank.

Marais, Hein. (2018). The Employment Crisis, Just Transition and Te Universal Basic Income Grant. Satgar, Vishwas. The Climate Crisis: South African and Global Democratic Eco-Socialist Alternatives, Wits University Press. Pp. 70 – 106.

Mumbunan, Sonny; Maitri, Ni Made Rahayu; Tazkiana, Dinna; Prajoso, Ari; SIHITE, Femme; Nabella Dhita Mutiara. (2021). Basic Income for Nature and Climate: On the first Basic Income proposal to conserve nature and combat climate change on the largest tropical island on Earth. Research Center for Climate Change Universitas Indonesia, Depok Indonesia, n.º 16424. P. 5. Retrieved from https://www.forclime.org/documents/Books/Mumbunan2021_Basic_Income_for_Nature_and_Climate_fi nal_versi0n.pdf

Nettle, Daniel. (2018). Getting your head around the Universal Basic Income, in Hanging on to the Edges: Essays on Science, Society and the Academic Life, Open Book Publishers. Pp. 163 – 180.

Queiroz, Cristina. (2006). Direitos Fundamentais Sociais: Funções, Âmbito, Conteúdo, Questões Interpretativas E Problemas De Justiciabilidade. Coimbra: Coimbra Editora.

Smith, Matt; Danson, Mike; Goodman, Cleo; Pugh, Michael; Cooke, Jamie; Smith, Michael; Forget, Evelyn; and Gibson, Marcia. (2021). Peace of Mind: Exploring Basic Income´s Potential to Improve Mental Health, May. P.1. Retrieved from https://www.scottishinsight.ac.uk/Programmes/UNGlobalGoals/UniversalBasicIncomeandMentalHealth.aspx

IV

Basic Income in German-Speaking Countries

Das Bedingungslose Grundeinkommen im deutschsprachigen Raum

Ulrich Schachtschneider

Grundeinkommen: Ein gastliches Umfeld für Postwachstum?

Eine erste Annäherung an ein neues Forschungsfeld

Das bedingungslose Grundeinkommen (BGE) wird im aktuellen Diskurs hauptsächlich als Automatisierungsdividende, Armutsverhinderung, Umverteilung nach unten, Entbürokratisierung, Kreativitätsförderung sowie als demokratiefördernde Teilhabegarantie propagiert. Diese Qualitäten sind zweifelsohne wichtige Argumente. Es fehlt jedoch in der bisherigen Debatte weitgehend die ökologische Herausforderung und eine Erörterung der Wirkung eines BGE für eine sozial-ökologische Transformation. In diesem Zusammenhang stellt sich die Frage, inwieweit das Grundeinkommen auch geeignet sein könnte zur Unterstützung einer Ökonomie und Gesellschaft jenseits immerwährenden Wirtschaftswachstums.

Nötig sein könnte dies, um die radikale Reduktion unseres Ressourcenverbrauchs, etwa um den Faktor zehn, wie wir es seit längerem – vom Wissenschaftler bis zum Schulkind – wissen, realisieren zu können. Eine solche große Transformation ist nicht nur durch technische Veränderungen, durch mehr PV-Anlagen, Elektroautos und Recyclingwirtschaft zu erreichen. Vielmehr bedarf es einer großen kulturellen Transformation bzw. „Reformation": Es geht möglicherweise um ein neues In-der-Welt-Sein und damit auch um ein neues Verhältnis zur Arbeit, die wesentlicher Teil unserer Auseinandersetzung mit der Welt ist. Beides weist auf mögliche Zusammenhänge mit dem Grundeinkommen hin. Im Beitrag werde ich diese skizzieren. Dabei kann es zunächst nur um Behauptungen von Zusammenhängen und Wirkungen gehen, die – nach dem gegenwärtigen Stand der Forschung – allenfalls kursorisch illustriert und indiziert werden können. Ansätze zur Erforschung der möglichen Zusammenhänge werden im Anschluss kurz umrissen.

Ausgangspunkt aller Überlegungen ist zunächst, dass für die Option auf Nicht-Wachstum (Engl.: „Degrowth"), verstanden hier als Möglichkeit auch der Schrumpfung des BIP, zwei Dinge dauerhaft ohne Krisenerscheinungen

(Degrowth by Design statt Degrowth by Desaster) möglich sein müssen: Es muss möglich sein, dauerhaft weniger Erwerbsarbeit nötig zu haben und es muss möglich sein, dauerhaft mit weniger Konsumtion, weniger bezahlten Waren und Dienstleistungen auszukommen.

Wie kann dies realisiert werden? Nötig wäre eine gesellschaftliche und ökonomische Struktur, in der wir

1. weniger Jobs annehmen müssen (weniger „Produktivismus" vorherrscht),
2. weniger Konsumieren müssen (weniger „Konsumismus" entsteht).

Im Folgenden werde ich kurz thesenartige Überlegungen darüber aufstellen, warum ein Grundeinkommen beide Anforderungen erfüllen könnte.

1. Grundeinkommen versus Produktivismus

Ein bedingungsloses Grundeinkommen (BGE) kann – so die erste These - einen Prozess in Gang setzen, bei dem das gesellschaftlich nach wie vor dominante Paradigma des Produktivismus zurückgedrängt wird. „Produktivismus" meint in diesem Zusammenhang nicht die möglichst effiziente Erstellung von Waren oder Dienstleistungen, sondern Produzieren als Selbstzweck[1]: Um möglichst viel Arbeitsplätze zu erhalten und zu schaffen, wird Wirtschaftswachstum begrüßt, erhofft und gefördert. Es bleibt auch dann Produktivismus, wenn auf diesen Arbeitsplätzen öko-effiziente Produkte hergestellt werden (grüner Produktivismus) oder Dienstleistungen anstelle von Waren erbracht werden (Dienstleistungs-Produktivismus).

Viele längst als ökologisch schädlich, sozial zweifelhaft oder die individuelle Entfaltung behindernd erkannte Produktionen oder Dienstleistungen werden heute nolens volens akzeptiert, wenn nicht sogar gefördert, weil daran in der kapitaldominierten Ökonomie elementar die ökonomische persönliche Existenz gekoppelt ist. Mit einem BGE im Rücken kann jede(r) zu solchen zweifelhaften Arbeitsangeboten eher „Nein" sagen. Ökonomische Aktivitäten, die heute ausschließlich zu existenzsichernden Erwerbszwecken vorgenommen werden, werden sich mit der höheren ökonomischen Basis-Sicherheit durch Grundeinkommen als unattraktiver darstellen. Die Menschen werden dann tendenziell nur noch an denjenigen ökonomischen Tätigkeiten teilnehmen (wollen), die aus ihrer Sicht Sinn machen – in ökologischer, sozialer und selbstverwirklichender Hinsicht. Sie werden weniger, aber authentischer.[2] Was auch immer übrig bleibt an Erwerbsaktivitäten, sie werden eher dem Denken und Fühlen der Menschen entsprechen.

Der Zusammenhang gilt auch auf gesellschaftlicher Ebene: Wir wissen inzwischen längst, dass wir aus klimaschädlichen Industrien (wie etwa Braunkohle oder einem immensen Ausmaß der Autoindustrie) aussteigen müssen. Dennoch werden diese mit Mehrheit als notwendig anerkannten Schritte immer wieder verzögert, wenn nicht sogar verhindert, da an diesen Arbeitsplätzen ökonomische Existenzen hängen. Die Widerstände der Betroffenen und die Angst der Politik, diese vor den Kopf zu stoßen, sind höchst verständlich. Nur ist es eine Struktur, die kontraproduktiv ist. Mit einem Grundeinkommen könnte die Loslösung von ihr mit sehr viel weniger Ängsten vollzogen werden. Auch ein Degrowth, in diesem Fall ein Abbau dieser Alt-Industrien ohne die Entwicklung von Ersatzarbeitsplätzen mit gleichem Arbeits- bzw. Verdienstvolumenvolumen, wäre dann eher möglich.

Für eine Weniger-Erwerbsarbeit-Wirkung des Grundeinkommens gibt es ein kleines empirisches Indiz: Ein Ergebnis etwa des von 1974 bis 1978 in Kanada durchgeführten Grundeinkommensexperiments „Mincome" war, dass das Arbeitsangebot der Grundeinkommen Beziehenden um ein bis sieben Prozent zurückging (Forget 2011). Dies ist freilich ein nicht in weiteren Versuchen untersuchtes und reproduziertes Resultat. Ein weiteres Indiz dafür, dass mit mehr ökonomischer Gleichheit des Grundeinkommens weniger Erwerbsarbeit zu erwarten wäre, ist folgender Zusammenhang: Je ungleicher die Gesellschaften – hier gemessen als Einkommensungleichheit – sind, desto mehr Arbeitsstunden werden geleistet (Pickett und Wilkinson (2010).[3] Offensichtlich sind Menschen bei Ungleichheit, die sowohl mit absoluter Armut als auch mit verstärktem Aufstiegswillen auf allen Stufen der gesellschaftlichen Leiter verbunden ist, eher materiell oder sozial gezwungen, jeden Job anzunehmen. Natürlich gilt auch hier: Die Koinzidenz von Ungleichheit und jährlichen Arbeitsstunden kann natürlich auch anders verursacht sein, aber das kulturübergreifende Resultat (die Autoren bezogen verschiedenste Gesellschaften der „entwickelten" Welt in die Untersuchung ein) ist zumindest ein Hinweis, dass an diesem Zusammenhang etwas dran sein könnte.

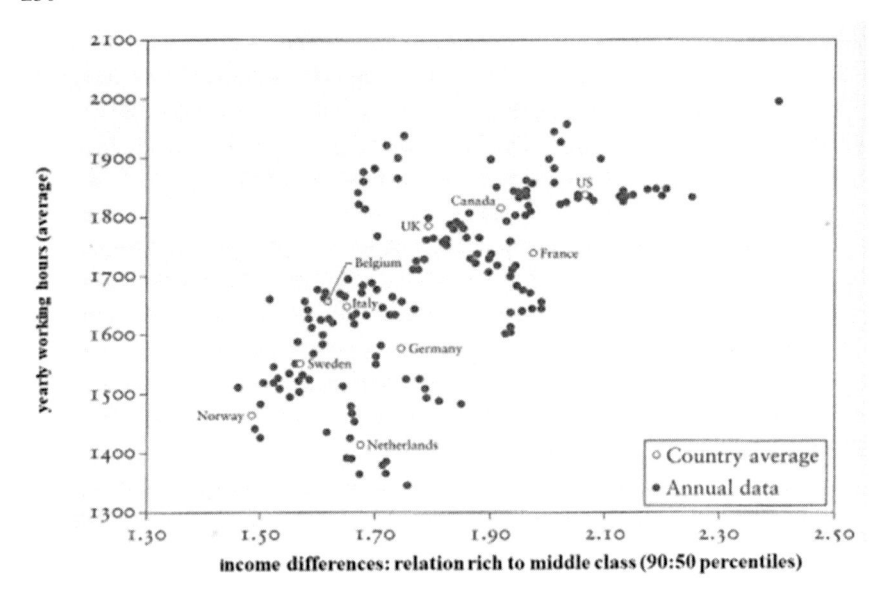

[Grafik: Streudiagramm mit y-Achse "yearly working hours (average)" von 1300 bis 2100 und x-Achse "income differences: relation rich to middle class (90:50 percentiles)" von 1.30 bis 2.50. Länder markiert: US, Canada, UK, Belgium, Italy, France, Germany, Sweden, Norway, Netherlands. Legende: Country average, Annual data.]

Grafik 1: Ungleichheit und Arbeitsstunden (Wilkinson und Pickett 2010)

3.1 (Work-)lifestyles of Degrowth

Der wachstumskritische Ökonom Niko Paech schlägt in seinem Modell der Postwachstumsökonomie eine Halbierung des (bezahlten) Konsums und der Erwerbsökonomie vor (Paech 2012). Damit wurde ei der Keynes'schen Vision einer 15 Std Woche (Keynes 1930) schon relativ nahekommen – zumindest was die Erwerbsarbeitszeit angeht. Paech aber geht davon aus, dass die freiwerdenden 20 Stunden für Subsistenzpraktiken genutzt werden: Für die Organisierung gemeinschaftlicher Nutzung, für Pflege und Reparatur sowie für Eigenproduktion. Damit würde jede(r) unabhängig(er) von der Industrieproduktion, von Markt- und Geldzwängen.

Kritisch anzufragen an eine solche Vision ist allerdings, welche neuen Abhängigkeiten von Gemeinschaften, von Netzwerken, wir uns damit einhandeln würden – die manche begrüßen, andere aber vielleicht nicht wollen oder auch nicht zustande bekommen. Dabei ist von einer Degrowth-Perspektive aus gesehen mehr Subsistenz keineswegs zwingend. Das „Weniger" der Produktion

Grundeinkommen: Ein gastliches Umfeld für Postwachstum ?

kann auch schlicht durch weniger, aber nicht durch Eigenarbeit substituierte Erwerbstätigkeit realisiert werden. Zum Zeitwohlstand gehört wesentlich die Freiheit, die Art der Arbeit, die wir „wirklich" möchten, zu wählen.
Das BGE erlaubt uns – dies wäre die zweite These –, unseren individuellen Mix aus Erwerbsarbeit, Bürger*innenarbeit und Subsistenz zu wählen. Ich kann als Spezialist*in erfüllt zwanzig Stunden in der Industrie arbeiten und ergänzend zehn Stunden subsistent und gemeinschaftlich tätig sein. Ich kann aber auch fünf Stunden die Woche irgendwo gegen Geld erwerbstätig sein und 30 Stunden in Gemeinschaft oder selber produzieren. Beides passt zum Ziel einer Postwachstumsökonomie, da der Output an Produkten und Dienstleistungen geringer wäre als der jetzige bei 40 Stunden Erwerbstätigkeit. Es wäre eine Postwachstumsökonomie, die mit der Pluralität der Lebensstile in der fortgeschrittenen Modernen kompatibel ist, mehr noch: die diese Pluralität stärker ermöglicht.

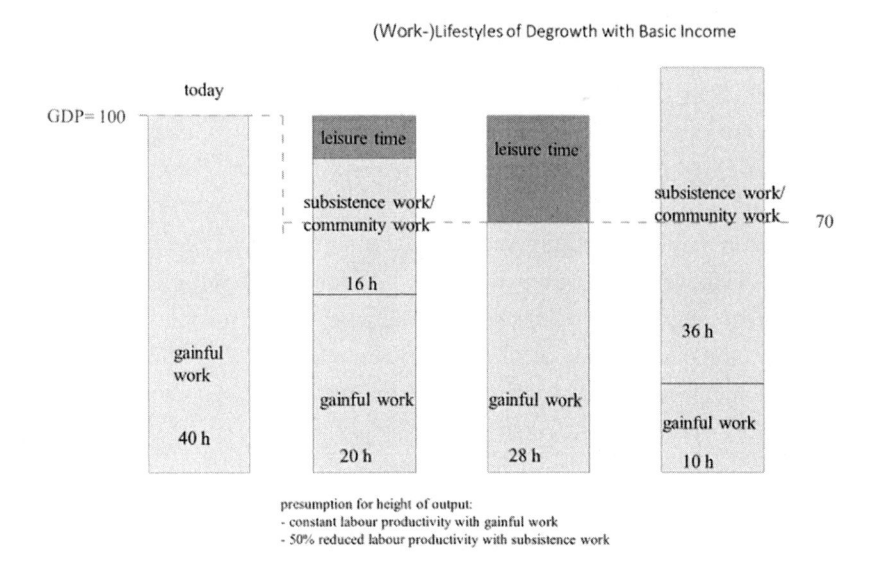

Grafik 2: (Work-)Lifestyles bei Degrowth mit Grundeinkommen

3.2 Finanzierung bei Degrowth?

Was aber wäre mit der Finanzierung eines BGE bei einer dadurch ausgelösten deproduktivistischen Wirkung? Werden weniger Güter erwerbsmäßig produziert, wird zwar das Steueraufkommen für das Grundeinkommen sinken. Sein Anteil an der Gesamtwertschöpfung (das BIP) aber könnte dann konstant bleiben– und damit womöglich auch seine soziale Wirkung. Es werden zum Beispiel Regelungen vorgeschlagen, die Höhe der Auszahlung an die Entwicklung des BIP zu koppeln. Bei weniger Erwerbstätigkeit wird es dann weniger monetäres Grundeinkommen geben. Gleichzeitig vollzieht sich aber ein Wandel zu einer Kultur des Weniger und/oder zu unbezahlten Tätigkeiten, mehr Eigenarbeit, Gemeinschaftsarbeit etc. Der Grad einer solchen Demonetarisierung von Arbeit kann nicht vorausgesagt werden, jedoch erlaubt ein Grundeinkommen hier eine große Bandbreite. Die soziale Sicherheit würde dann aus einem monetarisierten und einem demonetarisierten Anteil bestehen, deren Gewichte nicht vorausgesagt werden können und die im historischen Verlauf und regional variabel sein werden.

In welcher Sphäre der Arbeit auch immer sich die Menschen als weniger entfremdet empfinden, die Wahlfreiheit des Grundeinkommens könnte die Möglichkeit, unser Arbeitsleben in der „Existenzweise des Seins" (Fromm 1979) zu führen, stärken:

Der Sozialpsychologe Fromm verstand darunter (in Gegensatz zur Existenzweise des „Habens") eine Lebensweise der „Aktivität" („voller Freude" Fähigkeiten nutzen statt „Geschäftigkeit"), der „Liebe" (für jemanden oder etwas sorgen statt ihn oder es zu kontrollieren) und des „Werdens" (seine Persönlichkeit bilden statt von Ereignis zu Ereignis zu taumeln). Was bedeutet diese Existenzweise des Seins für die Arbeit?

„Voller Freude" meine Fähigkeiten nutzen – dies kann ich eher, wenn ich mich mit dem Produkt und seiner Produktion identifizieren kann. Alle frei gewählten (Work-)Lifestyles of Degrowth können so die Haben-Orientierung der reinen „Geschäftigkeit" abbauen. Mehr „Sein" in der Arbeit ist die Basis für die Realisierung unseres elementaren Bedürfnisses nach Resonanz: Nur wer durch frei gewählte Tätigkeiten Selbstwirksamkeitserfahrungen macht, kann auf dieser Identitätsgrundlage mit der dinglichen und sozialen Welt in einen inspirierenden Austausch treten (Rosa 2016) – eine Voraussetzung für einen Abbau der

Haben-Orientierung, auch jenseits der Arbeit, die elementarer Bestandteil für weniger Konsumismus ist.

2. Grundeinkommen versus Konsumismus

Das ökonomisch notwendige Passstück zum Produktivismus ist der Konsumismus. Die kulturelle Orientierung am „Immer Mehr" aufgrund eines Knappheitsgefühls ist weitgehend ungebrochen, wenn auch das „Mehr" nicht mehr im „Immer Gleichen" (Gronemeyer 2002), sondern im „Immer Neuem" besteht. Der Versuch, das begrenzte Leben auf Erden mit einem Maximum an Konsum und an Events zu füllen, die „Verheißung der Beschleunigung" (Rosa), ist zwar in den letzten Jahren in die Kritik geraten. Der Wunsch nach Entschleunigung taucht nicht nur mit Blick auf die eigene Lebensqualität auf, auch in der ökologischen Debatte wird seit langem ein ressourcenleichter Lebensstil des Weniger propagiert. Doch offensichtlich übersetzt sich dieser seit 20 Jahren von vielen zivilgesellschaftlichen und auch staatlichen Institutionen (etwa: Umweltbundesamt) mit viel medialem Aufwand betriebene Appell jenseits kleiner avantgardistischer Gruppen nicht nennenswert in die Alltagspraxen.

Damit kommen wir zu der dritten These: Ein BGE mit seiner ökonomischen Basissicherheit kann das ändern: Es vergrößert den Raum für das Ausprobieren anderer Lebensstile und eröffnet allen, aus der Tretmühle „Erwerbsarbeit-Konsum-Erwerbsarbeit" zunächst auf Probe auszusteigen. Die Fallhöhe beim Scheitern oder Nicht-Gefallen wäre nicht so groß wie heute, wo die Aufgabe eines Jobs den Anfang eines langen sozialen Abstiegs bedeuten kann. Neue Lebensstile des „Weniger", des „Zeitwohlstands" und des „Gemeinsam" hätten eine Chance, auch jenseits von randständigen Milieus bzw. Avantgarden mit höherem Problembewusstsein, Selbstwirksamkeitserwartungen und Risikoakzeptanzen ausprobiert und geschätzt zu werden. Auch die mit BGE eher mögliche Reduktion von Erwerbsarbeitszeit kann die Suche nach Lebenslauf-Alternativen fördern. Erich Fromm schrieb: „Bisher war der Mensch mit seiner Arbeit zu sehr beschäftigt (oder er war nach der Arbeit zu müde), um sich ernsthaft mit den Problemen abzugeben: ‚Was ist der Sinn des Lebens?', ‚Woran glaube ich?', ‚Welche Werte vertrete ich?', ‚Wer bin ich?' usw. Wenn er nicht mehr ausschließlich von seiner Arbeit in Anspruch genommen ist, wird es ihm entweder freistehen, sich ernsthaft mit diesen Problemen auseinander zu setzen oder er wird aus unmittelbarer oder kompensierter Langeweile halb verrückt werden." (Fromm 1999[1966]:310)

Ein sicheres Grundeinkommen könnte zudem die sozialpsychologischen Voraussetzungen für ein Gefühl der Fülle und damit eine dekonsumistische Einstellung schaffen. Fromm weiter: „Eine Psychologie des Mangels erzeugt Angst, Neid und Egoismus, [...]" (ebd.). Erst jenseits dieser Ängste des Zurückbleibens bzw. des Abgehängt-Werdens könnten Sinnfragen nicht mehr mit einer Steigerung des Konsums von Gegenständen, Urlauben, Intimbeziehungen etc. beantwortet werden. Das für eine weniger konsumistische Einstellung notwendige Gefühl der Fülle ist indes nicht nur abhängig vom Vorhandensein einer materiellen Basissicherheit.

Das Zufriedenheitsgefühl des Einzelnen hängt ebenso von der Stellung innerhalb der Hierarchie einer Gesellschaft ab beziehungsweise von ihrer Hierarchieförmigkeit. Je ungleicher sie ist, desto weniger kann sich ein Gefühl der Fülle einstellen, und zwar auf allen Hierarchiestufen. Pickett und Wilkinson (2010) fanden heraus: Je ungleicher Gesellschaften sind, desto geringer ist die Sparquote. Sie geben dafür eine einleuchtende Erklärung: Mit Waren und Dienstleistungen können die Menschen ihren Status anzeigen. Wer unten ist oder sich dort wähnt, kann diesen durch demonstrativen Konsum etwas erhöhen, koste es was es wolle. Auch wer sich in der Mitte positioniert, versucht dies durch statusgemäße Ausstattung zu beweisen. Um mitzuhalten oder sogar zu zeigen, dass er eigentlich ein bisschen höher steht, setzt er alle verfügbaren finanziellen Mittel ein und ist sogar bereit, sich dafür zu verschulden. Die eigenen Bedürfnisse werden mit Blick auf die „Nachbarn" definiert: Nach einer Untersuchung von Hemenway und Solnick (2005) würde die Hälfte der Befragten auf fünfzig Prozent ihres Einkommens verzichten, wenn sie dafür mit anderen gleichgestellt wären.

Ungleichheit als Konsumtreiber sollte keineswegs nur in ökonomischer Hinsicht verstanden werden. Wer sich in seinen sozialen Beziehungen, bei der Arbeit, in der Politik etc. unterdrückt sieht, wird dies womöglich eher durch Konsum kompensieren (wollen) als Zufriedenere. Das „Jetzt gönne ich mir auch mal etwas" entsteht bei Menschen, die sich in ihren Zusammenhängen aufgehoben und gewürdigt fühlen, weniger. Es wäre dann nicht nur die Modernekultur der Verheißung maximaler Lebensausfüllung, die die Menschen nach möglichst viel Konsum von Gütern und Erlebnissen streben lässt[4], sondern auch die Ungleichheit und die Herrschaftsförmigkeit einer Gesellschaft.

Daraus würde folgen: Soll das Weniger-Konsumieren nicht nur für besondere Milieus attraktiv sein, muss die Gesellschaft weniger herrschaftsförmig werden. Ein genügsamerer Lebensstil, eine „Eleganz der Einfachheit" (Sachs) kann sich nur entwickeln auf der Basis freiheitlicher Lebensalltage. Wer sich in welcher Weise auch immer unterdrückt fühlt, ständig ein Gefühl der Knappheit empfindet und seine Arbeit als entfremdet wahrnimmt, wird sich nicht zu neuer Bescheidenheit überzeugen lassen. Zur Kompensation benötigt man vielmehr demonstrativen Status-Konsum, entschädigende Erlebniswelten und führt Aufholjagden.

Ein BGE – so die vierte These – könnte das ökonomische und das sozialpsychologische Gefühl der Gleichheit stärken und damit den Konsum um das „Haben-Müssen" aufgrund der Unzufriedenheit mit der eigenen sozialen Stellung reduzieren. Die Motive für erwerbsökonomische Aktivitäten der Menschen würden mit BGE weniger überformt durch unsichere und hierarchische Verhältnisse.

Nun kann eingewendet werden, dass auch bei Abwesenheit solcher Motivlagen authentischere Bedürfnisse nach mehr Konsum und mehr dafür nötige Erwerbsarbeit entstehen können – dass das BGE sich also entgegen der hier abgeleiteten Weniger-Dynamik als Wachstumsimpuls herausstellt. In der Tat können wir dies keineswegs ausschließen. Ein solches Wachstum erfolgte dann aber auf der Basis erweiterter sozialer und ökonomischer Handlungsfreiheit. Postwachstumsgesellschaft bzw. „Degrowth" meint genau dies: Die Abwesenheit von Wachstumszwängen und -drängen, die die Option auf eine Verkleinerung des ökonomischen Produkts ermöglicht, aber nicht erzwingt.

3. Ausblick

Es lassen sich also sowohl für eine Veränderung hin zu „Weniger Erwerbsarbeit" als auch für das notwendige Pendent „Weniger Konsum" Theoreme aufstellen, nach denen Grundeinkommen diese Entwicklungen befördert. Die behaupteten Wirkungen sind zweistufiger Natur: Grundeinkommen soll zunächst Optionen für multiple Arbeits- und Lebensstile eröffnen. Im zweiten Schritt wird dann erwartet, dass die Subjekte unter den neuen, durch das Grundeinkommen geschaffenen gesellschaftlichen Bedingungen diese Optionen umsetzen in weniger Erwerbsarbeit. Grundeinkommen soll zunächst für weniger Herrschaftlichkeit in der Sphäre der Arbeit und in der Gesellschaft sorgen und im zweiten Schritt soll diese geringere Herrschaftsförmigkeit in weniger Konsumbedürfnis münden.

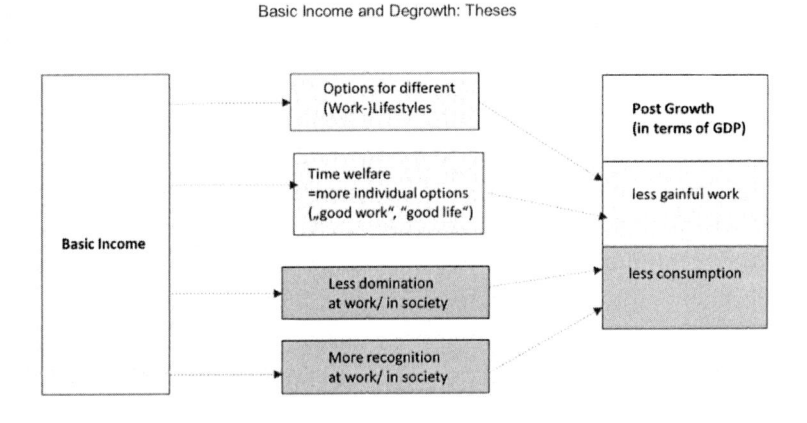

Basic Income and Degrowth: Theses

Grafik 3: Grundeinkommen und Degrowth: Theoreme

Diese zweistufigen Wirkungen sind zunächst nur Annahmen. Alle einzelnen Wirkungen sind Gegenstand zukünftiger Forschung zum Zusammenhang Grundeinkommen und Degrowth. Da direkte empirische Untersuchungen aufgrund nicht vorhandener realer Grundeinkommensgesellschaften nicht möglich sind, sind sie auf „Krücken" angewiesen: Zum einen gibt es Experimente, in denen sich zumindest ansatzweise die behaupteten Wirkungen zeigen. Ein weiterer Ansatz wäre die Auswertung von Situationen von Menschen, die sich heute schon in grundeinkommensähnlichen Situationen befinden wie etwa

Rentner, Erben, Kommunarden. Zu fragen wäre: Inwieweit ändern diese Situationen, meistens an den Rändern der Gesellschaft, den gegenwärtig hegemonialen Habitus der Affirmation der Erwerbsarbeitsgesellschaft (vgl. Ketterer 2019). Zudem müssen Ergebnisse aus Forschungen über hier enthaltene allgemeine Zusammenhänge bezüglich der Motivation für Arbeit und Konsum, die zunächst nicht auf Grundkommen oder äquivalente Lebenssituationen bezogen sind, noch sehr viel genauer in den Blick genommen werden wie zB: Wie ist Status-Konsum motiviert? Welche kompensatorischen Konsumhandlungen gibt es und was sind die Gründe dafür. In wie weit leiden Menschen unter herrschaftlichen Bedingungen und Nicht-Entfaltung in ihrer Erwerbstätigkeit? Welche Motive für Erwerbsarbeit jenseits der ökonomischen Existenzsicherung gibt es? Was sind die Voraussetzungen für eine Habitus-Transformation?

Anmerkungen

[1] Der Begriff in diesem Sinne wurde ursprünglich vom frz. Ökonomen und Regulationstheoretiker Alain Lipietz verwendet, auch von Andre Gorz

[2] „Authentisch" kann zweifelsohne nicht substantiell definiert werden: Als diese oder jene bestimmte Arbeit. Was die Einzelnen als authentisch definieren bzw. empfinden wird sehr unterschiedlich sein. Ich verwende den Begriff dennoch: als Zustand der Abwesenheit von seinem Gegenteil, einem Zustand der Entfremdung: Wenn die Ursachen für Entfremdung (verschiedene Arten von Zwängen Arbeit annehmen zu müssen etc.) wegfallen kann davon ausgegangen werden, dass die dann angenommenen Arbeiten authentischer sind.

[3] Die Autoren wählten hier den Quotient aus 90% und 50% Perzentil als Ungleichheitsmaß: 90% Perzentil: Das Einkommen, das 10% überschreiten. 50% Perzentil: Das Einkommen, das 50% überschreiten. Je größer der Quotient, je größer ist der Abstand zwischen diesen beiden Einkommen.

[4] So die Erklärung des Soziologen und Beschleunigungskritikers Hartmut Rosa (Rosa 2012).

Literatur

Forget, Evelyn: The Town with no Poverty, University of Manitoba 2011.

Fromm, Erich: Haben oder Sein. Die seelischen Grundlagen einer neuen Gesellschaft, München 1979.

Fromm, Erich: Psychologische Aspekte zur Frage eines garantierten Einkommens für alle, in: Gesamtausgabe in zwölf Bänden, Band V, S. 309-316. München 1999. Original): The Psychological Aspects of Guaranteed Income, New York 1966.

Gronemeyer, Marianne (2002): Die Macht der Bedürfnisse. Überfluss und Knappheit. Darmstadt

Hemenway, David / Solnick, Sarah: Are Positional Concerns Stronger in Some Domains Than in Others? American Economic Review 95(2)/ 2005, pp. 147-151.

Ketterer, Hanna 2019: Bedingungsloses Grundeinkommen als materielle und symbolische Ermöglichungsstruktur von Praktiken für die gesellschaftliche Transformation. In: Dörre, K. et al.: (Hg.) 2019 Große Transformation? Zur Zukunft moderner Gesellschaften. Sonderband des Berliner Journals für Soziologie.

Keynes, John Maynard: "Economic Possibilities for our Grandchildren (1930)," in Essays in Persuasion (New York: Harcourt Brace, 1932), 358-373

Paech, Niko: Befreiung vom Überfluss, München 2012.

Pickett, Kate / Wilkinson, Richard: Gleichheit ist Glück. Warum gerechte Gesellschaften für alle besser sind, Berlin 2010. Original: Kate Pickett, Richard Wilkinson, The Spirit Level. Why More Equal Societies Almost Do Better. London 2009.

Rosa, Hartmut: Weltbeziehungen im Zeitalter der Beschleunigung. Umrisse einer neuen Gesellschaftskritik, Frankfurt/M. 2012

Ronald Blaschke

Grundeinkommen: Positionen von Parteien und Zugänge von sozialen Bewegungen in Deutschland

Europäische Bürgerinitiative (EBI) Bedingungsloses Grundeinkommen in der gesamten EU

Mit dem Beitrag sollen die Definition des Grundeinkommens sowie Bestimmungsmöglichkeiten für die Höhe des Grundeinkommensbetrages erläutert, sowie die Positionen von Parteien und Zugänge von sozialen Bewegungen in Deutschland zum Grundeinkommen nachgezeichnet werden. Die Europäische Bürgerinitiative (EBI) Bedingungsloses Grundeinkommen in der gesamten EU wird vorgestellt. Ergänzend zum Beitrag wird auf die PowerPoint-Präsentation zum Thema verwiesen (vgl. Blaschke, 2021a).

1. Grundeinkommen: Definition

Grundlage der Darstellung und Diskussion im Folgenden ist die in Deutschland weitgehend anerkannte Definition des Grundeinkommens vom Netzwerk Grundeinkommen:

„Das bedingungslose Grundeinkommen ist ein Einkommen für alle Menschen, das Existenz sichernd ist und gesellschaftliche Teilhabe ermöglicht, auf das ein individueller Rechtsanspruch besteht, das ohne Bedürftigkeitsprüfung und ohne Zwang zu Arbeit oder anderen Gegenleistungen garantiert wird." (vgl. Netzwerk Grundeinkommen, o. J. a)

Beim Grundeinkommen handelt es sich also um ein universelles, d. h. allen Individuen bedingungslos zustehendes Einkommen, das deren Existenz sichert und gesellschaftliche Teilhabe ermöglicht. Ähnlich und mit dem Zusatz der regelmäßigen Zahlung versehen, definiert das europäische Netzwerk Unconditional Basic Income Europe (UBIE) das Grundeinkommen wie folgt: „Unconditional Basic Income (UBI) is an amount of money, paid on a regular basis to each individual unconditionally and universally high enough to ensure a material existence and participation in society." (Unconditional Basic Income Europe, o. J.)

Diese Definitionen unterscheiden sich von der Definition durch das Basic Income Earth Network (BIEN, o. J.) insbesondere dadurch, dass der Begriff Grundeinkommen bzw. bedingungsloses Grundeinkommen (hier und im weiteren synonym verwendet) ein Bestimmungsmerkmal bezogen auf die Höhe beinhaltet: Der Einkommensbetrag ist ausreichend, um die (materielle) Existenz zu sichern und gesellschaftliche Teilhabe jedes Einzelnen zu ermöglichen. Die Definition von BIEN beinhaltet dagegen keinerlei Angabe zur Höhe des Betrags. Ein "Grundeinkommen" nach dessen Definition könnte auch einen Cent oder 5000 Euro betragen. Mit dieser Definition von BIEN ist es daher auch unmöglich, irgend welche Aussagen zu Wirkungen des Grundeinkommens hinsichtlich des Arbeitsmarkts, des Sozialen, der Umverteilung, des (Sozial-)Psychischen usw. usf. zu treffen. Die Definition durch BIEN lässt offen, ob tatsächlich ein Grundeinkommen oder nur ein partielles Grundeinkommen angestrebt wird: Letzteres ist ein nicht ausreichender, im Sinne von nicht die (materielle) Existenz und gesellschaftliche Teilhabe sichernder, monetärer Transfer (Netzwerk Grundeinkommen, o. J.b). An dieser Stelle sei nur kurz darauf verwiesen, dass partielle "Grundeinkommen" vielen emanzipatorischen Ansprüchen, die mit dem Grundeinkommen verbunden werden, nicht gerecht werden können.

Grundsätzlich muss das Grundeinkommen auch von Grundsicherungen unterschieden werden. Grundsicherungen sind (sozialadministrativ) bedürftigkeitsgeprüfte und in der Regel nicht individuell garantierte Geldtransfers. Diese sind, sofern sie für Erwerbsfähige vorgesehen sind, auch an eine Bereitschaft bzw. einen Zwang zur Übernahme einer Lohn- bzw. Erwerbsarbeit gekoppelt. Grund- und Mindestsicherungen können bei Verletzungen der Mitwirkungs- bzw. Arbeitsübernahmeverpflichtung vollständig oder teilweise verwehrt werden. Es handelt sich also um nicht universelle, nicht bedingungslos gewährte und nicht individuell garantierte Transfers, die in der Regel auch nicht die Existenz sichern und nicht die gesellschaftliche Teilhabe ermöglichen. Beispiele für Grundsicherungen sind in Deutschland die Grundsicherung für Arbeitsuchende für Erwerbsfähige (Hartz IV), das Sozialgeld für nicht erwerbsfähige

Mitglieder in Hartz-IV-Haushalten, die Grundsicherung im Alter und bei Erwerbsminderung sowie die Hilfe zum Lebensunterhalt für eingeschränkt Erwerbsfähige (vgl. Netzwerk Grundeinkommen, o. J. b).

2. Sozialdividende oder Negative Einkommensteuer?

Ein Grundeinkommen kann sowohl als Sozialdividende als auch als Negative Einkommensteuer konzipiert werden. In beiden Fällen besteht ein Anspruch eines jeden einzelnen Menschen auf ein bedingungslos gewährtes Einkommen ohne jegliche Bedürftigkeitsprüfung in einer Höhe, die die (materielle) Existenz sichert und gesellschaftliche Teilhabe ermöglicht. Sozialdividenden oder Negative Einkommensteuern, die diese Merkmale nicht aufweisen, können nicht als Grundeinkommen bezeichnet werden. Unter der Voraussetzung, dass das Grundeinkommen über eine Einkommensteuer finanziert wird, unterscheiden sich Sozialdividende und Negative Einkommensteuer lediglich darin, dass bei der Sozialdividende eine gleich hohe, evtl. auch altersabhängig unterschiedlich hohe, Auszahlung an alle erfolgt und die Einkommensteuer auf die anderen Einkommen gesondert erhoben wird. Bei der Negativen Einkommensteuer wird dagegen die fällige Einkommensteuer auf die anderen Einkommen sofort mit dem Grundeinkommensanspruch, hier im Sinne einer Steuergutschrift, verrechnet. In beiden Fällen ist ein Grundeinkommen garantiert: bei der Sozialdividende als ausgezahlter Betrag, bei der Negativen Einkommensteuer als Steuergutschrift (negative Steuer). Einen gleich hohen Steuersatz vorausgesetzt, verbleibt unterm Strich dem Einzelnen der gleiche Gesamtnettoeinkommensbetrag – ob nun mit Grundeinkommen als Sozialdividende oder als Negative Einkommensteuer (vgl. Netzwerk Grundeinkommen, o. J.b). Für Deutschland wurden Grundeinkommensmodelle als Sozialdividende oder als Negative Einkommensteuer entwickelt, ein Grundeinkommensmodell auch für beide Auszahlungsvarianten (Netzwerk Grundeinkommen, o. J.c).

Exkurs: Bestimmung der Höhe des Grundeinkommensbetrages

In Deutschland existieren unterschiedliche Möglichkeiten die Höhe eines Geldbetrages zu bestimmen, der demjenigen, der in Deutschland lebt, ein gewisses Maß an Existenzsicherung und Ermöglichung der gesellschaftlichen Teilhabe zusichern soll.

Die bekannteste Möglichkeit ist diejenige, die der Gesetzgeber derzeit zur Bestimmung des sogenannten soziokulturellen Existenzminimums nutzt. Das „menschenwürdige Existenzminimum" gilt als „einheitliche grundrechtliche Garantie, die sowohl die physische Existenz des Menschen, also Nahrung, Kleidung, Hausrat, Unterkunft, Heizung, Hygiene und Gesundheit [...], als auch die Sicherung der Möglichkeit zur Pflege zwischenmenschlicher Beziehungen und zu einem Mindestmaß an Teilhabe am gesellschaftlichen, kulturellen und politischen Leben umfasst, denn der Mensch als Person existiert notwendig in sozialen Bezügen [...]." (Bundesverfassungsgericht, 2010, Rn 135). Das Bundesverfassungsgericht der Bundesrepublik Deutschland hat im Jahr 2010 geurteilt, dass der Gesetzgeber zur Ermittlung des Anspruchumfangs eines Transfers zur Sicherung des soziokulturellen Existenzminimums „alle existenznotwendigen Aufwendungen in einem transparenten und sachgerechten Verfahren realitätsgerecht sowie nachvollziehbar auf der Grundlage verlässlicher Zahlen und schlüssiger Berechnungsverfahren zu bemessen" (Bundesverfassungsgericht, 2010, 3. Leitsatz) hat. Das Bundesverfassungsgericht hat in seinem Urteil klargestellt, dass zur Ermittlung des soziokulturellen Existenzminimums sowohl die bis Anfang der 90er Jahre geltende Warenkorbmethode als auch die seitdem gewählte Methode der Ableitung aus einer Verbrauchsstatistik möglich ist (vgl. Bundesverfassungsgericht, 2010, Rn 166). Ebenso gesteht das Bundesverfassungsgericht dem Gesetzgeber bei der Bemessung des soziokulturellen Existenzminimums unter Berücksichtigung des jeweiligen Entwicklungsstands der Gesellschaft und den bestehenden Lebensbedingungen einen Gestaltungsspielraum zu (vgl. Bundesverfassungsgericht, 2010, 2. Leitsatz). Der Gesetzgeber nutzt derzeit zur Bestimmung des soziokulturellen Existenzminimums für Alleinstehende die Ableitung aus den Verbräuchen Alleinstehender der unteren 15 Prozent in der Einkommenshierarchie gemäß der Einkommens-

und Verbrauchsstichprobe (EVS) – nach Herausrechnung der Grundsicherungs-/Sozialhilfebeziehenden. Diese Verbräuche ergeben nach Abzug der Kosten für die Unterkunft der Heizung und weiterer nicht als regelbedarfsrelevant erklärten Verbräuche den Regelbedarf von Alleinstehenden. Zusammen mit den Kosten der Unterkunft und Heizung ergibt der Regelbedarf das sogenannte soziokulturelle Existenzminimum. Dieses ist wiederum die Grundlage der Ableitung des steuerrechtlichen Existenzminimums. Im Jahr 2021 betrug das durchschnittliche soziokulturelle Existenzminimum für Alleinstehende 858 Euro (die Summe aus dem Regelbedarf in Höhe von 446 Euro und durchschnittlich anerkannten Kosten der Unterkunft und Heizung in Höhe von ca. 412 Euro). Dies war der durchschnittliche monatliche Nettobetrag, der alleinstehenden Hartz-IV-Beziehenden ausgezahlt wurde, die über kein anrechenbares Einkommen verfügen. Die für die Auszahlung der Grundsicherung zuständigen Ämter zahlen darüber hinaus in der Regel die Beiträge für die Kranken- und Pflegeversicherung an die jeweiligen Kranken- bzw. Pflegekassen. Die grundsätzliche Kritik an dieser Methode der Bestimmung des sogenannten soziokulturellen Existenzminimums lautet:

1. Die Ableitung von den unteren 15 Prozent in der Einkommenshierarchie ist vollkommen willkürlich.

2. Die unteren 15 Prozent in der Einkommenshierarchie sind alle von Einkommensarmut und viele von sozialer Ausgrenzung betroffen. Die Regelbedarfe könnten genauso von den Ausgaben der unteren 10 bis 30 Prozent oder von den Ausgaben der Einkommensmitte der Alleinstehenden abgeleitet werden. Nur um die Auswirkung der willkürlich gewählten Referenzgruppe zur Ermittlung des Regelbedarfs zu verdeutlichen: Bezogen auf die Ausgaben der unteren 10 bis 30 Prozent und unter Anerkennung von rund 90 Euro höherer Kosten der Unterkunft und Heizung würde sich ein bedeutend höheres soziokulturelles Existenzminimum ergeben, ca. 1.360 Euro netto pro Monat. Mit diesem Betrag würde in Deutschland auch das Risiko der Einkommensarmut beseitigt, eine Zielsetzung der Europäischen Union seit Jahrzehnten. Außerdem würde dies den Entschließungen des Europäischen Parlaments entsprechen, dass Mindesteinkommen mindestens die Höhe der jeweiligen nationalen Armutsrisikogrenze haben müssen (vgl. Blaschke, 2021b).

Neben der hier skizzierten problematischen Bestimmung des sogenannten soziokulturellen Existenzminimums können andere Bestimmungsmöglichkeiten zur Höhe des Grundeinkommens genutzt werden, so zum Beispiel die Armutsrisikogrenze. Das würde den Ansprüchen der Europäischen Union bzw. des Europäischen Parlaments genügen, Armut oder soziale Ausgrenzung in der EU wesentlich zu minimieren bzw. ganz zu beseitigen. Die Armutsrisikogrenze nach EU-Standard lag für Alleinstehende in Deutschland nach o. g. EVS im Einkommensjahr 2018 bei 1.364 Euro (netto, im Monat). Nach dem Sozioökonomischen Panel des Deutschen Instituts für Wirtschaftsforschung lag diese Armutsrisikogrenze im Einkommensjahr 2018 bei 1.216 Euro (netto, im Monat), nach den European Union Statistics on Income and Living Conditions (EU-SILC) bei 1.176 Euro (netto, Monat) (vgl. Grabka, 2021, S. 313; Bundesregierung Deutschland, 2021, S. 477ff.). Nutzt man also die Armutsrisikogrenze nach EU-Standard für die Bestimmung der Höhe des Grundeinkommens, wären derzeit weit über 1.200 Euro bis rund 1.450 Euro netto angemessen. Mit dieser Höhe würde auch sichergestellt, dass das Grundeinkommen in allen Fällen netto höher ist, als der derzeitige maximale Grundsicherungsnettobetrag (Regelbedarf plus maximal anerkannte Kosten der Unterkunft und Heizung) von über 1.200 Euro. Das heißt, ein solcher Grundeinkommensbetrag würde sicherstellen, dass das bisherig geltende soziokulturelle Existenzminimum in keinem Fall unterschritten würde. Auch ein mit der Warenkorbmethode ermitteltes Grundeinkommen würde hochgerechnet auf die heutige Situation in etwa diesen derzeit notwendigen Betrag von über 1.200 Euro ergeben (vgl. Blaschke 2015).

Ohne auf die unterschiedlichen Begründungen für folgende andere Höhen von Mindesteinkommen einzugehen, die die Existenz und gesellschaftliche Teilhabe absichern sollen, seien hier noch die Pfändungsfreigrenze (derzeit 1.259,99 Euro) und der Betrag genannt, der eine Freistellung von der Rückzahlung des BAföG-Darlehens legitimiert (derzeit 1.330 Euro). Hierbei handelt es sich ebenso um monatliche Nettobeträge für Alleinstehende. Einen weiteren Zugang, um die Höhe eines Betrags zu bestimmen, der die Existenz und gesellschaftliche Teilhabe sichern soll, bietet der Ansatz der subjektiven Einkommensarmut. Hierbei werden über Umfragen Mindesteinkommen ermittelt (vgl. Andreß 1999, S. 96ff.), zum Beispiel im Rahmen des Sozioökonomischen Panels (SOEP) des Deutschen Instituts für Wirtschaftsforschung Berlin. Folgende Frage wurde gestellt: „Welches Haushaltseinkommen würden Sie persönlich – unter Ihren Lebensumständen – als das notwendige Mindesteinkommen betrachten? Gemeint ist der monatliche Nettobetrag, den ihr Haushalt unbedingt braucht, um zurechtzukommen." 1-Personen-Haushalte gaben für das, was sie unbedingt brauchen, im Jahr 2017 im Durchschnitt einen Betrag von 1.467 Euro an (Auskunft von Jürgen Schupp, Deutsches Institut für Wirtschaftsforschung Berlin, am 7.2.2022).

Egal, ob man die Armutsrisikogrenze, die Pfändungsfreigrenze, die Freistellungsgrenze bzgl. der Rückzahlung des BAfÖG-Darlehens oder das erfragte Mindesteinkommen (subjektive Armut) als Grundlage der Bestimmung der Höhe des Grundeinkommens wählt, Fakt ist: Alle diese möglichen Quellen zur Bestimmung der Höhe eines Mindest- bzw. Grundeinkommens weisen einen Betrag aus, der weit über dem derzeitigen sogenannten soziokulturellen Existenzminimum liegt, welches weder Armut noch soziale Ausgrenzung beseitigt, sondern beides zementiert.

3. Positionen der Parteien in Deutschland

In Deutschland gibt es viele Parteien, die sich in ihren Wahl- und Parteiprogrammen für die Einführung eines Grundeinkommens aussprechen. Bisher sind das kleinere Parteien, die derzeit keine Chance auf einen Einzug in den Bundestag oder in Landesparlamente haben, bzw. die nicht zu den Bundestags- bzw. Landtagswahlen antreten. Dazu gehören zum Beispiel die Tierschutzpartei (Wahlergebnis Bundestagswahl 2021: 1,5 Prozent), DIE PARTEI (1,0 Prozent), die Piratenpartei (0,4 Prozent), die Partei der Humanisten (0,1 Prozent), die V-Partei3 (0,1 Prozent), die Partei Demokratie in Bewegung (0,0 Prozent) sowie die nicht zur Bundestagswahl 2021 angetretenen Parteien Bündnis Grundeinkommen, Grundeinkommen für alle, Allianz Zukunft, Freiparlamentarische Allianz.

Festzustellen ist, dass alle genannten Parteien, außer den monothematischen Parteien Bündnis Grundeinkommen und Grundeinkommen für alle, neben dem Grundeinkommen weitere gesellschaftspolitische Reformen und radikale gesellschaftliche Veränderungen anstreben. Das Grundeinkommen ist also eingebettet in verschiedene Reformvorhaben. Selten wird von den genannten Parteien ein ausgearbeitetes Grundeinkommenskonzept vorgelegt.

Nur in zwei im Bundestag vertretene Parteien gibt es eine nennenswerte Bewegung bzw. Strömung pro Grundeinkommen: In der Partei BÜNDNIS 90/DIE GRÜNEN ist es das Grüne Netzwerk Grundeinkommen, in der Partei DIE LINKE die Bundesarbeitsgemeinschaft (BAG) Grundeinkommen in und bei der Partei DIE LINKE. Das Grüne Netzwerk Grundeinkommen hat im Gegensatz zur BAG Grundeinkommen DIE LINKE kein ausgearbeitetes Grundeinkommenskonzept vorzuweisen. Das Konzept der BAG Grundeinkommen DIE LINKE ist als Sozialdividende als auch als Negative Einkommensteuer konzipiert und durchgerechnet worden. Es ist explizit eingebettet in eine gesellschaftstransformatorische Perspektive. Die BAG Grundeinkommen DIE LINKE hat darüber hinaus ein Konzept eines Not-Grundeinkommens entwickelt, welches vor dem Hintergrund der Corona-Pandemie entwickelt wurde (vgl. Bundesarbeitsgemeinschaft Grundeinkommen in und bei der Partei DIE LINKE, 2021).

BÜNDNIS 90/DIE GRÜNEN trifft im Grundsatzprogramm folgende Aussage zum Grundeinkommen: „Existenzsichernde Sozialleistungen sollen Schritt für Schritt zusammengeführt und langfristig soll die Auszahlung in das Steuersystem integriert werden. So schaffen wir einen transparenten und einfachen sozialen Ausgleich. Verdeckte Armut wird überwunden. Dabei orientieren wir uns an der Leitidee eines Bedingungslosen Grundeinkommens." (BÜNDNIS 90/DIE GRÜNEN, 2020, S. 89). Im letzten Wahlprogramm der Partei BÜNDNIS 90/DIE GRÜNEN ist festgehalten: „Wir streben an, die soziale Sicherung schrittweise weiter zu vereinfachen, indem wir die existenzsichernden Sozialleistungen zusammenlegen und ihre Auszahlung in das Steuersystem integrieren. Wir begrüßen und unterstützen Modellprojekte, um die Wirkung eines bedingungslosen Grundeinkommens zu erforschen." (BÜNDNIS 90/DIE GRÜNEN, 2021, S. 121). Im Wahlprogramm der Partei DIE LINKE für die Bundestagswahl 2021 heißt es: „Alle in der Partei DIE LINKE sind dem grundlegenden Ziel verpflichtet, alle Menschen sicher vor Armut zu schützen und gesellschaftliche Teilhabe zu garantieren. Diese Garantie macht für viele die Idee eines Grundeinkommens attraktiv. Viele andere halten diese Idee dagegen für ungeeignet. Für uns ist dieses Ziel der Grund, uns für ein sanktionsfreies Mindesteinkommen von 1.200 Euro einzusetzen, für alle, die es brauchen: ob in Rente, Kurzarbeit, Erwerbslosigkeit oder im Studium – kein volljähriger Mensch soll weniger haben. Wir führen die gesellschaftlichen Diskussionen über ein bedingungsloses Grundeinkommen kontrovers und entscheiden im kommenden Jahr mit einem Mitgliederentscheid, ob wir unsere Haltung dazu ändern." (DIE LINKE, 2021, S. 28). Die Aussage, dass das Grundeinkommen kontrovers in der Partei DIE LINKE diskutiert wird, findet sich bereits im Parteiprogramm von 2011: „Teile der LINKEN vertreten darüber hinaus das Konzept des bedingungslosen Grundeinkommens, um das Recht auf eine gesicherte Existenz und gesellschaftliche Teilhabe jedes Einzelnen von der Erwerbsarbeit zu entkoppeln. Dieses Konzept wird in der Partei kontrovers diskutiert. Diese Diskussion wollen wir weiterführen." (DIE LINKE, 2011, S. 44) In den „Programmatischen Eckpunkten", dem programmatischen Gründungsdokument der Partei DIE LINKE anlässlich des Zusammenschlusses von WASG und Linkspartei.PDS im Jahr 2007, wurde diese Aussage getroffen: „Wir diskutieren mit unterschiedlichen Partnern weiter über Vorschläge für ein bedingungsloses Grundeinkommen." (DIE LINKE, 2007, S. 9) Schon damals wurde keine Antwort auf diese Frage gegeben: „Ist es ausreichend, eine bedarfsorientierte soziale Grundsicherung für Menschen in sozialer Not zu fordern, oder ist ein bedingungsloses individuelles Grundeinkommen als Rechtsanspruch für alle Bürgerinnen und Bürger zu verlangen?" (DIE LINKE, 2007, S. 19)

Sollte der Mitgliederentscheid in der Partei DIE LINKE dieses Jahr pro Grundeinkommen ausgehen, wäre die Partei DIE LINKE die erste im Bundestag vertretene Partei, die im Programm ein Grundeinkommen fordert. Sollte der Mitgliederentscheid gegen die Aufnahme des Grundeinkommens in das Parteiprogramm ausgehen, würde die kontroverse Debatte um das Grundeinkommen fortgesetzt.

In der CDU/CSU gibt es derzeit keine Bewegungen bzw. Strömungen pro Grundeinkommen. In der Antwort auf die Wahlprüfsteine des Netzwerks Grundeinkommen zur Bundestagswahl 2021 seitens der CDU/CSU heißt es: „Wir sehen es im Sinne der Hilfe zur Selbsthilfe als zielführender an, die Bürgerinnen und Bürger mit Blick auf ihre konkrete Lebenssituation finanziell zu unterstützen und Anreize für Beschäftigung zu setzen, anstatt ein bedingungsloses Grundeinkommen zu zahlen." (Christlich-Demokratische Union/Christlich-Soziale Union, 2021a, S. 3) Im Programm zur letzten Bundestagswahl ist zu lesen: „Ein bedingungsloses Grundeinkommen wird es mit uns [...] nicht geben." (Christlich-Demokratische Union/Christlich-Soziale Union, 2021b, S. 61)

Die FDP lehnt das Grundeinkommen ab: „Wir Freie Demokraten lehnen ein bedingungsloses Grundeinkommen ab. [...} Ein Grundeinkommen wäre leistungsfeindlich, teuer und ungerecht." (Freie Demokratische Partei, 2021) Diese Sätze von der Website der FDP zur Bundestagswahl 2021 sind allerdings im FDP-Bundestagswahlprogramm nicht zu finden. Das Konzept des „Liberalen Bürgergeldes", was auch zur Bundestagswahl propagiert wurde, stellt hinsichtlich geltender Verpflichtung zur Erwerbs-/Lohnarbeit, durchgesetzt zum Beispiel durch Sanktionen, klar: „Wer dagegen Sanktionen grundsätzlich abschaffen will, verabschiedet sich von diesem Grundprinzip unseres Sozialstaats, der Hilfen für diejenigen vorsieht, die sie brauchen und nicht für diejenigen, die sich nicht einbringen wollen. Sanktionen abzuschaffen, wäre schlichtweg unfair gegenüber allen, die diese Hilfen finanzieren. [...] Wir brauchen ein klares System, das sinnvolle Sanktionen vorsieht, deren Ziel der Weg in den Arbeitsmarkt ist." (FDP-Bundestagsfraktion, 2019). Das „Liberale Bürgergeld" soll außerdem einkommens- und vermögensgeprüft sein (vgl. FDP-Bundestagsfraktion, 2019).

Es ist nicht auszuschließen, dass sich die FDP, die sich offen für das Liberale Bürgergeld im Sinne einer Negativen Einkommensteuer zeigt, im Schulterschluss mit BÜNDNIS 90/DIE GRÜNEN in folgende Richtung bewegt: Zusammenfassung bzw. Bündelung verschiedener steuerfinanzierter Sozialleistungen und Integration der Existenzsicherung in das Steuersystem. Strittige Punkte werden dabei die Höhe der Absicherung, der Grad der Individualisierung, der Zwang zur Erwerbs-/Lohnarbeit bzw. zu Gegenleistungen und/oder verbleibende Elemente der sozialadministrativen Bedürftigkeitsprüfung sein. Die Klärung dieser Punkte können dann Aufschluss darüber geben, ob sich eine solche Vorgehensweise in Richtung Grundeinkommen bewegt oder ob weiterhin eine Grundsicherung präferiert wird.

Die Sozialdemokratische Partei Deutschlands lehnt klar ein Grundeinkommen ab: „Deutschland ist und bleibt eine Arbeitsgesellschaft. Durch den technologischen Wandel wird uns die Arbeit nicht ausgehen, sie wird sich nur stark und immer schneller verändern. Unsere Antwort darauf ist das ‚Recht auf Arbeit'. Das bedeutet, dass sich die Solidargemeinschaft dazu verpflichtet, sich um jeden Einzelnen zu kümmern und jedem Arbeit und Teilhabe zu ermöglichen – statt sich durch ein bedingungsloses Grundeinkommen von dieser Verantwortung freizukaufen. Wir teilen das Anliegen, Einkommenssicherheit im Lebensverlauf und mehr Zeitsouveränität zu schaffen. Doch wir halten das bedingungslose Grundeinkommen für falsch, denn es wird den Bedürfnissen der meisten nicht gerecht." (Sozialdemokratische Partei Deutschlands 2019)

In der SPD streiten vereinzelte Mitglieder und Gremien der Partei für ein Grundeinkommen, so zum Beispiel der SPD-Kreisverband Rhein-Erft (vgl. vorwärts 2016; Rhein-Erft-SPD 2010) und die Initiative „Grundeinkommen in der SPD" (vgl. Grundeinkommen in der SPD, o. J.) Seit Jahren wird auf dem Blog „vorwärts" die Diskussion über das Grundeinkommen geführt (vgl. vorwärts o. J.). Die Friedrich-Ebert-Stiftung hat sich vor Jahren intensiv mit dem Thema Grundeinkommen beschäftigt (vgl. Friedrich-Ebert-Stiftung, Abteilung Wirtschafts- und Sozialpolitik 2009).

Grundsätzlich gilt für alle parteipolitischen Ansätze in Richtung Grundeinkommen oder Beschlussfassungen zum Grundeinkommen: Sie sind außer bei monothematischen Parteien Bestandteil eines politischen Konzepts der Veränderung der Gesellschaft in die eine oder andere Richtung. Dies ist bei allen Diskussionen und Forschungen zum Grundeinkommen zu berücksichtigen. Es gibt nicht „das" Grundeinkommen. Es gibt verschiedene Grundeinkommenskonzepte als Bestandteil unterschiedlicher gesellschaftspolitischer Strategien. Die Ergebnisse sowohl von Feldversuchen und Pilotprojekten zur Einführung als auch von Simulationen der Einführung von Grundeinkommen haben vor diesem Hintergrund eine äußerst begrenzte Aussagekraft. Denn wenn Parteien ein Grundeinkommen einführen, würden sie im Kontext anderer gesellschaftspolitische Veränderungen eingeführt, die wiederum Einfluss auf die Wirkungen des Grundeinkommens haben. Außerdem hätten sich in diesem Falle Einstellungen, Verhaltensdispositionen und Positionierungen vieler zum Grundeinkommen verändert, sonst würden diese Parteien nicht entsprechende Machtpositionen erreichen.

4. Zugänge der sozialen Bewegungen in Deutschland

Im Folgenden sollen anhand von zwei ausgewählten sozialen Bewegungen Diskussionen und Zugänge der sozialen Bewegungen zum Grundeinkommen dargestellt werden. Dazu wird auf Überblicksliteratur verwiesen, ebenso auf detaillierte Beiträge und Positionen. Ein Anspruch auf Vollständigkeit wird dabei nicht erhoben. Der Begriff soziale Bewegung umfasst hier im Folgenden mehr oder weniger und unterschiedlich organisierte, kollektive, aber nicht homogene politische Akteure, die mit unterschiedlichen Strategien gesellschaftliche Wandlungsprozesse anstreben, solche umkehren oder verhindern wollen.

Ziel der Degrowth-Bewegung ist die Senkung der Produktion und Konsumtion, damit des Verbrauchs natürlicher Ressourcen, und der Erhalt der natürlichen Lebensgrundlagen. Profit-/Renditeorientierung statt Bedürfnisorientierung wird als ein wesentlicher Treiber des Wachstums von Produktion und Konsumtion ausgemacht. In der Degrowth-Bewegung wird das Grundeinkommen als ein wichtiger Bestandteil des dazu notwendigen gesellschaftlichen Transformationsprozesses wahrgenommen. Mehrere Gründe werden genannt: Ein Grundeinkommen befördere zeitlich und materiell das demokratische Engagement der Menschen, in allen gesellschaftlichen, auch in ökonomischen Bereichen. Das heißt, es bestünde die Möglichkeit, Ökonomie demokratisch und bedürfnisorientiert auszurichten. Mit einem Grundeinkommen wäre darüber hinaus die Möglichkeit der Individuen und kollektiver Akteure verbunden, Nein zu sagen zu nicht nachhaltiger Produktion, und Ja zu sagen zu solidarischer, nachhaltiger Ökonomie. Ein Grundeinkommen verschaffe zu Letzterem die nötigen materiellen und auch Zeitressourcen. Außerdem befördere es generell die individuelle und kollektive Arbeitszeitverkürzung, stellt also einen Beitrag zur notwendigen Minimierung der Produktion und Konsumtion dar. Ein Grundeinkommen würde aufgrund der Ermöglichung einer frei gewählten und selbstbestimmten Tätigkeit übermäßigen Konsum als Folge unbefriedigender, entfremdeter Arbeit bzw. Tätigkeit minimieren, so die weitere Annahme. Ein Grundeinkommen würde darüber hinaus, sofern es von oben nach unten umverteilt und somit für mehr Einkommensgleichheit sorgt, die Ersatzdroge Wachstum zurückdrängen (vgl. Wilkinson/Pickett, 2010, S. 253). Eine Umverteilung vom reichen globalen Norden in den armen globalen Süden könnte einer weiteren Ausplünderung der Ressourcen im globalen Süden entgegenwirken, ebenso dem Missbrauch dieser Länder als billiger Müllabladeplatz. Außerdem könnte ein Ökobonus als Bestandteil eines Grundeinkommens bzw. die (Teil-)Finanzierung des Grundeinkommens durch Nachhaltigkeit befördernde Steuern einen Beitrag zur nachhaltigen und ressourcenminimierenden Produktion und Konsumtion leisten (vgl. Blaschke, 2012; Blaschke, 2013; Blaschke, 2017a; Blaschke, 2017b; Blaschke, 2020). Aufgrund dieser grundlegenden Annahmen und Überlegungen, die das Soziale und Ökologische auf verschiedenen Ebenen verbindet, gibt es langjährige Kooperation zwischen Degrowth- und Grundeinkommensbewegung (vgl. Blaschke, 2016; Blaschke, 2018).

Dies kann ebenso bezüglich des Verhältnisses zwischen der feministischen bzw. postpatriarchalen Care-Bewegung und der Grundeinkommensbewegung gesagt werden (vgl. Blaschke, 2017c; Blaschke, Praetorius, Schrupp, 2016; Verein zur Förderung des bedingungslosen Grundeinkommens e. V., 2020). Die feministische und postpatriarchalische Care-Bewegung strebt gesellschaftliche Veränderungen in Richtung Sichtbarmachung und ausreichender Anerkennung bezahlter und unbezahlter Care-Arbeit sowie in Richtung einer carezentrierten Gesellschaft und Ökonomie an. Das Grundeinkommen wird in dieser Bewegung von vielen als ein Mittel der zeitlichen und materiellen Absicherung unbezahlter Care-Arbeit (nicht Entlohnung) und der Beförderung der geschlechtergerechten Verteilung der unbezahlten Care-Arbeit angesehen, ebenso als ein Mittel der angemessenen Absicherung der Existenz und gesellschaftlichen Teilhabe der Careempfangenden. Diese Absicherung ersetze nicht die infrastrukturelle Absicherung der Care-Arbeit, sondern sei mit deren Ausbau und Demokratisierung verbunden. Auch ersetze das Grundeinkommen nicht den notwendigen Ausbau der den individuellen Bedürfnissen angepassten Sonderleistungen für Care-Empfangende. Der in der Grundeinkommensdebatte oft in Frage gestellte Vorrang der Erwerbs- bzw. Lohnarbeit gegenüber anderen Formen der gesellschaftlichen Arbeit (zum Beispiel der unbezahlten Care-Arbeit) ist ein weiteres, die beiden Bewegungen verbindendes Element. Betont wird in der Care-Bewegung auch, dass das Grundeinkommen eine bessere Verhandlungsbasis für die Aushandlung der Bedingungen bezahlter Care-Arbeit biete. Das Grundeinkommen wird in der Care-Bewegung oft als ein Mittel der Beförderung bzw. als ein Baustein einer Care-zentrierten bzw. solidarischen Gesellschaft und Ökonomie diskutiert – einer Gesellschaft und Ökonomie, die sowohl die Befriedigung der Bedürfnisse aller Menschen als auch die selbstbestimmte Mitwirkungsmöglichkeit an der Realisierung der Bedürfnisbefriedigung in den Mittelpunkt stellt (vgl. Appel, Gubitzer, Wohlgenannt, 2013; Blaschke, 2014; Winker 2015; Winker, 2021). Abgelehnt wird in dieser Hinsicht, insbesondere im postpatriarchalen Diskurs, ein Dualismus von Freiheit einerseits und Abhängigkeit bzw. Bezogenheit andererseits (vgl. Schrupp, 2013; Praetorius, 2016). Über die zwischenmenschliche und gesellschaftliche Ebene hinaus wird von Feminist*innen das Sorge-Konzept auch auf das Verhältnis von Mensch/Gesellschaft und Natur ausgeweitet. Der sorgsame Umgang mit den natürlichen Lebensgrundlagen ist die andere Seite der Medaille des sorgsamen Umgangs mit anderen Menschen und mit zukünftigen Menschengenerationen im gesellschaftlichen Kontext (vgl. Biesecker, Wichterich, v. Winterfeld, 2012). Anschlussfähig werden diese feministischen bzw. postpatriarchalen Positionen inkl. dem Grundeinkommen damit auch an die Positionen der Degrowth-Bewegung.

Als ein Beispiel für die bewegungsübergreifende Positionierung zu Zukunftsfragen, die auch die Grundeinkommens-, die Degrowth- und die Care-Perspektive beinhaltet, kann das Buch „Zukunft für alle – Eine Vision für 2048. gerecht – ökologisch - machbar" (oekom-Verlag, 2021) gelten. Die darin zusammengefassten und aufeinander bezogenen Veränderungsvorschläge und Visionen wurden in Zukunftswerkstätten erarbeitet.

5. Europäische Bürgerinitiative (EBI): BGE in der EU

Mit einer Europäischen Bürgerinitiative (EBI) können die Europäische Kommission als auch das Europäische Parlament verpflichtet werden, sich mit dem Ziel und Gegenstand der jeweiligen Bürgerinitiative auseinander zu setzen. Konkret wird die Europäische Kommission mit einer EBI aufgefordert, einen Vorschlag für einen legal act für die Umsetzung des in der EBI Vorgeschlagenen vorzulegen. Sie muss dies aber nicht. Das Europäische Parlament muss sowohl die EBI als auch die Handlungsweise der Europäischen Kommission aufgrund der EBI bewerten. Es kann die EBI auch unterstützen. Die Aktivitäten der Europäischen Kommission und des Europäischen Parlaments und die

Anhörung der Initiator*innen der EBI durch die Kommission und durch das Parlament sind erst dann zwingend, wenn die EBI mindestens 1 Million Unterstützer*innen bei den EU-Bürger*innen findet und darüber hinaus in mindestens sieben EU-Mitgliedsstaaten eine Mindestanzahl an Unterstützer*innen erreicht wird. Erfolgreich ist die EBI letztlich erst dann, wenn das in der EBI Geforderte in der EU umgesetzt wird. Die im September 2020 gestartete und coronabedingt bis Juni 2022 laufende EBI „Bedingungslose Grundeinkommen in der gesamten EU" („Start Unconditional Basic Incomes throughout the EU") lautet: „Subject Matter: Our aim is to establish the introduction of unconditional basic incomes throughout the EU which ensure every person's material existence and opportunity to participate in society as part of its economic policy. This aim shall be reached while remaining within the competences conferred to the EU by the Treaties. Objectives: We request the EU Commission to make a proposal for unconditional basic incomes throughout the EU, which reduce regional disparities in order to strengthen the economic, social and territorial cohesion in the EU. This shall realize the aim of the joint statement by the European Council, the European Parliament and the European Commission, stated in 2017, that ‚the EU and its member states will also support efficient, sustainable and equitable social protection systems to guarantee basic income in order to combat inequality." (European Citizens' Initiative Unconditional Basic Incomes throughout the EU, o. J.). Im Annex der EBI wird das Grundeinkommen gemäß der o. g. Definition bestimmt (European Citizens' Initiative Unconditional Basic Incomes throughout the EU, Annex, o. J.). Bezüglich der Mindesthöhe des Grundeinkommens wird auf die jeweilige nationale Armutsrisikogrenze verwiesen. Die konkrete Formulierung der EBI ist abhängig von der jeweiligen EU-Vertragssituation und den darin verankerten Möglichkeiten der Umsetzung. Ohne diesen vertragsrechtlich hinreichenden Bezug würde keine EBI seitens der Kommission zugelassen. So wäre ein sozialpolitischer Bezug der EBI Grundeinkommen nicht möglich gewesen, da die EU bzgl. der Sozialpolitik der EU-Mitgliedsländer nur sehr eingeschränkte Gestaltungsmöglichkeiten hat. Es wirken an dieser EBI Vereine, Organisationen und Initiativen aus 25 EU-Mitgliedsländern mit. In Deutschland sind 38 Verbände, Initiativen, Parteien bzw. Zusammenschlüsse in Parteien im Kampagnenbündnis zur Beförderung der EBI organisiert. Neben der Umsetzung des in der EBI Geforderten werden folgende weitere Ziele der EBI Grundeinkommen beschrieben: Vernetzung der EBI-Aktivist*innen und mit anderen sozialen Bewegungen in der EU und in den EU-Mitgliedsländern (vgl. EU-Sign-Day, 2021), Verstärkung der öffentlichen Aufmerksamkeit und der pro-Positionen für das Grundeinkommen in der EU und in den EU-Mitgliedsländern (vgl. Europäische Bürgerinitiative Grundeinkommen, o. J.). Wie auch andere Europäische Bürgerinitiativen wird auch die EBI Grundeinkommen von drei hemmenden Faktoren beeinflusst. Es gibt erstens keine finanzielle Unterstützung der Aktivist*innen bei der Vorbereitung und Durchführung der länderübergreifenden EBI durch die EU. Zweitens ist das Beteiligungsinstrument EBI in der EU-Bevölkerung so gut wie nicht bekannt. In Deutschland liegt der Bekanntheitsgrad des Instruments der EBI mit 1,4 Prozent am niedrigsten, in Portugal mit 4,1 Prozent am höchsten bezogen auf eine Befragung in vier EU-Mitgliedsländern (vgl. EBI Grundeinkommen, Pressemitteilung 2021; ECI UBI, press release, 2021). Drittens verhindert der in vielen EU-Mitgliedsländern weit verbreitete EU-Skeptizismus die erfolgreiche Umsetzung der Europäischen Bürgerinitiativen.

Folge ist, dass seit der Einführung dieses Beteiligungsinstruments im Jahr 2012 lediglich sieben von 87 Europäischen Bürgerinitiativen die hohen Unterschriftenhürden nehmen konnten. Erfolgreich im Sinne der Umsetzung der Ziele war bisher nur eine EBI, und dies auch nur sehr eingeschränkt: Die EBI „Right2water".

Das Europäische Parlament kritisiert bestehende Formen der Beteiligung der Bürger*innen der EU an der Ausgestaltung der EU als vollkommen unzureichend (vgl. Europäisches Parlament 2021). Das trifft auch auf die Europäischen Bürgerinitiativen zu. Sicher auch ein Grund für den weit verbreiteten Europaskeptizismus. Das muss sich ändern.

Literatur und Quellen

Andreß, H.-J. (1999). Leben in Armut: Analysen der Verhaltensweisen armer Haushalte mit Umfragedaten, Wiesbaden: Springer Fachmedien.

Appel, M., Gubitzer, L., Wohlgenannt, L. (2013). Primär mehr – geschlechtergerecht und ressourcenschonend. in: Blaschke, R., Rätz, W. (Hrsg.): Teil der Lösung Plädoyer für ein bedingungsloses Grundeinkommen. Rotpunktverlag: Zürich, S. 99-114

Basic Income Earth Network (o. J.); (source: https://basicincome.org/, 15.01.2022)

Biesecker, A., Wichterich, C., v. Winterfeld, U. (2012). Feministische Perspektiven zum Themenbereich Wachstum, Wohlstand, Lebensqualität. Hintergrundpapier zur Enquete-Kommission im Deutschen Bundestag, Bremen, Bonn und Wuppertal; (source: https://www.rosalux.de/fileadmin/rls_uploads/pdfs/sonst_publikationen/Biesecker_Wichterich_Winterfeld_2012_FeministischePerspe.pdf, 26.02.2022)

Blaschke, R. (2012). Postwachstumsgesellschaft und Grundeinkommen. in: Woynowski, B., Becker, P., Bertram, A., Bhandari,S., Burger, J., Haver, M., Janssen, A., Lange, J., Miyazaki, J., Peters, G., Ruf, F., Schneider, J., Sempach, J., Wang C. C. (Hrsg.). Wirtschaft ohne Wachstum?! Notwendigkeit und Ansätze einer Wachstumswende. Freiburg: Albert-Ludwigs-Universität, S. 137-151, (source: https://www.ife.uni-freiburg.de/wachstumswende/woynowski-boris-et-al.-2012-wirtschaft-ohne-wachstum-notwendigkeit-und-ansatze-einer-wachstumswende.pdf, 26.02.2022)

Blaschke, R. (2013). Postwachstumsgesellschaft und Grundeinkommen; (source: https://www.postwachstum.de/postwachstumsgesellschaft-und-grundeinkommen-20130422, 26.06.2022)

Blaschke, R. (2014). Grundeinkommen und Carearbeit, in: Arbeit am Leben – Care-Bewegung und Care-Politiken. Widersprüche. Zeitschrift für sozialistische Politik im Bildungs-, Gesundheits- und Sozialbereich, Nr. 134, S. 113-127; (source: https://www.ronald-blaschke.de/wp-content/uploads/2014/12/Grundeinkommen_und_Carearbeit.pdf, 26.02.2022)

Blaschke, R. (2015): Aktuelle Studie zum Existenzminimum von Lutz Hausstein; (source: https://www.grundeinkommen.de/01/06/2015/aktuelle-studie-zum-existenzminimum-von-lutz-hausstein.html, 26.02.2022)

Blaschke, R. (2016). Hamburger Vernetzungskonferenz. Grundeinkommen und Degrowth; (source: https://www.grundeinkommen.de/15/02/2016/hamburger-vernetzungskonferenz-grundeinkommen-und-degrowth.html, 26.02.2022)

Blaschke, R. (2017a). Keine nachhaltige ökologische Transformation ohne bedingungslose soziale Sicherung aller Menschen, in: Konzeptwerk Neue Ökonomie e. V., DFG-Kolleg Postwachstumsgesellschaften (Hrsg.). Degrowth in Bewegung(en). 32 alternative Wege zur sozial-ökologischen Transformation. München: oekom-Verlag, S. 200-211; (source: https://degrowth.info/de/about-us/project/grundeinkommensbewegung-2, 26.02.2022)

Blaschke, R. (2017b). Sustainable ecological transition is impossible without unconditional social security for all people; (source: https://degrowth.info/en/about-us/project/unconditional-basic-income, 26.02.2022)

Blaschke, R. (2017c). Care-Revolutionieren mit Grundeinkommen; (source: https://www.grundeinkommen.de/28/08/2017/care-revolutionieren-mit-grundeinkommen.html, 26.02.2022)

Blaschke, R. (2018). Umverteilen statt Vermehren; (source: https://www.grundeinkommen.de/03/10/2018/umverteilen-statt-vermehren.html, 26.02.2022)

Blaschke, R. (2020). Klimaschutz braucht Grundeinkommen; (source: https://www.klimareporter.de/gesellschaft/klimaschutz-braucht-ein-bedingungsloses-grundeinkommen, 26.02.2022)

Blaschke, R. (2021a). Grundeinkommen. Positionen von Parteien und sozialen Bewegungen in Deutschland. Europäische Bürgerinitiative (EBI) Bedingungslose Grundeinkommen in der gesamten EU, Powerpoint zum Vortrag am 12.10.2021 auf der FRIBIS Jahreskonferenz 2021; (source: https://www.ronald-blaschke.de/wp-content/uploads/2022/03/21-10-12-Fribis.pdf, 26.02.2022)

Blaschke, R. (2021b). Der Regelsatz-Skandal; (source: https://www.grundeinkommen.de/30/03/2021/der-regelsatz-skandal.html, 15.01.2022)

Blaschke, R. (2021c). Was sagen die Wahlprogramme der Parteien zum Grundeinkommen?; (source: https://www.grundeinkommen.de/17/08/

2021/was-sagen-die-wahlprogramme-der-parteien-zum-grundeinkommen.html, 26.02.2022)

Blaschke, R.; Praetorius, I.; Schrupp, A. (Hrsg.) (2016). Das Bedingungslose Grundeinkommen. Feministische und postpatriarchale Perspektiven. Sulzbach am Taunus: Ulrike Helmer Verlag.

BÜNDNIS 90/DIE GRÜNEN (2020). Grundsatzprogramm; (source: https://cms.gruene.de/uploads/documents/20200125_Grundsatzprogramm.pdf, 06.02.2022)

BÜNDNIS 90/DIE GRÜNEN (2021). Bundestagswahlprogramm 2021; (source: https://cms.gruene.de/uploads/documents/Wahlprogramm-DIE-GRUENEN-Bundestagswahl-2021_barrierefrei.pdf, 06.02.2022)

Bundesarbeitsgemeinschaft Grundeinkommen in und bei der Partei DIE LINKE (2021). Konzepte; (source: https://www.die-linke-grundeinkommen.de/konzept/, 06.02.2022)

Bundesregierung der Bundesrepublik Deutschland (2021). Lebenslagen in Deutschland. Der Sechste Armuts- und Reichtumsbericht der Bundesregierung; (source: https://www.armuts-und-reichtumsbericht.de/SharedDocs/Downloads/Berichte/sechster-armuts-reichtumsbericht.pdf?__blob=publicationFile&v=6, 15.01.2022)

Bundesverfassungsgericht (2010). Urteil des Ersten Senats vom 09.02.2010 – 1 BvL 1/09 -, Rn. 1-220; (source: https://www.bundesverfassungsgericht.de/SharedDocs/Entscheidungen/DE/2010/02/ls20100209_1bvl000109.html, 15.01.2022)

Christlich Demokratische Union/Christlich-Soziale Union (2021a). Antworten der Christlich Demokratischen Union Deutschlands (CDU) und der Christlich-Sozialen Union in Bayern (CSU) auf die Fragen des Netzwerks Grundeinkommen; (source: https://www.grundeinkommen-ist-waehlbar.de/2021-de/wp-content/uploads/sites/18/2021/09/Grundeinkommen_CDU_CSU.pdf, 06.02.2022)

Christlich Demokratische Union/Christlich-Soziale Union (2021b). Das Programm für Stabilität und Erneuerung. Gemeinsam für ein modernes Deutschland; (source: https://www.csu.de/common/download/Regierungsprogramm.pdf, 26.02.2022)

DIE LINKE (2007). Programmatische Eckpunkte. Programmatisches Gründungsdokument der Partei DIE LINKE; (source: https://archiv2017.die-linke.de/fileadmin/download/dokumente/alt/programmatische_eckpunkte.pdf, 06.02.2022)

DIE LINKE (2011). Programm der Partei DIE LINKE; (source: https://www.die-linke.de/fileadmin/download/grundsatzdokumente/programm_formate/programm_der_partei_die_linke_erfurt2011_druckfassung2020.pdf, 06.02.2022)

DIE LINKE (2021). Wahlprogramm zur Bundestagswahl 2021; (source: https://www.die-linke.de/fileadmin/download/wahlen2021/Wahlprogramm/DIE_LINKE_Wahlprogramm_zur_Bundestagswahl_2021.pdf, 15.01.2022)

EBI Grundeinkommen, Pressemitteilung (2021). Bürgerinnen und Bürger kennen ihre Mitbestimmungsrechte in der EU-Politik nicht; (source: https://www.ebi-grundeinkommen.de/pressemitteilungen/pressemitteilung-7-4-2021/, 26.02.2022)

ECI UBI, press release (2021), New survey: ECI unknown in most European Contries; (source: https://eci-ubi.eu/new-survey-eci-unkown-in-most-european-countries/, 26.02.2022)

Europäische Bürgerinitiative Grundeinkommen (o. J.); (source: https://www.ebi-grundeinkommen.de/, 26.02.2022)

Europäisches Parlament (2021): Entschließung des Europäischen Parlaments vom 7. Juli 2021 zu dem Bürgerdialog und der Beteiligung der Bürger an der Entscheidungsfindung in der EU (2020/2201(INI)); (source: https://www.europarl.europa.eu/doceo/document/TA-9-2021-0345_DE.html, 26.02.2022)

European Citizens' Initiative Unconditional Basic Incomes throughout the EU (o. J.); (source: https://eci.ec.europa.eu/014/public/#/screen/home, 26.02.2022)

European Citizens' Initiative Unconditional Basic Incomes throughout the EU, Annex (o. J.); (source: https://europa.eu/citizens-initiative/initiatives/details/2020/000003_en, 26.02.2022)

EU-Sign-Day (2021); (source: https://eusignday.eu/, 26.02.2022)

FDP-Bundestagsfraktion (2019). Grundsicherung modernisieren – Chancen ermöglichen – Liberales Bürgergeld einführen; (source:

https://www.fdpbt.de/sites/default/files/2019-02/190221_Beschluss_liberales%20B%C3%BCrgergeld.pdf, 26.02.2022)

Freie Demokratische Partei (2021). Kein bedingungsloses Grundeinkommen; (source: https://www.fdp.de/forderung/kein-bedingungsloses-grundeinkommen, 26.02.2022)

Friedrich-Ebert-Stiftung, Abteilung Wirtschafts- und Sozialpolitik (2009). Das Grundeinkommen in der gesellschaftspolitischen Debatte, WiSo Diskurs März 2009; (source: https://library.fes.de/pdf-files/wiso/06193.pdf, 26.02.2022)

Grabka, M. M. (2021). Einkommensungleichheit stagniert langfristig, sinkt aber während der Corona-Pandemie leicht, DIW-Wochenbericht 18/2021, S. 308-316; (source: https://www.diw.de/documents/publikationen/73/diw_01.c.817473.de/21-18-1.pdf, 15.01.2022)

Grundeinkommen in der SPD (o. J.); (source: https://www.facebook.com/groups/grundeinkommeninderspd/, 26.02.2022)

Netzwerk Grundeinkommen (o. J.a). Die Idee; (source: https://www.grundeinkommen.de/grundeinkommen/idee, 15.01.2022)

Netzwerk Grundeinkommen (o. J.b). Grundbegriffe; (source: https://www.grundeinkommen.de/grundeinkommen/grundbegriffe, 15.01.2022)

Netzwerk Grundeinkommen (o. J.c). Modelle; (source: https://www.grundeinkommen.de/grundeinkommen/modelle, 15.01.2022)

Netzwerk Grundeinkommen (o. J.d). Definition of Basic Income; (source: https://www.grundeinkommen.de/english, 26.02.2022)

oekom-Verlag (Hrsg.) (2021): Zukunft für alle – Eine Vision für 2048. gerecht – ökologisch – machbar. , München: oekom-verlag; (source: https://zukunftfueralle.jetzt/buch-zum-kongress/, 26.02.2022)

Praetorius, I. (2016). Ökonomie der Geburtlichkeit. Wer das bedingungslose Grundeinkommen will, muss Wirtschaft vom menschlichen Anfang denken. in: Blaschke, R.; Praetorius, I.; Schrupp, A. (Hrsg.). Das Bedingungslose Grundeinkommen. Feministische und postpatriarchale Perspektiven. Sulzbach am Taunus: Ulrike Helmer Verlag, S. 31-45

Sozialdemokratische Partei Deutschlands (2019). Arbeit – Solidarität – Menschlichkeit. Ein neuer Sozialstaat für eine neue Zeit. Teil I: Arbeit;

(source: https://www.spd.de/fileadmin/Bilder/SPDerneuern/201902_PV-Klausur/20190210_Neuer_Sozialstaat.pdf, 26.02.2022).

Rhein-Erft-SPD (2010). Beschluss. Mitglieder-Parteitag der Rhein-Erft-SPD vom 06.11.2010; (source: https://www.rhein-erft-spd.de/wp-content/uploads/sites/200/2010/11/doc_31427_2010117225052.pdf, 26.06.2022)

Schrupp, A. (2013). Erkenne, was notwendig ist. in: Blaschke, R., Rätz, W. (Hrsg.): Teil der Lösung Plädoyer für ein bedingungsloses Grundeinkommen. Rotpunktverlag: Zürich, S. 83-97; (source: http://www.antjeschrupp.de/notwendigkeit, 26.02.2022)

Unconditional Basic Income Europe (o. J.). Who we are; (source: https://www.ubie.org/who-we-are/, 15.01.2022)

Verein zur Förderung des bedingungslosen Grundeinkommens e. V. (2021). Care-Revolutionieren mit Grundeinkommen; (source: https://www.grundeinkommen.de/wp-content/uploads/2020/08/BGECARE_Doku_200807_WEB.pdf, 26.02.2022)

vorwärts (2016). Grundeinkommen und SPD: Wie geschaffen füreinander; (source: https://www.vorwaerts.de/artikel/grundeinkommen-spd-geschaffen-fuereinander, 26.06.2022)

vorwärts (o. J.). Schlagwort Grundeinkommen; (source: https://www.vorwaerts.de/schlagwort/grundeinkommen, 26.06.2022)

Wilkinson, R., Pickett, K. (2010). Gleichheit ist Glück. Warum gerechtere Gesellschaften für alle besser sind, Berlin: Tolkemitt Verlag.

Winker, G. (2015). Care-Revolution. Schritte in eine solidarische Gesellschaft, Bielefeld: Transcript Verlag.

Winker, G. (2021). Solidarische Care-Ökonomie. Revolutionäre Realpolitik für Care und Klima, Bielefeld: Transcript Verlag.

Florian Wakolbinger, Elisabeth Dreer, Friedrich Schneider

Konsumfinanziertes BGE in Österreich

Finanzierungsbedarf und Preiswirkungen

Wir betrachten die Einführung eines BGE von 1000 Euro pro Monat in Österreich, welches ausschließlich durch Konsum- und Exportsteuern finanziert wird. Alle bisher geltenden Steuern, insbesondere Einkommensteuern und Sozialabgaben, werden in unserem Modell abgeschafft. Die Leistungen des Staates (Bildung, Infrastruktur, etc.) bleiben vollständig erhalten, allerdings werden Haushaltstransfers wie Sozialhilfe oder Arbeitslosengeld durch das BGE ersetzt. Ferner wird das BGE in unserem Modell additiv, d.h. zusätzlich zu den Löhnen aus Erwerbsarbeit oder Pensionen, ausbezahlt. Allerdings ist es Arbeitgebern und pensionsauszahlenden Stellen zunächst erlaubt, Löhne/Pensionen um den BGE-Betrag zu kürzen, bevor sie mit Arbeitnehmer- und Pensionistenvertretern neu verhandelt werden. Über die Ergebnisse dieser Verhandlungsprozesse bilden wir zwei unterschiedliche Szenarien. In Szenario 1 verbleiben die Löhne/Pensionen im Durchschnitt auf dem gekürzten Niveau, in Szenario 2 gehen sie auf das ursprüngliche, ungekürzte Niveau, zurück. In Szenario 2 steigen die Konsumgüterpreise aufgrund der Einführung des BGE und der damit verbundenen höheren Steuerbelastung zur Finanzierung desselben um etwa ein Drittel gegenüber dem Status Quo, in Szenario 1 bleiben die Konsumgüterpreise in etwa konstant.

1. Einleitung

Die Idee eines bedingungslosen Grundeinkommens (BGE) ist mittlerweile in der öffentlichen Diskussion[1] angekommen. Ein Grundeinkommen ist ein monetärer Transfer, dessen Höhe die Existenz des Individuums absichert und seine Teilhabe an der Gesellschaft ermöglicht. Die Auszahlung erfolgt ohne Bedürftigkeitsprüfung (= sozialadministrative Prüfung von Einkommen und Vermögen) und ohne Zwang zur Erwerbsarbeit oder anderen Gegenleistungen. Es stellt damit eine bedingungslose und regelmäßig zu gewährende, individuelle staatliche Transferleistung dar.[2] Mit dem Grundeinkommen würden zumindest Teile des bestehenden Systems der sozialen Sicherung ersetzt werden (vgl. Neumann, 2008, S.3).

Unsere Studie analysiert ein konsumsteuerfinanziertes BGE – in Anlehnung an das Modell des Vereins für Bedingungsloses Grundeinkommen (Modell „Verein Generation Grundeinkommen"; www.füreinander.jetzt). Unser Modell unterscheidet sich von den gängigen Finanzierungskonzepten (insb. Negative Einkommensteuer, Sozialdividende und Abschöpfung) und setzt an der Idee von Götz Werner (Finanzierungsbasis Konsumsteuer) an. Ebenso werden in unserem Modell alle direkten und indirekten Steuern, insbesondere aber Einkommensteuern und Sozialbeiträge abgeschafft und durch eine umfassende Konsumsteuer ersetzt. Dabei bleiben die bislang mit der Abgabenbelastung verbundenen Sozialleistungen (abgesehen von Leistungen der Arbeitslosenversicherung) in vollem Umfang erhalten (siehe Abschnitt 2.1)

Einschränkend muss betont werden, dass sich die Berechnungen am Status Quo orientieren, d.h. etwaige Anpassungsreaktionen, insbesondere im Hinblick auf das Arbeitsangebot bzw. die Arbeitsnachfrage nicht getroffen wurden – sie sind nach Einführung des BGEs jedoch wahrscheinlich. Langfristige Auswirkungen, etwa in zukünftigen Generationen, die mit einem Grundeinkommen bereits aufwachsen, sind noch schwieriger abzuschätzen.

Unser Modell und das des Vereins Generation Grundeinkommen setzen den Fokus – allerdings nicht ausschließlich (siehe Abschnitt 2.1) auf Konsumbesteuerung, da hier Ausweichhandlungen, wie die Verschiebung von Gewinnen, nicht möglich sind. Die Konsumenten tragen in unserem Modell (wie auch jetzt schon zum größeren Teil) die Steuerlast. Sämtliche Steuern und Abgaben sind auch jetzt schon Teil der Kalkulation für den Endpreis.

Ziel unserer Studie ist sowohl die Darstellung als auch die Berechnung der Finanzierbarkeit eines BGE-Modells via Konsumsteuern, sowie die Analyse einiger Auswirkungen davon. Sie gliedert sich wie folgt:

Der erste Abschnitt der vorliegenden Studie spezifiziert den Vorschlag des Vereins „Generation Grundeinkommen" und stellt das Untersuchungsdesign vor. Im zweiten Abschnitt werden die Umschichtungen im Steuer- und Transfersystem, die bei einer Umstellung auf Konsumsteuerfinanzierung anfallen, beschrieben. Im dritten Abschnitt wird der (gegenüber dem Status Quo) zusätzliche Finanzierungsbedarf einer Umstellung auf Konsumsteuer quantifiziert, während im vierten Abschnitt zur Finanzierung eines BGE notwendige Steuersätze und Abgabenquoten berechnet werden. Im fünften Abschnitt werden mögliche Effekte auf das Niveau der Konsumgüterpreise quantifiziert, und im sechsten Abschnitt wird ein kurzes Fazit gezogen.

2. Spezifikation des Vorschlags „Generation Grundeinkommen"

In unserem Modell wird der Vorschlag des Vereins „Generation Grundeinkommen", das BGE zunächst im österreichischen Bundesgebiet einzuführen, aufgegriffen. Alle nachfolgenden Berechnungen gehen daher von der Annahme aus, dass das BGE nur in Österreich eingeführt wird, während es in den restlichen Ländern zu keiner Systemänderung kommt. Daraus folgt, dass die Einkaufspreise von Importwaren durch die Systemumstellung zunächst unverändert bleiben.[3]

2.1 Das Konsumsteuersystem

In unserem Modell, wie auch im Modell des Vereins Generation Grundeinkommen, gibt es keinerlei Abgaben auf Einkommen - Bruttoeinkommen und Nettoeinkommen bzw. Brutto- und Nettolöhne sind daher ident. Die Finanzierung sämtlicher Staatsaufgaben erfolgt hauptsächlich über umsatzbezogene Steuern, vor allem über eine umfassende Konsumsteuer, die auf den Nettopreis der Produkte und Dienstleistungen, der – anders als im Status Quo – keinerlei Einkommens- und sonstige Abgaben umfasst, aufgeschlagen wird. Die bestehende Umsatzsteuer wird, wie auch alle weiteren bestehenden Steuern, durch die Konsumsteuer ersetzt. Dabei wird in zwei Steuersätze differenziert.[4] Die klassische Konsumsteuer gilt für im Inland verkaufte Produkte und Dienstleistungen, während die Exportsteuer auf den Nettopreis der Exportgüter aufgeschlagen wird. Ergänzend zur Konsum- bzw. Exportsteuer tragen ggf. eine Vermögensteuer, eine Finanztransaktionssteuer oder spezifische Verbrauchssteuern (z.B. Energie- oder CO2-Steuern) zur Finanzierung des Staates bei. Letztere werden im Rahmen der vorliegenden Studie nur insoweit thematisiert, als sich im Anhang eine allgemeine Diskussion der wissenschaftlichen Literatur zum möglichen Aufkommen einer Vermögensteuer und einer Finanztransaktionssteuer und den zur Verfügung stehenden Bemessungsgrundlagen in Österreich findet.

Inlandskonsum und Exporte unterliegen unterschiedlichen Steuersätzen, da die Exportsteuer so kalibriert wird, dass die Verkaufspreise der Exportgüter trotz Umstellung von Einkommens- auf Konsumbesteuerung im Durchschnitt über alle exportierten Produkte und Dienstleistungen konstant bleiben. Dies deshalb, da die Konkurrenzfähigkeit österreichischer Firmen auf den internationalen Märkten und im Ausland, in dem es annahmegemäß zu keinen Systemänderungen kommt, zumindest im Durchschnitt gewährleistet bleiben soll.

2.2 Höhe und Empfängerkreis des BGE

Die Höhe des BGE soll laut Definition „menschenwürdiges Leben ermöglichen". Sie beträgt im hier analysierten Vorschlag 1000 Euro pro Monat (12x jährlich netto) für erwachsene Personen, die im österreichischen Bundesgebiet wohnen.[5] Für Minderjährige unter 18 Jahren beträgt das BGE 500 Euro pro Monat. Das BGE wird monatlich ohne weitere Bedingungen an jedes Mitglied der österreichischen Wohnbevölkerung vom Staat ausbezahlt. Als Wohnbevölkerung gelten jene Menschen mit Hauptwohnsitz in Österreich.[6]

Erwähnt werden soll in diesem Zusammenhang, dass es abseits der durch das BGE ersetzten Haushaltstransfers (siehe Abschnitt 0 zu keinen Kürzungen oder Einstellungen öffentlicher Leistungen kommt. Unter dem Begriff „öffentliche Leistungen" werden im Rahmen der vorliegenden Studie vereinfachend auch Leistungen der Sozialversicherung, insbesondere der Krankenversicherung, subsummiert. Das bedeutet, dass beim Vorschlag der Generation Grundeinkommen insbesondere Gesundheitsdienstleistungen ohne weitere Versicherungsprämien (Krankenversicherung) zugänglich sind.

2.3 Art der Auszahlung und die Art der Einführung

Das BGE wird in unserem Modell nach seiner Implementierung additiv, also unabhängig von weiteren Einkommen (insbesondere Erwerbseinkommen) ausbezahlt.

Allerdings werden die heutigen Nettoeinkommen in der Einführungsphase zunächst gekürzt. Unmittelbar danach werden die Nettoeinkommen jedoch wieder den Lohnverhandlungen auf den jeweiligen Arbeitsmärkten überlassen (siehe Abschnitt 0Durch diese Vorgehensweise kann der Vorschlag des Vereins „Generation Grundeinkommen" mit einer substitutiven Auszahlung eines BGE verwechselt werden. Dies, obwohl die Kürzung der Einkommen lediglich in der Einführungsphase passiert und durch nachfolgende Verhandlungen wieder rückgängig gemacht werden kann.[7]

Bei einer substitutiven Auszahlung würden nur jene Personen vom Staat ein BGE erhalten, deren monatliche Nettoeinkommen kleiner als der BGE-Satz sind. Gewissermaßen würde das BGE, ähnlich der Sozialhilfe, die individuellen Nettoeinkommen auf den BGE-Satz anheben. Die substitutive Auszahlung wäre nicht bedingungslos, da für die Auszahlung das Einkommen kleiner als der BGE-Satz sein muss.

Die Finanzierung einer substitutiven Auszahlung wäre naturgemäß leichter zu bewerkstelligen als die Finanzierung einer additiven Variante. Eine substitutive Auszahlung würde beispielsweise für Österreich bei ansonsten konstanten Staatsausgaben (abgesehen vom Wegfallen der durch das BGE zu ersetzenden Haushaltstransfers) zusätzliche Budgetmittel von jährlich etwa 15 Mrd. Euro bzw. etwa 4% des Bruttoinlandsproduktes erfordern (ATTM (2018)).

2.4 Ersatz versus Ergänzung von Sozialtransfers

Das BGE ersetzt jene Sozialtransfers, die im gegenwärtigen System von Haushalten bezogen werden können. Dazu zählen insbesondere die Familienbeihilfe, das Kinderbetreuungsgeld, das Arbeitslosengeld, die Notstandshilfe und die Sozialhilfe (vormals Bedarfsorientierte Mindestsicherung). Weitere Leistungen wie z. B das Pflegegeld bleiben erhalten und werden weiterhin auf Antrag nch Prüfung der Sachlage ausbezahlt.

Pensionszahlungen bleiben erhalten, da sie Ansprüche aus vorangegangenen Leistungen von Pensionsversicherungsbeiträgen darstellen. Sie werden aber – wie die Erwerbseinkommen – bei Einführung mit der ersten Auszahlung des BGE so weit gekürzt, dass das Gesamt-Nettoeinkommen der Pensionisten inkl. BGE mindestens so hoch ist wie vor der Einführung (siehe den folgenden Abschnitt 0). Der Verlauf der Höhe der Pensionen nach Implementierung des BGE unterliegt wie bisher Verhandlungen der Pensionisten-Vertreter mit der Regierung.

2.5 Verhandlung von Erwerbseinkommen nach der Einführungsphase

Unser Vorschlag zur Implementierung eines BGE beinhaltet zwei Schritte. Schritt 1 "Wandlung" sieht vor, Erwerbseinkommen mit der ersten Auszahlung des BGE so weit zu kürzen, dass das Gesamt-Nettoeinkommen der Erwerbstätigen[8] inkl. BGE mindestens so hoch ist wie vor der Einführung. Das bedeutet, dass Nettoeinkommen, die unterhalb des BGE-Satzes von 1000 Euro pro Monat liegen, zunächst gänzlich durch das BGE ersetzt werden.

Würde dieser Schritt so umgesetzt, so entspräche das einer durchschnittlichen Kürzung der Nettoerwerbseinkommen um 44%.[9].

Schritt 2 „Verhandeln" sieht vor; nach Kürzung der Erwerbseinkommen und Wiederherstellung bzw. Erhöhung des Gesamteinkommens durch das BGE, dass Gehälter – wie bisher – individuell oder durch kollektive Verhandlungen vereinbart werden. Allerdings unter geänderten Voraussetzungen.

Einerseits werden für die Arbeitgeber die Löhne und Gehälter durch den Entfall aller Steuern und Abgaben auf den Faktor Arbeit wesentlich kostengünstiger. Andererseits ist die Verhandlungsposition der ArbeitnehmerInnen durch die Auszahlung des BGE gestärkt (siehe auch Calsamiglia und Flamand, 2019). Die unbedingte Notwendigkeit der Einkommenserzielung durch Erwerbsarbeit ist nicht mehr so stark gegeben bzw. fällt in vielen Fällen weg. Zudem könnte aufgrund der finanziellen Ausstattung durch das BGE auch die Bereitschaft, für geringe Löhne zu arbeiten, steigen.

Das Ergebnis der Lohnverhandlungen und somit das Niveau der Nettoerwerbseinkommen nach der hier skizzierten Einführungsphase ist daher unbestimmt und wird im Rahmen der vorliegenden Berechnungen nicht prognostiziert. Stattdessen werden in den nachfolgenden Berechnungen zwei Szenarien aufgespannt. Für Pensionen wird dabei angenommen, dass ihre Höhe der Entwicklung der Erwerbseinkommen folgt.

S1: Erwerbseinkommen / Pensionen bleiben nach Kürzung unverändert
S2: Erwerbseinkommen / Pensionen bewegen sich nach Kürzung auf ihr ursprüngliches Niveau zurück, vergleichbar einer initial additiven Auszahlung des BGE.

Szenario 1 stellt jene Situation dar, in der die verfügbaren Einkommen, d.h. die für Konsum / Ersparnis verwendbaren Einkommen, im Vergleich zum Niveau vor der Einführung unverändert bleiben (für Personen mit gegenwärtigem Nettoeinkommen ≥ BGE-Satz) bzw. erhöht werden (für Personen mit gegenwärtigem Nettoeinkommen < BGE-Satz). Die Autoren der vorliegenden Studie erwarten allerdings, dass – insbesondere aufgrund der verbesserten Verhandlungsposition der Arbeitnehmer*innen bei den Lohnverhandlungen – die Löhne und Gehälter nach einer allfälligen Einführung des BGE gemäß dem hier analysierten Vorschlag, gegenüber dem Niveau von Szenario 1 steigen würden. Es ist wahrscheinlich, dass die Arbeitnehmer*innen ihre gestärkte Position zur Wiedererlangung ihrer vormaligen Erwerbseinkommen nützen würden.[10] Im Gegenzug könnten überzogene Lohnforderungen der Arbeitnehmer*innen als Anlass zur Automatisierung genommen werden, um die Nachfrage nach Arbeitskräften zu verringern. Zum Vergleich wird daher auch Szenario 2 gerechnet, in dem die Erwerbseinkommen und auch die Pensionen nach der Einführungsphase wieder auf ihr ursprüngliches Niveau zurückkehren. Beide Szenarien sind nach unserer Meinung Eck- oder Randszenarien; sehr wahrscheinlich wird sich eine stabile Gleichgewichtslösung dazwischen einstellen.

Unklar ist, wie viel Zeit Schritt 2 „Verhandeln" in Anspruch nehmen wird, bis er vollständig abgeschlossen ist. Die Autoren der vorliegenden Studie gehen davon aus, dass – sollte es zu einer Durchführung des hier skizzierten Vorschlags kommen - das Datum der Einführung eines BGE im Vorhinein bekannt sein wird. Weiterhin gehen sie davon aus, dass bereits vor dem Einführungsdatum Arbeitnehmer- und Arbeitgebervertreter bzw. auch Arbeitnehmer*innen und Arbeitgeber*innen individuell in Verhandlungen für die Zeit nach der Einführung treten werden. Es ist daher davon auszugehen, dass Schritt 2 zum Großteil bereits vor dem Einführungsdatum des BGE, in dem Schritt 1 in Kraft tritt, abgeschlossen sein wird. Dennoch gehen wir davon aus, dass die gesamte Umstellung bis zu einem Zeitpunkt, in dem die Nettoerwerbseinkommen je Branche bzw. Beruf wieder weitgehend stabil sind, mindestens 3 – 5 Jahre dauern wird.

2.6 Weitere Annahmen bezüglich Konsum- und Erwerbsverhalten

Wie in der Ökonomie üblich, müssen zur Berechnung unseres Modells einige Annahmen getroffen werden:

(1) Die vorliegenden Berechnungen unterliegen der Annahme, dass die auf den Güter- und Dienstleistungsmärkten umgesetzten Mengen trotz allfälliger Preisveränderungen keinen Schwankungen unterliegen. D.h. die angenommene Nachfrageelastizität beträgt für alle thematisierten Güter und Dienstleistungen null.

(2) Weiterhin wird angenommen, dass zur Produktion von jeweils einer Einheit von Gütern und Dienstleistungen vor und nach der Einführung eines BGE gemäß dem hier skizzierten Vorschlag Arbeits- und Kapitalinput in gleicher Höhe notwendig ist. D.h. die Effizienz der Produktion bzw. eine Änderung der Kapital- oder Arbeitsintensität der Produktion wird im Rahmen der vorliegenden Studie nicht berücksichtigt.

(3) Hinsichtlich der Importstruktur wird für die vorliegende Analyse angenommen, dass die Importanteile der jeweiligen in Österreich verarbeiteten und angebotenen Güter und Dienstleistungen durch die Einführung des BGE unverändert bleibt.

Die Berechnungen erfolgen differenziert auf der Ebene von insgesamt 65 Wirtschaftssektoren (in etwa ÖNACE-Zweisteller), die Daten dazu wurden der Input-Output-Tabelle für Österreich (IOT, 2020) entnommen. Im Folgenden werden allerdings ausschließlich Überblicksergebnisse, die nicht in Sektoren gegliedert sind, dargestellt.

Abgaben auf Erwerbseinkommen	Aufkommen 2018
SV-Beiträge der Arbeitgeber (inkl. Lohnnebenkosten)	€ 37 Mrd.
SV-Beiträge der Arbeitnehmer	€ 23 Mrd.
SV-Beiträge der Selbständigen	€ 4 Mrd.
Lohnsteuer (auf Erwerbseinkommen)	€ 20 Mrd.
Einkommensteuer/KÖSt.	€ 21 Mrd.
Summe Abgaben auf Erwerbseinkommen	**€ 104 Mrd.**
Sonstige Abgaben	
Produktionsabgaben und Gütersteuern (z.B. MÖSt., Tabaksteuer, Energieabgaben)	€ 16 Mrd.
SV-Beiträge der Pensionisten	€ 4 Mrd.
Lohnsteuer auf Pensionen	€ 9 Mrd.
USt. in derzeitiger Form	€ 29 Mrd.
Sonstige direkte Steuern (z.B. motorbezogene Versicherungssteuer, ORF-Gebühren etc.)	€ 3 Mrd.
Summe sonstige Abgaben	**€ 61 Mrd.**
Gesamtsumme aller entfallenden Abgaben	**€ 165 Mrd.**

Tabelle 3.1 Abgaben, die nach Einführung eines Konsumsteuersystems entfallen
Quelle: Statistik Austria (2018), eigene Berechnungen.

3. Umstellung auf ein Konsumsteuersystem

Unser Vorschlag, und der Vorschlag der „Generation Grundeinkommen" sieht ein Konsumsteuersystem vor, in dem sich der Staat – anders als bisher – weitgehend aus beim Konsum anfallenden Abgaben finanziert. Darüber hinaus werden beim Konsumsteuersystem gemäß dem vorliegenden Vorschlag ergänzend eine Exportsteuer, eine Vermögensteuer und eine Finanztransaktionssteuer eingehoben.

3.1 Berechnungsbasis und Untersuchungsannahmen

Das Bruttoinlandsprodukt Österreichs im untersuchten Zeitraum 2018 betrug 386 Milliarden Euro. Die Summe an Steuern, Abgaben, Gebühren und Zöllen betrug für den gleichen Zeitraum 165 Milliarden EUR.

Bei vorliegender Modellierung einer Steuersystemumstellung auf Konsumbesteuerung und BGE fallen zunächst alle gegenwärtig gültigen Abgaben insbesondere jedoch Einkommensteuern und die ausschließlich auf Erwerbseinkommen anfallenden Sozialversicherungsbeiträge, weg. Tabelle 3 zeigt diesbezüglich das Abgabenaufkommen, das gegenwärtig jährlich anfällt und bei einer Systemumstellung ersetzt würde. Die gegenwärtig gültige Umsatzsteuer (USt.) wird durch eine Konsumsteuer gleicher Funktionsweise ersetzt. In Tabelle A1 im Anhang findet sich eine detaillierte Liste der Steuern und Abgaben, die bei einer Einführung des BGE gemäß dem hier diskutierten Vorschlag durch eine Konsumsteuer / Exportsteuer ersetzt würden.

3.2 Bemessungsgrundlage einer Konsum- und Exportsteuer

Im hier analysierten Vorschlag der „Generation Grundeinkommen" werden Güter, die im österreichischen Bundesgebiet angeboten werden, mit einer Konsumsteuer belegt. Jene Güter, die (zum Teil) in Österreich produziert werden und von österreichischen Anbietern an ausländische Nachfrager verkauft werden, werden hingegen mit der Exportsteuer belegt. Die Bemessungsgrundlage

von Konsumsteuer als auch Exportsteuer bestehen in beiden Fällen aus den Nettopreisen der Produkte, d.h. der Summe aus
- den Kosten des Faktors Arbeit[11] sowie den kalkulierten Unternehmensgewinnen (vor Abschreibungen) sowie
- den Preisen importierter Zwischenprodukte, die in den in Österreich gefertigten Gütern enthalten sind bzw. den Preisen importierter Endprodukte, die in Österreich angeboten werden.

Die Konsumsteuer wird somit auf „echte Nettopreise" - ohne jegliche andere bereits einkalkulierte Abgaben - erhoben, anders als die Bemessungsgrundlage der gegenwärtig gültigen Umsatzsteuer.[12] Da die Konsumsteuer (zusammen mit Exportsteuer, Vermögensteuer und Finanztransaktionssteuer) weitgehend alle bisher gültigen Abgaben ersetzt, und ihre Bemessungsgrundlage wie erwähnt „echte Nettopreise" sind, muss der Steuersatz deutlich höher sein als der Satz der Umsatzsteuer des gegenwärtigen Systems.

Investitionsgüter, die in Österreich nachgefragt werden, sind analog dem heutigen Umsatzsteuersystem auch bei der Konsumbesteuerung zur Vorsteuer abzugsberechtigt, daher nicht mit der Konsumsteuer belegt. Dies bedeutet, dass Investitionen im hier vorgeschlagenen Konsumsteuersystem keinerlei Besteuerung mehr unterliegen, während im gegenwärtigen System in Investitionsgüterpreisen insbesondere Abgaben auf Erwerbseinkommen, enthalten sind. Daraus folgt, dass Investitionsgüter im hier vorgeschlagenen Konsumsteuersystem um durchschnittlich ein Viertel (IOT, 2020) kostengünstiger sind als im gegenwärtig gültigen System. In weiterer Folge bedeutet dies, dass die Abschreibungen im Konsumsteuersystem ebenfalls um etwa ein Viertel reduziert werden.

4. Zusätzlicher Finanzierungsbedarf des Staates

Bei der Ermittlung des zusätzlichen Finanzierungsbedarfes des Staates bei Einführung eines BGE spielt naturgemäß dessen Höhe sowie die Höhe der durch das BGE ersetzten Sozialtransfers eine Rolle. Zudem ist wesentlich, dass der Staat an seine Angestellten (Beamte und Vertragsbedienstete) aufgrund des Wegfalls von Steuern und Abgaben auf den Faktor Arbeit nur noch Nettolöhne, nicht jedoch die Einkommensbestandteile zahlen muss, die von den staatlichen Angestellten als Lohnsteuern und SV-Beiträge entrichtet werden.

Unmittelbar nach der Einführung (siehe Abschnitt 0) können zudem die erwähnten vom Staat ausbezahlten Nettogehälter um den BGE-Betrag reduziert werden. Dies erleichtert zusätzlich die Finanzierung des BGE, da die freiwerdenden Mittel zur Finanzierung des BGE herangezogen werden können. Allerdings ist unklar, inwieweit diese Lohnreduktion bei den an die Einführungsphase anschließenden Lohnverhandlungen bestehen bleibt (siehe dazu den Unterschied zwischen Szenario 1 (S1) und Szenario 2 (S2)).

	Szenario 1	Szenario 2
BGE	€ 96 Mrd.	€ 96 Mrd.
SV-Arbeitgeberabgaben auf Gehälter staatl. Angestellter	-€ 8 Mrd.	-€ 8 Mrd.
SV-Arbeitnehmerabgaben auf Gehälter staatl. Angestellter	-€ 4 Mrd.	-€ 4 Mrd.
SV-Abgaben auf Pensionen	-€ 4 Mrd.	-€ 4 Mrd.
Lohnsteuern auf Gehälter staatlicher Angestellter	-€ 5 Mrd.	-€ 5 Mrd.
Lohnsteuern auf Pensionen	-€ 9 Mrd.	-€ 9 Mrd.
Haushaltstransfers	-€ 11 Mrd.	-€ 11 Mrd.
Produktionsabgaben	-€ 2 Mrd.	-€ 2 Mrd.
Summe	€ 53 Mrd.	€ 53 Mrd.
+/- Veränderung Nettogehälter staatl. Angestellter/Nettopensionen	-€ 25 Mrd.	+-0 Mrd.
FINANZIERUNGSBEDARF DES STAATES	**€ 28 Mrd.**	**€ 53 Mrd.**

Tabelle 4.1: Zusätzlicher jährlicher Finanzierungsbedarf des Staates als Saldo an- und entfallender Beträge Die Angaben beziehen sich auf das Jahr 2018 sowie ein BGE von 1000 bzw. 500 Euro monatlich gemäß Spezifikation in Abschnitt 2.3 (Quelle: Eigene Berechnungen)

Wird – wie im hier analysierten Vorschlag – gleichzeitig mit der Einführung eines BGE das Sozialsystem von (hauptsächlicher) Einkommensteuer- und Beitragsfinanzierung auf Konsumsteuerfinanzierung umgestellt, ist ferner relevant, dass die Gehälter der staatlichen Angestellten sowie die Pensionen gegenwärtig direkten Steuern und Abgaben unterliegen, in einem konsumsteuerfinanzierten System jedoch nicht mehr.

Dies hat zunächst zur Folge, dass die Gehälter und Pensionen, die der Staat selbst ausbezahlt, die Einkommensabgaben (typischerweise Steuer und SV-Abgaben), die der Staat unmittelbar nach Auszahlung selbst wieder einhebt, nicht mehr enthalten müssen. Vordergründig sinkt durch diese Umstellung auf Konsumbesteuerung der Finanzierungsbedarf des Staates, allerdings sind die Gehälter der staatlichen Angestellten und die Pensionen auch keine Bemessungsgrundlage mehr zur Einhebung von Steuern und Abgaben.

Daher ist zur Ermittlung des zusätzlichen Finanzierungsbedarfes die Entwicklung der Gehälter der staatlichen Angestellten sowie der Pensionen nach Implementierung des BGE maßgeblich. Diese wird im Rahmen der vorliegenden Studie wie erwähnt nicht prognostiziert, stattdessen werden zwei unterschiedliche Szenarien über diese Entwicklung gebildet und berechnet (siehe Abschnitt 2.5).

Schließlich ist die Preisentwicklung der Konsumgüter, die der Staat bezieht, zu berücksichtigen. Steigen (fallen) die Preise dieser Konsumgüter aufgrund der Systemumstellung, so steigt (fällt) der zusätzliche Finanzierungsbedarf.[13]

Tabelle 4.1 stellt zunächst die bei einer Einführung jedenfalls zusätzlich anfallenden den jedenfalls entfallenden Posten gegenüber. Wie ersichtlich würde der BGE-Betrag, der jährlich an alle Mitglieder der österreichischen Wohnbevölkerung ausbezahlt würde, sich auf rund 96 Mrd. Euro pro Jahr belaufen. Abzüglich der oben erwähnten entfallenden Sozialtransfers sowie der Abgaben in den Löhnen der staatlichen Angestellten und Pensionen, die aufgrund der Umstellung des Sozialsystems auf Konsumfinanzierung entfallen können, verbleibt zunächst ein zusätzlicher Finanzierungsbedarf von jährlich 53 Mrd. Euro. Wenn im Zuge der Systemumstellung und der daran folgenden Neuverhandlungen die Pensionen und Gehälter von staatlichen Angestellten gegenüber dem Status Quo unverändert bleiben (Szenario 2), stellen diese 53 Mrd. Euro jährlich den zusätzlichen Finanzierungsbedarf dar.

Von diesem Betrag wären jene Lohn- und Pensionsbestandteile abzuziehen, die bei einer „wandelnden" Einführung des BGE (Szenario 1) durch das BGE ersetzt werden.

Wie aus Tabelle 4.1 ersichtlich würde die Reduktion der Gehälter von staatlichen Angestellten und Pensionen in Szenario 1 25 Mrd. Euro jährlich betragen. Der zusätzliche Finanzierungsbedarf des Staates beträgt in diesem Szenario somit 28 Mrd. Euro.

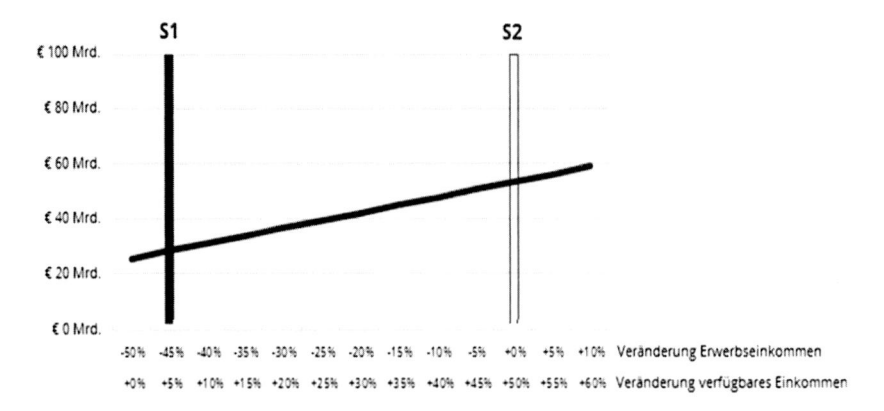

Abbildung 4.1: Zusätzlicher Finanzierungsbedarf in Abhängigkeit des Lohnniveaus
Quelle: Eigene Berechnungen, die Angaben beziehen sich auf das Jahr 2018.
S1: BGE + gekürzte Einkommen, S2: BGE + ungekürzte Nettoeinkommen

Abbildung 4.1 zeigt den zusätzlichen Finanzierungsbedarf für die zwei berechneten Szenarien sowie Situationen, die zwischen den beiden Szenarien liegen. Auf der X-Achse ist sowohl die Veränderung der Erwerbseinkommen (und Pensionen) als auch die Veränderung der verfügbaren Einkommen (Erwerbseinkommen/Pensionen + BGE – durch das BGE ersetzte Sozialtransfers) abgetragen. Szenario 1 (S1) zeigt, wie erwähnt, den Finanzierungsbedarf unmittelbar zur Einführung des BGE, in dem die Erwerbseinkommen und Pensionen so weit gekürzt werden, dass die verfügbaren Einkommen inkl. BGE nicht unter das ursprüngliche Niveau fallen. Dieser beträgt 28 Mrd. Euro.

Wie in Abschnitt 2.5 ausgeführt, entspricht S1 einer Kürzung der Erwerbseinkommen um etwa 44%. Gleichzeitig entspricht es einer Erhöhung der Gesamtheit aller verfügbaren Einkommen um etwa 5%. Für Personen, deren Nettoeinkommen vor der Einführung über dem BGE-Satz lag, bleibt das verfügbare Einkommen gleich, für Personen mit ursprünglichem Einkommen kleiner als der BGE-Satz erhöht sich das verfügbare Einkommen hingegen.

Kehren die Löhne und Pensionen auf das Niveau vor der Einführung zurück (S2), so beläuft sich der zusätzliche Finanzierungsbedarf auf 53 Mrd. Euro (siehe auch Tabelle 4.1). In diesem Szenario würde die Gesamtheit aller verfügbaren Einkommen jedoch mit der Auszahlung des BGE zusätzlich zu den Erwerbseinkommen und abzüglich ersetzter Sozialtransfers um etwa 50% steigen.

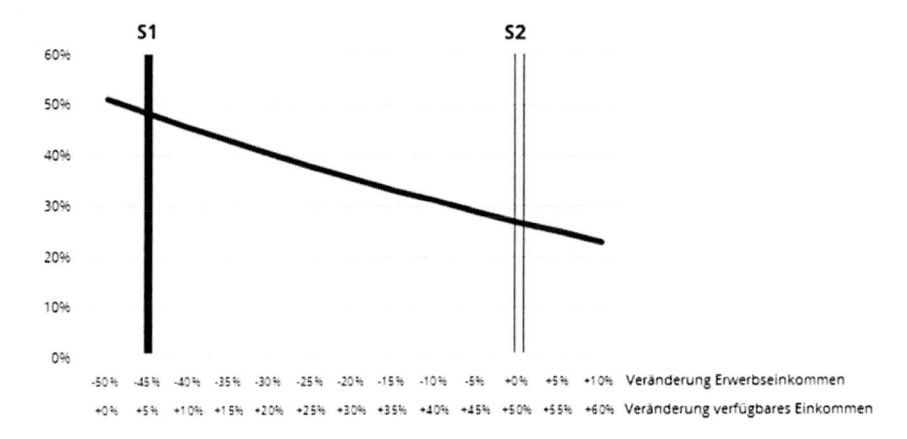

Abbildung 5.1: Möglicher Prozentsatz der Exportsteuer in Abhängigkeit des Lohnniveaus
Quelle: Eigene Berechnungen, die Angaben beziehen sich auf das Jahr 2018.
S1: BGE + gekürzte Einkommen, S2: BGE + ungekürzte Nettoeinkommen

5. Steuersätze und Abgabenquoten

Der folgende Abschnitt zeigt das mögliche Aufkommen der Konsumsteuer und Exportsteuer nach einer Einführung eines BGE gemäß den Forschungsfragen des Vereins „Generation Grundeinkommen". Die Aufkommen einer Vermögensteuer und Finanztransaktionssteuer, die im Vorschlag ebenfalls vorgesehen sind, werden im Rahmen der vorliegenden Studie nicht bewertet, jedoch im Anhang diskutiert.

Das Aufkommen von Exportsteuer und Konsumsteuer hängt dabei maßgeblich vom Lohn- und Erwerbseinkommensniveau ab, das sich nach Einführung des BGE einstellt. Denn die Löhne und Erwerbseinkommen sind Bestandteile der Güter- und Dienstleistungspreise und bestimmen daher die Bemessungsgrundlage der beiden Steuern. Daher werden die Aufkommenswirkungen für Konsumsteuer und Exportsteuer differenziert für die zwei unterschiedlichen Szenarien über die Entwicklung von Einkommen und Pensionen dargestellt.

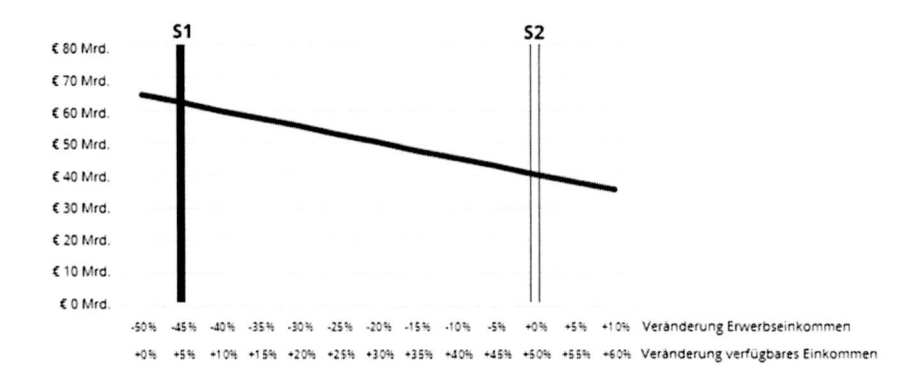

Abbildung 5.2: Aufkommen der Exportsteuer in Abhängigkeit des Lohnniveaus
Quelle: Eigene Berechnungen, die Angaben beziehen sich auf das Jahr 2018.
S1: BGE + gekürzte Einkommen, S2: BGE + ungekürzte Nettoeinkommen

5.1 Exportsteuer

Die Exportsteuer wird wie oben erwähnt (siehe Abschnitt 0) so kalibriert, dass das durchschnittliche Preisniveau österreichischer Exportgüter gegenüber dem Status Quo unverändert bleibt. Dies bedeutet, dass bei steigenden Löhnen der Prozentsatz der Exportsteuer geringer werden muss, da ansonsten das durchschnittliche Preisniveau des Status Quo nicht gehalten werden kann. Denn die Exportsteuer generiert im Durchschnitt über alle Produktgruppen genau das Aufkommen der direkten Steuern, die gegenwärtig in den Preisen enthalten sind (v.a. Einkommensteuern und SV-Abgaben) und nach der Umstellung auf ein Konsumsteuersystem entfallen würden.

Die in Abhängigkeit des Lohnniveaus möglichen Export-Steuersätze sind in Tabelle 5.1 dargestellt und betragen im Szenario 1 (S1) durchschnittlich +48% und in Szenario 2 (S2) 27%.

Konsumfinanziertes BGE in Österreich

Das resultierende Aufkommen einer Exportsteuer ist, wiederum in Abhängigkeit des sich auf den Arbeitsmärkten entwickelnden Lohnniveaus, in Abbildung 5.2 dargestellt und sinkt prozentuell mit zunehmendem Lohnniveau um jeweils auf die heutigen Netto-Exportpreise zu kalibrieren.

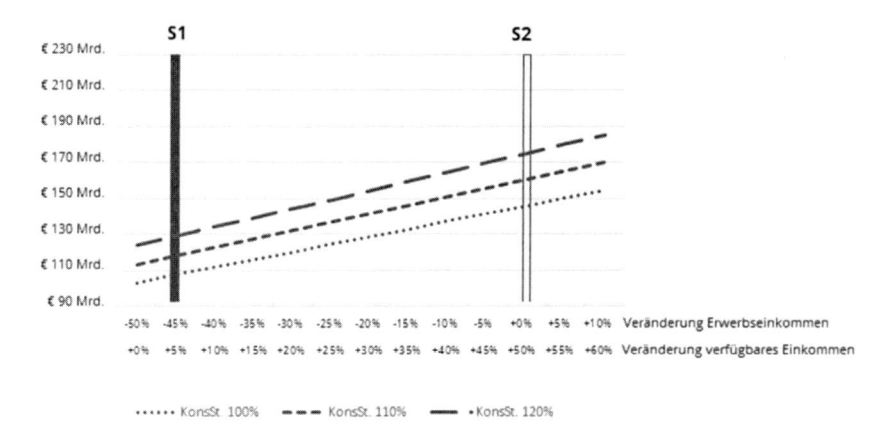

Abbildung 5.3: Aufkommen der Konsumsteuer in Abhängigkeit des Lohnniveaus
Quelle: Eigene Berechnungen, die Angaben beziehen sich auf das Jahr 2018.
S1: BGE + gekürzte Einkommen, S2: BGE + ungekürzte Nettoeinkommen

5.2 Konsumsteuersätze

Das Aufkommen der Konsumsteuer ist bei gegebenem Prozentsatz – unter den für die vorliegende Studie getroffenen Annahmen – ebenfalls abhängig vom sich auf den Arbeitsmärkten nach Einführung des BGE einstellenden Lohnniveaus. Abbildung 5.3 zeigt das Aufkommen einer Konsumsteuer, das bei Konsumsteuer-Prozentsätzen von 100%, 110% und 120% unter der getroffenen Annahme, dass die nachgefragten Gütermengen gegenüber dem Status Quo unverändert bleiben, generiert wird. Die Prozentsätze wurden in der Bandbreite gewählt, sodass das generierbare Aufkommen - inkl. Exportsteuer - in etwa dem für die Einführung des BGE inkl. Umstellung auf Konsumsteuersystem notwendigen Aufkommen entspricht. Die Betrachtung inkludiert mit 100% den einfachsten Konsumsteuersatz, da er, die jeweilige Steuerlast beim Kauf eines Produktes durch einfache Kopfrechnung berechenbar macht. Das erforderliche Aufkommen sowie die von Exportsteuer und Konsumsteuer (differenziert in die Steuersätze 100%, 110% und 120%) in Abhängigkeit von der Lohnentwicklung generierten Aufkommen sind in Abbildung 5.4 dargestellt. Wie ersichtlich steigt das erforderliche Aufkommen mit steigenden Lohnniveaus. Dies deshalb, da die Gehälter der staatlichen Angestellten und die Pensionen annahmegemäß derselben Entwicklung folgen wie die Löhne und Einkommen auf den privaten Arbeitsmärkten. Bleiben auf diesen Arbeitsmärkten die Löhne nach der Kürzung im Zuge der Einführung des BGE (S1) unverändert, so beträgt das für ein BGE erforderliche Aufkommen etwa 192 Mrd. Euro jährlich. Bewegen sich die Löhne der staatlichen Angestellten / Pensionen nach der im vorliegenden Vorschlag vorgenommenen Kürzung im Rahmen der Einführung des BGE wieder auf ihr ursprüngliches Niveau zurück (S2), so steigt der Finanzierungsbedarf entsprechend.

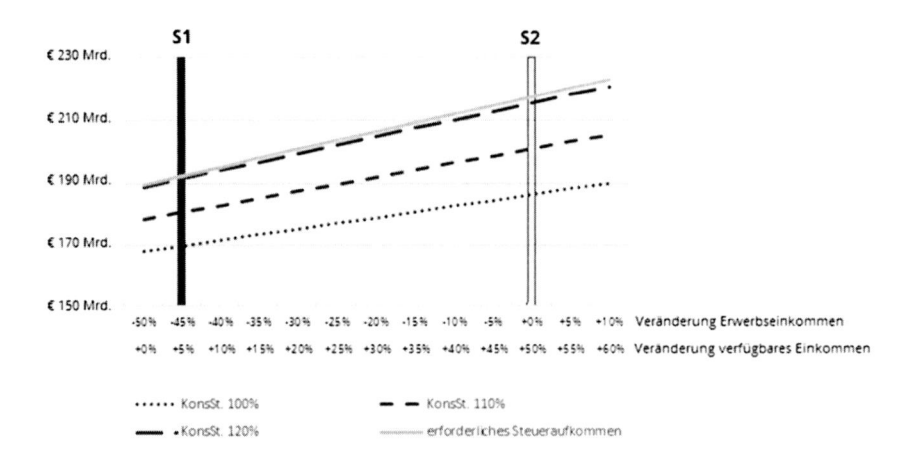

Abbildung 5.4: Aufkommen von Konsum- und Exportsteuer gegenüber dem für ein BGE erforderlichem Aufkommen; Quelle: Eigene Berechnungen, die Angaben beziehen sich auf das Jahr 2018. S1: BGE + gekürzte Einkommen, S2: BGE + ungekürzte Nettoeinkommen

Wie aus Abbildung 5.4 ersichtlich, würde eine Konsumsteuer von 120% zusammen mit einer Exportsteuer die Finanzierung des BGE gemäß dem Vor-

Konsumfinanziertes BGE in Österreich 279

schlag des Vereins „Generation Grundeinkommen" ohne weitere Steuerquellen annähernd gewährleisten. Ein (einfacher) Satz von 100% würde zusätzliche Steuereinnahmen im Ausmaß von etwa 23 Mrd. Euro jährlich (6% des Bruttoinlandsproduktes) erfordern, etwa aus den im Anhang diskutierten Vermögensteuern und Finanztransaktionssteuern bzw. auch aus spezifischen Verbrauchssteuern wie einer Energie- oder CO_2-Steuer.

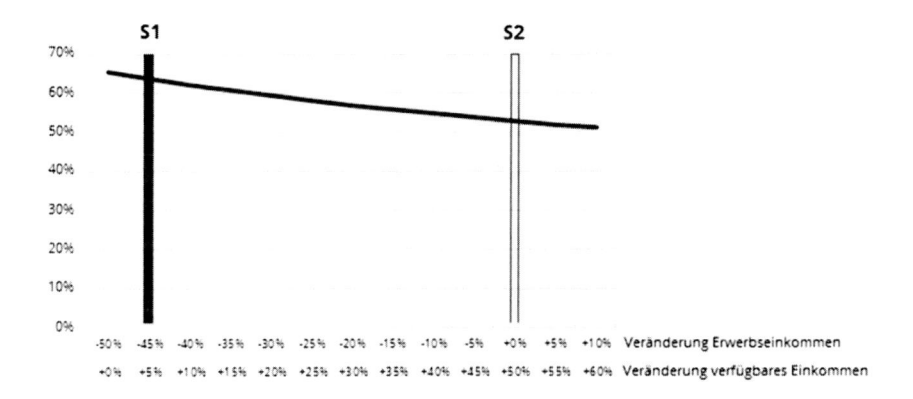

Abbildung 5.5: Zur Finanzierung eines BGE notwendige Abgabenquote
Quelle: Eigene Berechnungen, die Angaben beziehen sich auf das Jahr 2018.
S1: BGE + gekürzte Einkommen, S2: BGE + ungekürzte Nettoeinkommen

Im Anhang zur vorliegenden Studie wird die existierende wissenschaftliche Literatur zur möglichen Einführung einer Vermögensteuer- und einer Finanztransaktionssteuer in Österreich diskutiert. Gemäß den vorliegenden Untersuchungen dürfte mit einer umfassenden Vermögensteuer aufgrund signifikanter Ausweichreaktionen ein maximales Aufkommen von etwa € 5 Mrd. jährlich zu erzielen sein. Eine Finanztransaktionssteuer könnte den vorliegenden Untersuchungen zufolge ein Aufkommen von etwa € 1,5 Mrd. jährlich erzielen. Ein Konsumsteuersatz von 100% erscheint daher – auch wenn zusätzlich zur Vermögensteuer und Finanztransaktionssteuer spezifische Verbrauchssteuern wie Energie- oder CO_2-Steuern eingeführt werden, zur Finanzierung des BGE zu niedrig. Der dafür notwendige Steuersatz dürfte – in Abhängigkeit von der konkreten Ausgestaltung der zugezogenen Vermögensteuern, Finanztransaktionssteuern und Energiesteuern, bei 110% bis 120% liegen.

5.3 Abgabenquote

Die zur Finanzierung eines BGE gemäß dem Vorschlag des Vereins „Generation Grundeinkommen" notwendige Abgabenquote (in % des BIP) ist in Abbildung 5.5 dargestellt. Sie sinkt mit steigendem Niveau von Erwerbseinkommen, da diese die Basis der Abgabenquote, das BIP, beeinflussen. Im Szenario 1 mit um das BGE gekürzten Erwerbseinkommen (dieses gilt unmittelbar nach der Einführung des BGE gemäß dem hier analysierten Vorschlag) sinkt das Bruttoinlandsprodukt auf unter 300 Mrd. Euro. Der BIP-Rückgang ist vor allem darauf zurückzuführen, dass Investitionsgüter sowie die Gehälter der staatlichen Angestellten nach Umstellung auf Konsumsteuer vollständig von Abgaben befreit sind. Letzteres wirkt sich auch auf die Abschreibungen aus, die im BIP enthalten sind. Lohnerhöhungen sowie die insgesamt höhere Steuerbelastung wirken sich hingegen BIP-erhöhend aus. Die Summe der beiden Effekte ergibt das BIP-Niveau nach Einführung eines BGE gemäß dem hier analysierten Vorschlag. Die entsprechenden Werte sind in Abbildung 5.6 dargestellt.

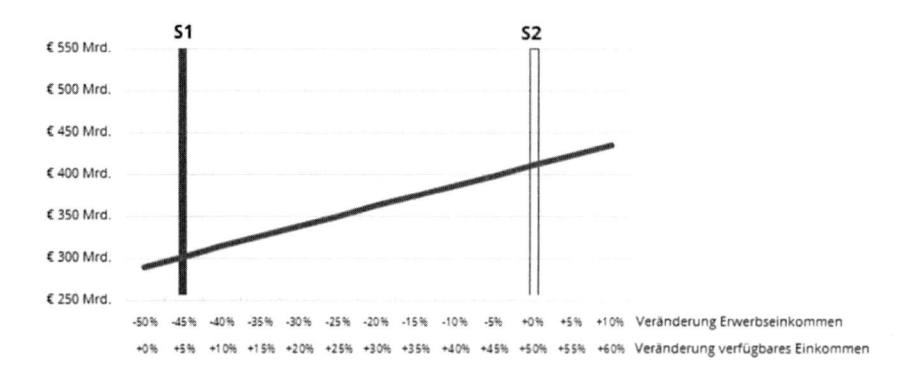

Abbildung 5.6: BIP-Niveau nach Einführung eines BGE
Quelle: Eigene Berechnungen, die Angaben beziehen sich auf das Jahr 2018.
S1: BGE + gekürzte Einkommen, S2: BGE + ungekürzte Nettoeinkommen

Bewegen sich die Löhne nach Einführung des BGE wieder auf ihr ursprüngliches Niveau zurück (S2), so würde die notwendige Abgabenquote noch knapp über 50% betragen. Allerdings müsste in diesem Fall von Preissteigerungen ausgegangen werden, wodurch die Kaufkraft des BGE sinkt (siehe Abschnitt 6).

6. Effekte auf das Preisniveau

Im vorliegenden Abschnitt wird dargestellt, wie eine Einführung eines BGE gemäß dem Vorschlag des Vereins „Generation Grundeinkommen" das Preisniveau der Konsumgüter beeinflussen würde. Effekte auf das Preisniveau sind durch die Umstellung des Steuersystems von weitgehender Einkommens- auf weitgehende Konsumfinanzierung denkbar. Denn eine Konsumsteuer wirkt vor allem über die Preise der Produkte, die mit der Konsumsteuer belegt sind. Eine Einkommensteuer tut dies – unter der Annahme konstanter Bruttolöhne bzw. Bruttoeinkommen – nicht. Stattdessen wirkt eine Einkommensteuer auf die Nettoeinkommen. Real, d.h. bezüglich der Gütermengen, die für eine Einheit Nettoeinkommen erhältlich sind, sind Konsumsteuer und Einkommensteuer äquivalent, nominell (d.h. bezüglich der monetären Beträge von Preisen und Nettoeinkommen) jedoch nicht.

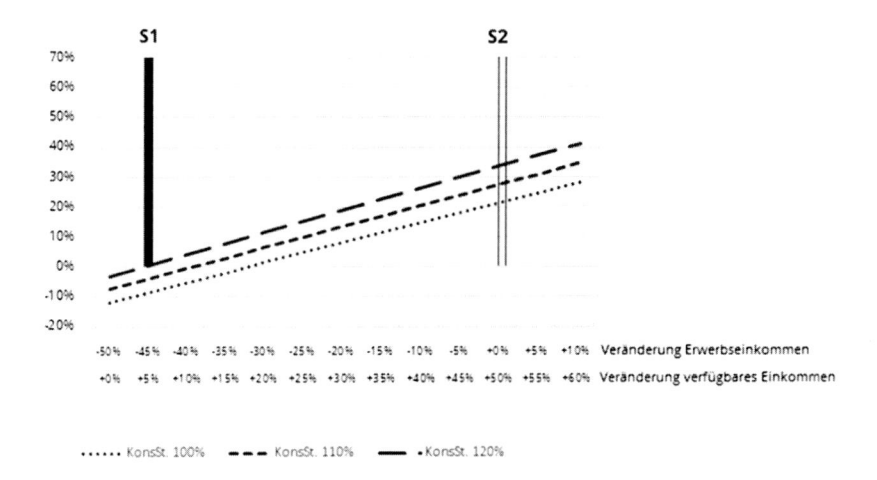

Abbildung 6.1: Veränderung des Preisniveaus nach Einführung eines BGE
Quelle: Eigene Berechnungen, die Angaben beziehen sich auf das Jahr 2018.
S1: BGE + gekürzte Einkommen, S2: BGE + ungekürzte Nettoeinkommen

Produktkategorie	Preisniveau S1	Preisniveau S2	Anteil 1. Dezil	Anteil 10. Dezil	Differenz
Tatsächliche Mietzahlungen	76	132	10,1%	3,1%	6,9%
Nahrungsmittel	113	147	14,2%	8,3%	5,9%
Wasserversorgung und andere Dienstleistungen im Zusammenhang mit der Wohnung	100	136	5,9%	3,4%	2,5%
Strom, Gas u.a. Brennstoffe	105	140	6,4%	3,8%	2,5%
Tabakwaren	111	142	2,1%	0,6%	1,5%
Andere Dienstleistungen, a.n.g.	113	143	0,5%	1,6%	-1,1%
Ambulante Gesundheitsdienstleistungen	83	133	1,1%	2,2%	-1,1%
Bekleidung	131	150	3,3%	4,5%	-1,2%
Versicherungsdienstleistungen	97	135	3,6%	4,9%	-1,3%
Waren und Dienstleistungen für den Betrieb von Privatfahrzeugen	78	118	6,7%	8,1%	-1,4%
Verpflegungsdienstleistungen	86	129	6,0%	7,6%	-1,7%
Regelmäßige Instandhaltung und Reparatur der Wohnungen	98	134	3,0%	5,1%	-2,1%
Kauf von Fahrzeugen	99	131	4,5%	7,5%	-3,0%
Pauschalreisen	85	128	3,1%	7,9%	-4,8%

Tabelle 6.1: Preisniveau bei Produktkategorien, deren Konsum stark einkommensabhängig ist
Quelle: Eigene Berechnungen, basierend auf der Konsumerhebung 2014/15 von Statistik Austria (2018). S1: BGE + gekürzte Einkommen, S2: BGE + ungekürzte Nettoeinkommen Angenommen wird ein Konsumsteuersatz von 110%. Die Berechnungen beziehen sich auf das Jahr 2018.

6.1 Durchschnittliches Preisniveau

Zur Ermittlung des Preisniveaus der Konsumgüterpreise wurden die Nettopreise herangezogen, die sich aus den Importanteilen der jeweiligen Güter und den (österreichischen) Netto-Erwerbseinkommen, die in den Szenarien S1 und S2 je nach Lohnentwicklung variieren, ergeben. Die Nettopreise wurden in weiterer Folge mit Konsumsteuersätzen von 100%, 110% und 120% belegt. Die Analyse erfolgt differenziert für 65 Produktgruppen, die in Abbildung 6.1 dargestellte Veränderung des Preisniveaus gegenüber dem Status Quo wird auf Basis des gewichteten Durchschnittes der Preisveränderungen bei den jeweiligen Produktgruppen errechnet. Als Gewichte werden die Anteile der jeweiligen Produktgruppen am gesamten privaten Konsum in Österreich gemäß Input-Output-Tabelle (2018) verwendet. Die Analyse erfolgt unter der Annahme, dass die Preisveränderungen die konsumierten Gütermengen nicht beeinflussen (Preiselastizität der Nachfrage = 0, siehe Abschnitt 2.6).

Die gezeigten Änderungen werden auch dadurch beeinflusst, dass die Konsumsteuer gemäß dem hier analysierten Vorschlag alle Produkte umfasst und auch alle Produkte mit dem gleichen Steuersatz belegt sind, während im Status Quo bestimmte Produkte von der Besteuerung ausgenommen sind (z.B. Dienstleistungen von Banken) oder einem reduzierten Steuersatz unterliegen (z.B. Lebensmittel).

Wie ersichtlich ist die Änderung des Preisniveaus abhängig vom unterstellten Szenario über die Lohnentwicklung. Der Vorschlag des Vereins „Generation Grundeinkommen" sieht vor, im Rahmen der Einführung des BGE die Löhne so weit zu kürzen, dass das Gesamt-Nettoeinkommen gegenüber dem Status Quo mindestens konstant bleibt (bzw. sich für Nettoeinkommen, die kleiner als der BGE-Satz sind, erhöht). Kommt es nach dieser Maßnahme auf den Arbeitsmärkten zu keiner weiteren Erhöhung der Erwerbseinkommen, so ändert sich das Preisniveau gegenüber dem Status Quo kaum. Bewegen sich die Erwerbseinkommen allerdings wieder auf ihr ursprüngliches Niveau zurück (S2), so ist mit Preissteigerungen von etwa 30% zu rechnen.

6.2 Einkommensabhängiges Preisniveau

In weiterer Folge stellt sich die Frage, ob Haushalte mit unterschiedlichem Einkommen, da sie unterschiedliche Konsumgewohnheiten aufweisen, durch die Preisänderungen in unterschiedlichem Ausmaß betroffen wären. Beispielsweise ist allgemein bekannt, dass Haushalte mit geringen Einkommen anteilsmäßig mehr für Lebensmittel ausgeben als Haushalte mit hohen Einkommen. Die Preisveränderung bei Lebensmitteln wirkt sich daher bei Haushalten mit geringen Einkommen entsprechend stärker aus.

Tabelle 6.1 listet diesbezüglich jene Produktgruppen auf, deren Konsum stark einkommensabhängig ist.[14] Zusätzlich dazu werden die jeweiligen Anteile am Gesamtkonsum für das 1. Dezil der Haushalts-Einkommensverteilung (d.h. die ärmsten 10% der Haushalte) sowie für das 10. Dezil (d.h. die reichsten 10% der Haushalte) und die Differenz dieser Anteile ausgewiesen. Darüber hinaus wird das produktgruppenspezifische Preisniveau nach Einführung eines BGE gemäß dem hier analysierten Vorschlag im Vergleich zum Status Quo (Wert 100) ausgewiesen.

Dezil	Preisniveau S1	Preisniveau S2
1	99,8	135,3
2	99,5	135,1
3	99,8	135,4
4	99,3	134,9
5	98,6	134,4
6	98,3	134,2
7	98,7	134,3
8	98,5	134,2
9	97,6	133,7
10	97,2	133,4

Tabelle 6.2: Durchschnittliche Änderung des Preisniveaus (Status Quo = 100) nach Einkommensdezilen; Quelle: Eigene Berechnungen, die Angaben beziehen sich auf das Jahr 2018. S1: BGE + gekürzte Einkommen, S2: BGE + ungekürzte Nettoeinkommen

Wie ersichtlich besteht bei Wohnungsmieten und Nahrungsmitteln eine erhebliche Differenz dahingehend, dass die Anteile bei ärmeren Haushalten höher sind. Allerdings werden Wohnungsmieten nach Einführung des BGE aufgrund niedriger Importanteile tendenziell billiger (S1) bzw. verteuern sich weniger stark (S2), Nahrungsmittel mit höheren Importanteilen jedoch sowohl in S1, vor allem aber in S2 teurer. Die Effekte gleichen sich insofern aus, als das durchschnittliche Preisniveau je Einkommensgruppe wenig variiert. In Szenario 1 (S1) bleibt es für alle hier gelisteten Einkommensgruppen in etwa auf dem ursprünglichen Niveau, in Szenario 2 (S2) erhöht sich das Preisniveau wiederum für alle gelisteten Einkommensgruppen um etwas mehr als 30%.

Bei Produkten mit stark steigenden Preisen ist davon auszugehen, dass Konsumnachfrage ins benachbarte Ausland abfließt (Stichwort Border-Shopping). Insbesondere wenn das Lohngleichgewicht am Arbeitsmarkt sich in Richtung Szenario 2 (S2) bewegt, ist von einem drastischen Nachfrageabfluss auszugehen. Derartige Abflüsse werden im Rahmen der vorliegenden Untersuchung allerdings nicht prognostiziert.

7. Fazit

Abschließend seien die Ergebnisse unseres Modells und der daraus folgenden Berechnungen in Tabelle 7.1 übersichtlich aufgeführt.

Wie ersichtlich beträgt der zusätzliche Finanzierungsbedarf dann, wenn die Netto-Erwerbseinkommen um das BGE gekürzt werden und somit die Gesamteinkommen – nach der BGE-Einführung aus dem BGE selbst und den Netto-Erwerbseinkommen – konstant bleiben, 28 Mrd. Euro jährlich und somit etwa 8% des gegenwärtigen BIP-Niveaus. In Szenario S2, wo es zu keinen Nettolohn-Kürzungen im Zuge der BGE-Einführung (S2) kommt, ist der zusätzliche Finanzierungsbedarf naturgemäß höher (53 Mrd. Euro jährlich). Der Grund ist, dass annahmegemäß die Lohnveränderungen auch für die Gehälter der Angestellten des Staates gelten.

Die Finanzierung des hier diskutieren Vorschlags soll – zusätzlich zur Konsumsteuer – über eine Exportsteuer, eine Vermögensteuer, eine Finanztransaktionssteuer und noch näher zu spezifizierende Energie- bzw. CO2-Steuern erfolgen.

	S1	S2
Erforderliches Steueraufkommen	€ 192 Mrd.	€ 217 Mrd.
erforderliche Abgabenquote	64%	53%
zusätzlich zum Status Quo erforderlich	€ 28 Mrd.	€ 53 Mrd.
Exportsteuer - Prozentsatz	48%	27%
Exportsteuer - Aufkommen	€ 62 Mrd.	€ 40 Mrd.
Konsumsteuer - Aufkommen Steuersatz 100%	€ 107 Mrd.	€ 146 Mrd.
Konsumsteuer - Aufkommen Steuersatz 110%	€ 118 Mrd.	€ 160 Mrd.
Konsumsteuer - Aufkommen Steuersatz 120%	€ 129 Mrd.	€ 175 Mrd.
Finanzierungslücke Export- + Konsumsteuer 100%	€ 23 Mrd.	€ 31 Mrd.
Finanzierungslücke Export- + Konsumsteuer 110%	€ 12 Mrd.	€ 17 Mrd.
Finanzierungslücke Export- + Konsumsteuer 120%	€ 1 Mrd.	€ 2 Mrd.
Veränderung Preisniveau bei KSt. 100% gegenüber Status Quo	-9%	+22%
Veränderung Preisniveau bei KSt. 110% gegenüber Status Quo	-4%	+28%
Veränderung Preisniveau bei KSt. 120% gegenüber Status Quo	+1%	+34%
Mögliches Aufkommen von Vermögensteuer und Finanztransaktionssteuer	€ 5-7 Mrd.	€ 5-7 Mrd.

Tabelle 7.1: Hauptergebnisse zu S1 (Löhne bleiben nach Einführung eines BGE gekürzt) und S2 (Löhne steigen nach Einführung eines BGE auf ursprüngliches Niveau) Quelle: Eigene Berechnungen, die Angaben beziehen sich auf das Jahr 2018. S1: BGE + gekürzte Einkommen, S2: BGE + ungekürzte Nettoeinkommen

Das mögliche Aufkommen einer Exportsteuer wurde im Rahmen der vorliegenden Studie berechnet, es beträgt 62 Mrd. Euro jährlich in Szenario 1 und 40 Mrd. Euro jährlich in Szenario 2. Die Aufkommen einer Vermögensteuer und Finanztransaktionssteuer können basierend auf der existierenden wissenschaftlichen Literatur mit 5 Mrd. Euro jährlich bzw. 1,5 Mrd. Euro jährlich beziffert werden (siehe Anhang). Das Aufkommen von möglichen Energie- bzw. CO2-Steuern wird in der vorliegenden Studie nicht beziffert.

Angesichts der Berechnungen erscheint eine Finanzierung eines BGE gemäß dem Vorschlag des Vereins „Generation Grundeinkommen" durch eine Exportsteuer, einer Vermögensteuer, eine Finanztransaktionssteuer, spezifischen Energie- bzw. CO2-Steuern und eine Konsumsteuer im Ausmaß von 110% bis 120% realistisch. Dies unabhängig von der Entwicklung der Erwerbseinkommen und Pensionen nach der Einführungsphase.

Ebenfalls aus Tabelle 7.1 ersichtlich ist, dass die Entwicklung der Nettolöhne im Zusammenspiel mit dem Konsumsteuersatz maßgeblich das Preisniveau der Konsumgüter beeinflusst. Verbleiben nach der Einführung des BGE die Gesamteinkommen – bestehend aus dem BGE selbst und den Netto-Erwerbseinkommen – auf dem Niveau von vor der Einführung (d.h. es kommt zu Kürzungen der Nettolöhne um das BGE (S1)) so wird sich das Preisniveau bei einem zur Finanzierung des BGE notwendigen Konsumsteuer-Satz von 110% bis 120% nur unwesentlich verändern. Bewegen sich die in der Einführungsphase um das BGE gekürzten Löhne allerdings auf ihr ursprüngliches Niveau zurück (S2) so kommt es zu deutlichen Preissteigerungen von mehr als +30% gegenüber dem Status Quo.

Anhang

Im Folgenden wird – anhand der zur Verfügung stehenden wissenschaftlichen Literatur – diskutiert, inwieweit und in welchem Ausmaß eine Vermögensteuer und eine Finanztransaktionssteuer zur Finanzierung eines BGE beitragen könnte. Dies vor dem Hintergrund der Tatsache, dass, wie oben beschrieben, neben einer Exportsteuer zur Finanzierung des BGE eine Konsumsteuer von 110% bis 120% notwendig wäre. Will man einen geringeren Steuersatz implementieren, beispielsweise 100%, so entstünde ein Fehlbetrag von je nach Lohnentwicklung 20 bis 30 Mrd. Euro, der aus alternativen Quellen gedeckt werden müsste. Dazu kämen eben eine Vermögensteuer, eine Finanztransaktionssteuer bzw. ggf. auch spezifische Verbrauchssteuern wie Energie- oder CO2-Steuern in Frage.

Vermögensteuer

Eine umfassende Berechnung des möglichen Aufkommens von Vermögensteuern, die im Rahmen einer Umstellung auf ein konsumfinanziertes Steuersystem eingeführt werden könnten, ist im Rahmen der vorliegenden Studie nicht möglich. Die Autoren beschränken sich daher auf eine Diskussion der diesbezüglich relevanten Literatur.

Grundsätzlich ist das Aufkommen einer Vermögensteuer oder auch einer Finanztransaktionssteuer naturgemäß abhängig vom Steuertarif und der Bemessungsgrundlage. Allerdings spielen gerade bei diesen beiden Steuerarten Ausweichreaktionen eine große Rolle, im Rahmen derer die Bemessungsgrundlage der Besteuerung entzogen wird (etwa indem Finanzvermögen in ein Land mit günstigerer Besteuerung transferiert wird).

Hinsichtlich einer Vermögensteuer existieren für Österreich Schätzungen, wonach ein progressiver Steuertarif von 1% auf Haushalts-Nettovermögen über 1 Mio. Euro und 1,5% auf Haushalts-Nettovermögen über 5 Mio. Euro jährlich ein Aufkommen von 4,9 Mrd. Euro generieren würde (Krenek und Schratzenstaller, 2017). Der verwendete Steuertarif wurde von Piketty (2014) vorgeschlagen. Bei der Berechnung wurde die Haushaltsgewichte am oberen Rand der Vermögensverteilung aus der Household Finance and Consumption Survey (HFCS) der Zentralbanken dergestalt angepasst, dass sie an diverse Listen (z.B. Trend-Liste 100 reichste Österreicher) angenähert werden. Es ist diesbezüglich bekannt, dass Befragungen den oberen Rand der Vermögensverteilung (d.h. die reichsten Haushalte) typischerweise nur ungenügend abbilden. Durch die Anpassung erhöht sich der Schätzwert für Bemessungsgrundlage (Nettovermögen der österreichischen Haushalte) einer Vermögensteuer von etwa einer Billion Euro auf etwa 1,3 Billionen Euro. Je nach Ausgestaltung des Steuertarifes, insbesondere des Grundfreibetrages (pro Haushalt), ist naturgemäß nur ein mehr oder weniger hoher Anteil der gesamten Bemessungsgrundlage steuerpflichtig.

Zudem wurde bei den Schätzungen die von Brülhart et al. (2016) für die Schweiz ermittelte Elastizität der Bemessungsgrundlage bezüglich des Steuersatzes verwendet. Demgemäß sinkt die Bemessungsgrundlage bei einer Erhöhung des Steuersatzes um einen Prozentpunkt aufgrund von Ausweichreaktionen der Besteuerten um 35%. Krenek und Schratzenstaller (2017) bezeichnen dies als „enorm, aber plausibel". Brülhart et al. (2016) verwenden für ihre Schätzungen Individualdaten im Zusammenspiel mit Kantonaldaten über Vermögensbestände aus den Jahren 2003 bis 2012. Sie nutzen die hohe Heterogenität der Vermögensbesteuerung zwischen den Schweizer Kantonen.

Eckerstorfer et al. (2013) vergleichen drei verschiedene Steuertarife. Ein progressiver Tarif mit Steuersätzen von 0,25% bis 0,67% ab einem persönlichen Freibetrag von 1 Mio. Euro würde demgemäß in einem jährlichen Vermögensteueraufkommen von 3,86 Mrd. Euro resultieren, ein linearer Tarif von 0,5%, ebenfalls ab einem persönlichen Freibetrag von 1 Mio. Euro, in einem jährlichen Aufkommen von 3,57 Mrd. Euro. Die Vorgehensweise hinsichtlich der Bemessungsgrundlage (Anpassung der Gewichte der Befragungsdaten) ist ident zu Krenek und Schratzenstaller (2017), allerdings berücksichtigen Eckerstorfer et al. (2013) keine Ausweichreaktionen.

Ein Vergleich der Ergebnisse von Krenek und Schratzenstaller (2017) und Eckerstorfer et al. (2013) zeigt, wie maßgeblich die Berücksichtigung von Ausweichreaktionen das Ergebnis beeinflusst. Werden die beiden progressiven Steuertarife verglichen, so zeigt sich, dass der progressive Tarif bei Krenek und Schratzenstaller (2017) Steuersätze aufweist, die mehr als doppelt so hoch sind wie jene des von Eckerstorfer et al. (2013) verwendeten Tarifs. Bei gleicher Datenbasis ist das von Krenek und Schratzenstaller (2017) ermittelte Steueraufkommen jedoch nur um etwas mehr als ein Viertel höher als das von Eckerstorfer et al. (2013) ermittelte Aufkommen.

Lassen sich die von Brülhart et al. (2017) für die Schweiz ermittelten Ergebnisse über die Ausweichreaktionen der Besteuerten – wie von Krenek und Schratzenstaller (2017) gemacht – auf Österreich anwenden, so lassen auch höhere Steuersätze als die von Piketty (2014) vorgeschlagenen 1% und 1,5% (ab 5 Mio. Netto-Haushaltsvermögen) kein wesentlich höheres Steueraufkommen als die von Krenek und Schratzenstaller (2017) ermittelten 4,9 Mrd. Euro jährlich erwarten.

Finanztransaktionssteuer

Für eine Steuer auf Finanztransaktionen gilt – ähnlich wie für eine Vermögensteuer – dass Ausweichreaktionen der Besteuerten das Steueraufkommen potenziell stark beeinflussen. Schulmeister (2007) beispielsweise unterstellt, dass Derivattransaktionen bei einem Steuersatz von 0,1% um 60% - 90% zurückgehen würden, und bei einem Steuersatz von 0,01% um 10% bis 40%. Er führt Aufkommens-Schätzungen für Deutschland und Großbritannien durch und schätzt für Deutschland einen Ertrag aus einer Transaktionssteuer auf Spot-Transaktionen, Derivat-Transaktionen und OTC-Transaktionen von 1,6% des BIP.

Dieser Wert ist allerdings nicht ohne Weiteres aus Österreich umlegbar, denn wie Schäfer (2015) zeigt, beträgt der Umsatz etwa des Derivatehandels in Deutschland mit 230 Mrd. Euro jährlich etwa das 28-fache des Umsatzes in Österreich (8,1 Mrd. Euro). Demgegenüber beläuft sich das BIP Deutschlands etwa auf das 10-fache des österreichischen BIP. Der Umsatz des Derivatehandels macht in beiden Ländern etwa 95% des Umsatzes aller für eine Besteuerung in Frage kommenden Finanztransaktionen aus. Ausgehend von einem Steuersatz von 0,1% für Wertpapier-Transaktionen und 0,01% für Derivat-Transaktionen geht Schäfer (2015) von einem Steueraufkommen von 18 bis 44 Mrd. Euro für Deutschland (variierend nach Annahmen über Ausweichreaktionen) und einem Steueraufkommen von 0,7 bis 1,5 Mrd. Euro für Österreich aus.

Tab. A1 Abgaben, die nach Einführung eines BGE entfallen & durch Konsumbesteuerung ersetzt werden

SV-Beiträge der Arbeitgeber (inkl. Lohnnebenkosten)	Aufkommen
Dienstgeberbeiträge zum AFFB/FLAF	€ 5,4 Mrd.
Kommunalsteuer	€ 3,3 Mrd.
U-Bahnabgabe	€ 0,1 Mrd.
Arbeitslosenversicherungsbeiträge	€ 3,5 Mrd.
Beiträge zur Bauarbeiter-Urlaubs- und Abfertigungskasse (BUAK)	€ 0,1 Mrd.
Beiträge nach dem Insolvenz-Ausfallgeldgesetz (IESG)	€ 0,4 Mrd.
Beiträge an Krankenfürsorgeanstalten	€ 0,2 Mrd.
Beiträge zur Krankenversicherung	€ 5,0 Mrd.
Dienstgeberbeiträge zur Pensionssicherung der Beamten	€ 0,2 Mrd.
Beiträge zur Pensionsversicherung	€ 15,6 Mrd.
Unfallversicherungsbeiträge	€ 1,6 Mrd.
Imputierte Sozialbeiträge	€ 1,8 Mrd.

SV-Beiträge der Arbeitnehmer

Arbeitslosenversicherungsbeiträge	€ 3,5 Mrd.
Beiträge an Krankenfürsorgeanstalten	€ 0,2 Mrd.
Beiträge zur Krankenversicherung	€ 5,0 Mrd.
Pensionssicherungsbeiträge der Beamten	€ 1,6 Mrd.
Beiträge zur Pensionsversicherung	€ 12,6 Mrd.

SV-Beiträge der Selbständigen

Beiträge zur Krankenversicherung	€ 1,0 Mrd.
Beiträge zur Pensionsversicherung	€ 2,6 Mrd.
Unfallversicherungsbeiträge	€ 0,1 Mrd.
Lohnsteuer auf Erwerbseinkommen	**€ 19,6 Mrd.**

Produktionsabgaben und Gütersteuern

Zölle	€ 0,3 Mrd.
„Rotterdam"-Zuschlag	€ 0,2 Mrd.

Alkoholsteuer	€ 0,2 Mrd.
Biersteuer	€ 0,2 Mrd.
Energieabgabe	€ 0,9 Mrd.
Mineralölsteuer	€ 4,4 Mrd.
Normverbrauchsabgabe	€ 0,5 Mrd.
Tabaksteuer	€ 1,9 Mrd.
Grunderwerbsteuer	€ 1,2 Mrd.
Kraftfahrzeugzulassungssteuer	€ 0,2 Mrd.
Konzessionsabgabe	€ 0,3 Mrd.
Spielbankenabgabe	€ 0,1 Mrd.
Feuerschutzsteuer	€ 0,1 Mrd.
Versicherungssteuer	€ 1,2 Mrd.
Altlastenbeitrag	€ 0,1 Mrd.
Fremdenverkehrsabgabe	€ 0,2 Mrd.
Werbeabgabe	€ 0,1 Mrd.
Flugabgabe	€ 0,1 Mrd.
Gewinne, Glückspielmonopol	€ 0,2 Mrd.
Grundsteuer B	€ 0,7 Mrd.
Kammerbeiträge, Landwirtschaftskammer	€ 0,1 Mrd.
Invalidenausgleichstaxfonds	€ 0,2 Mrd.
Kammerbeiträge	€ 0,4 Mrd.
Emissionszertifikate	€ 0,2 Mrd.
Gebrauchsabgabe	€ 0,3 Mrd.
Kraftfahrzeugsteuer	€ 0,1 Mrd.
Motorbezogene Versicherungssteuer, Anteil Unternehmen	€ 0,4 Mrd.
Sonstige Abgaben	€ 0,1 Mrd.
Übrige Gebühren (ohne Gewinstgebühr)	€ 0,2 Mrd.
Stabilitätsabgabe	€ 0,3 Mrd.
Haftungsentgelte Bund	€ 0,2 Mrd.
Beiträge an Single Resolution Fund (EU)	€ 0,2 Mrd.
Zahlungen an Einlagensicherungsfonds	€ 0,2 Mrd.

SV-Beiträge der Pensionisten und Nicht-Erwerbstätigen	
Beiträge zur Krankenversicherung	€ 3,0 Mrd.
Pensionssicherungsbeiträge der Beamten im Ruhestand	€ 0,3 Mrd.
Beiträge an Krankenfürsorgeanstalten	€ 0,2 Mrd.
Freiwillige Beiträge zur Krankenversicherung	€ 0,1 Mrd.
Freiwillige Beiträge zur Pensionsversicherung	€ 0,2 Mrd.
Lohnsteuer auf Pensionen	**€ 8,7 Mrd.**

USt. in derzeitiger Form	**€ 29,3 Mrd.**

Sonstige direkte Steuern (z.B. Motorbezogene Versicherungssteuer, ORF-Gebühren etc.)	
Kunst-/Kulturförderungsbeitrag, Anteil private Haushalte	€ 0,2 Mrd.
Rundfunkgebühren, Anteil private Haushalte	€ 0,1 Mrd.
Motorbezogene Versicherungssteuer, Anteil private Haushalte	€ 2,0 Mrd.
Abgabenstrafen und Resteingänge sonstiger weggefallener Steuern	€ 0,1 Mrd.
Übrige Gebühren inkl. Stempelmarken etc.	€ 0,2 Mrd.
ORF-Programmentgelt, Anteil private Haushalte	€ 0,7 Mrd.
Summe	**€ 165,1 Mrd.**

Literatur

ATTM (2019). Austrian-Tax-Transfer Model. Mikrosimulationsmodell der Gesellschaft für Angewandte Wirtschaftsforschung (GAW) zur Analyse von Reformen des österreichischen Steuer- und Sozialsystems.

Autor, D. (2015). Why are There Still so Many Jobs? The History and Future of Workplace Automation. Journal of Economic Perspectives 29(3), 3-30.

Autor, D., Levy, F., Murnane, R. (2003). The Skill Content of Recent Technological Change: An Empirical Exploration. Quarterly Journal of Economics 118(4), 1279-333.

Boccadoro, N. (2014). Non-Take-up of Minimum Income Schemes by the Homeless Population. Analysis and Road Map for Adequate and Accessible Minimum Income Schemes in EU Member States. Brussels, European Commission.

Brülhart, M., Gruber, J., Krapf, M., Schmidheiny, K. (2016). The Elasticity of Taxable Wealth: Evidence from Switzerland. NBER Working Paper 22376.

Calsamiglia, C., Flamand, S. (2019). A Review on Basic Income: A Radical Proposal for a Free Society and a Sane Economy by Philippe Van Parijs and Yannick Vanderborght. Journal of Economic Literature 2019, 57(3), 644-658.

Conesa, J.C., Li, B., Li., Q. (2020). Universal Basic Income and Progressive Consumption Taxes. Working Paper 2020-01, Stony Brook University.

Daigneault, P.-M., Jacob, S., Tereraho, M., (2012). Understanding and Improving the Take-up of Public Programs: Lessons Learned from the Canadian and International Experience in Human Services. International Journal of business and Social Science 3(1), 39-50..

Eckerstorfer, P., Steiner, V., Wakolbinger, F. (2013). Steuerreformvorschläge in der Diskussion: Eine Mikrosimulationsanalyse der Aufkommens-, Beschäftigungs- und Verteilungswirkungen für Österreich.

EU-SILC (2018). European Survey on Income and Living Conditions. Mikrodaten, repräsentativ für die österreichischen Haushalte, Welle 2018. Bereitgestellt durch Statistik Austria.

Haigner, S., Höchtl, W., Jenewein, S., Schneider, F., Wakolbinger, F. (2012a). Keep On Working: Unconditional Basic Income in the Lab. Basic Income Studies 7(1).

Haigner, S., Jenewein, S., Schneider, F., Wakolbinger, F. (2012b). Ergebnisse der ersten repräsentativen Umfrage in Deutschland zum Bedingungslosen Grundeinkommen. In: Werner, G., Eichhorn, W., Friedrich, L. (2012). Das Grundeinkommen, Würdigung, Wertungen, Wege. KIT Scientific Publishing.

IOT (2020). Input-Output-Tabelle für Österreich. Entnommen aus der Eurostat-Datenbank. Werte für das Jahr 2016, mit BIP-Wachstum hochgerechnet auf das Jahr 2018.

Jones, D., Marinescu, I. (2018). The Labor Market Impacts of Universal and Permanent Cash Transfers: Evidence from the Alaska Permanent Fund. NBER Working Paper 24312.

Krenek, A, Schratzenstaller, M. (2017). Sustainability-oriented Future EU Funding: A European Net Wealth Tax. Fair-Tax Working Paper Series No. 10.

Neumann, F. (2008). Gerechtigkeit und Grundeinkommen, Ruprecht-Karls-Universität Heidelberg.

Piketty, T. (2014). Capital in the 21st Century. Cambridge M.A. Harward University Press.

Schäfer, D. (2015). Fiscal and Economic Impacts of a Limited Financial Transaction Tax. DIW Politikberatung kompakt., Deutsches Institut für Wirtschaftsforschung.

Schneider, F., Dreer, E. (2017). Grundeinkommen in Österreich? Studie im Auftrag der Initiative Wirtschaftsstandort Oberösterreich (IWS).

Schulmeister, S. (2007). Eine generelle Finanztransaktionssteuer. Konzept, Begründung, Auswirkungen. WIFO Working Paper 352.

Schupp, J. (2020). Bedingungsloses Grundeinkommen: Viel Zustimmung, aber auch große Ablehnung. Wirtschaftsdienst 100 (2), 112-116.

Statistik Austria (2018). Mikrodaten der von Statistik Austria 2014/15 durchgeführten Konsumerhebung.

UK Department of Work and Pensions (2017). Income-Related Benefits: Estimates of Take-up: Financial Year 2015/16. UK Official Statistics. September 14.

Van Parijs, P., Vanderborght, Y., F. (2017). Basic Income: A Radical Proposal for a Free Society and a Sane Economy, Harvard University Press.

Vobruba, G. (2017). Das Grundeinkommen in der Utopiefalle. Der Standard am 3. November 2017.

Anmerkungen

[1] Auch die wissenschaftliche Diskussion zum Thema ist bereits weit fortgeschritten, wie ein Artikel im renommierten Journal of Economic Literature (Calsamiglia und Flamand, 2019) über eine umfassende Monographie zum BGE von Van Parijs und Vanderborght (2017) beweist. Hinsichtlich der Finanzierbarkeit bzw. möglicher Quellen zur Finanzierung eines BGE zeichnet sich in der wissenschaftlichen Diskussion kein einheitliches Bild ab (siehe z.B. Schupp, 2020, oder Conesa et al., 2020). Calsamiglia und Flamand (2019) führen das auf die Unterschiedlichkeit der verschiedenen BGE-Konzepte zurück. Breit diskutierte Aspekte sind zum einen die Vorteile eines BGE gegenüber „herkömmlichen" Haushaltstransfers im Hinblick auf die einfachere Verwaltung und die Reduktion des „Non-Take-up", d.h. das Problem, dass Sozialtransfers nicht bezogen werden, obwohl Anspruch bestünde (siehe z.B. Boccadoro, 2014, Daigneault et al., 2012, UK Department of Work and Pensions, 2017). Zum anderen ist die Literatur zu den Arbeitsmarkteffekten der Automatisierung / Digitalisierung relevant. Vielfach wird postuliert, dass die Arbeitsnachfrage aufgrund zunehmender Automatisierung sinken wird, und in weiterer Folge ein BGE umzusetzen wäre, da wesentlich mehr Menschen als bisher auf Transfereinkommen angewiesen sein werden. Autor (2003) bzw. Autor et al. (2015) bezweifeln allerdings, dass die Automatisierung die Arbeitsnachfrage drastisch sinken lassen wird. Schließlich nimmt die Diskussion zu den Effekten des BGE auf das Arbeitsangebot breiten Raum ein. Haigner et al. (2012a, 2012b) bzw. Jones und Marinescu (2018) zeigen in diesem Zusammenhang, dass das angebotene Stundenausmaß durch ein BGE sinkt, die Partizipation am Erwerbsarbeitsmarkt jedoch annähernd konstant bleibt. Schneider und Dreer (2017) geben einen Überblick über die in der jüngeren Vergangenheit entwickelten BGE-Konzepte.

[2] Da jedoch die Anspruchsberechtigten geografisch begrenzt sind, müsste der Begriff „bedingungsloses" Grundeinkommen eigentlich durch die Bezeichnung „garantiertes" Grundeinkommen ersetzt werden, da der Wohnort zumindest eine Bedingung darstellt (vgl. Vobruba, 2017). Einschränkungen des Anspruchs auf die Staatsbürgerschaft, einen längeren Wohnsitz bzw. einen legalen Aufenthaltsstatus von berechtigten Personengruppe, sind weitere Aufweichungen des Prinzips der Bedingungslosigkeit.

[3] Der Verkaufspreis in Österreich bzw. der Wiederverkaufspreis nach Bearbeitung durch österreichische Firmen ändert sich aufgrund der hier angenommenen Umstellung des österreichischen Steuer- und Sozialsystems auf Konsumsteuerfinanzierung und BGE. Im Regelfall erhöhen sich dadurch die Verkaufspreise von Importgütern und -dienstleistungen.

4 Etwaige Besteuerung einzelner Güter mit zusätzlichen Steuern (z.B. Energie- oder CO2-Steuern) werden in der vorliegenden Analyse nicht berücksichtigt.

5 Die vorgeschlagene Höhe des BGE ist somit etwas höher als der Richtsatz für Alleinstehende der Sozialhilfe/Mindestsicherung von 917 Euro (2020), bzw. der Ausgleichszulagenrichtsatz für alleinstehende Pensionisten von ebenfalls netto (=abzüglich KV-Beitrag) 917 Euro (2020). Die Armutsgefährdungsschwelle, definiert als 60 % des Medianeinkommens, betrug in Österreich für einen Einpersonenhaushalt 1.259 Euro monatlich, für einen Paarhaushalt 1.888 Euro monatlich. Somit wird die Armutsgefährdungsschwelle bei einem Einpersonenhaushalt, der ausschließlich BGE bezieht, unterschritten, bei einem Paarhaushalt mit ausschließlich BGE als Einkommensquelle jedoch überschritten.

6 Es sei erwähnt, dass auch Obdachlose gem. §19 Meldegesetz, einen Hauptwohnsitz geltend machen können, und somit BGE beziehen können.

7 Eine substitutive Variante bei Einkommen bis zur Höhe des BGE würde implizit eine Einkommensteuer von 100 % darstellen. Wenn beispielsweise das monatliche Netto-Erwerbseinkommen um 100 Euro steigt, so sinkt das BGE aufgrund der substitutiven Auszahlung um diesen Betrag. Das Gesamteinkommen bleibt konstant, obwohl Erwerbseinkommen erzielt wird. Dahingehend ist eine substitutive Auszahlung nicht mit einem Konsumsteuersystem vereinbar, da das Konsumsteuersystem per definitionem auf die Besteuerung von Einkommen verzichtet.

8 Der Vorschlag zielt grundsätzlich auf die Einkommen unselbständig Beschäftigter ab, da die Einkommen selbständig Beschäftigter sich aus den am Markt erzielten Umsätzen ableiten und daher nicht gekürzt oder erhöht werden können. Für die nachfolgenden Berechnungen wird angenommen, dass die Einkommen selbständig Erwerbstätiger denselben Schwankungen unterliegen wie die Einkommen unselbständig Erwerbstätiger.

9 Der Prozentsatz wurde mit den EU-SILC Daten (EU-SILC, 2018) erhoben. EU-SILC ist eine repräsentative Befragung von ca. 6.800 österreichischen Haushalten zu Einkommen (unter anderem Netto-Einkommen aus unselbständiger Beschäftigung) und Lebensbedingungen.

10 Denkbar ist auch, dass sich die Arbeitnehmer*innen mit dem gekürzten Erwerbseinkommen zwar zufriedengeben, allerdings ihr Arbeitsstunden-Ausmaß reduzieren. Dies wäre ebenfalls eine Rückführung der Erwerbseinkommen in Richtung ursprüngliches Niveau. Denn die reduzierten Arbeitsstunden müssen – wenn schon nicht zur Gänze so sicherlich zum Teil – durch zusätzliche Arbeitnehmer*innen aufgefüllt werden.

11 Diese sind aufgrund der wegfallenden Steuern und Abgaben auf den Faktor Arbeit deutlich niedriger als im Status Quo.

[12] In der Bemessungsgrundlage der gegenwärtig gültigen Umsatzsteuer (=Nettoverkaufspreis) sind hingegen Einkommensteuern und Sozialversicherungsbeiträge der am Produktionsprozess beteiligten Personen sowie weitere Abgaben wie Produktionssteuern und Gütersteuern (z.B. Mineralölsteuer, Tabaksteuer, Energieabgaben etc.) enthalten.

[13] Für die vorliegende Analyse wurde angenommen, dass die Preisentwicklung der Konsumgüter, die der Staat bezieht, der durchschnittlichen Preisentwicklung der Güter des privaten Konsums, die berechnet wurde, entspricht.

[14] Die Auswertung erfolgte auf Basis der Mikrodaten der Konsumerhebung (2016) von Statistik Austria, die eine Einteilung der Haushalte nach Einkommensgruppen (Dezilen) erlaubt.

Simon März

A Critical Analysis of a Proposed Basic Income Pilot Study in Germany

An Argument for Another UBI Pilot in Germany

UBI has been extensively researched through multiple experiments and policy introductions. Amid this vast literature, every new UBI pilot study should provide fresh insights on UBI and its effects on its recipients. The paper takes a critical look at the UBI experiments of the last 60 years in upper-middle and high-income countries. It finds that most experiments lack substance in their research design, implementation and the thoroughness of the follow-ups to be able to transfer their results onto a national level. To remedy this, the proposed basic income pilot from the NGO Expedition Grundeinkommen aims to include a well-designed study, federal and local state actors, and the implementation of the pilot study through direct democracy. Once carried out, the study has the potential to further the cause of introducing Universal Basic Income as a policy in Germany.

1. Introduction

Universal Basic Income (UBI) is a controversial policy proposal that has been fiercely debated over the last decades, especially since the dawn of the new millennium (Widerquist 2019b). The same holds for UBI experiments, UBI pilot studies and early experiments which received substantial media backlash in the 1970s and 1980s. The idea of handing money out to people for free to deal with low-income-related social issues was far from popular in the 1970s in the US, where early Basic income experiments were conducted. But the times are changing, and socioeconomic circumstances and an openness to new ideas are changing with them. That does not mean that large swathes of the population insist on an implementation of UBI, but that the openness toward UBI or similar social policy concepts has grown significantly in the last 20 years, particularly amongst younger age groups (Parolin and Siöland 2020). However, changing attitudes towards policy proposals and their testing methods do not automatically mean that the facilitation of these measures is the most advisable path forward for economic policy innovation. Before scientists can argue for the conduct of a new experiment, they must thoroughly examine the insights gained from old UBI pilots/experiments before concluding that a new UBI pilot study would be scientifically, politically and/or economically beneficial. This has been done with a UBI pilot proposal from the German NGO Expedition Grundeinkommen in this paper. This work gives an overview of UBI pilot studies/experiments, both completed as well as in progress, that are located either on the North American continent or in high-income countries in Europe.

The paper starts by discussing the political economy's role in constructing and conducting a new pilot study before moving on to elaborate on the reception of UBI pilots in general and on the need for researchers to be aware of certain pitfalls. The following chapter then discusses various issues that UBI pilot studies cannot address due to inherent limitations. From there the paper moves on to investigate older and ongoing UBI experiments, policy implementations and pilot studies. It concludes that the UBI pilot study proposed by Expedition Grundeinkommen will be scientifically valuable and may also be important from a political economy standpoint. The latter, however, is difficult to determine scientifically ex-ante.

1.1 The Concept of Universal Basic Income

Universal Basic Income (UBI) is a policy proposal that advocates for the governmental provision of a sufficiently high unconditional basic income to its citizens, regardless of their economic circumstances, status of employment, age, gender and health (Van Parijs 2004). Most proponents of UBI argue that it should not be paid in kind but as a cash transfer (Van Parijs 2004) to be paid out to its recipients individually (Torry 2013).

UBI is not a new concept to alleviate precarious socioeconomic circumstances. Dating back to as early as the 18th century, political theorists and activists have argued for various forms of a granted income for all citizens (Thomas Paine 1797; Howson and Meade 1988; Charlier J. 1848; Meade 1993). In the 20th century, famous civil rights activists like Martin Luther King, Jr.

(King 2010) and James Boggs (Boggs 2009) saw a guaranteed income as a viable means to confront systemic racial inequalities, whilst the economist Milton Friedman famously introduced his Negative Income Tax (NIT) concept in the 1960s. This concept shows many similarities to the UBI when it comes to combating endemic poverty. With the NIT, he envisioned a flat taxing system, where low-income households would consistently get tax rebates from the state up to a certain threshold. Once that threshold was bypassed by a household's income, the household would pay a flat income tax rather than receive tax rebates (Friedman 2020). In introducing this taxing scheme, Friedmann saw a chance to simultaneously eradicate poverty, avoid welfare traps and limit the extent of the state's bureaucracy while ensuring a high level of autonomy for the entire population (Friedman and Friedman 1980). This bureaucracy would be otherwise needed for conventional social assistance measures.

The introduction of the NIT model sparked a wave of discussions on a potential restructuring of social welfare. This led to numerous NIT-based Basic Income (BI) experiments being conducted in the United States and Canada in the 1960s, 1970s and 1980s. The next wave of discussions, which brought the issue much further into the forefront of the public eye and spills over into the current UBI discourse, was sparked off by the publication of Philippe Van Parijs's 1991 Paper "Why Surfers Should Be Fed: The Liberal Case for an Unconditional Basic Income" and his book "Real Freedom for All" in 1995.

In the last 10 years, UBI has thrown off its spell of obscurity to increasingly become a hotly debated policy proposal (Widerquist 2019b). In line with a Swiss referendum for a country-wide UBI introduction (Bundeskanzlei 2015) in 2016, the popular economists Robert B. Reich and Varoufakis outspokenly supported UBI (Hornemann and Steuernagel 2017). Silicon Valley's support for UBI has also become substantial (Guardian 2016, Business Insider 2017, Financial Times 2017). Many political analysts believe that it could well have been their support for UBI which was a decisive contributing factor for Andrew Yang to get as far as he did in the Democratic Party presidential primaries in the 2020 US election. As first laid out in his book (Yang 2018), Yang pivoted his primary campaign around his perceived economic necessity of a UBI introduction into the US American society.

The Covid-19 crisis unearthed many economic illnesses that lay dormant beneath a soil of public disengagement for decades and shifted them into the spotlight. Rising income inequality (Piketty 2014; Atkinson 2018; OECD 2015; Ken-Hou Lin and Donald Tomaskovic-Devey 2013) accompanied by rising job precarity (Kalleberg 2011; Straubhaar 2017; Yang 2018), entrenched poverty, especially in an ethnic context (Flournoy 2021; Neubeck and Cazenave 2002), and health inequalities (Wilkinson and Pickett 2009; Forget 2011a; Pickett and Wilkinson 2015 became publicly debated topics. These problems have led many to speak up in favour of a basic income in the past (Standing 2016b, 2016a; Bidadanure 2013, 2019; Ståhl and MacEachen 2021; Patel and Kariel 2021; Painter 2016; Atkinson 2018). Considering the current global economic difficulties, many more will most likely do so in the future.

Apart from the above-mentioned arguments for introducing a UBI as a socioeconomic policy, several other future socioeconomic challenges are often mentioned to underscore the necessity for a UBI in industrialized nations. According to the German economist Thomas Straubhaar, an ageing population will lead to an ever-increasing financial burden for the young age cohorts in Germany and other western societies (Straubhaar 2017). Furthermore, Straubhaar predicts that the ongoing artificial intelligence (AI) revolution will significantly lower the demand for human labour. He points out that the premise upon which many western social welfare systems were built – the working father, nursing mother premise – has become statistically obsolete (Straubhaar 2017). Since our societies are becoming increasingly individualistic, there is a need for an individually tailored universal social safety net (Straubhaar 2017). This could provide its participants with real economic freedom (Van Parijs 1997) and may help deal with the issue of gender inequality at the same time (Bidadanure 2019).

Naturally, psychological reasons for a UBI are also invoked, like the fact that cognitive abilities can be impeded by scarcity (Mullainathan and Shafir 2014) and that mental health conditions improved in numerous guaranteed income experiments (Forget 2011a; Gupta et al. 2021; Ruckert et al. 2018). Furthermore, moral arguments in favour of a UBI are brought forth, like socio-ethical or ethical justifications for a UBI (Meireis 2015; van Parijs 1992). Yet moral and ethical arguments have not gotten the same public attention as economic or psychological ones.

UBI has also been extensively researched through numerous experiments and policy introductions. (Widerquist 2018; Merrill et al. 2022; Gibson et al. 2018a;

Pinto et al. 2021; Mathebula 2021) Amid this vast sea of results and literature, ideally, every new UBI experiment should provide fresh insights on a UBI and its effects on its recipients. Additionally, it ought to demonstrate how it furthers the cause of introducing UBI as a valid policy response.

This essay, therefore, examines the rationality of carrying out a new UBI pilot study in Germany, as advocated for by the German NGO Expedition Grundeinkommen (Expedition Basic Income). The proposed pilot study will run across several German municipalities and encompass a treatment group of 10,000 participants. The study is scheduled to commence in 2023 and is set to run for three consecutive years. Each participant will receive a basic income covering their basic living costs from their municipality. This basic income will also cover all formerly received social benefits so that a recipient does not receive any further social welfare payments. To simulate the tax effects of a UBI, the NGO suggests an NIT guaranteed income payment scheme pegged to a 1200 Euros after-tax threshold. Should an individual have, therefore, no income, they would receive the full 1200 Euros. However, if a treatment correspondent's income was above 1200 Euros, they would receive no payments (in a NIT model they would, strictly speaking, be net taxpayers). All income in between these two benchmarks will receive payments according to the following formulas:

The entire income of the treatment group is taxed with a fictional tax (with a yet to be defined marginal tax rate; in other models it ranges from 40 to 50 per cent). The fictional net income of a UBI recipient in the pilot study would then be as follows:

Net income fictional = Net income before taxes x (1 - marginal tax rate)

What every treatment group participant will receive in the end will then be:

Entitlement UBI = UBI + Net incomefictional - Net income real, with treatment = max (Entitlement UBI,0)

Sums under 0 will not be considered. Therefore:

Treatment = max [(Entitlement UBI,0) + Net income fictional − Net income real]

To determine how scientifically and financially prudent it is to conduct a new UBI pilot study in the light of the results from past UBI experiments, this paper analyses the most notable UBI experiments of the last 60 years in industrialized or partly industrialized countries. Before this can be done however, it is imperative to discuss the political economy's role in the implementation of a UBI pilot study. In the then following chapter, the paper elaborates on how their results were often misunderstood, misinterpreted (spinning effects), or sensationalized. After this, it discusses a number of questions that their methodologies are unable to answer.

2. Political Economy of a UBI Pilot Study Implementation

The introduction of a UBI pilot experiment does not happen in a political vacuum. Every time such an intervention is proposed, some forces are either in favour of an implementation of a UBI experiment or against it. Both sides are prone to ideological bias (Jordan et al. 2022; Parolin and Siöland 2020) and may argue with extreme arguments at times (Gibson et al. 2018b; BBC 2017). In recent years there has been a multitude of public and political discussions on various UBI experiments in Europe and the US. The most recent ones were in Great Britain, particularly in Wales and Scotland, but also in Ireland (Crisp et al. 2022).

Calls for UBI trials have significantly increased in the aftermath of the 2008-2009 financial crises (Widerquist 2019b). However, many proponents of a UBI policy seem to support a UBI trial mainly due to a politically beneficial value that they attribute to it (Widerquist 2018; Merrill et al. 2022). They hope that a scientific study will attract more benign attention and create a sufficiently strong momentum to introduce UBI as a policy. By doing this, many have neglected to specify what specifically they wanted to have researched through a study (Widerquist 2018). This in turn has led to heightened research design and data collection difficulties for accompanying researchers in the past. Moreover, their hopes have yet to materialize since not a single UBI has been introduced into policy.

Therefore, even though many BI experiments may be regarded as purely scientific undertakings from the outside, it is more appropriate to see them as input of a "political process" (Merrill et al. 2022, p.124). Due to this process, substantial risks are involved with an introduction of a UBI pilot study. The least likely risk is that policymakers would agree to a UBI trial to use its results to portray it as an invalid social policy option (Widerquist 2018). From thereon, even if it was driven by a policymaker's scientific curiosity, its introduction could be limited to a too narrow range of UBI socioeconomic variables or too limited sample sizes to test for a national UBI, of which the Wales UBI pilot is the most recent example. Moreover, politicians in favour of a BI trial may back it to be able to raise more support for it amongst their constituents. Even when a politician favours a UBI policy, considering the significant opposition such a policy faces, they may also regard a UBI pilot introduction as a convenient way to gain the support of UBI supporters (Wispelaere and Yemtsov 2019) without immediately needing to vouch for an introduction of UBI into national law (Van Parijs and Vanderborght 2017). Thus, a UBI trial study could sap the momentum of an otherwise potentially successful drive towards full policy implementation. There is also the danger that once politicians are in a position to approve a UBI trial, they can just as quickly call it off (Merrill et al. 2022; Gibson et al. 2018b, 2018a).

3. The Reception of the UBI Pilot Study Results

Even though the media perception of UBI pilot studies has been positive or neutral in recent years, this was often not the case in the past. The notion that unconditional financial support would incentivize recipients to become lazy has often evoked a hostile reaction from the media and the political spectrum (Widerquist 2019a; Gibson et al. 2018b). This made clear that how researchers frame their Basic Income experiment and their findings and how they construct their experiment matters greatly in the sphere of public discussion (Kangas 2021; Merrill et al. 2022).

Consequently, researchers need to take the public discussion and policy implications into account when designing their field experiments. As shown by Banerjee and Duflo (2020), field experiments also examine how the institutional context they are introduced into reacts to the introduced policy experiment (Banerjee and Duflo 2020).

Communicating science to the public is challenging (Lupia 2013; Cheng et al. 2008). Researchers are required to walk a tightrope between presenting their research simply enough for the public to understand it while at the same time needing to communicate the necessary details as well as the complexity of the research to give an accurate picture of their work. Widerquist (2018) identifies, therefore, three key challenges in the "specialist-non-specialist communication" (Widerquist 2018, p.147) for UBI field experimenters that need to be overcome.

Firstly, ethical and econometric issues often become easily mixed up in the public discourse but need to be addressed separately. The public discussion around the UBI trial studies is of a heated nature and the opposing side is prone to attach their spin to the results of the experiment. To avoid this, instead of framing the study neutrally, Widerquist advises researchers to provide useful information to their audience beforehand. This information should contain different ethical views of UBI. They should also initiate a discourse on those differing views that are related to the experiments. Secondly, many public stakeholders are interested in the long-term impacts of the different variables studied. But, due to study time frame limitations, studying those impacts often is outside of the scope of UBI pilot studies. This means that the researchers should refer this interest to another discussion that goes beyond the one on the experiments. This discussion must then be substantiated by additional information outside of the experiment's findings. Thirdly, researchers need to be upfront about the questions their field experiments cannot answer and clarify how this study contributes to the overall understanding of UBI's impacts on its recipients. The aim here is to make sure that their research helps to answer important policy-related questions, like whether a UBI is feasible and advisable to implement, rather than resorting to testing easier to test variables that are irrelevant for policy deliberations.

Furthermore, to avoid spinning and sensationalizing of the results, a clarification of the relevance of their findings by the researchers, can significantly lower the likelihood of a misunderstanding or misinterpretation of their research. On the other hand, however, Journalists and writers also would do well to invest the necessary time to understand the intricacies of the implications of UBI experimental results (Merrill et al. 2022).

4. Topics a UBI Pilot Study Cannot Address

UBI trials generally aim to research, to varying extents, how a Universal Basic Income implementation would play itself out in the various spheres of our society. Given the ambitious scope of this goal, it is inevitable that there are many questions that field UBI trials cannot answer (Gibson et al. 2018b).

From an empirical perspective, due to their time and sample size limitations, Basic Income experiments will offer limited or negligible insight into how a UBI will affect important long-term microeconomic and macroeconomic factors (Gibson et al. 2018a). For example, one might ask how a paid-out UBI will affect an individual's behaviour and decision making – even more so in a community context – in the long run. Claims that UBI would be an economic stimulus or an impediment, that people would become more innovative or lazier, can, therefore, be either true or false if they are not able to be supported by adequate results or research. A small-scale, short-term-focused pilot study cannot answer these claims in any meaningful way. Gibson et al. 2018b state that a person's long-term behaviour – in a community context – could be modelled through agent-based modelling (ABM), but the extent to how scalable these simulations are, is very dependent on the set-up of those models. Furthermore, modelling is always limited by the extent to which its basic assumptions hold up to real live data.

Widerquist 2018, therefore, provides a further list of issues a UBI experiment cannot test for. He claims that a UBI will ultimately either lead to more worker exploitation or lower the likelihood of it. It can be both true and false at the same time, depending, for example, on the definition of exploitation. Furthermore, since the bulk of UBI experiments were set up as Randomised Control Trials (RCTs), they could say very little about the influence of structural inequities like rising/falling social inequality, and localised macroeconomic factors causing endemic poverty etc., on the results of the experiments. This would have to be researched in other separate studies. Potential effects like the eradication of the social stigma attached to welfare payments are similarly very difficult to quantify accurately, even though some may argue the contrary (Calnitsky 2016), since such stigma is attached to a recipient individual/group by either the society in its entirety or by groups of society. Since the entire society is not included in the test setup, this cannot be accurately controlled for (Widerquist 2018).

Since there are several other aspects of UBI that should be tested for but are difficult to quantify (Widerquist 2018) researchers need to be aware of their experiment-specific limitations before they launch their studies. Moreover, these limitations need to be well communicated to the public – repeatedly if necessary – to ensure that the UBI pilot study is perceived in the right light from the get-go.

5. But Is a New UBI Pilot Study Really Necessary? What Can We Learn from Previous Studies?

Having discussed the political background, its reception and other issues that a Basic Income pilot cannot sufficiently deal with, the question remains if a new trial study, like the one suggested by the German NGO Expedition Grundeinkommen (Expedition Basic Income), would be able to contribute to the knowledge pool on UBI that already exists from former studies.

To determine this the paper will conduct a review of studies on the most notable UBI experiments and on the design of the experiments themselves in the last 60 years in the upper-middle and highly industrialized countries (for clarity on the country classifications please refer to The World Bank 2022). UBI experiments, whose contexts differ considerably from the western industrialized context, i.e. low-income countries and lower-middle-income countries, will not be included in the review. Furthermore, all completed studies that had a specific target group or compared an Unconditional Cash Transfer (UCT) with a conditional one are considered to have limited relevance to the proposed new UBI experiment introduction and have therefore been left out. Like Gibson et al. 2018b's review, all included studies feature "universality, permanence, unconditionality and payments which are fixed in value (in relation to other income) and provide for basic subsistence" (Gibson et al. 2018b, p.19). They deem these features the most important ones to understand the impacts of a 'full' basic income. This paper shares their opinion.

As mentioned before, most of the UBI experiments are RCTs, but some are also qualitative studies, quasi-experiments and before and after studies. In some studies, however, a Basic Income is not paid out to individuals but on a household basis instead. All in all, this paper will examine 5 completed Basic Income experiments in detail as well as several ongoing ones. Their settings range from North America in the 1970s to present-day Germany.

All completed studies on the UBI experiments indicated an impact on the labour market participation of their participants. However, this impact has highly varying degrees and is varying in its conclusiveness (Widerquist 2005, 2018). The older studies on the NIT experiments reported a small decrease in working hours by primary earners by an average of 5% to 7.9% (Burtless, 1986, Keeley 1981, Robins, 1985). This effect is mainly driven by a longer period between ending one job and starting another (R. A. Levine, H. Watts, Robinson G. Hollister, W. Williams, A. O'Connor, and K. Widerquist 2005). Furthermore, older studies suggested that secondary earners (0% to 27% work hours' reduction) and single parents (15% to 30% work hour's reduction) opted to spend more time at home (Widerquist 2019a). This was singled out as the main reason why there was a small reduction in their work hours as well (Burtless 1986; R. A. Levine, H. Watts, Robinson G. Hollister, W. Williams, A. O'Connor, and K. Widerquist 2005; Robins 1985). More recent studies on NIT and later experiments however indicated either a very small negative effect (e.g. a 10% income increase by NIT recipients leading to a 1% decrease in labour supply) (Marinescu 2018), no effect or a small positive effect (Bibler et al. 2019; Jones and Marinescu 2018) of BI payments on labour supply.

The empirically established link between household income and child development (Blau 1999; Duncan and Brooks-Gunn 1997; Chaudry and Wimer 2016; Dahl and Lochner 2008) tentatively suggests a potentially positive impact of UBI payments on child development factors like cognitive abilities, educational attainment, social behaviour and the likelihood to engage in criminal behaviour or not. The completed UBI experiments confirm this suggestion, even though they do so with reservation (see "Topics UBI experiments cannot address"). There is evidence that children/teenagers stayed in school longer than their peers from their comparison groups if their parents receive BI payments (McDonald and Jr. 1979; Maynard and Murnane 1979; Akee et al. 2010) and were on average much less likely to engage in criminal behaviour (Akee et al. 2010). Furthermore, these effects were the most pronounced in low-income or at-risk groups and were "sometimes even stronger than typical effects of interventions directly targeting these outcomes"(Gibson et al. 2018b, p.11).

Several studies on the completed UBI experiments reported moderately positive effects on the health outcomes of UBI recipients. This included better health and mental health, a significantly lower rate of doctor visitations, a better diet and higher birth weight (Forget 2010; Forget 2011b; Kelly and Singer 1971; Kershaw and Skidmore 1974; Costello et al. 2016). The health findings, however, are less consistent than the labour market participation findings, which is most likely due to differences in sampling of the different experiments (Gibson et al. 2018b).

Wherever UBI payments were paid to affect large populations in one single place, spill-over effects and community-level effects could be detected. However, these effects can only be found in saturation studies or wide-scale policy trials, which are conducted with a group of respondents all of whom need to live near each other. According to the country inclusion criteria for this paper established before, the studies that analyse these effects are limited to one study that focused on the town of Dauphin in Manitoba, Canada. In this town Forget (2013) reported a significant reduction in hospital admissions and a larger percentage of the reduction of labour supply compared to other RCT- or qualitative NIT studies. In the other UBI experiments, those effects were limited because many employed scattered samples or due to specific targeting of social groups.

UBI experiments in general, however, do not only report positive effects of NIT guaranteed payments for its recipients. Evans and Moore (2011) found that once a year pay-out in Alaska led to increased alcohol consumption which they linked to an increase in the state's mortality rate. However, they also found the same pattern with other forms of pay-out of one-off payments like tax rebates, military salaries etc. The same pattern is also reported by Jones and Marinescu (2018) and it was also detected in a tribal casino income experiment

(Bruckner et al. 2011). The authors of the later study conclude that, even though long-term income payments were shown to have health-improving effects, large sudden income gains increase the likelihood of risk-taking in the short term.

These findings, however, need to be interpreted with caution. The Bruckner et al. (2011) study struggles with statistical inconclusiveness. Furthermore, if these experiments were conducted in an environment with an above-average alcohol consumption in the population, the propensity for a recipient to spend their newly-gained income on alcohol could well be higher.

Furthermore, the Seattle/Denver Income Maintenance Experiment (SIME/DIME) studies reported an increase in the divorce rate of 40-60%. This lead the researchers to assume that the NIT guaranteed payments would help the women who wanted to leave their marriages (Hannan et al. 1977). However, a later study, including a 5-year data set and an analysis of the separated NIT recipient groups, found that the NIT payments did not affect marriage stability (Cain and Wissoker 1990).

Having summarized the main findings of completed UBI experiments, the paper continues by examining these experiments and their associated studies in detail.

6. Assessment of Old Experiments in Detail: The Negative Income Tax Experiments

The NIT experiments were conducted by U.S. and Canadian Governments between 1968 and 1980. In total, there were five studies: The New Jersey Graduated Work Experiment (NJ) (1968-72), the Rural Income Maintenance Experiment (RIME) (1969-73), the Seattle/Denver Income Maintenance Experiment (SIME/DIME) (1970-80), the Gary Income Maintenance Experiment (Gary) (1971-74), and the Manitoba Basic Annual Income Experiment (1975-79). More detailed information about these studies can be found in Annex A.

The NIT experiments were set up as large RCTs, where a subsistence level basic income was provided to recipients on a household basis across large areas. However, the NJ and RIME NIT experiments also tested a guaranteed income which was 50% of the poverty line income then, which would not be considered sufficient enough for a Basic Income today. The experiments were large-scale and econometric testing of social policy was still a very novel approach to policymakers at that time. Furthermore, the NIT experiments were introduced into a political context that widely supported a guaranteed BI (see Chapter: The concept of Universal Basic Income). Their implementation was approved and supported by the federal governments of the US and Canada. Their administration and research were conducted by several universities and research institutions. The US government chose their experiment sites carefully since it expected these areas to be the most likely to be eligible for NIT payments if the concept was to be implemented (Watts, Harold W., Bawden D.L. 1978). Each experiment tested an NIT approach as a guaranteed income approach for low-income family households. This didn't mean they targeted low-income families. Rather, if a household's income dropped beneath a certain level in the testing areas, an NIT guaranteed income would help to raise it back up to that level. Furthermore, they also tested the different levels of guaranteed income and taxable income would be taxed with different tax rates (details in Table 1 in Annex A) The various combinations of guarantee rates and tax rates were employed to determine the effectiveness, in terms of work incentives and disincentives, of each combination for the working efforts of the recipients (Widerquist 2019a). Data on other effects, however, was also collected and analysed (R. A. Levine, H. Watts, Robinson G. Hollister, W. Williams, A. O'Connor, and K. Widerquist 2005).

The New Jersey Graduated Work Experiment (NJ) (1968-72) sites, in New Jersey and Pennsylvania, were both industrial urban areas in decline (Burtless 1986), with certain districts with higher household income poverty rates (Greenberg and Halsey 1983). In general, even when they were on a NIT plan, initially only low-income single parents were eligible to receive child-related welfare benefits, but shortly after the beginning of the experiment low-income two-parent households also became eligible. Those were the Aid to Families with Dependent Children (AFDC) and AFDC-Unemployed Parent (AFDC-UP) packages, which were "more generous than most of the NIT plans" (Gibson et al. 2018b, p.30). Different to the control group, however, the NIT recipients could not apply for additional Medicaid and food stamps. Hence NIT recipients assigned to lower guarantee plans were more likely to drop out of the program to be able to receive these benefits. This, however, changed significantly in 1971 due to a significant cut in welfare spending by the US federal government (Garfinkel 1974). Suddenly most NIT plans were more financially beneficial for low-income households to stay on than to drop out of them.

The Rural Income Maintenance Experiment (RIME) (1969-73) was the NIT experiment with the smallest sample and was carried out in a poor rural setting, different to the NJ experiment in that regard (Bawden et al. 1979). Also contrary to the NJ experiment, the states where the RIME experiment where conducted had ethnically varied rural poor populations. On the site in North Carolina, Dublin county, 67,9% of the sample was Coloured, while in Pocahantas County in Iowa, the sample consisted of an almost entirely Caucasian ethnic background (Maynard 1977b). The sample was further split into single parents, farmers and non-farmers (Maynard 1977a). In both states, the treatment and control groups did not receive any welfare benefits since there were not any available.

The Seattle/Denver Income Maintenance Experiment (SIME/DIME) (1970-80) was the largest NIT experiment with an experimental group of approximately 4,800 participants, spread out across the metropolitan areas of Seattle and Denver. Whilst Seattle's labour market – the labour market being dominated by the aerospace industry – experienced a lot of fluctuation, the Denver labour market did not. The experiment was originally scheduled to end after six years but was cancelled after 9 years in 1980, even though the participants all the while believed they would be part of it for the next 20 years (Widerquist 2019a).

The Gary Income Maintenance Experiment (1971-74) predominantly singled out black families, many of them single-parent units (60% of them) in Gary, Indiana, to receive a NIT guaranteed income for three years. Gary, once the site of a heavy steel industry, was much like the NJ site, an urban area in heavy decline (Kelly and Singer 1971).

The Manitoba Basic Annual Income Experiment (1975-79) incorporated three different samples in the Canadian state of Manitoba. One urban sample in Winnipeg, one rural sample of the surrounding areas and one saturation sample in the small town of Dauphin. Due to the particularly unstable job situation in Dauphin, up to 30% of the town received NIT payments at some point during the experiment (Forget 2013). Even though the experiment was received very well in the beginning, the Canadian government cancelled it before much of the data could be analysed. This was only done much later (Forget 2013).

Since policymakers are meant to be directly involved in the proposed experiment by the Expedition Grundeinkommen, the impact that they had on the experiment design is therefore of interest. Their role can, however, at best be described as problematic.

Firstly, there was the choice of study sites. All but for the SIME/DIME experiment in the US were introduced in poorer areas. Furthermore, all studies, even the Canadian ones, predominantly drew their samples from a low-income group/job sector (Widerquist 2019a). This income group is most likely to reduce their working hours more significantly than average since the granted income is comparatively high concerning their income (Widerquist 2019a). Their work hours response is therefore bound to be higher than that of a nationwide program (Moffitt 1979). The specific choice of experiment location also impedes the generalizability of the results, even though some of their samples were very well diversified outside of the household income criteria (Greenberg et al. 2003).

The fact that policymakers wanted to test so many different payment plans was a source of confusion for recipients and researchers alike. Furthermore, since they wanted to understand the effect of an NIT on many different types of socioeconomics groups, they insisted on the inclusion of so many subgroups that some of these became statistically irrelevant when it came to analysing the results. This can be seen very well in the Gary experiment (Greenberg and Shroder 2004). Here they also introduced additional social welfare measures for the treatment group, which further lowers the explanatory power of the findings.

In the case of the NJ and RIME experiments, the federal authorities were involved while the state-level ones were left out. This enabled many in the NJ experimental group to still be eligible for welfare benefits throughout the study. On top of that, during that time the state's social spending was severally cut, which furthermore raises doubts about the validity of the experiment's results. Furthermore, due to political pressure, the NJ researchers had published their results much earlier than they anticipated. This pressure, in combination with negative press, created significant stress for the participants (Kershaw et al. 1976) which can distort the effects of the research results even further.

Apart from the negative political influence on the study outcome, the studies were also plagued by several methodological issues. An underreporting of employment often led to an overestimation of the negative labour supply responses. In SIME/DIME, therefore, the effects on male primary, female secondary earners and youth employment ought to be lower than reported (Greenberg and Halsey 1983). In Gary's experiment, accounting for underreporting, the effects would subsequently be nullified (Burtless 1986). On top of that, the researchers used the Conlisk-Watts allocation, which was considered an optimal design for simultaneous equation models at that time (Aigner 1979) to randomly allocate participants to different treatment plan brackets. Using this method, however, made it more likely for people with a higher household income to be allocated to a treatment plan with a higher pay-out rate (Gibson et al. 2018b). This increased the risk that treatment group responses could be attributed to inherent test subject characteristics rather than be attributed to NIT effects. Another point of debate in the past was the short study period of most experiments. Some considered a three-year time frame long enough (Watts, Harold W., Bawden D.L. 1978; Choudhry and Hum 1995) while others had doubts about this (Christophersen et al. 1983).

Furthermore, the experiments were unable to control for important factors like the influence of the general economic situation on the study respondents/results. They also did not add a second study to control for these factors. Widerquist 2019a argues, that since these factors were not controlled for, in an economic environment where there were much fewer good jobs, the control group would be more desperate to work in less attractive jobs than a treatment group with a guaranteed income (Widerquist 2019a). The NIT experiments also did not control for demand responses (which was not feasible when the samples are scattered over wide areas) (Calnitsky and Latner 2017). These would, according to simple economic theory, lead to higher wages and inevitably reduce incentives to work less. Simulations by Greenberg and Halsey (Greenberg and Halsey 1983) report a small demand effect and a positive effect on low-skill wages (Bishop 1979). However, as argued before, as much as simulations are an important tool in social policy research, their setup includes assumptions which need to hold in a real-life scenario. Therefore, their results can be seen more as an indicator of direction rather than as hard evidence.

7. Unconditional Cash Transfers

When researching Universal cash transfers, one comes across three ongoing Unconditional cash transfers (UCTs) that many do not see as "full" basic income experiments. The Alaska Permanent Fund (APDF) (1982-), Macau's wealth partaking scheme (1999-) and the Iran Fuel subsidy (2010-). Even though there is significant social support of over $1000 for each state citizen each year through the APDF, which, cumulated on a household basis, becomes even more impactful, this paper still deems the amounts as too low for subsistence. The same holds for the wealth partaking scheme of Macao, which entitles permanent residents of Macao to varying payments of around 650 Euros and non-permanent residents to around 320 Euros (Merrill et al. 2022) per year.

The Iranian fuel subsidy was 45$ per person per month (Tabatabai 2012) or 90$ - adjusted for purchasing power - per household in 2011. This equalled 29 % (Salehi-Isfahani and Mostafavi 2017) of the Iranian median household income and was higher than 2.8 million Iranian household expenditures in 2011 (Salehi-Isfahani 2014). It, therefore, meets the inclusion criteria of this paper. However, due to a combination of sanctions and economic mismanagement, the country experienced strong inflationary pressures in the years following 2011. Thus, the value of the subsidies was only a third of its initial value in 2014 (Salehi-Isfahani and Mostafavi 2017). Hence, this work also excludes the Iran Fuel subsidy from its considerations.

Unlike the above-mentioned policies, which are similar to the UBI payment policies, the tribal casino dividends and their studies do meet the inclusion criteria. In 1988, the US Congress passed the Indian Regulatory Act that enabled US Native American tribes to run gambling businesses on their reservations. As of 2020, 248 (National Indian Gaming Commission 2020) of those tribes are running such businesses and at least 120 of them are giving parts of their revenues back to tribal members (Akee et al. 2015). The value of these payments varies between the different tribes but is in the following four studies at subsistence level or higher. Most of those payments were not paid out monthly. They are paid into a trust fund for young tribal members and later paid out in lump sums. Young Native Americans of the concerned tribes can access that money once they turn 18.

Foley (2005) researched a tribal casino dividends pay-out scheme of the Meskawki nation in Iowa. From casino proceeds, they would hand out 1800 $ to all adult tribal members biyearly and $200,000 to young people who had completed their high school after turning 18. The qualitative study however only contained 60 non-randomly chosen tribal members and a "control group" of 20 non-Native Americans. Therefore, their results are not generalizable with absolute certainty for a bigger population and are considered irrelevant for this paper. The same goes for Kodish et al. 2016 who conducted qualitative interviews with only 12 tribal chiefs and 24 members. (Kodish et al. 2016)

The last concluded tribal casino dividends study was published by Conner and Taggart in 2013. They set out to compare the aggregated economic data of 330 Native American nations on gaming-related pay-out schemes. These 330 Native American nations sample is split up into nations without gaming operations, nations with gaming operations, but no dividend payments, and nations with gaming operations and dividend sharing schemes. However, this sample split created very small and numerically unequal subsamples (n=29/n=41), which limits the meaningfulness of their comparability. Moreover, Gibson et al. (2018b) also report substantial amounts of missing data in that study. Hence this paper considers the explanatory power of their results rather limited and chooses not to consider them any further.

Since 3 out of the 4 studies have statistically invalid results, that leaves the Bruckner et al (2011) study. The Bruckner 2011 study researched the Casino dividend payments of the Eastern Cherokee Indian nation. The study utilised accidental death data from 57,000 individuals from North Carolina. They applied a Poisson Regression to a period between 1990 and 2006, totalling 204 months (Bruckner et al. 2011). Their results have already been discussed briefly (see Chapter: Is a new UBI pilot study even necessary? What can we learn from older studies?). Their baseline sample includes the entire population from 3 counties totalling 57,000. To establish a link between dividend payments and mortality rates, they compared 70 interviewees, where it is not clear if they are representative of the population, to the baseline sample, which is statistically unsound. Therefore, this study also struggles with an unspecified method description and a small sample. Furthermore, a study by Wolfe et al. (2012), applied a difference-in-differences approach to annual data from 1988 to 2003 on all tribal gaming operations and pay-outs in the US to research the causal relationship between Casino dividend payments and health indicators. They found that those payments had significant positive effects on the recipient's health, nutrition and even access to health care. Their study, even though it does include non-subsistence-level BI payments, does not struggle to the same extent from econometric weaknesses as Bruckner et al (2011) study and draws the opposite conclusions.

8. Pilot Studies

Several UBI pilot studies have been conducted since the early 2000s and some of them are still in progress. However, since Expedition Grundeinkommen's UBI tests a full UBI given to all groups of society in a high-income country, many of these studies will be excluded. This does not mean that these results are not important when looking at UBI experiments in general. It simply means that due to the specifications of the planned German UBI pilot, these findings are deemed irrelevant because of their lacking applicability.

Therefore, studies like the ones in Massachusetts, Oakland, Stockton and Maricá, Brazil will be excluded. But more importantly, this does not include UBI pilot studies that have received extensive media coverage, like the ones in Utrecht, the Netherlands, in Barcelona, Spain, the Youth Basic Income Policy in South Korea, the Give Directly Basic Income Experiment in Kenya, the Stockton BI experiment and the Kela Experiment in Finland. The Ontario Basic Income Pilot cannot be considered either because it was terminated in the year of its implementation in 2018. Furthermore, numerous UBI pilots are either completed, planned or in progress in the US ((Crisp et al. 2022). These UBI programs are targeted UBI programs and are therefore also not included in the considerations of the paper.

Unlike these, there are ongoing pilot studies that are of strong interest and importance to consider when implementing the proposed German pilot. Since they are still ongoing, however, there are no results that would render – in terms of potential insights gained and advocation for policy implementation of UBI – the proposed German pilot study obsolete. Opponents of the Expedition study can rightfully argue to wait for the results to come out and be thoroughly discussed. But on the other hand, proponents of it also have valid arguments as to why this UBI pilot should be launched in the next years. To get better clarity on the validity of both sides of the argumentation, this paper will look at some of the ongoing and planned UBI pilot studies.

In examining the validity of both sides of the argumentation, one has to keep in mind that all these pilots are either in their planning or early implementation stage. Therefore, the academic and public discussion about them is still limited. Thus, this paper cannot claim to provide an exhaustive insight into the quality of its research. This can only be done in the years to come.

There are three UBI pilot programs that are interesting when deliberating whether to conduct the pilot study in Germany. The BI pilot, funded by Y Combinator, the planned UBI income pilot in Scotland and the ongoing "Pilotprojekt Grundeinkommen" in Germany.

All these pilot programs have clearly established research design structures. Furthermore, they are aware of a potential conflict of their BI payments with social benefits and the issue of taxing to refinance a UBI. They can therefore avoid some of the major points of contention that plagued the NIT studies. However, their research design also leaves room to argue for another large Basic Income pilot.

The BI pilot funded by Y Combinator is conducted by the research organisation Open Research. It sources its researchers from several prominent North American universities, such as the Universities of Chicago, Michigan, California, Harvard and Toronto. The pilot program started in 2019 and is set to end in 2024. The Basic Income pilot assigns $1500 to a randomly selected group of 1000 participants in two US states. Their control group consists of 2000 people, each of whom receives $50 a month. Furthermore, their samples are stratified random samples of individuals between 21 and 40 years (OpenResearch 2020). Participants who are eligible for social benefits will not receive social benefits during the study but as soon as it stops they can get back onto their social benefit plans if they wish to do so (OpenResearch 2020).

This pilot design, however, differs in several vitally important aspects from the proposed pilot of the Expedition Grundeinkommen. The predefined age range of the Y Combinator pilot limits the representativeness of its results for a full Basic Income for the entire population, something the pilot of the Expedition Grundeinkommen is seeking to establish. Second, the pilot is limited to two US states, which significantly raises the likelihood of geography-specific effects interfering with the potential effect of UBI payments. Thirdly, and most importantly, the pilot specifically singles out individuals out of households who are below the national median income. The researchers of the pilot study argue for this because higher-income households will inevitably not profit as much from UBI payments since much of those benefits would have to be paid back to the state in the form of taxes anyway. The marginal effect of such additional income would then be so small for that group that including the income group in the sample would lead to an underestimation of the effects of a basic income. However, they do admit that one can indeed test UBI payments to all groups of society (OpenResearch 2020) yet call it "unaffordable and an inefficient use of [...] resources" (OpenResearch 2020, p. 13).

Nevertheless, one does not have to pay a BI to wealthier individuals and therefore "waste" resources to test the effects of BI payment on all members of society. By proposing an NIT approach to BI payments, the Expedition pilot can research UBI effects on the entirety of the population without squandering resources, whilst accounting for taxation related effects as well.

If the Scottish UBI pilot would be implemented, it would only be the second UBI experiment to be set up as a saturation experiment. Saturation studies, as mentioned before in this paper, enable the researchers to determine the community effects of UBI payments. However, they also underlie the danger that the potential positive effects of UBI payments can be diluted by locally specific economic effects. The researchers are aware of this danger, yet specifically want to research those effects. If the proposed study were to be implemented, it would be implemented in Edinburgh, a not yet specified town in the region of Fife, Glasgow and a not yet specified town in the region of North Ayrshire. Like the pilot from the Expedition Grundeinkommen, it is planned to be conducted for three years and employs an NIT like UBI pay-out approach.

Due to an already completed feasibility study in the different locations, local authorities will be much more adequately prepared for the challenges of such a study than they were during the NIT trials. In their publications, Expedition Grundeinkommen has not mentioned a feasibility study that supersedes their UBI pilot implementation yet (see Expedition Grundeinkommen 2021), but factually similar studies will have to be done in the research locations before the study will be conducted to coordinate well with local officials. This will help to involve and prepare policy-makers, the public and government officials alike for the future UBI pilot studies. Compared to the Expedition Grundeinkommen pilot, the Scottish pilot does not simulate an NIT payment scheme in which the recipient receives payments in line with his reported net income. Rather, all recipients' income is included in the income calculation, which then has a tax bracket of £12,500 (Project Steering Group 2020).

The Scottish UBI trial is shown to have two potential weaknesses when it comes to its design and future implementation. On one hand, the conductors propose two different kinds of UBI payment plans, one of which matches almost one-to-one with the current Scottish welfare benefit payments (details in Table 2 in Annex B). By suggesting a payment that is equal to already existing social benefit payments, they have given opposing lawmakers ample reasons to argue for a non-implementation of the pilot altogether. However, even more importantly, they have introduced a much lower bar for bargaining, one onto which it may very well be bargained down to in the case of collective bargaining.

The Scottish UBI pilot, on the other hand, is set up in a way that welfare payments are substituted by UBI payments. However, this does not apply to child support, housing support and disability payments (Project Steering Group 2020; Crisp et al. 2022). As much as those measures are ethically justifiable, they will also inevitably dilute and overestimate any effect that UBI payments will have on the general receiving population.

The last relevant currently running UBI pilot study is a UBI study in Germany itself. The Pilotprojekt Grundeinkommen is a study conducted by the NGO Mein Grundeinkommen and the Deutsches Institut für Wirtschaftsforschung (DIW) from the middle of 2021 until 2024. The NGO Mein Grundeinkommen has been providing UBI payments to individuals ever since 2014 and documented the results. In the Pilot, the treatment of 120 participants receives 1200 Euros monthly, whilst a control group of 1380 receives no payments. The Pilotprojekt Grundeinkommen randomly selected its treatment and control group out of a pool of 20.000 people, which in turn is randomly selected from one million applicants. Furthermore, they predetermined statistically that those 20,000 participants have similar attributes to the entire population of Germany (Mein Grundeinkommen 2020). At first glance, the results of this study could well nullify the necessity to conduct another even larger UBI pilot program in Germany. However, this is not the case and the researchers make this clear as well (Mein Grundeinkommen 2020). Even though they randomly selected their study participants out of one million applicants, the subsample of 20,000 which they randomly drew, was limited to people from the age of 21 to 40, single-person households, with a monthly net income not higher than 2,600 Euros. Therefore, the results are not generalizable for the entire German population.

This, however, is something that the proposed Pilot of the Expedition Grundeinkommen is setting out to rectify.

9. Conclusion

The demands for large-scale testing of a new UBI pilot study in Germany, as advocated for by the German NGO Expedition Grundeinkommen, coincides with the increased popularity of quantitative social policy testing in Europe (Morisi 2014). However, any new pilot study still needs to be justifiable. After closely examining older UBI pilot studies and experiments, the results of older and currently ongoing UBI experiments need to be considered when refining the research design of the Expedition Grundeinkommen pilot study. Nevertheless, the results of the examined BI experiments and their studies do not nullify the need to conduct further UBI pilot studies. On the contrary, their findings on positive effects for UBI recipients, but empirical shortcomings, even more so, encourage such an enterprise. If the Scottish UBI pilot is conducted and evaluated, its results and the findings from the proposed pilot study will create a much more solid empirical response to the question of how a UBI would influence its recipients in a Western European context, with its elaborate social systems and high-level taxing schemes.

However, to ensure that such a pilot study can be called a success, more factors need to be accounted for than included in the research design. Its success, from its implementation to the reception of the experiment, will also be decided by the level of competence in communicating the design, limitations, and aims of the BI pilot. The political economy around the implementation of a UBI plays an immensely important role and researchers would do well to take this into account and learn from the mistakes of the past. Much like the Scottish UBI pilot, however, when it comes to the realm of political discussion, the newly proposed German pilot has an ace up its sleeve. Its coordination and research efforts will go hand in hand with those of German municipal and federal governmental officials. Their close involvement in the pilot study will educate vital political stakeholders about the potential benefits and potential shortfalls of a UBI policy proposal first-hand. Many UBI supporters hope that this will be the missing link between UBI testing and a UBI introduction to policy. Only time will tell if this indeed will be the case.

Annex A
NIT Studies Research Sample Details from 1968-1980

The New Jersey Graduated Work Incentive Experiment (NJ)
New Jersey & Pennsylvania (1968-1972)

Sample size initial / (final)	1,216 (983)
Sample Characteristics:	Black, white and Latino; 2-parent families in urban areas with a male head aged 18-58 and income below 150% of the poverty line
Guarantee level / tax rate or level of payment	(1) 50% of poverty line guarantee, 30% tax rate (2) 50% guarantee, 50% tax rate (3) 75% guarantee, 30% tax rate (4) 75% guarantee, 50% tax rate (5) 75% guarantee, 70% tax rate (6) 100% guarantee, 50% tax rate (7) 100% guarantee, 70% tax rate (8) 125% guarantee, 50% tax rate

The Rural Income Maintenance Experiment (RIME)
Iowa & North Carolina (1970-1972)

Sample size initial (final)	809 (729)
Sample Characteristics	Both 2-parent families and female-headed households in rural areas with income below 150% of poverty line.
Guarantee level / tax rate or level of payment	(1) 50% of poverty line guarantee, 50% tax rate (2) 75% guarantee, 30% tax rate (3) 75% guarantee, 50% tax rate (4) 75% guarantee, 70% tax rate (5) 100% guarantee, 50% tax rate

The Seattle / Denver Income Maintenance Experiments (SIME/DIME)
Seattle & Denver (1970-1976; some up to 1980)

Sample size	4,800
Sample Characteristics	Black, white and Latino families with at least one dependent and incomes below $ 11,000 for single parents, $ 13,000 for two-parent families
Guarantee level / tax rate or level of payment	11 combinations of guarantee, tax rate and change in tax rate for $ 1000 income increase:

(1) 95%, 50%, 0%   (7) 120%, 70%, -2.5%
(2) 95%, 70%, 0%   (8) 120%, 80%, -2.5%
(3) 95%, 70%, -2.5%   (9) 140%, 50%, 0%
(4) 95%, 80%, -2.5%   (10) 140%, 70%, 0%
(5) 120%, 50%, 0%   (11) 140%, 80%, -2.5%
(6) 120%, 70%, 0%

The Gary, Indiana Experiment (Gary)
Gary, Indiana (1971-1974)

Sample size initial (final)	1,799 (967)
Sample Characteristics	Black households, primarily female-headed, head 18-58, income below 240% of poverty line
Guarantee level / tax rate or level of payment	(1) 75% of poverty line guarantee, 40% tax rate (2) 75% and 60% (3) 100% and 40% (4) 100% and 60%

The Manitoba Basic Annual Income Experiment (Mincome)
Winnipeg and Dauphin, Manitoba (1975-1978)

Sample size	1,300
Sample Characteristics	Families with head younger than 58 and income below $ 13,000 for a family of four
Guarantee level / tax rate or level of payment	8 combinations of maximum benefit level and tax rate:

(1) 3800, 35%   (5) 5,800, 50%
(2) 4,800, 35%   (6) 3,800, 75%
(3) 3,800, 50%   (7) 4,800, 75%
(4) 4,800, 50%   (8) 5,800, 75%

The Dauphin saturation site only tested one combination: 30% of Dauphin residents received Mincome during the study

Source: Reproduced from Widerquist (2005) and Gibson et al (2018b)

Annex B:
List of Payment Details for the Proposed Citizens' Basic Income (CBI) Pilot in Scotland

Age Range	Low CBI Level (per week)	High CBI Level (per week)
0 to 15 years	£84.54 (payment to main carer / parent)	£120.48 (payment to main carer / parent)
16 to 19 years	£84.54	£213.59
20 to 24 years	£57.90	£213.59
25 years to pension age	£73.10	£213.59
Pension age	£168.60	£195.90

Source: Project Steering Group 2020

References

Aigner, Dennis J. (1979): A brief introduction to the methodology of optimal experimental design. In: Journal of Econometrics 11 (1), pp. 7–26. DOI: 10.1016/0304-4076(79)90051-4.

Akee, Randall; Jorgensen, Miriam; Sunde, Uwe (2015): Critical junctures and economic development – Evidence from the adoption of constitutions among American Indian Nations. In: Journal of Comparative Economics 43 (4), pp. 844–861. DOI: 10.1016/j.jce.2015.08.004.

Akee, Randall K. Q.; Copeland, William E.; Keeler, Gordon; Angold, Adrian; Costello, Elizabeth J. (2010): Parents' Incomes and Children's Outcomes: A Quasi-Experiment. In: American economic journal. Applied Economics 2 (1), pp. 86–115. DOI: 10.1257/app.2.1.86.

Atkinson, Anthony B. (2018): Inequality. What can be done? Paperback edition. Cambridge, Massachusetts, London, England: Harvard Univ. Press.

Banerjee, Abhijit V.; Duflo, Esther (2020): 4. The Experimental Approach to Development Economics. In: Dawn Langan Teele (Ed.): Field Experiments and Their Critics: Yale University Press, pp. 78–114.

Bawden, D. L. and W. S. Harrar (1978). Design and Operation. ed.: J. Palmer and J. Pechman Welfare In: Rural Areas: The North Carolina-Iowa Income Maintenance Experiment. Washington DC, Brookings Institution.

Bawden, D.Lee.; Bryant, W.Keitb; Cain, Glen G.; Covert, Mary; Crawford, David L.; Evans, Lewis T. et al. (1979): The Rural Income Maintenance Experiment. With assistance of the Institute for Research on Poverty, University of Wisconsin. U.S.Department of Health, Education, and Welfare.

Bibler, Andrew; Guettabi, Mouhcine; Reimer, Matthew N. (2019): Short-Term Labor Responses to Unconditional Cash Transfers. In: SSRN Journal. DOI: 10.2139/ssrn.3357230.

Bidadanure, Juliana Uhuru (2013): The precariat, intergenerational justice and universal basic income. In: Global Discourse 3 (3), pp. 554–560. DOI: 10.1080/23269995.2014.898531.

Bidadanure, Juliana Uhuru (2019): The Political Theory of Universal Basic Income. In: Annu. Rev. Polit. Sci. 22 (1), pp. 481–501. DOI: 10.1146/annual-polisci-050317-070954.

Bishop, John H. (1979): The General Equilibrium Impact of Alternative Antipoverty Strategies. In: ILR Review 32 (2), pp. 205–223. DOI: 10.1177/001979397903200205.

Blau, David M. (1999): The Effect of Income on Child Development. In: Review of Economics and Statistics 81 (2), pp. 261–276. DOI: 10.1162/003465399558067.

Boggs, James (2009): The American revolution. Pages from a Negro worker's notebook. New edition. New York, NY: Monthly Review Press.

Bruckner, Tim A.; Brown, Ryan A.; Margerison-Zilko, Claire (2011): Positive income shocks and accidental deaths among Cherokee Indians: a natural experiment. In: International journal of epidemiology 40 (4), pp. 1083–1090. DOI: 10.1093/ije/dyr073.

Bundeskanzlei (2015): Eidgenössische Volksinitiative 'Für Ein Bedingungsloses Grundeinkommen.'. Bundesverwaltung, BK.

Burtless, Gary (1986): The work response to a guaranteed income: a survey of experimental evidence. In: Conference Series; [Proceedings] 30, pp. 22–59.

Cain, Glen G.; Wissoker, Douglas A. (1990): A Reanalysis of Marital Stability in the Seattle-Denver Income-Maintenance Experiment. In: American Journal of Sociology 95 (5), pp. 1235–1269. DOI: 10.1086/229428.

Calnitsky, David (2016): "More Normal than Welfare": The Mincome Experiment, Stigma, and Community Experience. In: Canadian review of sociology = Revue canadienne de sociologie 53 (1), pp. 26–71. DOI: 10.1111/cars.12091.

Calnitsky, David; Latner, Jonathan P. (2017): Basic Income in a Small Town: Understanding the Elusive Effects on Work. In Social Problems 64 (3), pp. 373–397. DOI: 10.1093/socpro/spw040.

Charlier J. (1848): Solution du Problème Social ou Constitution Humanitaire, Basée sur la Loi Naturelle, et Précédée de l'Exposé de Motifs. Brussels: G.J.A. Greuse.

Chaudry, Ajay; Wimer, Christopher (2016): Poverty is Not Just an Indicator: The Relationship Between Income, Poverty, and Child Well-Being. In: Academic paediatrics 16 (3 Suppl), S23-9. DOI: 10.1016/j.acap.2015.12.010.

Cheng, Donghong; Claessens, Michel; Gascoigne, Toss; Metcalfe, Jenni; Schiele, Bernard; Shi, Shunke (Eds.) (2008): Communicating Science in Social Contexts. Dordrecht: Springer Netherlands.

Choudhry, Saud A.; Hum, Derek P. J. (1995): Graduated work incentives and how they affect marital stability: the Canadian evidence. In: Applied Economics Letters 2 (10), pp. 367–371. DOI: 10.1080/758518991.

Christophersen, Gray.; Mathematica Policy Research, Inc.; SRI International. (1983): Final report of the Seattle-Denver income maintenance experiment. [Washington, D.C.: U.S. Dept. of Health and Human Services. Available online at //catalog.hathitrust.org/Record/000666543.

Costello, E. Jane; Copeland, William; Angold, Adrian (2016): The Great Smoky Mountains Study: developmental epidemiology in the southeastern United States. In: Social psychiatry and psychiatric epidemiology 51 (5), pp. 639–646. DOI: 10.1007/s00127-015-1168-1.

Crisp, Joe; Smyth, Laura; Stanfield, Claire; Pearce, Nick; France, Rachel; Taylor, Chris (2022): Basic Income experiments in OECD countries. A Rapid Evidence Review. Edited by EPPI Centre, UCL Social Research Institute, University College London. London.

Dahl, Gordon; Lochner, Lance (2008): The Impact of Family Income on Child Achievement: Evidence from the Earned Income Tax Credit. Cambridge, MA.

Duncan, Greg J.; Brooks-Gunn, Jeanne (1997): Consequences of Growing Up Poor: Russell Sage Foundation.

Evans, William N.; Moore, Timothy J. (2011): The short-term mortality consequences of income receipt. In: Journal of Public Economics 95 (11-12), pp. 1410–1424. DOI: 10.1016/j.jpubeco.2011.05.010.

Expedition Grundeinkommen (2021): Staatlicher Modellversuch zum bedingungslosen Grundeinkommen. Wie verändert ein Grundeinkommen unsere Gesellschaft? Wir möchten Fakten schaffen.

Flournoy, Edward Brian (2021): The rising of systemic racism and redlining in the United States of America. In: Journal of Social Change 13 (1), p. 6. Available online at https://scholarworks.waldenu.edu/jsc/vol13/iss1/6/.

Forget, Evelyn (2010): Abolishing poverty: the history and significance of the North American Guaranteed Annual Income Social Experiments. In: HISTORY OF ECONOMIC THOUGHT AND POLICY (1), pp Source: Reproduced from Widerquist (2005) and Gibson et al (2018b). 5–31. DOI: 10.3280/SPE2010-001001.

Forget, Evelyn L. (2011a): The Town with No Poverty: The Health Effects of a Canadian Guaranteed Annual Income Field Experiment. In: Canadian Public Policy 37 (3), pp. 283–305. DOI: 10.3138/cpp.37.3.283.

Forget, Evelyn L. (2011b): The Town with No Poverty: The Health Effects of a Canadian Guaranteed Annual Income Field Experiment. In: Canadian Public Policy 37 (3), pp. 283–305. DOI: 10.3138/cpp.37.3.283.

Forget, Evelyn L. (2013): New questions, new data, old interventions: the health effects of a guaranteed annual income. In: Preventive medicine 57 (6), pp. 925–928. DOI: 10.1016/j.ypmed.2013.05.029.

Friedman, Milton (2020): Capitalism and Freedom, with a New Foreword by Binyamin Appelbaum. With the assistance of Rose D. Friedman. Chicago, London: University of Chicago Press.

Friedman, Milton; Friedman, Rose D. (1980): Free to choose. A personal statement. New York, NY: Harcourt Brace Jovanovich.

Garfinkel, Irwin (1974): The Effects of Welfare Programs on Experimental Responses. In: The Journal of Human Resources 9 (4), pp. 504–529. DOI: 10.2307/144783.

Gibson, Marcia; Hearty, Wendy; Craig, Peter (2018a): Potential effects of universal basic income: a scoping review of evidence on impacts and study characteristics. In: The Lancet 392, S36. DOI: 10.1016/S0140-6736(18)32083-X.

Gibson, Marcia; Hearty, Wendy; Craig, Peter (2018b): Universal basic income; A scoping review of evidence on impacts and study characteristics. What Works Scotland.

Greenberg, David; Halsey, Harlan (1983): Systematic Misreporting and Effects of Income Maintenance Experiments on Work Effort: Evidence from the Seattle-Denver Experiment. In: Journal of Labor Economics 1 (4), pp. 380–407. DOI: 10.1086/298019.

Greenberg, David; Shroder, Mark (2004): The digest of social experiments. 3. ed. Washington, DC: Urban Inst. Press.

Greenberg, David H.; Linksz, Donna; Mandell, Marvin B. (2003): Social experimentation and public policymaking. Washington, D.C.: The Urban Institute Press.

Gupta, Rashmi; Jacob, Jemima; Bansal, Gaurav (2021): The Role of UBI in Mitigating the Effects of Psychosocial Stressors: A Review and Proposal. In:

Psychological reports, 332941211005115. DOI: 10.1177/00332941211005115.

Hannan, Michael T.; Tuma, Nancy Brandon; Groeneveld, Lyle P. (1977): Income and Marital Events: Evidence from an Income-Maintenance Experiment. In: American Journal of Sociology 82 (6), pp. 1186–1211. DOI: 10.1086/226463.

Hornemann, Börries; Steuernagel, Armin (2017): Sozialrevolution! Frankfurt: Campus Frankfurt / New York. Available online at http://www.content-select.com/index.php?id=bib_view&ean=9783593435756.

Howson, Susan; Meade, James E. (Eds.) (1988): The collected papers of James Meade. London: Unwin Hyman.

Jones, Damon; Marinescu, Ioana Elena (2018): The Labor Market Impacts of Universal and Permanent Cash Transfers: Evidence from the Alaska Permanent Fund. In: SSRN Journal. DOI: 10.2139/ssrn.3118343.

Jordan, Soren; Ferguson, Grant; Haglin, Kathryn (2022): Measuring and framing support for universal basic income. In: Social Policy & Administration 56 (1), pp. 138–147. DOI: 10.1111/spol.12760.

Kalleberg, Arne L. (2011): Good Jobs, Bad Jobs. The Rise of Polarized and Precarious Employment Systems in the United States, the 1970s-2000s: Russell Sage Foundation.

Kangas, Olli (2021): The feasibility of universal basic income. In: Experimenting with Unconditional Basic Income: Edward Elgar Publishing, pp. 187–196.

Keeley, Michael C. (1981): Labor Supply and Public Policy: A Critical Review. New York, N.Y.: Academic Press.

Kelly, Terence F.; Singer, Leslie (1971): The Gary Income Maintenance Experiment: Plans and Progress. In: American Economic Review 61 (2), pp. 30–38. Available online at http://www.jstor.org/stable/1816971.

Ken-Hou Lin and Donald Tomaskovic-Devey (2013): Financialization and U.S. Income Inequality, 1970–20081. In: American Journal of Sociology (5), pp. 1284–1329.

Kershaw, David; Fair, Jerilyn; Watts, Harold W.; Rees, Albert (1976): The New Jersey income-maintenance experiment. New York: Academic Press (Institute for Research on Poverty monograph series).

Kershaw, David; Skidmore, Felicity (1974): The New Jersey Graduated Work Incentive Experiment. Mathematica Policy Research Reports. Mathematica Policy Research. Available online at https://EconPapers.repec.org/RePEc:mpr:mprres:3b39f7503d74457ea6e37a3980762887.

King, Martin Luther (2010): Where Do We Go from Here. Chaos or Community? With the assistance of Vincent Harding, Coretta Scott King. Boston: Beacon Press (King Legacy Ser, v.2). Available online at https://ebookcentral.proquest.com/lib/gbv/detail.action?docID=6077370.

Kodish, Stephen R.; Gittelsohn, Joel; Oddo, Vanessa M.; Jones-Smith, Jessica C. (2016): Impacts of casinos on key pathways to health: qualitative findings from American Indian gaming communities in California. In BMC public health 16, p. 621. DOI: 10.1186/s12889-016-3279-3.

Lupia, Arthur (2013): Communicating science in politicized environments. In: Proceedings of the National Academy of Sciences of the United States of America 110 Suppl 3 (supplement_3), pp. 14048–14054. DOI: 10.1073/pnas.1212726110.

Marinescu, Ioana (2018): No Strings Attached: The Behavioral Effects of U.S. Unconditional Cash Transfer Programs. Cambridge, MA.

Mathebula, Brian (2021): The universal basic income grant (UBIG): A comparative review of the characteristics and impact.

Maynard, Rebecca A. (1977a): The effects of the rural income maintenance experiment on the school performance of children. In: American Economic Review 67 (1), pp. 370–375.

Maynard, Rebecca A. (1977b): The Effects of the Rural Income Maintenance Experiment on the School Performance of Children. In: American Economic Review 67 (1), pp. 370–375. Available online at http://www.jstor.org/stable/1815932.

Maynard, Rebecca A.; Murnane, Richard J. (1979): The Effects of a Negative Income Tax on School Performance: Results of an Experiment. In: The Journal of Human Resources 14 (4), p. 463. DOI: 10.2307/145317.

McDonald, John F.; Jr., Stanley P. Stephenson (1979): The Effect of Income Maintenance on the School-Enrollment and Labor-Supply Decisions of Teenagers. In: The Journal of Human Resources 14 (4), p. 488. DOI: 10.2307/145319.

Meade, James E. (1993): Liberty, equality, and efficiency. Apologia pro agathotopia mea. 1. publ. New York, N.Y.: New York Univ. Press. Available online at http://www.loc.gov/catdir/enhancements/fy0807/92034923-b.html.

Mein Grundeinkommen (2020): Pilotprojekt Grundeinkommen. Wie verändert ein Grundeinkommen unsere Gesellschaft? Wir wollen es wissen. Berlin.

Meireis, Torsten (2015): Bedingungsloses Grundeinkommen – eine protestantische Option? Ethik und Gesellschaft, Nr. 2 (2008): Rückkehr der Vollbeschäftigung oder Einzug des Grundeinkommens? DOI: 10.18156/eug-2-2008-art-5.

Merrill, Roberto; Neves, Catarina; Laín, Bru (2022): Basic Income Experiments. Cham: Springer International Publishing.

Morisi, David (2014): Testing social policy innovation, European Commission, Brussels.

Moffitt, Robert A. (1979): The Labor Supply Response in the Gary Experiment. In: The Journal of Human Resources 14 (4), p. 477. DOI: 10.2307/145318.

Mullainathan, Sendhil; Shafir, Eldar (2014): Scarcity. The true cost of not having enough. 1. Penguin Books ed. London: Penguin Books.

National Indian Gaming Commission (2020): 2020 INDIAN GAMING REVENUES OF $27.8 BILLION SHOW A 19.5% DECREASE. With the assistance of Marvis Harris. National Indian Gaming Commission. Washington, D.C.

Neubeck, Kenneth J.; Cazenave, Noel A. (2002): Welfare Racism: Routledge.

OECD (2015): In It Together. Why Less Inequality Benefits All. Paris: OECD Publishing. Available online at http://gbv.eblib.com/patron/FullRecord.aspx?p=3564375.

OpenResearch (2020): Basic Income Project Proposal.

Painter, Anthony (2016): A universal basic income: the answer to poverty, insecurity, and health inequality? In BMJ (Clinical research ed.) 355, i6473. DOI: 10.1136/BMJ.i6473.

Parolin, Zachary; Siöland, Linus (2020): Support for a universal basic income: A demand–capacity paradox? In Journal of European Social Policy 30 (1), pp. 5–19. DOI: 10.1177/0958928719886525.

Patel, Salil B.; Kariel, Joel (2021): Universal basic income and covid-19 pandemic. In: BMJ (Clinical research ed.) 372, n193. DOI: 10.1136/bmj.n193.

Pickett, Kate E.; Wilkinson, Richard G. (2015): Income inequality and health: a causal review. In: Social science & medicine (1982) 128, pp. 316–326. DOI: 10.1016/j.socscimed.2014.12.031.

Piketty, Thomas (2014): Capital in the twenty-first century. Cambridge, Massachusetts, London: The Belknap Press of Harvard University Press. Available online at https://www.jstor.org/stable/10.2307/j.ctvjnrvx9.

Pinto, Andrew D.; Perri, Melissa; Pedersen, Cheryl L.; Aratangy, Tatiana; Hapsari, Ayu Pinky; Hwang, Stephen W. (2021): Exploring different methods to evaluate the impact of basic income interventions: a systematic review. In International journal for equity in health 20 (1), p. 142. DOI: 10.1186/s12939-021-01479-2.

Project Steering Group (2020): Assessing the Feasibility of Citizens' Basic Income Pilots in Scotland: Final Report.

R. A. Levine, H. Watts, Robinson G. Hollister, W. Williams, A. O'Connor, and K. Widerquist (2005): A Retrospective On The Negative Income Tax Experiments: Looking Back At The Most Innovative Field Studies In Social Policy. In: The Ethics And Economics Of The Basic Income Guarantee, pp. 95–106.

Robins, Philip K. (1985): A Comparison of the Labor Supply Findings from the Four Negative Income Tax Experiments. In: The Journal of Human Resources 20 (4), p. 567. DOI: 10.2307/145685.

Ruckert, Arne; Huynh, Chau; Labonté, Ronald (2018): Reducing health inequities: is universal basic income the way forward? In: Journal of Public Health 40 (1), pp. 3–7. DOI: 10.1093/pubmed/fdx006.

Salehi-Isfahani, Djavad (2014): Iran's subsidy reform: From promise to disappointment. Economic Research Forum (Policy Perspective, 13).

Salehi-Isfahani, Djavad; Mostafavi, Mohammad-Hadi (2017): Cash Transfers and Labor Supply: Evidence from a Large-Scale Program in Iran. In: SSRN Journal. DOI: 10.2139/ssrn.2896702.

Ståhl, Christian; MacEachen, Ellen (2021): Universal Basic Income as a Policy Response to COVID-19 and Precarious Employment: Potential Impacts on Rehabilitation and Return-to-Work. In: Journal of occupational rehabilitation 31 (1), pp. 3–6. DOI: 10.1007/s10926-020-09923-w.

Standing, Guy (2016a): The Corruption of Capitalism. Why rentiers thrive and work does not pay. London: Biteback Publishing. Available online at https://ebookcentral.proquest.com/lib/kxp/detail.action?docID=4781386.

Standing, Guy (2016b): The precariat. The new dangerous class. Bloomsbury Revelations edition. London, New York: Bloomsbury Academic (Bloomsbury revelations).

Straubhaar, Thomas (2017): Radikal gerecht. Wie das bedingungslose Grundeinkommen den Sozialstaat revolutioniert. Hamburg: edition Körber-Stiftung. Available online at https://ebookcentral.proquest.com/lib/kxp/detail.action?docID=4810005.

Tabatabai, Hamid (2012): Iran: A Bumpy Road toward Basic Income. In: Richard K. Caputo (Ed.): Basic Income Guarantee and Politics. New York: Palgrave Macmillan the US, pp. 285–300.

The World Bank (2022): World Bank Country and Lending Groups. Available online at https://datahelpdesk.worldbank.org/knowledgebase/articles/906519-world-bank-country-and-lending-groups.

Thomas Paine (1797): Agrarian Justice. London: R. Folwell.

Torry, Malcolm (2013): Money for everyone. Why we need a citizen's income. s.l.: Policy Press The. Available online at https://search.ebscohost.com/login.aspx?direct=true&scope=site&db=nlebk&db=nlabk&AN=544850.

Van Parijs P. 1991. Why surfers should be fed: the liberal case for an unconditional basic income. Philos. Public Aff. 20(2):101–31.

Van Parijs, Philippe (1992): Arguing for Basic Income. Ethical foundations for a radical reform. 1. publ. London: Verso.

Van Parijs P. (1995): Real Freedom for All. Oxford, UK: Clarendon

Van Parijs, Philippe (1997): Real Freedom for All: Oxford University Press.

Van Parijs, Philippe; Vanderborght, Yannick (2017): Basic Income: Harvard University Press.

Van Parijs, Phillippe (2004): Basic Income: A Simple and Powerful Idea for the Twenty-First Century. In: Politics & Society 32 (1), pp. 7–39.

Watts, Harold W., Bawden D.L. (1978): "Issues and Lessons of Experimental Design. With the assistance of John L. Palmer and Joseph A. Pechman. The Brookings Institution. Washington DC: The Brookings Institution (Welfare in Rural Areas: The North Carolina-Iowa Maintenance Experiment).

Widerquist, Karl (2005): A failure to communicate: what (if anything) can we learn from the negative income tax experiments? In: The Journal of Socio-Economics 34 (1), pp. 49–81. DOI: 10.1016/j.socec.2004.09.050.

Widerquist, Karl (2018): A Critical Analysis of Basic Income Experiments for Researchers, Policymakers, and Citizens. Cham: Springer International Publishing.

Widerquist, Karl (2019a): The Negative Income Tax Experiments of the 1970s. In: Malcolm Torry (Ed.): The Palgrave International Handbook of Basic Income. Cham: Springer International Publishing (Exploring the Basic Income Guarantee), pp. 303–318.

Widerquist, Karl (2019b): Three Waves of Basic Income Support. In: Malcolm Torry (Ed.): The Palgrave International Handbook of Basic Income. Cham: Springer International Publishing (Exploring the Basic Income Guarantee), pp. 31–44.

Wilkinson, Richard G.; Pickett, Kate (2009): The spirit level. Why more equal societies almost always do better. 1. publ. London: Allen Lane.

Wispelaere, Jurgen de; Yemtsov, Ruslan (2019): The Political Economy of Universal Basic Income. With assistance of Ugo Gentilini, Margaret Grosh, Jamele Rigolini, and Ruslan Nemtsov. World Bank Group. Washington DC.

Wolfe, Barbara; Jakubowski, Jessica; Haveman, Robert; Courey, Marissa (2012): The income and health effects of tribal casino gaming on American Indians. In: Demography 49 (2), pp. 499–524. DOI: 10.1007/s13524-012-0098-8.

Yang, Andrew (2018): The war on normal people. The truth about America's disappearing jobs and why universal basic income is our future. First edition. New York, NY: Hachette Books.

Online sources

BBC (2017): Universal basic income 'worrying and expensive'. With the assistance of Cemlyn Davies. Available online at: https://www.bbc.com/news/uk-wales-politics-38770586, retrieved on 10.03.2022.

The Business insider (2017): Richard Branson just endorsed basic income — here are 10 other tech moguls who support the radical idea Available online at:https://www.businessinsider.com/entrepreneurs-endorsing-universal-basic-income-2017-3#sam-altman-4, retrieved on the 10.03.2022.

The Guardian (2016): Why Silicon Valley is embracing universal basic income, Available online at: https://www.theguardian.com/technology/2016/jun/22/silicon-valley-universal-basic-income-y-combinator, retrieved on the 10.03.2022.

The Financial Times (2017): Silicon Valley aims to engineer a universal basic income solution, Available online at: https://amp.ft.com/content/b0659404-0fea-11e7-a88c-50ba212dce4d, retrieved on the 10.03.2022.

Author's Biographies

Ronald Blaschke, geb. 19.03.1959, Diplom-Philosoph, Diplom-Pädagoge, Mitbegründer des deutschen Netzwerks Grundeinkommen und des europäischen Netzwerks Unconditional Basic Income (UBIE), Mitglied im deutschen Netzwerkrat und Koordinator der Europäischen Bürgerinitiative „Bedingungsloses Grundeinkommen in der gesamten EU", Mitherausgeber mehrerer Bücher und Autor zahlreicher Aufsätze und Beiträge zum Grundeinkommen und zu angrenzenden Themen, zum Beispiel: Blaschke, R., Otto, A., Schepers, N. (Hrsg.) (2010): Grundeinkommen. Geschichte – Modelle – Debatten. Berlin: Karl Dietz Verlag; Blaschke, R.; Praetorius, I.; Schrupp, A. (Hrsg.) (2016). Das Bedingungslose Grundeinkommen. Feministische und postpatriarchale Perspektiven. Sulzbach am Taunus: Ulrike Helmer Verlag. Webseite: https://www.ronald-blaschke.de/

Dr. Elisabeth Dreer, MSc.; Jahrgang 1965, studierte zwischen 1985 und 1990 Volkswirtschaftslehre an der Johannes Kepler Universität Linz und promovierte 1995 an der Alpen-Adria Universität Klagenfurt. Im Jahr 2001 absolvierte sie einen postgradualen Lehrgang in Business Administration mit Schwerpunkt Banking & Finance an der Donau[1]Universität Krems und der University of British Columbia in Vancouver. Sie arbeitete zwischen 1991 und 1995 als Universitätsassistentin an der Alpen-Adria-Universität Klagenfurt und anschließend am Forschungsinstitut für Bankwesen an der Johannes Kepler Universität Linz, wo sie zahlreiche Studien gemeinsam mit em. Univ. Prof. Dr. Dr. h. c. mult. Friedrich Schneider verfasste. Kontakt: Forschungsinstitut für Bankwesen, Johannes Kepler Universität Linz, Altenbergerstraße 69, 4040 Linz, T +43 732 2468 3296, elisabeth.dreer@jku.at

Marcel Franke is pursuing a Ph.D. at the GWP. The social debate about an unconditional basic income has undoubtedly flared up again. Scientific concepts and analyses can help to contribute to their progress. However, the risk of misunderstandings must be particularly taken into account in such accessible and comprehensive issues. Therefore, a basic explanation of what social sciences can contribute to this is given first. In compliance with and illustrating this, the demand of a universal basic income for possible attributes of a market economy society is discussed. Article: Franke M, Neumärker BKJ. A Climate Alliance through Transfer: Transfer Design in an Economic Conflict Model. World. 2022; 3(1):112-125. https://doi.org/10.3390/ world3010006

Leon Hartmann M.A., born in 1996, works on history and discourse of basic income and political Participation, history of knowledge, poststructuralism, discoure analysis, praxeology, Friedrich Nietzsche He is Research Assistant at Freiburg Institute of Basic Income Studies (FRIBIS) and leads the FRIBIS Team „Participation and Universal Basic Income – ‚Narratives' of the Future". His Doctoral thesis: The Futures of Democracy. On the Relationship Between Participation and UBI. Central publication on the topic: (together with Sebastian Kaufmann) Bedingungsloses Grundeinkommen und politische Partizipation als 'Zukunftsnarrative'. FRIBIS Policy Debate Paper 19.04.2022.

Alex Howlett, born in 1983, is an outsider to academia. He first started thinking about basic income in 2011 when he noticed some of the inefficient means by which government policy tries to ensure a source of money for consumers. Since then, he has been independently studying basic income, money and economics. He is the originator of what he calls "Consumer Monetary Theory." Alex understands the economy as a machine that produces goods and services for the people, and money as the means by which the people access the economy's output. He is a follower of economist Perry Mehrling's "Money View" of monetary economics as well as Moshe Hoffman's game theoretic functional description of social behavior. For over three years, Alex hosted the weekly Boston Basic Income YouTube live streaming discussion group that explored a variety of different topics as they related to basic income.

Tobias Jäger, born in 1989, Master of Science in Economics (Business), is the team coordinator for the Fribis BIP and WEF_FABI teams. His focus is on conflict economics and development economics. He is also pursuing a Ph.D. at FRIBIS /GWP. The topic of his Ph.D. thesis is UBI in a development context.

M.Sc. Lida Kuang, born in 1994 is currently a research associate at FRIBIS. She studied economics in Freiburg and Finance in Milan. Her Ph.D. topic is related to social contract laboratory experiments on UBI, to explore the socially acceptable conditions and rules for a basic income society.

Michael von der Lohe, Dipl. Ing. Photoingenieurwesen, geboren 1953, ist seit 2000 Mitarbeiter bei OMNIBUS FÜR DIREKTE DEMOKRATIE in der Deutschland gemeinnützige GmbH. Seit 2004 ist der dort Geschäftsführer. Er war von 1978-2014 selbstständig als Fotodesigner tätig und gewann 1988 den „Kodak European Award" für Profifotografen. 1992 entwickelte er ein chemisches Verfahren zum Einbrennen von Silber-Halogenid-Emulsionen auf keramischen Untergründen. 2000-06 war er Mitarbeiter beim Unternehmen „Wirtschaft und Kunst - erweitert" gemeinnützige GmbH in Frankfurt.

Simon März, born in 1988, M.Sc. Economics, studied economics at the University of Bayreuth, Cape Town and Freiburg. He is the team coordinator of the FRIBIS-team "Expedition Grundeinkommen" and researches in cooperation with the NGO Expedition Grundeinkommen. In his dissertation project, he researches the implementation of UBI pilot studies in Germany and their financing through the federal equalisation scheme.

Thiago Monteiro de Souza is natural from Rio de Janeiro, where he graduated in Law in the Rio de Janeiro Federal University. After his graduation, he moved to Lisbon, where he completed his Master's course in Political Science, in Nova de Lisboa University, producing a dissertation focused on the Bolsa Família Case and how can this experience foment the Universal Basic Income debate. Currently, Thiago is doing his Phd in Philosophy and Ethics, in Minho University, studying the Basic Income program of the city of Maricá, in Rio de Janeiro Brasil. Besides, Thiago works as a lawyer and as a political consultant in Brazilian electoral campaigns.

Bernhard Neumärker, Full Professor at the University of Freiburg since 2004, oncerns himself since many years with problems of social justice, economics of social conflict and political economy of reforms from a constitutional perspective. He applies his approaches of "New Ordoliberalism" and "Social

Sustainability" to the Universal Basic Income (UBI) from an interdisciplinary viewpoint integrating mainly new aspects of liberty and justice and testing UBI in the Social Contract Laboratory (SoCoLab). Since June 2019 he holds the "Götz Werner Chair of Economic Policy and Constitutional Theory" and since September 2019 he is Head of the new "Freiburg Institute for Basic Income Studies (FRIBIS)" both at the University of Freiburg. In his second main pillar the questions of energy transition, energy security and climate security, he works recently as PI, or, subproject leader on the research projects I4C (Intelligence for Cities), RES_TMO (Regional concepts for an integrated, efficient and sustainable energy supply and storage), and FRIAS Penn State Collaboration Development Program "Framing and analyzing novel interventions for sustainable communities in Africa".

Born in Portugal, **José H. Rocha** is a 29-year-old public servant in Valongo, with a book and some articles in Administrative, Health and Environmental Law. He holds a Master in Administrative Law from the Law School of the University of Minho in Braga, and a Law degree from the Law School of the Lusíada University of Porto, both in Portugal. He is going to start working on his Doctor´s degree, which is going to be dedicated to the perspective of a Universal Basic Income as a paradigm changing option in terms of it´s effects on the Laws of the portuguese nation, in particular as it concerns to the Social Security Net as a European and as a national.

Ulrich Schachtschneider, Dipl.-Ing. Dr. rer. pol., born in 1962, studied energy engineering, sociology and environmental policies and is working as energy consultant and freelance social scientist. His research fields are social-ecological transformation, sustainability and modern society, and policies of "Degrowth". He is member of board of Unconditional Basic Income Europe (UBIE) and advocating for an "Ecological Basic Income".
Publication on Basis Income: „Freiheit, Gleichheit, Gelassenheit. Mit dem ökologischen Grundeinkommen aus der Wachstumsfalle?" München 2014. Hives in Oldenburg, Germany. Website: www.ulrich-schachtschneider.de

Friedrich Schneider, em.o.Univ.-Prof. Dr. Dr.h.c.mult., war von 1986 bis 2017 Professor am Institut für Volkswirtschaftslehre an der Johannes Kepler Universität Linz; von 1996 bis 2007 war er Vizerektor für Außenbeziehungen der Johannes Kepler Universität. Der gebürtige Deutsche lehrte bereits an vielen Universitäten in Europa, Amerika und Australien. In der Forschung befasst er sich mit der ökonomischen Theorie der Politik, Finanzwissenschaft, Wirtschafts-, Umwelt- und Agrarpolitik; Schwerpunkte sind die Schattenwirtschaft und Steuer-hinterziehung, gesundheitspolitische Fragen und das BGE (bedingungsloses Grundeinkommen). Emeritiert seit 01.10.2017 Kontakt: Forschungsinstituts für Bankwesen, Johannes Kepler Universität Linz, Altenbergerstraße 69, 4040 Linz, T +43 732 2468 7340; friedrich.schneider@jku.at

Dr. Florian Wakolbinger studierte von 1998 bis 2004 Volkswirtschaftslehre an der Johannes Kepler Universität Linz und der Karlsuniversität Prag mit dem Schwerpunkt Angewandte Ökonometrie. Im Jahr 2007 promovierte er an der Universität Innsbruck im Bereich experimenteller Ökonomik. Seither ist er als selbständiger Ökonom bei der Gesellschaft für Angewandte Wirtschaftsforschung in Innsbruck tätig und befasst sich vorwiegend mit der Entwicklung mikro- und makroökonomischer Simulationsmodelle. Inhaltlich liegen seine Schwerpunkte im Bereich Regionalökonomik sowie im Bereich Steuer- und Sozialpolitik, wo er zahlreiche Studien zum Thema Kalte Progression, Finanzierung der Sozialversicherung und Bedingungsloses Grundeinkommen (BGE) mit-verfasste. Kontakt: Gesellschaft für Angewandte Wirtschaftsforschung, Sparkassenplatz 2/1/115, 6020 Innsbruck, T +43 0664 638 5993, wakolbinger@gaw.institute

Jette Weinel studied economics at the University of Freiburg and is team coordinator of the FRIBIS Basic Money Team. Her research at the Götz Werner Chair of Economic Policy and Constitutional Economic Theory focuses on the implications of the Basic Income on the utility function and tax revenue.